*William J. Fay*

*William J. Fay*

# NEW TESTAMENT
## APOLOGETIC

D1214437

# NEW TESTAMENT APOLOGETIC

The Doctrinal Significance of the
Old Testament Quotations

BARNABAS LINDARS, S.S.F.

SCM PRESS LTD
BLOOMSBURY STREET LONDON

334 01129 9
First published 1961
by SCM Press Ltd
56 Bloomsbury Street London
Second impression 1973

© SCM Press Ltd 1961

Printed in Great Britain by
Fletcher & Son Ltd, Norwich

To my Father
The Revd Walter St John Lindars, D.D.

# CONTENTS

# PREFACE

THE Old Testament quotations in the New Testament have frequently attracted the attention of scholars. In recent years interest in them has been considerably increased as a result of the discovery of the Dead Sea Scrolls. The following pages are in no sense an exhaustive study of them, but are intended as a contribution to the contemporary discussion.

The work of research into the origins of Christianity can proceed by two methods. There is first the *thesis*, in which a mass of data is assembled, the pattern is discerned, and firm conclusions are drawn. Secondly there is the *hypothesis*, in which a pattern is observed before the facts have been fully investigated. It is used as a key to a new understanding. Such a method can only proceed from a sure grasp of fundamental principles. It is not free from the dangers that always beset speculation. But it has its justification in opening up new perspectives. The *Formgeschichte* advocated by M. Dibelius forty years ago is an example of the hypothesis which has had far-reaching results in New Testament scholarship.

In adopting this second approach I am acutely conscious of my deficiencies for such a task. But the idea came almost by accident, and it had to be worked out. Others better qualified to judge have given me encouragement to believe that the work may have some value in the common task of advancing knowledge of early Christianity. And so it is offered for consideration by those interested in the problems of Christian origins.

The manuscript of this book was submitted to the University of Cambridge for the degree of Bachelor of Divinity, and I gratefully acknowledge the award of the degree.

I would like to record my gratitude to my brothers in the Society of St Francis, particularly to the Father Minister and the Chapter, who have waited patiently for me to show some fruit of my studies. It has not been easy, because the life of a religious house with pastoral commitments in both City and University leaves all too little time for such work.

I am especially grateful to the Rev. Professor C. F. D. Moule, who has never failed to be helpful and encouraging; and also to the members of his New Testament Seminar, who listened to the nucleus of the book at a very early stage, and made valuable and constructive criticisms.

I am also much indebted to Miss Jean Cunningham of the SCM Press, who patiently guided the book through the press, and whose vigilant care saved me from a number of errors.

Much further back a debt has been incurred to my father, who first taught me Hebrew and set me on the way of biblical studies. And so this book is dedicated to him with gratitude and affection.

*Cambridge*                                    BARNABAS LINDARS, S.S.F.
*November* 1960

A great deal of work has been done on the Old Testament quotations since this book was published twelve years ago. In some ways the views here expressed need to be modified in the light of more recent research. As present conditions do not permit a second edition, it is here reissued without change, apart from the correction of a few misprints, in the hope that it will still prove useful to students and scholars of the New Testament.

*Cambridge*                                    BARNABAS LINDARS, S.S.F.
*May* 1973

# ABBREVIATIONS

*Acc. Scrip.* C. H. Dodd, *According to the Scriptures*, 1952
*BASOR* Bulletin of the American Schools of Oriental Research
BH³ *Biblia Hebraica*, ed. R. Kittel, 3rd edn, ed. A. Alt and O. Eissfeldt, 1945
BZAW Beiheft zur *ZAW*
CD *The Damascus Document*
ET English translation
GCS Griechischen Christlichen Schriftsteller der ersten drei Jahrhunderte
ICC The International Critical Commentary
*JAOS* *Journal of the American Oriental Society*
*JBL* *Journal of Biblical Literature*
*JTS* *Journal of Theological Studies*
LXX The Septuagint Version
MT The Massoretic Text
*NTS* *New Testament Studies*
1QH *Hodayoth* or *Thanksgiving Psalms*
1QpHab *The Habakkuk Commentary*
1QS *The Manual of Discipline*
1QSa *The Two-Column Fragment*
par(r). and parallel(s)
*RB* *Revue Biblique*
SB H. L. Strack and P. Billerbeck, *Kommentar zum Neuen Testament aus Talmud und Midrasch*², 1922-56
SBT Studies in Biblical Theology
*SSM* K. Stendahl, *The School of St Matthew*, 1954
*TWNT* *Theologisches Wörterbuch zum Neuen Testament*, ed. G. Kittel, 1932 ff.
*ZAW* *Zeitschrift für die alttestamentliche Wissenschaft*
*ZNW* *Zeitschrift für die neutestamentliche Wissenschaft*

Old Testament references are to chapter and verse of the *Hebrew Bible*, where this differs from the Septuagint or English versions. In the Qumran literature, references are to the column and line.

# I

## TESTIMONIES

THE special characteristics of the Old Testament quotations in the New Testament invite the student to use them as a tool in the task of research into the origins of Christianity. We are here concerned with their value as evidence of the earliest formulation of Christian doctrine.

These quotations are commonly called Testimonies, especially since the publication of two slim volumes under that name by J. Rendel Harris.[1] In them he put forward the theory that there existed one or several documents containing collections of such testimonies, in the early days of the Church before the Epistles of St Paul. These were primarily used in anti-Judaic apologetic. This theory was widely held for some time, especially among British scholars, but is now generally discarded.[2] But the word remains a convenient way of describing the use which is made of these quotations in the New Testament. For they are constantly introduced to show how the Church's faith is rooted in the Old Testament revelation, and very frequently there is clearly an apologetic purpose. They are adduced to prove the Church's claims, when the unbelieving Jews contest them. They are thus testimonies to the truth of Christianity.

They may also be regarded as testimonies in another sense. Ancient writings vary widely in their worth as evidence of the facts which they profess to describe. But even where this must be rated at its lowest, the work retains its value as showing what men made

[1] *Testimonies* I and II (Cambridge, 1916-20).
[2] Cf. K. Stendahl, *The School of St Matthew*, 1954, pp. 207-17. This book (hereafter referred to in the notes as *SSM*) contains valuable summaries of the work of scholars on the Old Testament quotations. For this reason I have felt free to omit discussion of a number of issues which are fully reviewed in this book, but are not strictly relevant to my own purpose.

of the facts. Historians today lay increasing stress on the importance of such 'non-intentional data'.[1] It is in this way that the
quotations may be regarded as testimonies to early Christianity.
The choice of quotation, the form of the text, the method of interpretation, the context into which it is introduced, and comparison
of several citations of the same text, will all have to be taken into
consideration, and may yield valuable evidence.

In the last few years several books have given a new direction to
the study of the Old Testament quotations. In his Stone Lectures
Professor C. H. Dodd examined numerous quotations and allusions
in the light of the Old Testament contexts from which they are
drawn.[2] He showed that certain key passages of Scripture have
provided the principal testimonies, so that they belong together,
instead of being drawn from the entire Old Testament at random.
He thus inferred that these passages were thought through by the
first Christians, in their attempt to work out the meaning of the
redemptive action of Christ, so that they are the source of the
'regulative ideas' of the primitive theology. The use of these passages as a quarry for texts follows as a consequence of this as the
need arises, and very often a quotation is intended to evoke the
whole passage from which it has been selected. This convincing
study has struck the death-blow against the theory of a Testimony
Book put forward by Rendel Harris. The observations which
underlie his theory must now be explained in other ways.[3] The importance of Professor Dodd's work can hardly be over-estimated.
He has ascertained the passages which form 'the sub-structure of
all Christian theology', and has also shown the method which was
used by the first Christians in formulating it.

The lectures on which this book was based were delivered before
the first publication of the Dead Sea Scrolls from the Qumran
caves. The appearance of the *Habakkuk Commentary*, and subsequently of further scriptural commentaries, was quickly recognized

---

[1] Cf. Marc Bloch, *The Historian's Craft*, ET by P. Putnam, 1954, p. 61:
'There can be no doubt that, in the course of its development, historical
research has gradually been led to place more and more confidence . . . in
the evidence of witnesses in spite of themselves.'

[2] *According to the Scriptures: the Sub-Structure of New Testament
Theology*, 1952. Hereafter referred to as *Acc. Scrip.*

[3] For instance, the fact that recurrent citations in the NT agree against
the LXX and all other ancient texts has been explained by the fluidity of
the Greek text in the first century, by P. Kahle, *The Cairo Geniza*[2], 1959.
For another explanation by K. Stendahl, see next page.

to be of the first importance for the study of the testimonies. It is now possible to assert with confidence that these commentaries belong to the period 50 B.C. - A.D. 50.[1] Since they are all unique, and no duplicates have appeared in the thousands of Qumran fragments, it is reasonable to infer that they are all autograph works of members of the Sect. We can thus form a very nearly exact idea of their date and setting in relation to the rise of Christianity.

The importance of these commentaries for our purpose lies in the fact that they reveal a type of biblical interpretation quite distinct from that of the rabbinic tradition. In them a series of significant events, more or less contemporary with the writer, is regarded as the reality to which the prophecy points forward. If the prophecy is systematically applied to these events, it may be expected to reveal the divine meaning of them, because it is the inspired word of God. Of course it is impossible in practice to apply a prophecy verse by verse to a particular series of events. It is bound to involve a certain amount of wresting the text, to say the least. But in fact the Qumran exegetes use their interpretation to elucidate the obscurities of the text itself, so that in the course of their exposition they introduce delicate alterations and modifications to accord with their convictions.[2] One may say that these commentaries, and the life of the Sect revealed by the Scrolls as a whole and by the excavation of its buildings, indicate a continuous work of biblical study along these lines, constituting a 'school of exegesis'.

It is with this in mind that the bearing of the Scrolls on the study of the testimonies in St Matthew's Gospel has been examined by Professor Krister Stendahl.[3] The textual and exegetical phenomena of these quotations may now be explained by a tradition of Christian study, in which our Lord's work of redemption forms the reality to which all the inspired prophecies refer. It should be observed that we have to do with two things here, the 'school' of exegesis and the *pesher*[4] method of interpretation which it employs. It is not clear how far Professor Stendahl preserves this distinction.

[1] F. M. Cross, Jnr, *The Ancient Library of Qumran*, 1958, p. 84.

[2] E.g. 1QpMicah on Micah 1.6, where לְמַטָּעֵי of the text is interpreted as if it were derived from טָעָה =stray, instead of נָטַע =plant.

[3] *Op. cit.*

[4] So called because these commentaries, after citing each verse, begin the exposition with the word *pishrō* =its interpretation. An interpretative text-form can be conveniently called a *pesher* text, though this is not strictly correct.

Although the First Gospel may well be the resultant of the work of a school, it will be seen later in this study that Matthew inherits the formula-quotations without being aware of the issues which underlie the selection of them and are responsible for their text-forms. It is the same with the Fourth Gospel, which also has formula-quotations. Although the church in Ephesus was the setting of a common work of devotional study, resulting in the distinctive character of the Johannine literature, St John's Gospel bears throughout a personal impress which makes any theory of it as the product of a school inadequate.[1] On the other hand it appears that the writer knew and made use of traditions of exegesis, and that he accepted the general contentions of the *pesher* method.

Finally E. Earle Ellis has applied these results to the Old Testament quotations in the Epistles of St Paul.[2] He shows that the chief influence in St Paul's handling of the Scriptures is not rabbinic exegesis, whether Palestinian, Hellenistic or Alexandrian, but the Church's own version of the *midrash pesher*. It is something which he can take for granted in expounding the faith, and use creatively for his own purposes. This places the use of Scripture in the Pauline Epistles in the same category as that of the Fourth Gospel. It is not the work of a school, but the writer knows and uses such scholarly work; and he continues the tradition by his own positive contribution along the same lines. Consequently we can imagine that such exegetical study was an element in the life of the Church in all its chief centres, and that the more fruitful results of it were widely diffused by the apostolic missionaries and catechists. They would be useful in the work of preaching and teaching, and especially in the defence of the faith against the objections of unbelieving Jews in the synagogues where the kerygma was presented. St Paul's preaching in the synagogue at Pisidian Antioch (Acts 13.16-41) may not be an authentic record of his own work, but is still an excellent example of the way in which the early Church used scriptural exegesis.

These recent works on the Old Testament quotations have given us certain presuppositions to guide us in this present study. By drawing our attention to the blocks of material from which the testimonies have been drawn, Professor Dodd has shown that the

[1] Stendahl, *SSM*, pp. 31, 162f.
[2] *St Paul's Use of the Old Testament*, 1957. This book also contains much information on the history of the study of the quotations in general.

primary meaning must be ascertained by reference to the whole passage. Generally quotations in the New Testament have not been selected with complete disregard of the original context. Their meaning has been already fixed by the process of working over whole passages which seem most relevant to the Church's fundamental doctrines.[1] The analogy of the *Habakkuk Commentary* has suggested a definite rule of interpretation in this process: the events of redemption are the regulative factor, and provide the key to the meaning of scripture. Moreover we observed in the same source a distinctive method of exegesis, whereby this interpretation is clarified by means of subtle modifications of the texts which are used.

With these presuppositions in mind we can assess the phenomena which the quotations present. It becomes possible to trace the history of exegetical study which has produced the forms in which they are used in the New Testament. To do this is a valuable task, because it takes us behind our written sources to see the actual process of the Church's exegetical labours. So a window is opened for a glimpse into the doctrinal workshop. It may be hoped that the view of the process may point the way back to the origins of doctrinal formulation.

The task before us is a delicate one, demanding careful attention to detail. In the course of it two factors will have special claim for consideration. These are *shift of application* and *modification of text*. It will be worth while to explain these in some detail.

## I. SHIFT OF APPLICATION

In the first place, it seems, the Church selected whole passages of the Old Testament for study. A definite rule of interpretation is used. We should thus expect that, when a verse is quoted, its application should be closely related to this interpretation, and that this should be the same if it is quoted more than once. In fact, however, this is not so. When the various applications of a given text are compared, it is sometimes possible to arrange them progressively. In this way stages of interpretation can be discovered, corresponding to the developing thought and interest of the early Church.

A good example of this is the use of Isa. 6.9f.: 'Hear ye indeed, but understand not; see ye indeed, but perceive not', etc. This is

---

[1] Dodd thinks that this process begins in the creative mind of our Lord himself (*Acc. Scrip.*, p. 110).

a classic passage to account for the unbelief of the Jews. Its ramifications will be examined in a later chapter.[1] For our present purpose we may notice that in John 12.39f. it appears as the reason
why the response to the mission of Jesus, especially to his signs,
was so small; in Acts 28.25-28 it suggests the change of St Paul's
policy, turning from the Jews to the Gentiles; while in Mark 4.11f.
and parallels it is advanced as the reason for our Lord's method of
teaching by parables. All these are of course concerned with response. But none of them is quite the same, and from the point of
view of apologetic the Marcan example has strayed into an entirely
different field. It is doubtful whether the use of parables was a real
difficulty to those who actually listened to Jesus as he taught. It is
only later, when their context is lost and they are remembered as
isolated units, that the Church is both perplexed and embarrassed
by the traditional teaching of its Founder. Then, for apologetic
reasons, it becomes necessary to formulate a theory that the teaching was deliberately given in an intentionally obscure form, and
scriptural warrant is adduced in support of it. But the use of the
Isaiah text in John is concerned with a problem which is liable to
arise at a much earlier stage, the reason why the teaching of Jesus
did not compel belief. It thus seems reasonable to arrange the uses
of this quotation in order of development from the basic idea contained in the passage from which it is taken. This is first the problem of the hardness of heart which prevented many from believing
the Gospel, then the need to explain the rejection of the Jews in
favour of Gentile audiences, and finally the perplexity caused by
the presence of unexplained parables in the traditional body of
teachings.

This example is especially instructive, because the sequence of
interpretation is the direct opposite of the presumed order in which
the books themselves were written. John preserves the oldest application, Acts the second, and Mark the latest! This does not mean
that our estimate of the dates when these books were written must
now be radically revised. But it does provide a warning not to
evaluate a book by its date alone, for a later book may preserve
more primitive ideas. The shift of application shows the logical
sequence in the development of thought.

The shift of application is most likely to take place with quotations that have become generally accepted in Christian thought

[1] *Infra*, pp. 159-67.

and speech. It is a sure sign that an important issue has been at stake in the primitive period, even though the battle has been fought and won, and the original point of using the text has been largely forgotten.

It is, of course, always possible that the same text has been used by different authors entirely independently of a common background of exegesis. But the work of Professor Dodd shows that this is extremely unlikely. A text springs to mind because it is already in the memory through familiarity with the passage as a whole. It is key passages considered *in extenso* which are the starting-point of Christian exegesis. They are chosen because they immediately appear relevant to the matter in hand, that is, to some item in the proclamation of the Christian message. At first, no doubt, they would be referred to in general terms, with perhaps some allusions to evoke the whole passage. That would be enough in the ordinary work of preaching. But if the Church's interpretation is contested by the scholars of the synagogue, more exact reference must be made. Thus the Jews of the synagogue at Beroea 'examined the scriptures daily, whether these things were so' (Acts 17.11).

It thus seems likely that the use of Old Testament quotations belongs primarily to the apologetic element of the early preaching. The key passages have given some general theological positions, and from them specific quotations bring the point to bear on particular issues. In other words, these passages are an armoury, from which the appropriate weapon may be selected to be trained onto the target. But this is no arbitrary digging out of proof-texts, without taking the context into account. On the contrary, the context with its Christian interpretation has already defined the meaning of them. It is with this definite meaning that they are found to be useful at a particular stage in argument or discussion.

On the basis of this reasoning it seems legitimate to ask what is the original apologetic purpose of any given testimony. Presumably it answers some objection to the primitive kerygma, even if the New Testament application of it appears to be concerned with something quite different. By asking this question we can advance our study from the narrow limits of those quotations which occur more than once, to include those that are cited once only. In this case the shift of application is seen by comparing the *actual* use of the quotation with the *original* usage inferred from the Old

Testament context interpreted in relation to the basic kerygma.

To take a simple example, when we find a citation of words from Isa. 53, we may assume that they were referred in the first instance to the Passion of our Lord, even though they are concerned with something different in their present context. This is what has happened in the case of Isa. 53.4, cited in Matt. 8.17 as 'Himself took our infirmities, and bare our diseases.'[1]

That the shift of application may be traced in this way follows logically from taking Professor Dodd's theory of the quotations seriously. To do it is a delicate matter, inevitably involving subjective judgments on the part of the student. Like the true and false prophets, it must seek its justification in its fruits.

Beyond the limits of the New Testament canon, the shift of application may also be observed in early patristic writings. St Clement of Rome, writing to the Corinthians (*I Clem.* 4), gives a list of Old Testament examples of the consequences of envy. The greatest stress is laid on the first example, Cain and Abel, and Gen. 4.3-8 is quoted. The example of Moses and the strife between two Hebrews includes quotation of Ex. 2.14. All the examples tend to show that envy leads to persecution. In the New Testament this idea has a theological motive, for the Passion of Jesus was held to be a continuation of the treatment meted out to the prophets of old. The story of Cain is used in this way in a Q passage, which speaks of 'the blood of Abel' (Luke 11.51). In the parallel in Matt. 23.35 we find that he is 'righteous Abel'. This is a tendentious addition (perhaps older than the inclusion of the passage in Matthew) intended to invite comparison with the Crucifixion of Jesus. For at an early period the Church seems to have used ὁ δίκαιος as a special title of Jesus.[2] Now it is so used in Acts 7.52, a verse which both sums up the whole of St Stephen's speech and also bears a close resemblance to this Q passage. We may infer from this that the story of Abel was valued for its apologetic use, and that this is responsible for the addition of τοῦ δικαίου in Matthew. Moreover, whatever critical attitude we adopt towards the question of the authenticity of the speech in Acts 7, it clearly belongs to the same range of apologetic tradition, and it is remarkable that v. 52

---

[1] *Infra*, pp. 153f.

[2] K. Lake and H. J. Cadbury, *The Beginnings of Christianity*, I.IV, 1933, p. 83. It is derived from Isa. 53.11, and may be paralleled from *Ethiopian Enoch* 38.2, 47.1, 4, 53.6. Cf. SB I, p. 481; S. Mowinckel, *He that Cometh*, ET by G. W. Anderson, 1956, p. 366.

is closer to the developed Matthean form of the Q passage than to the Lucan. The speech itself does not include Abel, but does use the other incident of Moses and the two Hebrews, citing the same verse from Ex. 2 (Acts 7.27f.).

These two stories thus have an early Christian use as examples of persecution.[1] Clement is aware of this, but he has forgotten the apologetic motive which made them such telling examples. His motive is simply the moral one of showing that such is the consequence of envy, and therefore the Corinthians should try to avoid it. The shift of application from apologetic to homiletic has emptied the material of its theological significance.

In some cases it is possible that Clement retains a Jewish homiletic tradition, although he is at the same time aware of Christian theological usage. Thus in ch. 10 he quotes the Genesis passage about Abraham which St Paul had used in Galatians and Romans. He even speaks of the faith of Abraham—but only to show his limitations of thought by the telling phrase $\delta\iota\grave{\alpha}$ $\pi\acute{\iota}\sigma\tau\iota\nu$ $\kappa\alpha\grave{\iota}$ $\phi\iota\lambda o$-$\xi\epsilon\nu\acute{\iota}\alpha\nu$. The great Pauline passages are adduced simply as exhortation to the virtues. This precise Greek phrase is also used in ch. 12 to show how Rahab the harlot was 'saved'. Here again we have the moral motive, as in James 2.25, and there is nothing of the theological concept of faith found in Heb. 11.31. The background is likely to be Jewish homiletic,[2] but contact with specifically Christian thought reappears at the end of the chapter, where Clement speaks of the scarlet thread as a type of the Blood of Christ. This is the first mention of an idea beloved of the fathers

[1] It is possible that this usage lies behind the quasi-typological description of *righteous* Abel in Heb. 11.4, and even the reference to Cain and Abel in I John 3.12. These would thus be other examples of the shift of application. 'The way of Cain' in Jude 11 is, however, merely proverbial.

[2] The relation between Hebrews, James and Clement is very hard to determine. B. W. Bacon argued that the presence of the same OT examples in all three writings is not due to coincidence, but to deliberate doctrinal correction. Hebrews improves on Paul's doctrine of faith, James goes further and opposes Paul, while Clement gives greater fulness to the ideas of Hebrews—'The Doctrine of Faith in Hebrews, James, and Clement of Rome', *JBL* 19, 1900, pp. 12-21. But it is doubtful if a real literary connection can be established in this way. Our argument provides two explanations as alternatives to this: (a) early Christianity continued the Jewish homiletic tradition, in which the Patriarchs and other characters were prominent as examples; (b) the stock of written and unwritten material, used in apologetic, catechetical and homiletic work at the major church centres, was larger than the documentary remains that we have today.

from Justin onwards. Considering Clement's lack of theological interest it seems incredible that he has thought of this idea himself. It is more likely to be derived from a Christian work now lost.[1] Perhaps these moralizings are to be regarded as retained pre-Christian applications, rather than a simple shift from theology to homiletic. But in ch. 16 Clement quotes the great Passion passages, Isa. 53 and Ps. 22.6-8, without a hint of the theology of redemption. They are simply treated as descriptions of our Lord as the pattern of humility. We shall see the beginning of this shift of application in I Peter.

It is also instructive to follow a quotation through the New Testment into the early Fathers. St Paul in Rom. 2.24 quotes Isa. 52.5, 'And my name continually all the day is blasphemed'. In the original context this is because it appears that God is powerless to save his own people; the coming deliverance will take away the dishonour to God's name. In the Christian understanding this deliverance has now taken place in the Resurrection of Christ, so that the blasphemy only continues where the Jews persist in unbelief. This is the expected application of this text.[2] But Paul's use of it is different. It is the Jews' failure to keep the Law which causes scandal, rather than God's failure to act. Paul's words apply to Judaism before the work of Christ, to those who still refuse to believe now, and also to the Judaizers (whom he has constantly at the back of his mind). The scandal could have been removed, if they had heeded how God has in fact taken away the dishonour to his name. A shift of application has taken place in accordance with the change of circumstances—because, as a matter of fact, the cause of blasphemy is no longer God's inaction, but the fact that the Jews behave as if he still had not acted.

A further shift takes place when the text is used in a wholly Christian milieu. Then it is applied to the scandal of heresy

---

[1] J. B. Lightfoot, *The Apostolic Fathers*, Pt. I, Vol. II, 1890, p. 50, thinks it is derived from the scarlet wool in Heb. 9.19. But if so, it must surely be by way of *Ep. Barn.* 7.11, which uses it as a type of the Passion. But is *Ep. Barn.* older than *I Clem.*? Clement's comment (ὁρᾶτε, ἀγαπητοί, οὐ μόνον πίστις ἀλλὰ προφητεία ἐν τῇ γυναικὶ γέγονεν) may be compared with Origen's description of Rahab as προφῆτις ἀντὶ πορνῆς (*Hom. in Jos.* III.4, fragment from Procopius printed by Behrens, GCS VII, p. 621 [addendum to p. 305]). This does not necessarily entail acquaintance with *I Clem.*, but may indicate a common (Alexandrian?) source.

[2] Notice the close proximity of this verse to the important passage Isa. 52.13-53.12.

(II Peter 2.2) or the scandal of low moral standards among the Christians (1 Tim. 6.1, Titus 2.5, if they are allusions to this passage). This is the shift we should expect to find in Clement, but he does not use this text. However it does appear in just this moralizing way in the spurious *Epistle of Clement* 13. The text is extraordinary, for it is written twice over in slightly different forms, as if two separate but similar quotations were intended. This shows that the author has not selected the words from the Septuagint himself, but depends on memory for at least one version. The second one begins with the words οὐαὶ δι᾽ ὅν, which are not found in the Septuagint. This introductory οὐαὶ δι᾽ ὅν (or δι᾽ οὗ) reappears in Ignatius, *Trall.* 8, Polycarp, *Phil.* 10, and *Apost. Const.* I.10; III.5. J. B. Lightfoot regards the last three as all dependent on Ignatius.[1] The application in each case is to the scandal of heresy, except *Apost. Const.* I.10, which is moralistic. These are thus the normal ecclesiastical interpretations of this passage. It occurs a third time in *Apost. Const.* VII.24, but this time following the Septuagint more closely. It follows a full citation of the Lord's Prayer, and though it is used for pointing a moral, it shows an originality of treatment which suggests that the author has been reminded of it by the phrase 'hallowed be thy name' and actually referred to the true context before quoting it.

Meanwhile the more primitive apologetic use is likely to continue in the anti-Judaic literature. And so we find it in Justin's *Dialogue with Trypho* 17.2. The name of God is blasphemed by the Jews who go about condemning the godless sect (αἵρεσιν ἄθεον) of the Christians.[2] Tertullian uses it in *Adversus Marcionem* with reference to the Jews' refusal to believe (III 23) and to their persecution of our Lord which resulted from this unbelief (IV 14). These are the closest examples to what we argued was the probable primitive interpretation of Isa. 52.5.

The theory of Rendel Harris was that the postulated testimony-book was a collection specially intended for use in argument against the Jews.[3] Although we have seen reason to think that such a book

---

[1] *The Apostolic Fathers*, Pt. II, Vol. II², 1889, p. 172.

[2] Justin's quotation does not begin with οὐαὶ δι᾽ ὅν, but it is immediately followed by two more texts (Isa. 3.9-11, 5.18-20), comprising four sentences beginning with οὐαί. Perhaps we have here a relic of an early collection of Woes against the unbelieving Jews; and this may be the explanation of the non-LXX opening of Isa. 52.5 in Ignatius, etc.

[3] *Testimonies* I, p. 2. For further information on Isa. 52.5 cf. *Test.* II, pp. 15f.

is a development which follows rather than precedes the writing of the New Testament books, his observation that the primitive testimonies are often anti-Judaic in character is to be accepted. The expansion of the Church in the Gentile world creates new problems and new needs in the task of teaching the Christian faith and life. The history of the use of Isa. 52.5, which has just been traced, shows the shift of application at each stage of the Church's early development. But in the Christian dialogue with the Jews the same considerations remain operative as in the days when the Church was first being established in Jerusalem. There may be greater elaboration and subtlety of argument, but on the whole there is little likelihood of the shift of application. This suggests that there will be evidential value in Justin Martyr's *Dialogue with Trypho*, which on other grounds is gaining an increased respect from scholars today.[1] It is interesting to notice that in the course of this work he quotes extended passages and draws a general inference from them, before expounding particular texts, very much as Professor Dodd proves in the case of the earliest Christians from the biblical evidence. Justin is thus continuing a traditional method as well as a traditional exegesis.

## 2. MODIFICATION OF TEXT

In tracing the history of the use of Isa. 52.5 we were struck by the fact that it is quoted several times with non-canonical opening words. It is possible that this is to be ascribed to its inclusion in a series of Woes against the unbelieving Jews (cf. p. 23 n. 2). This means that the form of the text is a relic of the more original interpretation, which has nevertheless been discarded by the writers who quote the text in this form.

This is an example of the way in which the previous history of a quotation may be discovered by noticing the variations in the form of the text. As has been seen, such variations very often constitute part of the *midrash pesher* itself, so that, in addition to the

---

[1] The fragments of a Jewish Greek OT text discovered in the Qumran caves have affinities with Justin's quotations. See D. Barthélemy, 'Redécouverte d'un chaînon manquant de l'histoire de la Septante', *RB* 60, 1953, pp. 18-29. It was pointed out by Hilgenfeld as long ago as 1850 that in the extended quotations the copyist has used the ordinary LXX, so that Justin's peculiarities of text are there lost, cf. P. Katz, 'Septuagintal Studies in the Mid-Century', in W. D. Davies and D. Daube (edd.), *The Background of the New Testament and its Eschatology*, 1956, p. 206, n. 5.

caprice or inaccuracy of the writer, a conscious and deliberate
motive on his part may be present. In certain extreme instances
layers of successive interpretative modifications may be uncovered,
rather like archaeological excavations.

The most elaborate example of this kind of thing is the proof-
text concerning Judas Iscariot in Matt. 27.9. Professor Stendahl
has traced a process of exegesis, in which two versions of Zech.
11.13 have been worked over and combined with words from Jer.
18.1f. and 32.6-9.[1] By this means the texts are brought into line
with what actually happened when the high priest received the
money from Judas. It is thus a matter of making the words fit the
facts, rather than making the facts fit the words, as has so often
been assumed. But when the text is analysed in this way, and then
viewed in the light of the primitive apologetic, it becomes possible
to see a change of motive at each stage of the textual history. We
can see how the interest shifts from the fact that our Lord was sold
for money to the story of the fate of Judas. These are quite separate
issues. The first is an aspect of the scandal of the cross, in which it
must be shown that what was done to Jesus in no way conflicts
with the Church's claim that he is the Lord's Messiah. The second
is aimed at a more subtle criticism, which aims at throwing doubt
on this claim by showing up the ignorance and folly of Jesus in
including Judas in the number of the Twelve. This will have to be
shown in greater detail later on.[2] But perhaps enough has been said
to show the possibilities of watching the modification of text to
take us inside the mind of the early Church.

This is a fascinating method of research, and at first sight would
seem to promise convincing results. But this is not at all so clear
on further examination. The *Habakkuk Commentary* provides both
text and commentary for the student to compare with the standard
Massoretic Text of the Hebrew Scriptures. It can be shown, by
also taking into account the Versions, that the writer is making a
choice among a known variety of readings for the benefit of his
interpretation.[3] It is a work of the study, the *'scriptorium'*, where
texts are copied and variations may be noted. But it is not quite
the same with the New Testament. It may be plausibly argued
that this kind of scholarly work underlies *some* of the quotations,

[1] *SSM*, pp. 120-6, 196-8.
[2] *Infra*, pp. 116-22.
[3] Examples are given in Stendahl, *SSM*, pp. 185-90.

especially the formula-quotations in Matthew. But in fact the New Testament only gives us a few scattered fragments of such work. It is impossible to say that every variation from the Septuagint is an intentional modification or alternative reading. Every case has to be examined separately, and no single rule will be found to cover all. Where approximate dates of composition of documents are possible, it is noticeable that the later the date the greater is the appearance that the writer quotes from memory. In the early patristic literature one gets a very strong impression that variations are simply due to memory-quotation. This must not be allowed to affect our estimate of the greater significance of variations in the earlier literature.[1] It is intrinsically probable that, as the Church in various centres acquired a greater number of favourite texts for its different purposes, so the authors found themselves reverting to the traditional stock and trusting their memory more and more, rather than looking them up every time. When they wished to use less familiar material, they would naturally have to make sure of it.[2]

There is another difficulty. It is not always possible to tell whether a variation is due to the selection of a genuine variant reading or is a deliberate alteration of the text which lay before the

[1] The writer recently heard a patristic scholar express the view that the NT phenomena are largely due to memory-quotation.

[2] This observation seems specially likely in the case of Justin Martyr, and may account for some of the classic difficulties of his OT quotations. An excellent example is his treatment of the Palm Sunday testimony, Zech. 9.9. In *I Apol.* 35.11 he cites this in a form very similar to that of Matt. 21.5, except that the introductory words of Zech. 9.9 itself are used, instead of substituting Isa. 62.11 for them. But he ascribes the text to *Zephaniah*. There are two points to notice about this. (*a*) The opening words of Zech. 9.9 are identical with Zeph. 3.14 in the LXX. (*b*) The brief form of Zech. 9.9 given in John 12.15 takes its opening words from Zeph. 3.16 (MT). These facts suggest that we have to do with a *pesher* text, based on a deliberate correlation of the prophecies of Zechariah and Zephaniah. The similarity of Justin's version to Matthew's is not only due to direct borrowing, for that leaves the opening words and false ascription unexplained. But if Justin is using one of his memorized stock of *pesher* texts, then both difficulties are accounted for. He quotes this testimony again in *Dial.* 53.3. This time it is closer to the LXX, and correctly ascribed to Zechariah. The implication is that he has felt obliged to look it up, because of the erudition of his opponent. Similarly it is probable that all Justin's erroneous attributions are due to their previous history in the Church's *midrash pesher*. These are, besides *I Apol.* 35 just quoted, *ibid.* 51.8f. (Dan. 7.13, ascribed to Jeremiah), 53.10f. (Jer. 9.26, ascr. to Isaiah); *Dial.* 12.2 (Isa. 6.10, ascr. to Jeremiah), 14.8 (Zech. 12.10, ascr. to Hosea) and 49.2 (Mal. 4.5 [3.23], ascr. to Zechariah). We shall meet with several of these testimonies in the course of this study.

writer. One naturally hopes to have a fixed standard Septuagint
text as the basis of comparison. Although it may be hoped that
Septuagintal studies may eventually take us nearer to the recovery
of original texts, it has to be remembered that the history of recensional variations had already begun by New Testament times.[1] The
question is extremely complicated, and does not admit of a simple
solution. Evidence is now forthcoming that a Palestinian recension
of the Greek version existed, attempting to bring it into closer
accord with the Hebrew text.[2] This would be a precursor of the
versions of Aquila and Theodotion, and presumably they were
based on such previous work. On the other hand P. Kahle has
probably gone too far in taking the New Testament quotations as
themselves witnesses to current Greek texts which preceded the
standardizing of the Septuagint.[3] This would empty the variations
of all significance, except in so far as they may be due to deliberate
choice between two or more known texts. We may suppose that
the truth lies between the extremes. Some of the variations may be
due to some alternative Greek readings which have now perished,[4]
but others are to be regarded as deliberate alterations to point the
application.

There are thus three factors to be taken into account in esti-
mating the modification of text. These are deliberate alteration,
selection of reading, and memory-quotation. It is, of course, the
first of these three which offers the most promising possibilities
for our purpose. Such alterations are to be regarded as interpretative renderings, comparable to the Targums. Similarly one text
interprets another, and so conflate texts are formed. There was
nothing morally reprehensible about such treatment of the text,
because it was felt that the real meaning of the Scripture was being
clarified by it. This is because the Church's interpretation is based

[1] See P. Katz, *art. cit.*, and H. M. Orlinsky, 'On the Present State of
Proto-Septuagint Studies', *JAOS* 61, 1941, pp. 81-91, and 'Current Pro-
gress and Problems in Septuagint Research', in *The Study of the Bible
Today and Tomorrow*, ed. H. R. Willoughby, 1947, pp. 144-61.
[2] This is deduced from agreement of some details of NT citations with
the second-century Greek versions, and from some fragments of Greek
texts which can be assigned to a definitely Jewish origin. See D. Barthélemy, *art. cit.*
[3] *Op. cit.* The idea is worked out in detail by A. Sperber in *Tarbiz* 6,
1934, pp. 1-29, and 'The New Testament and the Septuagint', *JBL* 59,
1940, pp. 193-293.
[4] Some possible examples will be noted as the quotations are studied.

on the rule that what God has done in Christ is the key to the understanding of all the Scriptures.

The second factor, selection of reading, seems to the modern mind to be a more honest procedure. But in fact it presupposes an equally deliberate and tendentious manipulation of texts, as it is done to secure the same object, not to establish the '*Ur*-text'. At the same time, the recognition that variant readings are a possible source of textual variation also reduces the value of such phenomena. For the writer may not have known any other reading, and so would have used it without any special motive, as would have been the case if he had had to make a choice between two or more readings.

In the third group the significance is reduced still further. An error that is due to the fickleness of memory can only be given weight if the factor predisposing the writer to make this mistake can be found. There is thus a diminishing degree of certainty attainable for drawing conclusions from the modification of text.

We must conclude that this method will not stand alone, but requires the corroboration of the *rule of interpretation* and the *shift of application*. In other words, if the form of the text points to an interpretation in terms of the Church's claim that Jesus is the Messiah, or to one of the related items of the kerygma, it can be given the attention due to a deliberate modification of the text. It gains greatly in significance if the shift of application has taken place, the quotation being concerned with a derivative issue, so that the writer appears to be unaware of the implications of the form of the text he is using.

It may be seen from the above argument that modification of text may be used as an indicator in evaluating the quotations, in spite of the uncertainty which still surrounds the problem of the Greek texts used by the New Testament writers. As we have pointed out, the question that must be asked is what was the objection to the primitive kerygma which the testimony, taken in its context, was designed to meet. Very often the modification of text will be the deciding factor in answering this question.

The presuppositions and method of study have now been explained, and it may be hoped that by means of them a picture of the early Church can be gained—its immediate interests, and the process which led to the formulation of its dogmas. It will naturally

be an inadequate and partial picture, because it is the result of only
one line of enquiry. It is hoped that it will be of value to supplement other approaches to the subject, and both confirm them and
be confirmed by them. Anticipating some of the results, we may
say that this study shows that the Resurrection of Jesus is the
primary factor in the formation of Christian dogma. The messianic
titles are applied to him as a consequence of this fact, and defended
by appeal to it. There will also be a controversy concerning the
origins of Jesus, what they were, and whether they accord with
messianic expectations. But the controversy only arises as a result
of the messianic claims, which have been already made on the basis
of the Resurrection. The assertion of the virgin birth only follows
at a later stage still. How far this 'later stage' is really posterior in
time is extremely difficult to estimate. All that will be asserted in
these and suchlike results is a *logical sequence* in the development
of dogmatic expression. This can be linked to historical developments at some points, but not always. It is, then, the sequence of
thought in the period between the Resurrection and the writing of
the New Testament which this study illuminates.

The arrangement of the following chapters is largely dictated by
the logical sequence which appears from study of the quotations
along the lines we have laid down. But this cannot always be ad-
hered to, because some of the material is better presented in closely
related groups, and not all of it can be fitted into a tidy scheme.
It will be seen that the books of the New Testament most often
used are the four Gospels, Acts, I Peter, and the earlier Epistles of
St Paul. These books lie closest to the main stream of the development of Christianity, and also were found to yield the most fruitful
material for this study. It may be felt that this conjunction of facts
is not altogether fortuitous. The Epistle to the Hebrews has also
been used, though it is a highly individual biblical study in its own
right, so that its scriptural interpretation witnesses more to the
outlook of the author than to a previous apologetic tradition. The
Book of Revelation, which also contains a wealth of scriptural
quotations, is so poetical and allusive in its approach, and the date
of composition is so difficult to estimate, that it could be used only
rarely for confirmatory evidence of conclusions drawn from other
parts of the New Testament.

The method of this study has a close affinity to that of Form
Criticism. There the Gospels are first broken down into separate

literary elements. These are then classified according to their setting in life by comparison with the laws of the tradition of folk-
lore. From this it appeared that the preservation of these elements
in the Gospel could be ascribed to a particular usefulness in the
Church's missionary preaching. Sometimes a strictly apologetic
motive was observed. We have already seen reason to connect the
Old Testament quotations with apologetic, or to find in them an
implied apologetic as an aid to evaluating them. Throughout this
book this is the normally presumed life-setting of the material
which we are handling. Thus those testimonies which occur in the
Gospels are presumed to owe their *preservation* to this usage in the
early days, even if they are placed on the lips of our Lord, and if a
maximum view of the authenticity of the Gospel record is adopted.[1]
For it is by seeing the apologetic motive that the place of these
elements of Gospel tradition in the development of doctrine can be
gauged. C. H. Dodd holds that this theology, and the chief passages of Scripture which are its foundation, were laid down by our
Lord himself.[2] It may be that the tendency of this study to tear the
quotations from their contexts in the Gospels will make this seem
less probable. Yet it is not intended that this process should be
taken to imply a necessarily negative attitude to this question. But
it does appear that specific citations are less likely to be genuine
parts of the *ipsissima verba* in a number of instances. On the whole
one gains the impression that Jesus used the Bible or referred to it
as occasion arose, but generally preferred to teach in terms of real-
life situations without appealing to the written word. This may
well have contributed to the impression of authority which distinguished his preaching from that of the scribes (Mark 1.22).[3]

Finally it must be pointed out that the argument of this book is
cumulative. In any given instance it may be difficult to accept the
conclusions suggested by application of the methods of study out-
lined in this chapter. But the probability is increased by the fact

[1] Cf. H. Riesenfeld, *The Gospel Tradition and its Beginnings*, 1957. He
maintains that much of the Gospel material is Christian *halakah*, carefully
taught by Jesus himself, and transmitted by the disciples, in the manner
of the rabbinic schools.

[2] *Acc. Scrip.* p. 110.

[3] Notice also the personal authority over against the written word in
the Sermon on the Mount, 'But *I* say . . . '. On the other hand Luke may
have misunderstood Mark's description of our Lord in the synagogue,
when he ascribed to him a sermon on Isa. 61.1f. (Luke 4.16-21). It was
suggested by the Q passage Matt. 11.2-6 = Luke 7.19-23.

that these methods can be used fruitfully so frequently, and by the coherence and consistency of the picture that is built up. We have so little material at our disposal to enable us to see inside the minds of the first Christians, and to know what they made of it when God took action to save the world through his incarnate Son, that we cannot afford to neglect any way of handling it that may serve to increase our understanding of it. The Church had its *testimonia* to the faith—a faith that was newly revealed, yet rooted in the ancient biblical revelation—and we must use them as testimonies to discover the original content of that faith and the process by which it was developed.

# II

## THE RESURRECTION

IN the very first phase after the Resurrection there was probably some uncertainty exactly how what had been accomplished in Jesus should be interpreted. It was clear that all that he had said and done had now been triumphantly vindicated, in spite of the apparent failure. His preaching that the coming kingdom was near was proved to be true. Since he had risen from the dead, it was evident that he would still take the lead in the kingdom. In other words, there could be no doubt that he was to be identified with the Lord's Messiah. So much was overwhelmingly clear. But what was the position now? Was the kingdom still to come after a further short interval? If so, the Resurrection amounted to a divine declaration of the messiahship of Jesus. He is the *Messias designatus*, reserved in heaven for the time when he is to inaugurate the kingdom and usher in the age of the blessings of the Spirit.[1] Alternatively, was the kingdom already established? In this case Jesus, by his Resurrection, is the *Messias revelatus*, and the great future event is already past.

On the first view the Church has the task of undertaking an extremely quick evangelistic mission to complete the work of preparation.[2] The second view is consistent with the deeper and more realistic understanding that the work of preparation goes on alongside life in the kingdom now. This appears to accord best with our Lord's own teaching, in the parables of the leaven and the seed. This is the view that very quickly prevailed in the early Church.

Even though there was this hesitation about the proper interpre-

---

[1] This has left a trace in Acts 3.20f. Cf. J. A. T. Robinson, 'The Most Primitive Christology of all?', *JTS*, NS 7, 1956, pp. 177-89, now reprinted in his *Twelve New Testament Studies* (SBT), 1962, and the same writer's *Jesus and His Coming*, 1957, pp. 143-50.

[2] Cf. Matt 10.23; Mark 9.1.

tation of the actual events, all would agree that Jesus was the Messiah in one sense or the other, and this was the real issue between the Church and the unbelieving Jews. Their unbelief has to be met on their own ground, and so a scriptural argument must be used. In this chapter we shall examine what appear to be survivals of the most primitive argument for the messiahship of Jesus.

This is the argument from *literal fulfilment*. The Bible says that such and such will happen, and it *has* happened. This is the most direct exegesis. It has a simplicity that forestalls criticism and precludes further argument.

It is important to distinguish between this argument and a mere enumeration of correspondences (typology). It has to be common ground between the disputants that the passage of Scripture has a future redemptive, or specifically messianic, reference. If it is then shown that it has been literally fulfilled in Jesus, then it constitutes proof that he is the Messiah. In the New Testament this argument is only used in connection with the Resurrection. It is an event which literally fulfils messianic texts. It therefore proves that Jesus is the Messiah, and the event itself must be interpreted accordingly. This argument arises directly out of the actual situation, and presupposes no objection to the kerygma.[1]

The point may be illustrated from the use of the Passion Psalm 22. It is so frequently alluded to, and details of it are so closely woven into the texture of the Passion narrative of the Gospels, that one can say without hesitation that its usage belongs to the earliest period of the Church's constructive theology. It was quickly seized on for the apologetic purpose of accounting for the sufferings of Jesus. But can we go further, and say that the Church had previously used it to prove that Jesus is the Messiah, or inaugurator

[1] This tradition of argument is preserved in a much developed form in Justin's *Dialogue with Trypho*. He first gives at great length all the major christological passages, proving that they are to be given the future messianic interpretation, and that other commonly held Jewish interpretations are inadequate. Then in 39.7 Trypho stops him, and conceding the messianic interpretations, asks Justin to prove that Jesus is indeed the person to whom they properly apply. It is at this point that Justin begins his more elaborate exegesis, showing in detail how Jesus fulfils the OT types. He begins this with an example that can hardly be primitive, the two crossed spits of the manner of roasting the Passover as a type of the Crucifixion. Then he is sidetracked into another issue, before continuing the series of fulfilments in 49.2. It will be observed that the distinction between typology and the argument from literal fulfilment has in fact disappeared by the time of Justin.

of the coming kingdom? Has the process been first to establish the necessity of messianic interpretation, and then to say that Jesus is the Messiah, because his Passion literally fulfils details of the psalm? It is surely more likely that it was these astonishingly accurate details which first drew attention to the psalm, which was then declared to be messianic because it is fulfilled in Jesus, who is acclaimed as the Messiah *on other grounds*. Of course, once the application had been made in general, it was available for 'explaining' the facts of the Passion. So it is not surprising to discover a greater tendency to elaborate the correspondence in the *later* elements of the Passion narratives.[1] But we look in vain in the New Testament for any indication that the literal fulfilment of this psalm was used for the *construction* of the claim that Jesus is the Christ.

The reason for this is not hard to seek. The Passion needs no explanation unless the claim of messiahship has already been made. It follows that, however early this and other Passion prophecies began to be used, they can never be regarded as primary from the point of view of logical sequence. But with the Resurrection the case is different. The early Christians were able to point to passages of Scripture which required messianic interpretation and were visibly demonstrated in the Resurrection.

The most cogent examples of this primitive argument are to be found in the speech ascribed to St Peter in Acts 2. This may cause some surprise, as it is often held to be a comparatively late composition. But it is characteristic of the material studied in this book that traditions of exegesis are often much more primitive than their context, or their actual form, seems to suggest. In the following sections we shall examine the relics of the argument from literal fulfilment contained in this speech, and also the phrase 'the third day' which has an important bearing on it. The analysis will show how the fundamental tenets of the faith in Jesus were formulated, and the origin of certain basic theologumena which express them.

However, one preliminary objection must be faced. We do not need to take sides in the debate whether the speeches of Acts were composed by Luke himself or taken from a prior source.[2] We only

---

[1] W. L. Knox, *Sources of the Synoptic Gospels* I: St Mark, 1953, p. 144 n. 3.
[2] Full discussion in M. Dibelius, *Studies in the Acts of the Apostles*, ET 1956, pp. 138-85.

maintain that he was making use of the stock of biblical exegesis which was available to him, which would naturally contain both ancient and more recent material. But we cannot avoid the implications of the fact that he quotes from the standard Alexandrian text of the Septuagint almost exclusively, and shows little trace of the influence of the Hebrew text. This is not a real objection. All it means is that, in Luke's Greek-speaking milieu, the change to the exclusive use of this recension of the Septuagint has already taken place. It is the same as the process that may be observed in the manuscript tradition of Justin's *Dialogue* at a later date, except that this is the work of the 'school' *before* Luke made use of the material.[1] There are of course a few places where relics of previous forms of the text remain.[2] Even where the argument turns on the use of the Alexandrian text (the classic example is Acts 15.15-18), that only means that Luke is using one of the later items in the growing store of apologetic scriptures. And in this particular instance the form of the text still reveals a previous exegetical history, from which a useful deduction may be made.[3] We must be pre-

---

[1] Cf. *supra* p. 24 n. 1.

[2] It will be shown in the course of this chapter that the speech in Acts 2 still has a trace of the exegetical work on the *Hebrew* text of Ps. 16 in v. 24. It has been pointed out by M. Black, *An Aramaic Approach to the Gospels and Acts*, 1946, pp. 34-38, that the *casus pendens* in Acts 2.22f. is a sign of translation Greek. The influence of the Targum on a LXX-type phrase has been noted by N. A. Dahl, 'A People for his Name (Acts 15.14)', *NTS* 4, 1958, pp. 319-27.

[3] The crucial phrase is Acts 15.17a: ὅπως ἂν ἐκζητήσωσιν οἱ κατάλοιποι τῶν ἀνθρώπων τὸν κύριον.. Amos 9.12a LXX[B]: ὅπως ἐκζητήσωσιν οἱ κατάλοιποι τῶν ἀνθρώπων. MT: יִירְשׁוּ אֶת־שְׁאֵרִית אֱדֹם. LXX[A] has been influenced by the text of Acts. Presumably the LXX translator had read יִדְרְשׁוּ אֹתִי שְׁאֵרִית אָדָם, though the object με has not survived in our text of the LXX. If τὸν κύριον is an old reading, it points to אֶת י' for אֹתִי. It will be seen that the LXX rendering alone secures the desired universalistic interpretation. A prior exegetical history before Luke incorporated the text may be deduced from Acts 15.18: λέγει κύριος ποιῶν ταῦτα γνωστὰ ἀπ' αἰῶνος. This is a conflation of Amos 9.12: λέγει κύριος ὁ θεὸς ὁ ποιῶν ταῦτα with Isa. 45.21: ἀκουστὰ ἐποίησεν ταῦτα ἀπ' ἀρχῆς. This alters ποιῶν ταῦτα from being a straightforward verb, 'doeth these things', to becoming a causative auxiliary 'maketh these things known'. This makes perfectly good Greek, but would cause some surprise to those familiar with the Amos passage; hence the variants which attempt to undo the conflation. But it is important, because it links this passage with the universalistic prophecies of Deutero-Isaiah, which were a special source of scriptures in the Gentiles apologetic. In a LXX milieu Amos 9.11f. has been used as a comment on the more widely used prophecy of Deut.-Isa.

pared to find examples of very varied age and importance side by side in a single speech.

## 1. BELOW THE SURFACE OF THE SPEECH IN ACTS 2

In the speech ascribed to St Peter on the day of Pentecost there are two quotations used with the argument from literal fulfilment. These are Pss. 16.8-11 and 110.1. Before we consider them in detail, we shall analyse the whole speech from the point of view of a stock of biblical exegesis. Luke has selected what seemed to him suitable from this stock, without realizing what a varied history lies behind each different item.

The structure of the speech is as follows:

(a) The experience at Pentecost is identified with the outpouring of the Spirit in the last days. This is proved from Joel 2.28-32 (3.1-5) (Acts 2.14-21).

(b) The Resurrection is stated as the grounds for the belief that Jesus is 'both Lord and Christ'. This is proved from Ps. 16.8-11. Several other scriptures are referred to in the exegesis of this quotation, including Ps. 110.1, which is also quoted (Acts 2.22-36).

(c) After a pause, in which the response of the audience is mentioned, there is an invitation to them to repent and to be baptized. This includes the final words from Joel 2.32 (3.5), which had not been quoted in the first part of the speech (Acts 2.38f.).

The first thing to notice is that we can distinguish altogether between the first and second parts of the speech. In Acts 2.22 there is a new start. It is an appeal to the hearers, superficially similar to that made in v. 29. But in fact it bears no relation to the preceding quotation from Joel, whereas v. 29 begins the exposition of Ps. 16. This clean break is accompanied by a real difference of subject matter.

On the other hand the third part is necessarily to be taken closely with the first part, because of the integral connection of the quotation material. The quotation in the first part stops short after the first line of the last verse of a paragraph that seems to be complete in itself. Some at least of the missing words appear in Acts 2.39, conflated with words from Isa. 57.19. So we have πᾶσιν τοῖς εἰς μακράν (cf. Isa. 57.19: τοῖς μακρὰν καὶ τοῖς ἐγγὺς οὖσιν) ὅσους ἂν προσκαλέσηται κύριος (cf. Joel 2.32: οὓς κύριος προσκέκληται). A similar phenomenon will be shown later when we consider the scriptures of the second part.

These facts may be explained on the theory that Luke is joining together two separate speeches, a 'Pentecost speech' (parts (a) and (c) ) with a 'Resurrection speech' dovetailed into it. This would imply the combination of two written sources. But it is not necessary to suppose this. His sources may just as well have been two different ranges of scriptural material, *Joel 2.28-32 and its commentary*, and *Ps. 16.8-11 and its commentary*. We have to imagine something like the commentaries discovered at Qumran, consisting of text and comment after each verse, or group of verses.[1] The break in the Joel citation may be a sign that a comment was inserted here.

The argument of this study suggests that the latter alternative is to be accepted. This means that we have two major quotations, each with its commentary, and therefore each with its own exegetical history. It will be seen that both are the end of a process of some complexity, though in the case of Ps. 16 the primitive argument from literal fulfilment has been preserved. This will be shown in the next section. We may complete our present remarks by giving a brief history of the Joel quotation.

In the 'Pentecost speech' Luke has applied Joel 2.28-32 to the outpouring of the Spirit at Pentecost. This cannot be primitive, for it implies that right from the very beginning the Christians were able to plot the precise place of the events in which they were involved in a definite eschatological pattern. It is intrinsically probable that the passage should be used in a much more general way to begin with. It is one of many eschatological passages used by the early Christians in the course of time, to support their claim to be living in the Last Days and to possess the Spirit. No actual example of this general use of this prophecy survives in the New Testament.

A second stage is the use of this prophecy to justify the Church's mission to the Gentiles. On the basis of the general fulfilment of the whole passage, the final verse, which speaks of universal salvation, can receive this particular application. We thus find the first line of Joel 2.32 quoted in precisely this way in Rom. 10.13. It will be shown when we come to examine the quotations in St

[1] We are not here postulating the existence of commentaries of this kind in the primitive Church, none of which have survived. The evidence only suggests an accumulating stock of related texts with occasional explanatory remarks, which may have been oral rather than written for the most part.

Paul that this is only one of a number of eschatological passages which have been given this special application, notably from Deutero-Isaiah. It is an application which was elaborated in a Greek setting, for it takes advantage of the universalizing tendency of the Septuagint version of these prophecies.

These facts lead us to expect that Joel 2.32 might well have a comment on it in terms of a Deutero-Isaiah passage. This is precisely what we find in Acts 2.39. The comment is Isa. 57.19, perhaps the most appropriate of all texts for the preaching to the Gentiles. It is used for this purpose with great effect in Eph. 2.13f., 17.

When we turn to Luke's handling of this material, we see that his context requires this universal application to be restricted to the Diaspora Jews and proselytes of Acts 2.9-11. This is probably not an intentional change, but is due to the needs of the composition. By far the more important change is the application of the whole prophecy from the general experience of the Spirit in the Last Days to the particular event on the Day of Pentecost. It looks like an example of literal fulfilment, but in fact depends on Luke's own typical understanding of this episode as a special event in a post-Resurrection series. The prophecy has gone through at least two stages of Christian interpretation before Luke has used it as the basis of the 'Pentecost speech'.

## 2. PSALM 16 AND ITS COMMENTARY

The 'Resurrection speech' begins with a theological description of the work and death of Jesus (Acts 2.23f.). But v. 24 contains more than a statement of the Resurrection: 'Whom God raised up, having loosed the pangs of death: because it was not possible that he should be holden of it.' This is an *interpretation* of it in terms of the following quotation of Ps. 16.8-11, especially of the key-verse 'Neither wilt thou give thy Holy One to see corruption'. The quotation itself is then followed by a commentary which shows that this verse has been literally fulfilled in Jesus.

The quotation comprises the latter half of the psalm. It also exhibits the same peculiarity as the Joel quotation in that it stops short of the last phrase of the final verse, which should read (as given in RV at Acts 2.28):

'Thou madest known to me the ways of life;
Thou shalt make me full of gladness with thy countenance;
In thy right hand there are pleasures for evermore.'

We must reckon with the possibility that in the traditions known
to St Luke there were comments on the complete psalm. We can,
I believe, see a trace of a comment on an earlier part of it in Acts
2.24, the interpretation of the Resurrection; and the missing line
from the last verse has left a quite elaborate comment in v. 33.
The 'Resurrection speech' thus consists of (i) a comment on the
earlier part of Ps. 16 (v. 24); (ii) the main quotation and its commentary (vv. 25-32); and (iii) the final line of the psalm, used in
conjunction with Ps. 110.1, which also mentions God's right hand.
This analysis must now be shown in detail.

(i) In v. 24 the Resurrection is put in terms of a metaphor of
imprisonment. Jesus had been 'held' by the 'pangs of death', but
God has 'loosed' him from them. It is really a mixed metaphor, for
it speaks of 'pangs' where we should expect 'bonds'. This leads us
into a tantalizing exegetical problem. For the phrase 'pangs of death'
(τὰς ὠδῖνας τοῦ θανάτου) is taken from Ps. 18(17).5a = 116(114).3a,
translating the Hebrew חֶבְלֵי־מָוֶת. The word חבלי is the plural
of two distinct words, one meaning 'pangs' and the other 'cords'.
The whole phrase can be used in different contexts with a variety
of metaphors, the ideas oscillating between these two meanings.[1]
The Greek translator was not able to reproduce this play on words,
and so was forced to decide which meaning to adopt. The fact that
at times he has chosen what appears to be the inappropriate word
may be due to the use of the mixed metaphor (i.e. being bound by
pains) already in Greek literature.[2] This makes it very hard to
decide whether the mixed metaphor in this verse has been caused
by a translator's misconstruction of an Aramaic original, or is
merely fortuitous in an original Greek composition.[3]

[1] The metaphor may be the hunter's noose (Ps. 18.6; in v. 5 the
metaphor was lost when the original מִשְׁבְּרֵי־מָוֶת, preserved in II Sam.
22.5, was attracted to חֶבְלֵי־מָוֶת). It appears to be a cordon or net in
Ps. 116.3, though the parallel (if not corrupt) implies that the meaning
pain is also present. In 1QH 3.9 it is the pangs of childbirth. 1QH 3.28
appears to require the meaning torrents or currents of water, and so
attests the reading חבלי־מות in Ps. 18.5, from which it is clearly derived.
[2] T. E. Page, *The Acts of the Apostles*, 1886, refers to ὠδῖσι συνέχεσθαι,
Plato *Rep.* 574A. Cf. also Acts 28.8.
[3] C. C. Torrey supposed confusion from an Aramaic original, but this

Our theory of a previous exegetical history suggests a new solution to the problem. The first Christians had a special interest in the Psalms as prophecy of the events of redemption. It was natural to use the psalm-phrase 'pangs of death' in connection with the Passion. Ps. 16 is a prophecy of the Resurrection, but it contains the word חֲבָלִים in v. 6. But it is here used in a good sense, and *must* have the meaning 'cords' (*sc.* of life, i.e. lot or fate). The RV translates it: 'The *lines* are fallen unto me in pleasant places.' Here the Septuagint correctly uses σχοινία. The good news of the Resurrection proclaims that in Jesus the pangs of death have been transformed into the cords of a prosperous destiny, God-given life. Thus the Christian exegetes use Ps. 16.6 as a commentary on 'the pangs of death', a phrase already applied to the Passion. This exegetical work has been done with the Hebrew text, and is obscured when turned into Greek. That is why Luke has failed to see any reason for including v. 6 with his quotation.

(ii) What Luke really is interested in is to express the Resurrection in a way that will lead up to the argument based on the long quotation from Ps. 16. So he lays the emphasis, not on the fact that Jesus rose from the dead, but on the fact that the grave could not contain him. The verses quoted from Ps. 16 expound the Resurrection from this point of view.

To see the point of the exegesis, we need to have some idea of the meaning that might have been expected. Taking the psalm as it stands, it appears to be a psalm of trust in time of sickness. The psalmist is confident that his fears of death will not be realized, and that he will live to rejoice in the knowledge of God's providence. He expresses this in the idea of return from Sheol. But the metaphor of sickness and healing is frequently applied within the Old Testament itself to the weakness and revival of the nation. Inevitably such a psalm as this would be applied to national renewal in late Judaism. It might even be applied, with closer regard to the literal meaning, to the expectation of the resurrection of the dead which appears in Dan. 12.2 (cf. Matt. 27.52f.).

So much might be generally taken for granted. But this is not a properly literal interpretation, because it still involves thinking of the revival in collective terms. But v. 10 (the key-verse) is in the first person, and the psalmist describes himself as 'thy holy

is not followed by M. Black, who only refers to the possible indication of translation Greek, as noted above.

one'.[1] This means that it must refer to one individual, presumably David, who is the speaker. But David had died and was buried (v. 29).

The comment brings out the only alternative interpretation by adducing the messianic promise made to David. It makes reference to Ps. 132.11 and II Chron. 6.9f. (LXX). The psalm necessarily speaks of the coming Messiah (τοῦ Χριστοῦ). At this point (v. 31) the title is simply a technical term, and not yet specifically applied to Jesus. But even this messianic interpretation does not do full justice to the exact words of the psalm. There was no expectation of a dying and rising Messiah.[2] It still means taking the psalm metaphorically. The Church insists that it is to be taken messianically and to be taken literally. This is the point where the Christian exegesis parts company with any previous Jewish exegesis. Ps. 16 foretells the actual death and resurrection of the Messiah. Seeing that God actually raised Jesus from the dead, it follows that he is the Messiah.

This conclusion is not expressed in Acts 2.32, where it might be expected, because it is held over until v. 36, after the comment on the last line of the psalm has been given. But it is already implied, and in fact is inevitable and irresistible. We can imagine how compelling such an argument from literal fulfilment would be. It has no objections to answer, but simply gives the meaning of the staggering event of the Resurrection. It is a form of argument which is pre-apologetic, and it carries immediate conviction.

Nevertheless it cannot be asserted that it was precisely *this* psalm which was first used by the Church in this telling way. It is more probable that it is only one of several messianic psalms used with this argument.[3] Ps. 110, which we shall be studying in the next section, was probably in use before it. The New Testament does not give evidence of any wide use of Ps. 16. But it appears to have been important in Luke's milieu, because he uses it again in Acts 13.34-37. Here there is exactly the same argument from literal ful-

[1] τὸν ὅσιόν σου. MT חֲסִידְךָ according to the text of Ben Asher preserved in the Leningrad MSS used in BH³. The better-known text of Ben Chayyim has Kthibh חֲסִידֶיךָ and Qri חֲסִידְךָ. This at least shows that the singular was traditional here, a fact which is now confirmed.

[2] Cf. S. Mowinckel, *He that Cometh*, pp. 325-33, summarizing the evidence of literature of late Judaism. The recent attempts to prove the contrary from the Qumran literature are now generally held to be a failure.

[3] For messianic interpretation of Ps. 16 see SB II, p. 618.

filment, but he has made a different selection of accompanying messianic texts (Ps. 2.7, Isa. 55.3).

There can be no doubt that the argument is primitive. It is specially notable that it does not involve a claim that Jesus is actually descended from David. The oath mentioned in Acts 2.30 might imply this, but is really only included to secure the messianic interpretation of the psalm. It has nothing to do with the proof of the messiahship of Jesus, which rests on his fulfilment of the psalm in contrast to David. But of course, since Jesus is the Messiah, descent from David is desirable, and becomes imperative. We shall see how this came to the fore in the Church's apologetic in a later chapter (ch. V). Luke himself accepted the Davidic descent of Jesus. This makes it all the more significant that he omits to use it in the argument of this speech.

(iii) We must now turn to the comment on the words which were not included in the main quotation, i.e. Ps. 16.11c: τερπνότητες ἐν τῇ δεξιᾷ σου εἰς τέλος. The comment begins in Acts 2.33, which reads: 'Being therefore by (RVm at) the right hand of God exalted, and having received of the Father the promise of the Holy Ghost, he hath poured forth this, which ye see and hear.'[1] Thus the 'pleasures at God's right hand', which are the reward of the risen Messiah, consist in the Exaltation of Jesus and the Gift of the Spirit. These correspond to the two great events (in the Lucan scheme) that followed the Resurrection, i.e. the Ascension and Pentecost.

But it is not really as simple as this. For the idea of the Resurrection and Ascension (or Heavenly Session) as separate, successive events is a schematization devised by Luke for ease in the presentation of his material. Outside the Lucan literature all the evidence points to the conclusion that they were originally considered to be simultaneous, or rather as different aspects of one truth.[2] This was probably true in the underlying exegetical material. We therefore have to unravel v. 33 to discover the meaning of the exegesis before Luke used it in composing the speech: τῇ δεξιᾷ οὖν τοῦ θεοῦ ὑψωθεὶς τήν τε ἐπαγγελίαν τοῦ πνεύματος τοῦ ἁγίου λαβὼν

---

[1] J. A. T. Robinson, 'The Most Primitive Christology of all?', p. 185, suggested that the speech may have originally ended at this point, the citation of Ps. 110.1 and the peroration (v. 36) being added in the final editing. It will be seen that the evidence of the quotation material is decisive against this view.

[2] This is now an axiom of New Testament critical scholarship.

παρὰ τοῦ πατρὸς ἐξέχεεν τοῦτο ὃ ὑμεῖς καὶ βλέπετε καὶ ἀκούετε.

In this verse τὴν ἐπαγγελίαν and τοῦτο ὅ to the end are clearly Lucan words (cf. 1.4, 2.16). We can also strip off τοῦ πνεύματος τοῦ ἁγίου and ἐξέχεεν, because they have been introduced from the beginning of the Joel quotation in v. 17. All these words belong to Luke's composition and its context of the Pentecost experience. This leaves only τῇ δεξιᾷ οὖν τοῦ θεοῦ ὑψωθείς and λαβὼν παρὰ τοῦ πατρός as relics of the commentary on Ps. 16. These therefore belong to the exposition of Ps. 16 in terms of the Resurrection of Jesus.

The main part of Ps. 16, as we have seen, spoke of the Resurrection in terms of the impossibility of the grave to contain the Messiah, and the phrase 'pangs of death' from Pss. 18 and 116 was used in conjunction with it (v. 24). In the same way, this final stichos expresses the Resurrection in terms of the proper *place* of the Messiah, i.e. at God's right hand. So presumably it was used in conjunction with Ps. 110.1, κάθου ἐκ δεξιῶν μου, which is actually quoted in v. 34. Jesus, being raised from the dead, is *ipso facto* satisfied with pleasures at the right hand of God, where he sits.[1]

This interpretation necessarily attaches a local signification to τῇ δεξιᾷ in v. 33, as in RV margin. It is more commonly translated instrumentally. The question cannot be solved grammatically, but depends on the underlying quotations. The instrumental interpretation is suggested by the following verb ὑψωθείς, which makes the whole phrase reminiscent of Ps. 118(117).16, δεξιὰ κυρίου ὕψωσέν με. This seems plausible, seeing that the verb is passive. This means that 'by the right hand of God exalted' represents 'the right hand of God has exalted'. But this is not really the case. The only other place in the New Testament where τῇ δεξιᾷ occurs without preposition is Acts 5.31, τοῦτον ὁ θεός . . . ὕψωσεν τῇ δεξιᾷ αὐτοῦ. Here again it is usually translated instrumentally, but RV margin gives the alternative 'at'. It is self-evident that this passage has close affinities with Acts 2.33. In fact it is another case where Luke uses his biblical material a second time, just as he repeats the argument from Ps. 16 in ch. 13. The two passages can thus be used to interpret one another. We notice that Acts 5.31 has the same verb

---

[1] These pleasures might even be called the joy of victory, if the psalm was used with this interpretation in the original Hebrew, and נֶצַח received the same meaning as it bears in I Cor. 15.54. But this is pure speculation.

ὑψόω, but this time in the *active* voice, and God himself is the subject. This obviously makes the direct influence of Ps. 118.16 less likely. We are then justified in interpreting τῇ δεξιᾷ of place, because the real influences are Ps. 16.11 and Ps. 110.1, which are found or implied in the context of Acts 2.33.

This means that we must look elsewhere for the origin of ὑψωθείς in this verse. It is to be seen in connection with the other pre-Lucan words λαβὼν παρὰ τοῦ πατρός. Luke is probably right to say that the object of this verb is the Spirit. For it adds to the notion of the *place* of the Messiah that of his *function*. This is a second comment on the last line of Ps. 16. The first was Ps. 110.1, which has survived in Luke's composition. It is likely that the second was another psalm verse, Ps. 68(67).19, ἀνέβης εἰς ὕψος ... ἔλαβες δόματα ἐν ἀνθρώπῳ.[1] The verbal link is provided by λαβών, and it affords an alternative to account for ὑψωθείς. This may not seem very probable at first sight, but is strikingly confirmed by the very next verse, which goes on to say οὐ γὰρ Δαυιδ ἀνέβη εἰς τοὺς οὐρανούς. Moreover this verse can be shown to have influenced Acts 5.31, which continues with the thought of messianic gifts, especially that of the Spirit.

We need not discount the influence of Ps. 118.16 altogether. In the biblical material which Luke draws on for his composition one scripture interprets another. Ps. 118 was used in connection with the Resurrection from an early date (see ch. IV). But it cannot be held to be a primary influence in Acts 2.33 for the reasons already given. The basic thought is the place of the Messiah, and this leads into the thought of his function. It is the very primitive testimony Ps. 110.1, and also Ps. 68.19, which give expression to these ideas. They belong to the early creative stage, when dogmatic statement is emerging from specially valued testimonies.

The study of the intricate biblical background of the speech in Acts 2 has shown the survival of a very primitive argument for the messiahship of Jesus from the fact of the Resurrection. It has also shown how the Exaltation of Jesus could be an alternative way of speaking of the Resurrection, throwing the emphasis on the place at God's right hand. This in its turn was inseparable from the thought of the Messiah's function. The two testimonies which convey these ideas in the substratum of Acts 2.33 are each deeply

---

[1] I am indebted to Professor C. F. D. Moule for drawing my attention to this reference.

involved in the evolution of dogmatic formulation, and are at the foundation of the two theologumena of the Session at the Right Hand of God and the Gift of the Spirit. These will now be examined in the next two sections.

### 3. AT THE RIGHT HAND OF GOD

In the preceding section it has been suggested that Ps. 110.1 was the first of two comments on the last line of Ps. 16.11. But it was also pointed out that it was probably in use in the Church at a very much earlier date, and that it was perhaps the most important of the scriptures used with the argument from literal fulfilment. These two observations make it very desirable to trace the history of its use in the New Testament, and suggest that we should continue to use Acts 2 as our starting-point, where this primitive argument has still been preserved. We shall, of course, have to bear in mind that the Exaltation of which it speaks was originally an alternative way of talking about the Resurrection, though it slips into denoting a separate, successive act.

The argument is strictly parallel to that of Ps. 16. The psalm demands a messianic interpretation; it is not true of David himself; it has been literally fulfilled in the Resurrection of Jesus; therefore Jesus is the Christ.

In the text of Acts 2.33f. this is only hinted at. It is assumed that Ps. 110 is messianic.[1] Then comes the question whether it may be properly applied to David. The psalm states that 'The Lord said unto my lord, Sit thou on my right hand . . .'. The early Christian exegete supposes that, in order to sit at God's right hand, it is necessary first to go up to heaven, where God is. We may conjecture that the psalmist himself would have thought an earthly throne entirely adequate for this purpose, according to the usual conventions of the ancient 'enthronement psalms'.[2] But the Christian assumption would undoubtedly have been shared by all dis-

---

[1] This was frequent in late and rabbinic Judaism. See the *Excursus* in SB IV, pp. 452-65.

[2] For a recent appraisal of the theories of Gunkel and Mowinckel in connection with these psalms, see A. R. Johnson, 'Hebrew Conceptions of Kingship', in S. H. Hooke (ed.), *Myth, Ritual and Kingship*, 1958, pp. 204-35, especially p. 228. It is not necessary to accept the hypothesis that there was actually an annual enthronement festival after the Babylonian pattern, in order to see that old Israel could conceive of the virtual *equivalence* of the earthly and heavenly thrones in a way that was impossible to late Judaism.

putants, as it was the normal idea in late Judaism.[1] Therefore the words cannot apply to David himself, who only sat on an earthly throne and died a natural death. But Jesus passed from death to life. God raised him up through the gate of death to the place at his right hand. He is actually enthroned there, as literally as such a phrase will allow without degenerating into crude anthropomorphism. It is a risen and ascended Lord who has been seen by the chosen witnesses. On account of this literal fulfilment of Ps. 110.1, Jesus can be styled 'Lord', אֲדֹנִי.[2] So the argument of the 'Resurrection speech' can be summarized in v. 36: the Resurrection proves that Jesus is both Lord, the literal fulfiller of Ps. 110, and Christ, the literal fulfiller of Ps. 16.

Here again we notice that there is no question of basing our Lord's messiahship on real or supposed descent from David. That will arise later, because he is the fulfiller of this messianic psalm.

This brings us face to face with the use of Ps. 110.1 in the Gospel tradition at Mark 12.36 and parallels. This challenges our theory of the original use of it on two counts. It purports to go behind the primitive Church to the teaching of Jesus himself; and it is specifically concerned with the Davidic issue. This latter aspect differentiates it from all other references to this scripture in the New Testament. We must therefore give special attention to it.

In the *pericope* as given in Mark 12.35-37 our Lord takes up an opinion of the rabbis that the Messiah is son of David. He refutes it by citing Ps. 110.1, where David (the presumed speaker) calls the Messiah 'my lord'. Two interpretations of this are possible. (a) The traditional view is that Jesus is proving that the rabbis have a too narrow and mundane conception of messiahship. This is consistent with belief that the incident is authentic Gospel tradition. (b) Many modern critics hold that Jesus is refuting the necessity of descent from David to establish a messianic claim. In this case it may well belong to the controversy concerning the origins of Jesus, and so be a church-formation.[3]

For its provenance, W. L. Knox has shown that it 'came to Mark in its present form as an isolated unit or from a different collection of sayings'.[4] The motive of the *pericope* itself differs from

---

[1] Cf. S. A. Cook, *The Old Testament: a Reinterpretation*, 1936, pp. 205f.

[2] There is no warrant for supposing an implicit identification of the risen and exalted Jesus with יהוה (LXX ὁ κύριος) himself in this context.

[3] R. Bultmann, *Geschichte der Synoptische Tradition*[2], 1931, p. 145.

[4] *Sources of the Synoptic Gospels* I, p. 91.

the motive for the insertion of it into its present context. The latter is simply the fact that it provides an example of the worsting of the rabbis. No doubt Mark understood it according to the traditional interpretation. He failed to remove the ambiguity because he was only really interested in it as a sample of beating the rabbis with their own stick. It was for this reason that 'the common people heard him gladly' (v. 37), in spite of the fact that (on either interpretation) it was their own popular idea of messiahship that was being attacked!

Taking the passage by itself, we observe that the argument depends upon the gratuitous assumption that 'lord' is either inconsistent with, or greatly superior to, 'son of David'. The psalm apparently speaks of a lordship that was greater than anything that David could claim for himself. This is presumably defined by the remainder of the verse, i.e. the session at the right hand of God instead of merely on an earthly throne. The distinction between 'lord' and 'son of David' thus depends on precisely the argument used in Acts 2.34, which proved that the psalm is only truly fulfilled in the Resurrection of Jesus.

Viewed in this light, the whole *pericope* is evidently derived from the exegesis preserved in Acts 2. This means that we are bound to accept the verdict of many modern critics that it is a product of *Gemeindetheologie*. We can even go further, and show its place in the apologetic development. As it stands, it is a purely theoretical argument on the qualifications for messiahship. It fails to include the reference to Jesus himself. It ought to go on to say that Jesus does fulfil the qualification of lordship, and therefore he is the Christ. But this is assumed by the tradition, for it is implied in the very fact that this argument has been placed on the lips of Jesus. The reason for its omission is that the interest has shifted to another issue. Attention is concentrated on the fact that David himself did not qualify for the messianic claim in this way. The apologetic motive behind this is clearly the need to assert our Lord's messiahship in spite of the objection that he is thought not to be descended from David. We conclude that the argument in Acts 2 preserves the original and fundamental use of Ps. 110.1, and that the Gospel passage about David's son represents a slightly later stage, when the Davidic controversy has arisen. It thus shows the use of this testimony in a secondary and derivative application.

It is not necessary to go into the many other quotations and allusions to Ps. 110.1 in such detail, for their dependence on the argument in Acts 2 needs no demonstration. None of them shows any further interest in the Davidic issue, nor do they reveal the process of literal interpretation we have seen preserved in Acts 2. But they presuppose this process. For they use the phrase 'at the right hand of God' as an established theologumenon, an expression normally employed in the kerygma, an article of the Creed. This happens as early as Rom. 8.34. Other places in which it will be found are Eph. 1.20; Col. 3.1; Heb. 1.3, 13, 8.1, 10.12, 12.2; I Peter 3.22 (Mark 16.19).

Two places require closer attention, where the same phrase is conflated with words from the important Son of Man text, Dan. 7.13. These are Mark 14.62, and parallels, and Acts 7.55f. It is probable that in the earliest period the Daniel passage was used to express the vindication of Jesus in the Resurrection, regarded as the moment of declaration of his messiahship. In this case the verse is correctly treated as describing a coming *to* God, contrary to the usual way of interpreting it when it is used as a *messianic* text (coming to earth to set up the kingdom).[1] If this was how the Church first used it, then its meaning was exactly equivalent to that of Ps. 110.1a. Jesus, the Son of Man (whatever that meant), was declared to be the Messiah by virtue of his Exaltation.

This original use of the two equivalent texts is implied in the account of the Ascension in Acts 1.9, and actually seems to be preserved in Acts 7.55f.[2] As the close parallel of words and ideas in John 1.51 shows, Luke is here using conventional phraseology, and is no doubt unaware of its implications for discovering the original use of Dan. 7.13.

In Mark 14.62, our Lord's answer to the high priest, the original use has been overlaid by adaptation to meet a later reconsideration. The first half of the verse, ὄψεσθε τὸν υἱὸν τοῦ ἀνθρώπου ἐκ δεξιῶν καθήμενον τῆς δυνάμεως, expresses the original idea, if taken by itself. It gives a direct answer to the question 'Art thou the Christ?', i.e. 'I am, as you will see when my claim is vindicated

---

[1] J. A. T. Robinson, *Jesus and His Coming*, pp. 43-45. The view that Dan. 7.13 means a coming down to earth belongs not only to Christian apocalyptic, but also to rabbinic texts when the passage is referred to the *Messiah*. See H. K. McArthur, 'Mark 14.62', *NTS* 4, 1958, pp. 156-8.

[2] The use of ἑστῶτα rather than καθήμενον here is not significant for the interpretation, being equally suitable to express the *place* of the risen and exalted Jesus. Cf. Dodd, *Acc. Scrip.*, p. 35, note.

and I am declared to be the Christ at my exaltation to the right hand of God.'[1] The second half, ἐρχόμενον μετὰ τῶν νεφελῶν τοῦ οὐρανοῦ, is bound to refer to a coming *after* the Heavenly Session, and so necessarily implies the Parousia, when the kingdom is to be set up on earth, and all God's enemies will be punished. The Resurrection, as the moment of messianic declaration, is lost to view, and the whole verse becomes an apocalyptic prophecy. It ceases to *explain* the answer 'I am'. It merely adds to it a veiled threat. This is a common feature of the early apologetic.

On these grounds it seems necessary to regard the second half of Mark 14.62 as an addition to the original saying.[2] This does not mean that we regard it as an interpolation into the text of Mark, against the unanimous manuscript evidence and the parallel in Matt. 26.64. It is omitted in Luke 22.69, probably simply to get rid of the inconsistency.[3] There are textual features that show that this verse in Mark 14.62 is drawn from a different version of Dan. 7.13 from that used in the Little Apocalypse (Mark 13.26).[4] The adaptation has thus taken place before the saying reached Mark. The first half has some exceptional features, whereas the second half simply follows the text of Daniel as found in Theodotion.[5] It seems, then, that in the first place Ps. 110.1 has been conflated with Dan. 7.13 without change of the fundamental meaning that Jesus is declared to be Messiah by his Exaltation. But the allusion to Dan. 7.13 has later (but still in the pre-Marcan phase) exerted an increasing influence, resulting in expansion of the text to convey a new meaning.

We cannot leave study of Ps. 110.1 without a few remarks on the second half of the verse, 'Till I make thine enemies the footstool of thy feet.' In the earliest phase the striking words of the first half monopolize attention, although the first Christians would

---

[1] Taking τῆς δυνάμεως (sc. τοῦ θεοῦ) to be a periphrasis for God (cf. τοῦ εὐλογητοῦ in the preceding verse).

[2] E. Meyer, *Ursprung und Anfänge des Christentums* I, 1921, p. 194.

[3] Cf. his omission at 9.27 = Mark 9.1.

[4] Notice first the comparative freedom of Mark 13.26 from both LXX and Theodotion, not only ἐν νεφέλαις for ἐπὶ (Θ' μετὰ) τῶν νεφελῶν, but also μετὰ δυνάμεως πολλῆς καὶ δόξης, cf. LXX ἐξουσία . . . καὶ πᾶσα δόξα, Θ' ἡ ἀρχὴ καὶ ἡ τιμὴ καὶ ἡ βασιλεία. Contrast with this, in Mark 14.62a, the use of δυνάμεως in a different sense, and in the second half the full phrase μετὰ τῶν νεφελῶν τοῦ οὐρανοῦ.

[5] First half: the conflation with Ps. 110.1, and the use of δυνάμεως mentioned in last note. For second half, cf. Θ' ἰδοὺ μετὰ τῶν νεφελῶν τοῦ οὐρανοῦ ὡς υἱὸς ἀνθρώπου ἐρχόμενος ἦν.

no doubt think of it as standing for the meaning of the psalm as a whole. It is to be expected that derivative interpretations will be drawn from other parts of the psalm as time goes on. As we have observed when discussing Acts 2.33, the place and function of the risen Lord tend to be taken closely together. There, an allusion to Ps. 68.19 expressed his function. But Ps. 110.1b can also be used for this purpose. It is included in the quotation in Acts 2.34f., and also in Mark 12.36, but without comment. We find it actually used in quotations in I Cor. 15.25 and Heb. 10.13, and allusions in Eph. 1.22, Heb. 2.5-8 and I Peter 3.22. In all these places the meaning is the subjugation of *spiritual* enemies. Although this involves taking the words metaphorically, there is no suggestion here of allegory. It is simply the consequence of applying the first half of the verse to the Heavenly Session of the Messiah. His presence at the right hand of God necessarily entails the conquest of the spiritual powers. This is thus part of the *literal* fulfilment of the psalm, which, it is asserted, has taken place in the Resurrection of Jesus.

A notable feature of these references is that consideration of Ps. 110.1b often involves conflation with Ps. 8.7, 'Thou hast put all things under his feet'. Thus in I Cor. 15.25 the addition of πάντας, 'all thine enemies', is due to the quotation of Ps. 8.7 two verses later, which is already in St Paul's mind. Heb. 2.5-8 is exclusively concerned with an exposition of Ps. 8.5-7, but the way has been prepared for it by the unexpounded citation of Ps. 110.1 in 1.13. In Eph. 1.20-22, and in I Peter 3.22, only the *first* half of Ps. 110.1 is alluded to, the second being exclusively expressed in terms derived from Ps. 8.7. Only Heb. 10.13 is uninfluenced by Ps. 8.7, but here there is no comment. It is equally notable that Ps. 8.7 is nowhere expounded without the aid of Ps. 110.1. The only other allusion to it (Phil. 3.21) depends on the christology formulated by means of linking both these passages. Even the citation of Ps. 8.3 in Matt. 21.16 is probably dependent on this christological use of the psalm, for it has been introduced into the account of our Lord's triumphal entry at a comparatively late stage.[1] As literary dependence between the Paulines, Hebrews and I Peter can hardly be supposed, we must conclude that all three writers are drawing on the common stock of exegetical material.

[1] The use of this passage in this context turns on the LXX αἶνος for MT עז, cf. Stendahl, *SSM*, p. 134.

In this work Ps. 110 is primary and the use of Ps. 8 follows from it. This development marks a new stage in christology, which is presupposed by all three writers. It is a matter which will have to be studied further in a later chapter.[1]

The use of Ps. 110.4, 'a priest for ever after the order of Melchizedek', belongs exclusively to Hebrews. It is another derivative application of this psalm, which will be referred to again later.[2] It is not too much to say that the entire christology of this Epistle stems from the study of this psalm.

It is universally recognized that the christological application of Ps. 110.1 is of cardinal importance throughout the New Testament. The above analysis has shown that it gained this importance because it was seen from the first that it was literally fulfilled in the great event of redemption. It thus definitively explains this event, and has given the theologumenon of our Lord's Session at the Right Hand of God to the Christian vocabulary.[3]

## 4. THE GIFT OF THE SPIRIT

It will now be argued that Ps. 68.19, the other text alluded to in Acts 2.33, has also a place in the early history of Christian doctrine, and lies behind another theologumenon, the Gift of the Spirit. The evidence is slighter, and the results are less certain, than in the case of Ps. 110.1 which we have just studied. This time we cannot use the argument from literal fulfilment to achieve certainty that the psalm verse was actually used in the most primitive phase. It is more probable that it enters into the discussion at a slightly later stage.

In the text of Ps. 68.19 (EVV 18), it is the words 'Thou hast ascended on high . . . thou hast received gifts among men' which attracted the attention of the Church. They express both the Exaltation and the function of the Messiah. We have already seen that place and function are both to be found in the two halves of the Exaltation text, Ps. 110.1. It is thus most probably a comment on the more primitive testimony. As such, it adds nothing further to the idea of the Exaltation, and so all the interest passes to the phrase which describes the messianic function. In the earlier testi-

---

[1] Infra, pp. 167-69.     [2] Infra, p. 142.
[3] The theological implications of the references to Ps. 110.1 have been clearly set out by J. Daniélou, 'La Session à la droite du Père', in K. Aland, F. L. Cross et al. (edd.), Studia Evangelica (Texte und Untersuchungen 73), 1959, pp. 689-98.

mony this was the negative function of waiting for the subjection
of God's enemies. In this one there is the positive function of receiving gifts among men. It is in this phrase that a very significant
modification of text occurs.

The verse is quoted only once in the New Testament. This is in
Eph. 4.8, in the following form: ἀναβὰς εἰς ὕψος ᾐχμαλώτευσεν
αἰχμαλωσίαν, ἔδωκεν δόματα τοῖς ἀνθρώποις. There are several differences here from the Septuagint. At the end ἐν ἀνθρώπῳ (v.l. -οις)
has been changed to τοῖς ἀνθρώποις. This is more important than it
seems at first sight, as will appear later. The verbs have been
changed from second to third person. This is probably only due
to the needs of the context. But the last verb itself is a different
one, ἔδωκεν instead of ἔλαβες. This is a most significant alteration,
and requires careful study.

It has long been held that this change is due to the influence of
the Targum, which paraphrases the verse thus: 'Thou ascendest
up to the firmament, O Prophet Moses, thou tookest captives cap-
tive, thou didst teach the words of the law, thou *gavest* them as
gifts to the children of men.'[1] But as it is a matter of only one word,
and the Targum seems to have had no other influence either on
the form or the interpretation of the quotation in Ephesians, it is
probably better to suppose that this Targum and Eph. 4.8 both
witness to a Hebrew text which had 'gavest' for 'receivedst'. But
this cannot be proved.[2] It is much more likely that we have here a

---

[1] S. R. Driver's translation. The text is:

סלקתא לרקיע משה נביא שביתא שביתא אלפתא פתגמי
אוריתא יהבתא לון מתנן לבני נשא:

[2] H. St J. Thackeray, *The Relation of St Paul to Contemporary Jewish
Thought*, 1900, p. 182, suggested that there might have been a variant
חלקת for לקחת, but it is not likely that this would yield ἔδωκες in a
Greek text and יהבתא in the Targum. SB (III, pp. 596-8) quote *Aboth
RN2* (2a) and *Tr. Sopher* 16.10, which have full comments on this verse,
but both follow MT without a hint of the Targum tradition. The Peshitta
Syriac has also been claimed as a witness to this tradition, but this can
hardly be maintained. W. E. Barnes, in his edition of the Peshitta Psalms
1904), prints ܘܝܗܒܬ (*wᵉ-yahbhtᵉ*) in his text. The critical apparatus
gives ܘܢܣܒܬ (*wa-nᵉṣabhtᵉ*) as an alternative reading. In his introduction he discusses this reading at some length, because it is a crux for his
attempt to get behind the Jacobite and Nestorian recensions to the original
text. He notes that all the Jacobite texts have *wᵉyahbhtᵉ*, and all the
Nestorian *wa-nᵉṣabhtᵉ*. The Jacobite MSS are older, but this is not the
main criterion. It may be argued that the Jacobite has been influenced by
Eph. 4.8; alternatively that the Nestorian has been influenced by the LXX.

real case of coincidence, rather than actual dependence. The reason is not hard to find. The words 'thou hast received gifts among men' are too compressed to be understood unambiguously. It probably means 'received gifts by right of superiority over the people'. But it is easy to think of it as 'gifts *for* men', and then the receiving is evidently for the purpose of giving. There is thus nothing surprising when the word 'gifts' suggests expression of its own cognate verb, and then the receiving drops out altogether. In Eph. 4 the idea of giving dominates the whole context, which implies that the reading in the quotation has an interpretative motive. It is thus most probably a case of the *midrash pesher*,[1] and should be classified as an example of *modification of text*. Seeing that ἔδωκεν in the quotation is the keyword to the whole of the argument, it is probable that it already existed in the form of the text known to the writer of Ephesians. It is our contention that it does indeed go back to a much earlier time, and is the origin of the phrase 'the gift of the Spirit'.

The first thing to observe is that the three references to this text in the New Testament are concerned with the idea of the giving of the Spirit. Eph. 4 itself is about precisely the same *spiritual* gifts, or manifestations of the Spirit, as I Cor. 12. There is certainly a literary connection between the two passages, even if Ephesians is not by St Paul. The second reference is Acts 2.33, which is, as we have seen, related to the experience at Pentecost. The use of λαβών

In other places LXX influence can be demonstrated; NT influence remains unproven. Moreover Theodore follows LXX, and it is known that his works influenced the final form of the Peshitta. Therefore Barnes accepts *wᵉ-yahbhtᵉ* of the Jacobite as the original text, thinking that the Nestorian has conformed it to the LXX, perhaps following Theodore. This would give an independent tradition for 'gavest' in this verse. On the other hand it is *a priori* more probable that the original text was that common to both MT and LXX, which has survived in the Nestorian without the aid of actual influence of the LXX or of Theodore. It is surely the simplest solution to suppose that the original Syriac text had *wa-nᵉṣabhtᵉ*, which has survived in the Nestorian, but was corrupted to *wᵉ-yahbhtᵉ* in the exemplar which lies behind the Jacobite recension, not because of Eph. 4.8, but because (*a*) the two words are very similar to the eye, especially in the Estrangela script, and (*b*) the following *mauhbhāthā'* would easily exercise an attraction to the cognate verb on the part of the copyist. The Peshitta has so often been cited in support of the text in Eph. 4.8 that it ought to be better known that its value as evidence is extremely precarious.

[1] So Ellis, *St Paul's Use of the OT*, p. 144.

testifies to the unmodified text of Ps. 68.19. It is, however, possible that the following verb ἐξέχεεν replaces an original ἔδωκεν. It comes from the Joel quotation (Acts 2.17). This, we have argued, was the nucleus of a separate 'Pentecost speech', just as the 'Resurrection speech' was woven round Ps. 16. The word has therefore been inserted into v. 33 only in the final editing. If ἔδωκεν originally stood here, then we would have an intermediate stage, between the true text of Ps. 68.19 and the quotation in Eph. 4.8, where *both* the receiving *and* the giving are expressed. The third reference, Acts 5.31, lends support to this suggestion, for τοῦ δοῦναι immediately follows the description of the Exaltation, ὕψωσεν τῇ δεξιᾷ αὐτοῦ. It has already been shown that these words are probably derived from the same exegetical material, i.e. Ps. 110.1 with its comment, Ps. 68.19. Although the object of δοῦναι is μετάνοιαν τῷ 'Ισραὴλ καὶ ἄφεσιν ἁμαρτιῶν, this (and also v. 32a) is a typical Lucan amplification, to render the material suitable for its present context. The real object is contained in v. 32b, which awkwardly has to repeat the verb in the form of a relative clause: τὸ πνεῦμα τὸ ἅγιον ὃ ἔδωκεν ὁ θεός.

Next we have to distinguish between the general notion of the outpouring of the Spirit in the Age to Come and the specific gift of the risen and ascended Lord. The idea of a special outpouring of the Spirit was part of the general expectation of the Days of the Messiah. When he came, there would be a cleansing and sanctifying of the people, who would thus be ready to share in the blessings of the kingdom, including possession of the Spirit. This is already implicit in the glimpse of the Age to Come in the 'new covenant' passage of Jer. 31.31-34, and in the vision of the revived bones in Ezek. 37. It is the basis of the work of St John the Baptist, whose cleansing baptism is to be followed by the baptism of the Spirit when the Messiah appears. If the work of Jesus is interpreted as a preliminary to the inauguration of the kingdom, then the proper manifestation of the Spirit cannot be expected as yet, though some anticipations of what is to come may be observed. But as soon as his Resurrection is seen to be, not only the declaration that he is *Messias designatus*, but the actual inauguration of the kingdom itself, then the Spirit should be a present reality in those who have been cleansed and made members of the kingdom.

Thus belief that Jesus is indeed the Messiah goes hand in hand with belief that the Spirit is already given. But to interpret what has happened in this way creates fresh difficulties. It does not account for the sequence of events, in which the Messiah first dies and is buried, and then rises from the dead and sits at the right hand of God, before the general outpouring of the Spirit. The Heavenly Session is an idea proper to the Son of Man type of messianism, in which it denotes the consummation rather than the inauguration of the kingdom.[1] The manifestation of the Spirit ought to take place while the Messiah rules on earth, but it seems that he has gone too soon. The Church is the messianic kingdom without its Head. But his headship is vividly realized if the manifestation of the Spirit is closely associated with him as his specific 'gift'. The Messiah is unseen, but known in the experience of the outpouring of the Spirit. We shall thus expect to find that, along with more usual expressions, the New Testament can speak of the Spirit as given by the ascended Lord himself. This novel aspect of the matter finds its justification from Ps. 68.19, which specifies the Messiah's function in terms of gifts.

It thus becomes possible to see an apologetic motive in the use of this testimony. It is likely that in the earliest phase the first Christians thought of the Spirit as shed on them by God, and not as a messianic gift. But from the first the presence of the Spirit was something that was experienced in close connection with the conviction that Jesus was the Messiah by virtue of his Resurrection. Indeed this may be seen as a third equivalent of the Resurrection itself. It is not only the conquest of death and the raising of God's Messiah to his right hand, but also the moment of the manifestation of the Spirit. It is because Jesus is where he is that the signs of the Spirit are now seen in the life of the Church. There is an integral connection between his place in heaven and the presence of the Spirit. His achieving of that place has won the Spirit for those who are baptized into his name. It is natural to express this close association of ideas by ascribing the shedding of the Spirit to his mediation, and so to regard it as one of his messianic functions. The unbelieving Jews might well object that such an idea is unwarranted in Scripture. The Church has to give much thought to the problem of relating what has actually happened to current speculations and authoritative texts. Starting from belief in the Heavenly Session of Jesus, the Christian exegetes use Ps. 68.19 as a comment on this event. Then they show that it provides warrant

[1] Cf. Mowinckel, *He that Cometh*, p. 389.

for his mediation of the powers of the Age to Come, for it describes his function as a receiving in order to give gifts to men. It is but a step to apply this to the mediation of the Spirit in particular.

But this step has important consequences for theology. For the word used, 'gifts', inevitably carries with it the nuance of a concrete and separable entity. This militates against the true Hebraic idea of the Spirit as a fluid extension of God, which may be shed upon someone, or caused to rest on or in or among some person or persons, but is not detached from God himself. With the language of giving the Spirit a change begins. We can see this transformation taking place in the New Testament.

The earliest use of the phrase δίδωμι πνεῦμα ἅγιον is in I Thess. 4.8, where, in fact, the words are a quotation from Ezek. 37.14, δώσω τὸ πνεῦμά μου εἰς ὑμᾶς. Although the words come into the context quite casually, they serve a specific purpose. St Paul is reminding his readers that a high moral standard is expected of them, to accord with their baptismal cleansing and sanctification. 'Therefore', he says, 'he that rejecteth, rejecteth not man, but God, who giveth his Holy Spirit unto you.' This is the normal fluid idea. Bad behaviour drives out God, because it is incompatible with possession of his Spirit. Reference to the text of Ezekiel shows that the verb really means 'put' (so EVV), though the Septuagint has in this instance translated וְנָתַתִּי literally. This is also indicated in the use of εἰς ὑμᾶς, representing בָּכֶם, which is not a true indirect object, but is meant literally, 'into you'. Nevertheless the idea of a gift does seem to be present in Paul's citation. We seem to hear an undertone of Ps. 68.19, δόματα ἐν ἀνθρώπῳ (בָּאָדָם).

The next example is I Cor. 12.7. Here the influence of the christology which we have connected with Ps. 68.19 becomes more apparent. The fluid idea is carefully maintained, for it is essential to Paul's purpose to show that the diverse manifestations (χαρίσματα) of the Spirit flow from one undivided source. In the trinitarian verses (vv. 4-6) this outflow is traced back through the ministrations of the one Lord (as diverse as the charisms of the Spirit himself) to its origin in God. The use of the title κύριος goes with the form of confession in v. 3 Κύριος Ἰησοῦς. It is especially interesting, as it links the lordship of Jesus with the mediation of the Spirit, his *place* with his *function*, exactly as is implied in the allusion to Ps. 68.19 in Acts 2.33. There is no suggestion of the actual use of this testimony here, but the idea which it was used to formulate is evidently operative.

In II Cor. 1.22 and 5.5 Paul uses the phrase with the aid of a new expression, which he has coined to clarify his meaning: δοὺς τὸν ἀρραβῶνα τοῦ πνεύματος. This helps to explain how the giving of the Spirit, which is characteristic of the messianic age, has been partial and awaits greater fulness. It is correlative to the fact that Jesus has inaugurated the kingdom by his Exaltation, but it awaits its consummation. δίδωμι πνεῦμα ἅγιον occurs again in Rom. 5.5, and the same thought as we have just seen in II Corinthians is worked out more fully in Rom. 8.

In all these Pauline passages the fluid notion of the Spirit as an outflow from God is retained, though it is through the mediation of the exalted Jesus. The tendency towards a more concrete way of speaking of the Spirit appears when the thought is concentrated on the *effects* of the Spirit in the recipient.[1] So, when we turn to Eph. 4 we notice a distinct change. The chapter is a rewriting of I Cor. 12, which we have just looked at. The unity of the Spirit is mentioned, but when it comes to the description of the charisms, they are made out to be the direct gift of Christ, without mention of the Spirit. The gifts may not be *things*, but they are at any rate functions of the recipients rather than manifestations of the one Spirit. Ps. 68.19 is actually cited in v. 8. The two following verses expound the opening words of it in terms of the Exaltation, and then follows the exposition of the *pesher* reading ἔδωκεν. This is the moment to refer to the other modification of text, τοῖς ἀνθρώποις for ἐν ἀνθρώπῳ (בָּאָדָם). The gifts are not 'into' or 'among' men, but 'to' men. This tiny change is thrown into relief by the contrast of I Thess. 4.8, the earliest of our examples. We are here close to the concrete idea of a gift in the exact sense of the word.

This stage is reached in the Lucan literature. It is probable that Luke goes beyond the normal point of view of his own time. It is typical of his whole mentality to misunderstand or to rationalize the idea in this way. Consequently it is not surprising to find that he is the only New Testament writer to use the noun phrase 'the gift of the Spirit', or a variation of it (Acts 2.38; 8.20; 10.45; 11.17, all using δωρέα). It is interesting to compare Luke 11.13, 'How much more shall your heavenly Father give the Holy Spirit . . . ?'

---

[1] A similar tendency may be discerned in the use of ἐπιχορηγέω (Gal. 3.5) and ἐπιχορηγία (Phil. 1.19) in connection with the Spirit.

Here πνεῦμα ἅγιον has replaced the ἀγαθά (sc. δόματα) of the original preserved in Matt. 7.11. Luke's alteration is clearly interpretative, and one wonders whether it has been mediated by the occurrence of δόματα in Ps. 68.19. Luke uses the verb 'give' in Acts 5.32, 8.18, 11.17 and 15.8. When the verb occurs, the proper fluid idea is more easily preserved. But that Luke himself is guilty of intending the idea of a concrete gift may be inferred from the presence of the noun phrase in some of these contexts. In all these places the idea of the gift of the Spirit is an established theologumenon, presupposing the christology which is expressed in the Christian use of Ps. 68.19.

It remains to note the evidence of the Johannine literature. As so often, the Fourth Gospel does not employ the same words, but preserves the fundamental idea with remarkable accuracy. In John 7.39 the coming of the Spirit is closely connected with the glorifying of Jesus. It seems that John thought of Jesus as glorified in the act of death, though this is not separable from the thought of the Resurrection. Then the close link between the Exaltation and the Giving of the Spirit, themselves aspects of the Resurrection, is discernible in ch. 20. Moreover the theme of the living water in ch. 4 and 7.37 speaks of the Spirit as definitely the personal gift of Jesus. There is thus the same idea of the gift of the Spirit mediated by the exalted Christ. It reappears more clearly in the Last Discourses (compare 14.16 with 15.26 and 16.7). So true is it that the Spirit is the Messiah's own gift, that the departure of Jesus is the necessary condition for the coming of the Spirit. Moreover John is so much aware of the simultaneity of the component acts of the redemption (the Death, Resurrection, Exaltation and Giving of the Spirit), that he can even include a hint of the pentecostal outpouring in describing the actual moment of our Lord's death on the cross. For whereas Mark 15.37 and Luke 23.46 say ἐξέπνευσεν, and Matt. 27.50 uses the expression ἀφῆκεν τὸ πνεῦμα, John 19.30 has παρέδωκεν τὸ πνεῦμα. This carries a hint of handing over and passing on the Spirit which has been Jesus' own messianic endowment. John never loses the fluid way of speaking about the Spirit. It is also indicated by the partitive genitive in I John 4.13 (3.24 is ambiguous).

It is not possible to assess the actual point at which Ps. 68.19 was introduced to account for the Messiah's mediation of the Spirit. The use of the verb 'give' is natural, and has a precedent in Ezek. 37.14 (I Thess. 4.8), etc. It is probable that the idea was being canvassed first, and that Ps. 68.19 was subsequently adopted to support it. It does this presumably in a Greek-speaking milieu, as a scholarly comment on the second half of Ps. 110.1. But it has the effect of encouraging a more concrete, less truly Hebraic, conception of the Spirit, and is closely connected with the formation of the theologumenon 'the Gift of the Spirit'. It makes the christology in connection with the coming of the Spirit more precise. These developments may well have contributed materially to the evolution of the Christian idea of the Spirit as a separate Person of the Holy Trinity.[1]

## 5. THE THIRD DAY

The preceding sections of this chapter have all been concerned with evidence drawn in the first instance from the speech in Acts 2. We have seen there the argument from literal fulfilment, which first gives scriptural warrant to the Church's claims about Jesus. Only one of the testimonies examined, Ps. 110.1, could be regarded as itself certainly used in this way in the most primitive period of all. It was notable that the same fundamental testimony is also the origin of a cardinal theological expression. The thesis that we now put forward in this section is that a similar history lies behind the credal statement that Jesus 'rose again on the third day'. This

---

[1] In this discussion of Ps. 68.19 we have not alluded to the typology of Jesus as the true Moses, which would connect the early Christian exegesis closely with the interpretation of the Targum (also *Babylonian Shabbath* 89a). It is true that Matthew sees Jesus as the Teacher of the New Law, a figure resembling Moses. It is true also that Paul insists on the *spiritual* nature of the New Law, though he never compares Jesus to Moses even by implication. Ps. 68 belonged to the liturgy of Pentecost, which would link it with the setting provided by Luke for the speech in Acts 2. It could thus be argued that the idea of Moses giving the Law to the people was the model of the Church's theology of the exalted Christ shedding the Spirit. But the evidence for a Moses typology in the earliest period is very uncertain. Moreover the possibility of such a typology does not necessarily involve *this* Targum. And in Eph. 4.8, where this Targum has perhaps influenced the *text*, there is no hint of the New Moses theme in the *interpretation*. Our argument, that the text is an example of the *midrash pesher*, beginning as a comment on the much used Ps. 110.1, remains unaffected even if the typology of the New Moses was a factor in the wider background of thought. The passage is not discussed either from the rabbinic point of view by W. D. Davies, *Paul and Rabbinic Judaism*[2], 1955, or from the point of view of Moses typology by A. Descamps and P. Démann in their contributions to H. Cazelles *et al.*, *Moïse, l'homme de l'alliance* (Desclée & Cie, Tournai, 1955).

became a conventional phrase in the presentation of the kerygma at a very early date. We think that it owes its form to an underlying scriptural testimony, and its early currency to the argument from literal fulfilment.

That a Scripture text is the basis of it is implied by I Cor. 15.4, where Paul says that Jesus 'hath been raised on the third day according to the scriptures'. Unfortunately there is no indication what passage or passages of Scripture he has in mind. The majority of scholars hold that it is Hos. 6.2: 'After two days will he revive us: on the third day he will raise us up, and we shall live before him.' However this verse is never quoted in the New Testament, so that other possible passages have been suggested.[1] In an article on I Cor. 15.4, B. M. Metzger considers these various possibilities, and concludes that the quest is hopeless.[2] Instead he proposes to dissociate κατὰ τὰς γραφάς from the adverbial phrase τῇ ἡμέρα τῇ τρίτῃ, and to take it simply with the verbal idea. This means that any Resurrection text is sufficient without necessarily containing the idea of the third day. But in fact the parallel in v. 3 renders this suggestion improbable. For there also κατὰ τὰς γραφάς occurs, following a verb with a closely associated adverbial phrase, and the whole complex has a clear scriptural allusion: 'Christ died for our sins according to the scriptures.' The echo of the closing verses of Isa. 53 can hardly be missed.[3] Similarly a definite scriptural reference, which includes the third day, seems to be demanded by v. 4. Hos. 6.2 is surely the most likely one. It is our belief that it is the basis of the expression in question, and that the argument from literal fulfilment had shaped its conventional form. It will also be found in the course of the analysis that the complete absence of the actual testimony from the New Testament can be readily explained.

In the Passion predictions in the Synoptic Gospels, the rising on the third day is usually included. The preservation of these passages in the Gospel tradition is no doubt due to the Church's Passion apologetic, which we shall be studying in the next chapter. The phraseology has evidently been influenced by this apologetic to some extent. The question therefore arises whether the forecast

---

[1] Jonah 2.1 (cf. Matt. 12.40); II Kings 20.5; Lev. 23.11 (cf. I Cor. 15.20).

[2] 'A Suggestion concerning the Meaning of I Cor. 15.4b', *JTS*, NS 8, 1957, pp. 118-23.

[3] W. Zimmerli and J. Jeremias, *The Servant of God*, ET (SBT 20), 1957 ( =Art. Παῖς θεοῦ from *TWNT* V, 1952), p. 88.

of the Resurrection has been added at this stage in the transmission
of the tradition, or belongs, in some form or other, to the actual
words of Jesus.

If it really does go back to Jesus himself, the meaning must
surely have been something very similar to that of Hos. 6.2. There
the Hebrew idiom 'after two days . . . on the third day' is always
taken in the same sense as the better known תְּמוֹל שִׁלְשׁוֹם
(lit. 'yesterday, the third day') = 'heretofore', 'formerly', so that
the words in their context mean national revival in the near future.
The whole tenor of the prophecy throws the emphasis on this in
a way that implies that the renewal will happen in an unexpectedly
short time. If this is the kind of meaning which originally attached
to our Lord's Resurrection prediction, then he was probably expressing his belief that his death, though inevitable, would quickly
prove to be for the lasting benefit of God's people, inaugurating
the restored, spiritualized kingdom. In this case the three days
means 'a little while', exactly as we find it in John 16.16-22. We
may well ask whether the author is aware how correctly he has
conveyed the meaning which the dogmatism of the Synoptists has
obscured.[1] Moreover the idea of resurrection is being used as a
metaphor of national restoration just as it is in Hos. 6.2. Although
we are not at this point claiming that Jesus actually used this
passage as the basis of a prophecy about his own mission, we are
bound to regard it as probable, seeing that it provides the clue to
his meaning. It gives a reasonable basis for avoiding the necessity
of having to regard these words as a spurious addition to the
Passion prediction, merely a *vaticinium ex eventu*.

The probability is increased when we take into account the
elusive words preserved in Luke 13.32f.: 'Behold, I cast out devils
and perform cures today and tomorrow, and the third day I am
perfected. Howbeit I must go on my way today and tomorrow and
the day following: for it cannot be that a prophet perish out of
Jerusalem.' In this passage the Semitic idiom of the Hosea prophecy has been left untouched. Perhaps we may see a further
verbal link in ἰάσεις in v. 32 (cf. Hos. 6.1 ἰάσεται). The matter is
complicated, because there are signs that the original saying has
been edited with Hos. 6.2 in mind. It is probable that the original
nucleus was confined to the words ἰδοὺ ἐκβάλλω δαιμόνια καὶ ἰάσεις

---

[1] Compare the similar retention of primitive ways of thought in John's
handling of the idea of the Spirit, referred to in the preceding section.

ἀποτελῶ σήμερον καὶ αὔριον· πλὴν δεῖ με τῇ ἐχομένῃ πορεύεσθαι.[1]
The phrase καὶ τῇ τρίτῃ τελειοῦμαι has been added to the first
clause, in order to make the reference to the Resurrection explicit.
τῇ τρίτῃ is from the actual Hosea text, and τελειοῦμαι has no doubt
been suggested by ἀποτελῶ in the saying itself. This addition has
made it necessary to repeat σήμερον καὶ αὔριον before τῇ ἐχομένῃ.
Finally an explanatory clause has been added to bring in an overt
reference to our Lord's impending death. This also shows acquaintance with the Greek version of Hosea in the words προφήτην
ἀπολέσθαι[2] and provides the link with the Q saying which immediately follows (Luke 13.34f. = Matt. 23.37-39). It should also be
observed that the use of this chapter of Hosea by the early Church
is attested by the citation of Hos. 6.6 twice as *verba Christi*
(Matt. 9.13 and 12.7), and by a possible literary allusion to
Hos. 6.9, about robbers lying in wait, in the parable of the good
Samaritan.

The meaning of the passage is that Jesus has faith in the necessity of his own mission, and no personal danger will deflect him
from it. The proverbial mode of expression, with its probable
reference to Hosea even in the original short form, gives an air of
divine compulsion to the saying. In the full form πορεύεσθαι takes
its meaning from the 'perfecting' on the third day, and so is a
veiled reference to the Resurrection. But by itself it must be referred to the warning of death in v. 31, which presumably can be
faced calmly in the knowledge that the work is accomplished. It is
an understatement which has a touch of irony about it, astonishingly similar to the dialogue in John 7.33-36: 'Jesus therefore said,
Yet a little while (ἔτι χρόνον μικρόν) am I with you, and I go (ὑπάγω)
unto him that sent me. Ye shall seek me, and shall not find me:
and where I am ye cannot come. The Jews therefore said among
themselves, Whither will this man go (πορεύεσθαι) . . . ?' This is
repeated in John 16.16-22 with extraordinary emphasis on the
phrase 'a little while', as already noted. We now notice that the
Johannine 'go away' may also be a primitive feature.

The Lucan passage just studied shows that the idea of the third
day was linked with the theme of 'a little while' in the Gospel

[1] Cf. J. Wellhausen, *Das Evangelium Lucae*, 1904, *ad loc.*
[2] Hos. 6.5 LXX: ἀπεθέρισα τοὺς προφήτας ὑμῶν, ἀπέκτεινα αὐτούς. This
differs from MT, which makes the prophets God's instruments to slay
the people, to whom αὐτούς ought to refer.

tradition, and it is natural to hold that it always implies this Semitic idiom on the lips of Jesus. We now have to see how it was applied literally to the Resurrection. H. J. Cadbury contests the assertion that the Resurrection actually took place on the third day. The most that could be assigned to it is the first appearance of the risen Lord, seeing that no one witnessed the actual moment of rising. So he asks, 'Is the official date due merely to the literal understanding of the phrase "third day" used in the frequent but inexact sense of "soon"?'[1] This is to suggest that not even the first appearance can be dated on the third day with any certainty. On the other hand the emphasis on the first day of the week in the Resurrection narratives, and the early fixing of this day for the celebration of the Eucharist, make it very unlikely that the third day was taken literally instead of idiomatically without any foundation in the actual events.

In fact the same factors can be interpreted with a greater degree of probability in the opposite sense. It is surely more likely that it was the actual appearance of our Lord on the third day which caused the literal interpretation of the phrase. Knowing perfectly well that the Semitic phrase is an idiom for an unspecified span of time in the immediate future,[2] the disciples were dazzled by what really happened. The revival of which Jesus had spoken had not only come true in his own person, but the mysterious 'little while' had been literally fulfilled! There is no difficulty about the double meaning of the idea of resurrection. Our Lord may have been speaking of the restoration and renewal of the nation, but it is his personal Resurrection which inaugurates the messianic kingdom in which this becomes an accomplished fact. This was already implied in his teaching. He foresaw his own death, but prophesied that it would result in speedy revival. This prophecy, presumably drawing on Hos. 6.2, was couched in terms of his own Resurrection.

It follows that the Resurrection itself was a literal fulfilment of a prophecy that need not have been taken to be anything but metaphor. It is still more striking in that it includes the literal

[1] 'Acts and Eschatology', in *The Background of the NT and its Eschatology*, p. 303.
[2] It should be observed that there is nothing in the Semitic phrase itself to suggest that this would be a very *short* time, but the early Christian usage seems to imply this. This is no doubt due to the influence of the Hosea passage, where the context in which the phrase occurs evidently means that the revival will happen in an *unexpectedly short* time.

fulfilment of the mysterious third day. If a scriptural basis is required for the great event to which the apostles give witness, then Hos. 6.2 can be cited with compelling force. We can imagine that it would be used in the same way as the literal fulfilment of Ps. 110.1, enunciated with the same air of confidence and the same triumphant ring. Resurrection on the third day is an article of belief that is specially 'according to the scriptures' (I Cor. 15.4). And just as the literally fulfilled Ps. 110.1 was the origin of a conventional dogmatic phrase, so this also provides a phrase which belongs to the kerygma and takes its place in the creed. But there is one important difference. The connection of the idea of the Heavenly Session with its basic text is never lost, because the text itself remains central to the development and defence of christology. But although we have the evidence of I Cor. 15.4 that Resurrection on the third day must be linked to a basic text, there seems to be no certainty what the text referred to is. So we must ask, how is it that it has been lost, or rather has failed to become a great text of the dogmatic thinking of the early Church? Our discussion so far suggests two reasons. In the first place, unlike Ps. 110.1, the Hosea passage would not be claimed as a messianic passage, either by the Jews in general or by the first Christians. Secondly, and more important, we have seen reason to believe that Jesus did himself speak of revival on the third day in some form. Although his words are based on prophecy, the interest fastens on the fact that he had himself spoken it. It is thus the literal fulfilment of the words of Jesus as much as of prophecy which first fires the imagination of the disciples. He is risen on the third day 'as he said unto you' (Mark 16.7) as much as 'according to the scriptures'.

The disappearance of the text, and the development of the theologumenon, can be analysed further, if we attend to the form of the Greek words in which Resurrection on the third day is expressed. There is no fixed formula. Excluding the sayings about raising the temple in three days (which we shall consider in a moment), the commonest form is τῇ τρίτῃ ἡμέρᾳ ἐγερθῆναι (Matt. 16.21, 17.23, 20.19; Luke 9.22; Acts 10.40; I Cor. 15.4). The temporal phrase is once μετὰ τρεῖς ἡμέρας in Matthew (27.63), and the verb is three times ἀναστῆναι in Luke (18.33, 24.7, 46). Mark always uses μετὰ τρεῖς ἡμέρας ἀναστῆναι (8.31, 9.31, 10.34). Of course these are not certain statistics, because there are nearly always textual variants.

But they do show the predilection of each evangelist for the different forms.

It is probable that the original version is the commonest form, although it is not found in Mark. The others are stylistic alterations. Thus μετὰ τρεῖς ἡμέρας is smoother as a temporal clause, because it does not allow the possible misunderstanding 'third day in a series' (i.e. betrayal first day, crucifixion second, and resurrection third). At the same time it banishes the traces of the underlying Semitism, which the other still hints at. Similarly ἐγερθῆναι must be accepted as more original than ἀναστῆναι. When a transitive verb is required, ἐγείρω is the regular word. The only exceptions are the transitive use of ἀνίστημι in John 6 (four times) and in Acts (six times). We have seen that Luke has a preference for this root, and it is reasonable to assume that in both John and Acts it is used on stylistic grounds. Normally, however, the intransitive ἀναστῆναι is to be regarded as the passive of ἐγείρω. The change from ἐγερθῆναι to ἀναστῆναι goes with a change of emphasis. The real passive is a typical Semitic circumlocution to avoid the name of God (i.e. was raised = God raised), but it becomes a virtual intransitive (i.e. arose), and so becomes interchangeable with ἀναστῆναι. This shift of meaning accompanies the development of the use of the expression from a description of what happened to a theologumenon of the Resurrection. Seeing that Matthew and Luke had Mark before them, and that Mark uses the fully Hellenized form, it looks as if the process was reversed by the evangelists. The most likely reason is that so important a phrase had conventional forms in teaching and liturgy in the different localities where the Gospels were composed. The writers adapt the words to the form they commonly use. So, whereas Mark writes for Gentiles, Matthew writes for Christians of Semitic origin, and Luke for Hellenistic Jewish as well as Gentile readers.

In the Septuagint of Hos. 6.2 the verb is ἀναστησόμεθα. The original form of the phrase was thus arrived at directly from the Hebrew יְקִמֵנוּ. We notice that this is transitive with God for subject, whereas the Septuagint has changed it to the intransitive form. This helps to explain the disappearance of the testimony in the earliest strata of New Testament literature. The tendency to use ἀναστῆναι probably began without conscious adaptation to the Hosea text. In Luke, however, the connection has been perceived, and the version he gives in 18.33 is especially close.[1] We have already noticed that the Septuagint version of this passage has influenced the editing in Luke 13.33. By this time, then, it is coming back into use in Hellenistic circles, to take its place in the testimonies cited by the Fathers.[2]

We have now traced a prophecy of speedy renewal on the lips of Jesus, spoken in terms of the ideas of Hos. 6.2, through its adoption by the Church as a triumphant example of literal fulfilment, to its conventional use as a theologumenon of the Resurrection. The way in which the presumed underlying text first disappears, and then begins to creep back into theological writing, has also been shown. We must now turn our attention to an interesting parallel development, which failed to gain the same importance in dogmatic formulation. This is the prophecy of rebuilding the temple in three days. It occurs as a charge made by false witnesses at the trial of Jesus (Mark 14.58 = Matt. 26.61), as a taunt when he hangs on the cross (Mark 15.29 = Matt. 27.40), and on the lips of Jesus himself in John's account of the cleansing of the temple (John 2.19). Luke omits it altogether.

The saying as it stands in the Marcan account of the trial is hardly likely to be original, because it does not constitute a suitable charge. The declared intention of destroying the temple would certainly be viewed gravely, but when a promise to rebuild it in three days is added, it sounds captious and not worth serious consideration. We should expect the Sanhedrin to take up the charge of wishing to destroy the temple, but in fact nothing further is said about it. Even so, it may well have been a real factor at the trial of Jesus, as it was later in the cases of Stephen (Acts 6.14) and

---

[1] Luke 18.33: καὶ τῇ ἡμέρᾳ τῇ τρίτῃ ἀναστήσεται; Hos. 6.2: ἐν τῇ ἡμέρᾳ τῇ τρίτῃ ἀναστησόμεθα.

[2] Although it is not found in the earliest writers, it appears significantly in the anti-Judaic collections, which preserved so much of the primitive apologetic: Tertullian, *Adv. Jud.* 13 (cf. *Adv. Marc.* IV.43); Cyprian, *Ad Quirinum*: *Test. adv. Jud.* II.25; Lactantius, *Inst.* IV.19. The distinction of meaning between ἐγερθῆναι and ἀναστῆναι may perhaps also have a basis in the Hebrew הָקִים (=cause to stand) and הָקִיץ (=awaken). In another resurrection passage, Dan. 12.2, יָקִיצוּ is correctly translated ἐξεγερθήσονται by Theodotion, but LXX has ἀναστήσονται. Is the latter evidence of an otherwise unknown reading יָקוּמוּ? And is it possible that יְקצֵנוּ stood for יְקמֵנוּ in Hos. 6.2? If so, it would help to account for the early preference for ἐγερθῆναι and also contribute to the loss of the testimony in the primitive period.

Paul (Acts 21.28). For we have other evidence that Jesus prophesied the destruction of the temple in Mark 13.2 (= Matt. 24.2) and in Luke 19.44.

If, then, we accept the first part of the saying as a real charge against Jesus, can we point to any motive for expanding it into a text of christological importance by the addition of the second half? It is not difficult to see how the needs of apologetic make such a change desirable. For if there really had been a charge of this kind at the trial, it would still be in people's minds after the Crucifixion. It may well be that the Church had to suffer considerable embarrassment on account of it, seeing that the prophecy had not come true. This is an adequate motive for wishing to reinterpret it at any time up to the destruction of the temple in A.D. 70. It is of course possible that Jesus had actually said something to the effect that the temple would be rebuilt in three days, in the same sense as he spoke of rising on the third day, i.e. spiritual renewal in the immediate future. We may compare the implications of Matt. 12.6, 'One greater than the temple is here'. But if he did say something of this kind, it has been lost, for the form of the false witnesses' saying shows theological development in every case. It is better to regard it as frankly modelled on the Resurrection prediction, in order to meet the challenge of an unfulfilled prophecy of the destruction of the temple.

The reinterpretation takes the form of transferring the prophecy from the temple to the person of Jesus. We can actually catch a glimpse of the process in the Johannine account of the cleansing of the temple (John 2.13-22). In the next chapter a more complete analysis of this passage will be given. It will be shown that the key to it is to be found in the quotation from Ps. 69, which is one of the most important items of the Passion apologetic, and that the presentation of the whole incident is in close touch with the Church's apologetic at a very early stage, whatever may be thought of the date of composition of the Fourth Gospel. Ps. 69 is adduced because it explains why the Messiah suffered, contrary to expectation. When the psalm as a whole is applied to the Passion, it is natural to apply the final verses, which speak of the rebuilding of Zion and the cities of Judah, to the Resurrection and the spread of the Church. If this is taken in conjunction with the taunt that the temple is still standing, no difficult leap of thought is required to suggest that Jesus had never meant the temple as such, but that 'he spake of the temple of his body' (John 2.21). *This* temple certainly was destroyed, and yet has been rebuilt. It follows from this that the way is open for a doctrine of the supersession of the temple, which soon appears in the speech of Stephen (Acts 7).

It so comes about that the prophecy of Resurrection in three days is appended to that of the destruction of the temple, and thereby effects the necessary christological reinterpretation. For this reason we are inclined to think that John preserves the most original form of the saying (John 2.19): λύσατε τὸν ναὸν τοῦτον, καὶ ἐν τρισὶν ἡμέραις ἐγερῶ αὐτόν. This is not only the simplest version of the saying, but also has ἐγείρω, which we have argued belongs to the most primitive form of the Resurrection prediction. The saying is a special application of the literal fulfilment of that prediction, which also serves to take the treason out of the charge at the trial as well as answering hostile criticism.

Not unnaturally the verb ἐγερῶ is soon changed to οἰκοδομήσω, and further christological motives attach to the saying. In Mark there are really two distinct forms, the first (14.58) prophesying the rebuilding of an entirely new kind of temple (ἄλλον ἀχειρο-ποίητον), the second (15.29) implying by its failure to express the object that the *same* one is to be rebuilt. Although Mark may have been simply abbreviating the second time, and have intended the same meaning as before, Matthew has not taken it this way, but alters the first one to give the definite impression that it is the same temple that is to be rebuilt (26.61). His second version (27.40) is almost identical with Mark's. In both Gospels the basic form of the saying is the same as John's, except that the verb is οἰκοδο-μῆσαι.[1] This gives no surprise, for it is the expected idea. Mark thus gives an expanded version of the original saying, but Matthew in his turn abbreviates it once more. We must now attempt to find the reasons for these changes.

Mark's contribution is the addition of χειροποίητον and ἄλλον ἀχειροποίητον. The background of this is probably the stone cut out ἄνευ χειρῶν in Dan. 2.34, 45,[2] and so belongs to the whole

---

[1] At Mark 14.58 D it. have ἀναστήσω, showing the tendency of this text to revert once more to the Resurrection announcement. It is noteworthy that in the Resurrection announcements D changes ἐγερθήσεται to ἀναστή-σεται in nearly every case.

[2] Cf. the interpolation at Mark 13.2 found in D W it. Cypr. καὶ διὰ τριῶν ἡμέρων ἄλλος ἀναστήσεται ἄνευ χειρῶν. It is characteristic of the 'Western Text' to conform the text to the implied quotation.

nexus of 'stone' testimonies. The idea of the Rejected Stone in Ps. 118.22 is the foundation of this theme in the New Testament, which shows that the Passion apologetic is again at the root of the matter. This helps to explain how these words became part of the saying in Mark. But they have a Platonic ring about them, which suggests a more advanced christology and a Hellenistic background. It is not simply that the Resurrection of Jesus fulfils the restoration idea in the promise of rebuilding, but that his risen, heavenly, body is itself the new temple. Even before the temple of Herod has been destroyed, it can be said to be at an end, for it has been superseded. We here see how the practical difficulty of the unfulfilled prophecy of destruction of the temple is overcome by referring it to the Resurrection; and how this leads on to the thought of our Lord's risen body as the true temple. Such is the thought of Stephen and of the Epistle to the Hebrews, no doubt founded in part on pre-Christian speculation about the temple and its spiritual counterpart which is to come.[1] The only two other occurrences of ἀχειρο-ποίητος pursue the matter to further conclusions. In II Cor. 5.1 the members of the Body of Christ will receive resurrection bodies in a way analogous to the transformation from earthly to spiritual temple. In Col. 2.11 there is a spiritual circumcision corresponding to that of the old Law, which has been superseded. In both these instances the new, spiritual, temple is an established idea which can be used metaphorically. These developments are already implicit in the saying as it reached Mark. But it is doubtful whether he realized this, as he can cheerfully omit the operative words in 15.29. As a taunt of the enemies of Christ, it is clearly applied directly to the Resurrection with Johannine irony. The reader knows that the real temple was indeed rebuilt in three days.

It seems, then, that the motive of Mark was straightforward, and that he was not himself responsible for the development in the form of the saying. But Matthew has presumably simplified it again deliberately. In his narrative this has the effect of securing the same interpretation in terms of the fact of the Resurrection. But it is also possible that he has a typological interest, derived from Zech. 6.12: ᾿Ιδοὺ ἀνήρ, ᾿Ανατολὴ ὄνομα αὐτῷ, καὶ ὑποκάτωθεν αὐτοῦ ἀνατελεῖ, καὶ οἰκοδομήσει τὸν οἶκον κυρίου. In the next

---

[1] Cf. C. F. D. Moule, 'Sanctuary and Sacrifice in the Church of the NT', *JTS*, NS 1, 1950, pp. 29-41; M. Simon, 'Retour du Christ et reconstruction du Temple dans la pensée chrétienne primitive', in *Aux sources de la tradition chrétienne* (Mélanges Goguel), 1950, pp. 247-57.

chapter we shall consider the use of this book in the Passion apologetic. It is worth noting that John's account of the cleansing of the temple, which contains the rebuilding saying, also has a probable allusion to Zech. 14.21, כְּנַעֲנִי, in John 2.16, ἐμπορίου. As time goes on, more and more details are dug out of this prophecy by early Christian writers. The early chapters mention the high priest Joshua (LXX ’Ιησοῦς), which invites comparisons. It is not long before the church fathers delight to apply ’Ιδοὺ ἀνήρ, ’Ανατολὴ ὄνομα αὐτῷ to the Incarnation.[1] It is possible that Matthew alludes to this in Matt. 2.2, τὸν ἀστέρα ἐν τῇ ἀνατολῇ, besides the principal reference to Num. 24.17. The final words of this verse, καὶ οἰκοδομήσει τὸν οἶκον κυρίου, have perhaps influenced the rebuilding saying in Matt. 26.61: δύναμαι καταλῦσαι τὸν ναὸν τοῦ θεοῦ καὶ διὰ τριῶν ἡμερῶν οἰκοδομῆσαι. Here Matthew has not only omitted τὸν χειροποίητον, etc., from Mark, but has added τοῦ θεοῦ to ναόν (instead of Mark's τοῦτον). Another allusion to Zech. 6.12 may be detected in Matt. 16.18, οἰκοδομήσω μου τὴν ἐκκλησίαν, where the Church is described in terms of the temple (cf. Eph. 2.20-22).

There is other evidence that Matthew was aware of the christological interpretation of the Zechariah passage in his handling of the tradition about the crowning with thorns. Mark 15.17 reads: καὶ ἐνδιδύσκουσιν αὐτὸν πορφύραν καὶ περιτιθέασιν αὐτῷ πλέξαντες ἀκάνθινον στέφανον. In Matt. 27.28f. this is considerably expanded: καὶ ἐκδύσαντες αὐτὸν χλαμύδα κοκκίνην περιέθηκαν αὐτῷ, καὶ πλέξαντες στέφανον ἐξ ἀκανθῶν ἐπέθηκαν ἐπὶ τῆς κεφαλῆς αὐτοῦ. Matthew has thus transferred Mark's verb (περιτιθέασιν) from the act of crowning to the act of putting on the robe. This leaves him free to add words clearly based on Zech. 6.11, καὶ ποιήσεις στεφάνους καὶ ἐπιθήσεις ἐπὶ τὴν κεφαλὴν ’Ιησοῦ.[2] It is the verse that

---

[1] Justin, Dial. 106; 121; Hippolytus, Comm. in Prov. (on Prov. 30.18f.).

[2] There is other evidence that the early Church saw in the crowning with thorns a fulfilment of Zech. 6.11. In John 19.2 the words πλέξαντες στέφανον ἐξ ἀκανθῶν ἐπέθηκαν αὐτοῦ τῇ κεφαλῇ are evidently much closer to Matthew than to Mark. Commentators generally deny any literary connection between John and Matthew, though they often allow that John may have read Mark. If we accept this opinion, then the coincidence between John and Matthew in this instance can be explained by allusion to Zech. 6.11 independently of each other. And if there really is this allusion in John (as seems probable), then it is permissible to see a further allusion to the opening of Zech. 6.12 in John 19.5, ἰδοὺ ὁ ἄνθρωπος (I owe the latter suggestion to the Rev. E. A. Amand de Mendieta). We find the same reference again (though perhaps simply dependent on Matthew) in Ev. Petri 3.8: καί τις αὐτῶν ἐνεγκὼν στέφανον ἀκάνθινον ἔθηκεν ἐπὶ τῆς κεφαλῆς τοῦ κυρίου.

immediately precedes the one we have just been studying. This is not the kind of allusion which the reader is expected to pick up, in order to discover the real meaning of the passage. The irony that the true King of Israel is mocked as a king is sufficiently marked without Matthew's alterations. But to include words derived from the symbolic-prophetic coronation of one who bore the same name is a thing that is sure to appeal to a writer who is interested in 'fulfilments', as Matthew undoubtedly is.[1]

These traces of a typology based on Zech. 6 give to the saying about rebuilding the temple a richer messianic significance. Seeing that Joshua the son of Jehozadak was the anointed high priest, not king, it is bound to belong to the later stage when priestly traits are included in the concept of the messiahship of Jesus (as in Hebrews). But there is no trace of the spiritualizing of the saying which we saw in Mark.

Luke omits the saying, possibly because of another factor. He knows that the destruction of the temple has actually happened (i.e. in A.D. 70), but that it has not been rebuilt in the specified three days. There are possibilities of confusion here which make it safer to omit all mention of it! Instead he has elsewhere incorporated prophecies of destruction which subsequent events have certainly fulfilled.[2]

This issue of the temple has led us so far afield, that it may be useful to give a very brief summary of the dogmatic developments of the idea of Resurrection on the Third Day. It has seemed to us probable that the teaching of Jesus contained a prophecy of re-

---

[1] The crown of thorns was probably an imitation of the radial crown shown on some Roman imperial coins of this period, rather than an instrument of torture. This has been argued convincingly by H. St J. Hart, 'The Crown of Thorns in John 19.2-5', *JTS*, NS 3, 1952, pp. 66-75. This observation makes the connection between the crowning of Jesus and Zech. 6.11f. more straightforward. For when the LXX translator chose to use Ἀνατολή for the Hebrew messianic title צֶמַח in v. 12, he may have been thinking of it in terms of the *Sol invictus*. With such a title, those who were nurtured on the Greek Scriptures would normally picture Joshua wearing a radial crown when they read these verses. Joshua and Jesus were thus alike, not only in name, but also in the crown which each wore.

[2] Luke 19.41-44; 21.20-4. C. H. Dodd has shown that these prophecies are composed of OT phrases, and so cannot be held to be actually descriptive of the events of A.D. 70, as has often been assumed ('The Fall of Jerusalem and the "Abomination of Desolation"', *Journal of Roman Studies* 37, 1947, pp. 47-54). But it remains probable that Luke's preference for them was dictated by his knowledge of what had happened.

newal in terms of Hos. 6.2. His rising on the third day was seen to be the literal fulfilment of the prophecy, all the more stirring and convincing because it was not precisely expected. The fact that this is 'according to the scriptures' is not forgotten, though interest attaches more to the fulfilment of the words of Jesus than to that of a particular text. Thereafter there are two developments. On the one hand the literal fulfilment becomes a theologumenon of lasting importance in the presentation of the kerygma and the symbol of belief. On the other hand it is immediately available for coping with an objection raised by the Church's enemies that another prophecy of Jesus—that the temple would be destroyed—had not been fulfilled. This involves certain elaborations of exegesis which belong to the beginnings of the theology of the Body of Christ. But the original issue was altogether obscured by the subsequent destruction of the temple at the fall of Jerusalem.

## 6. THE FOUNDATION OF FAITH

In this chapter we have wandered down labyrinthine paths in the attempt to find the logical sequence of the textual modifications and shifts of application of testimonies used by the early Church. The result has been to show how a striking event—the Resurrection—became the foundation of a dogmatic faith. It is not our concern here to argue whether the Resurrection did or did not happen. It is certain that the first Christians *believed* that it had happened. There never was a time when Christianity existed as an interpretation of Judaism without the Resurrection as the fundamental belief.[1]

On this basis we can arrange the order of development. The first thing is the literal fulfilment of the prophecy of Resurrection on the Third Day. This means that all that Jesus had claimed about himself and his work has been proved true. As it is not a specifically messianic text, it does not imply that any theory of messiahship is yet imposed upon the bare facts. On the other hand it is highly

---

[1] The supreme theological importance attached to the Resurrection from the beginning is consistent with the fact that the *appearances* of the risen Jesus are the earliest evidence for it, and precede the tradition of the empty tomb. See the persuasive argument in John Knox, *Christ the Lord*, 1945, pp. 62ff. It is a book which coincides to a considerable degree with the argument of the present work as regards the order of development of dogmatic formulation, but on the basis of a wider range of NT studies, presented in more general terms.

probable that Jesus was regarded as the Messiah in some sense from the first.

The second stage is the *proof* of the messiahship of Jesus from the literal fulfilment of Ps. 110. Even when this is conflated with Dan. 7.13, it still leaves it an open question whether Jesus is merely *Messias designatus*, or is *Messias revelatus* already inaugurating the kingdom.

At an early date this issue was decided in favour of the latter view. Ps. 110.1 becomes the classic text for a new idea of the Heavenly Session of the Messiah, who reigns in heaven while his followers remain on earth until a later consummation. As such he has already fought their spiritual battles by his conquest over death.

This way of understanding the Exaltation necessitated reinterpretation of the idea of the manifestation of the Spirit in the messianic age. It is worked out from the actual experience of the church, which does not quite accord with preconceived notions. At some point in the process Ps. 68.19 is used, and helps to form the idea of the Gift of the Spirit.

These developments involve belief in a special relationship between the Christians and the risen Lord, which is expressed in the idea of the Body. This idea itself is derived primarily from reflection on the meaning of the Resurrection of the person of Jesus.

Other issues have also entered into the process of development. The question has been raised whether Jesus is, or needs to be, a descendant of David. The idea of our Lord's messiahship has been enriched by typological details, notably the features of the priestly Messiah. The relationship of his risen body to the Christians themselves has been worked out with the aid of the spiritualizing concepts of Hellenistic speculation.

All these developments are the fruit of trying to understand and to defend a given fact from within a living experience. It is clear that Jesus himself refused to fit into preconceived or systematic messianic ideas; the difficulty is to be sure that he was ever claiming to be the Messiah at all. The apostles were convinced of it, but only after he had arisen from the dead. They then took their stand in direct opposition to the decision of the Jewish and Imperial authorities. Their claim was bound to be subjected to every kind of test. Much of what we have studied in this chapter has been pre-apologetic, i.e. derivative from the basic Resurrection faith. But right from the very beginning this faith had to be refined and articulated by the process of meeting the objections of the Church's enemies. Through it all deeper and fuller understanding of the fundamental faith was reached, that 'Jesum Christum . . . tertia die resurrexisse, in caelos ereptum sedisse ad dexteram Patris, misisse vicariam vim Spiritus Sancti.'[1]

[1] Tertullian, *De Praescriptione Haereticorum* 13.

# III

## PASSION APOLOGETIC

IN the preceding chapter a sounding was taken in the fairly late composition of St Peter's speech in Acts 2. It was found possible to disengage the biblical quotations and their comments, and to show a developing process of biblical exegesis. This proceeded *pari passu* with the development of doctrine, so that the most primitive forms of exegesis coincided with the earliest attempts at the formulation of Christian dogma. In this chapter we shall have a simpler procedure. It has long been recognized that one of the first tasks which the Church had to undertake in defence of its claims was to explain the suffering and death of Jesus the Messiah. The Old Testament quotations are frequently concerned with this issue. It is thus not difficult to collect these quotations and to make useful deductions from them.

The primitive character of the Passion apologetic is vouched for by the fact that the Resurrection is the kernel of the original kerygma. It is impossible to speak of the Resurrection without attaching some positive significance to the death as well. As a messianic proclamation, it demands adherence to the theory of a dying and rising Messiah. Although such an idea is found in some sense in late Judaism,[1] it was not the generally accepted expectation, and undoubtedly formed the chief object of attack by the unbelieving Jews. It was a position which the Church had to defend

---

[1] The evidence is extremely difficult to determine. The idea of a *suffering* Messiah can be detected from the nuances of the translation of Isa. 53 by LXX, Peshitta, and Targum, the 'leprous' Messiah of Aquila, *B. Sanhedrin* 98, and a few other rabbinic texts (cf. W. Zimmerli and J. Jeremias, *The Servant of God*, pp. 41, 60-75). A *dying* Messiah (the military Messiah ben Joseph) appears in *Test. Benjamin* (Armenian) 3.8, and is referred to in *B. Sukkah* 52a. The two conceptions are not fused. There is really nothing corresponding to the dying and rising of Jesus preached by the Church. Cf. S. Mowinckel, *He that Cometh*, pp. 326-8.

against a constant barrage of taunts and criticisms. Some of these will appear as we study the scriptures adduced by New Testament writers.

The whole question of a suffering Messiah in pre-Christian thought remains extremely obscure. It is well known that the Targum of Isa. 53, although it gives a messianic interpretation, excludes the idea of death in spite of the plain meaning of the chapter. But this is certainly due to conscious opposition to Christianity, a counter-apologetic to what we are now considering. It is more important to observe that the Targum does not deny the messianic interpretation. If that is a fairly old tradition, it may be presumed that the idea of the Messiah's death was originally included, and removed only later for apologetic reasons. This has been convincingly argued by J. Jeremias in his study of the Servant of the Lord.[1] He also adds other evidence from late Jewish and rabbinic sources for a belief that the Messiah's work would culminate in his expiatory death on behalf of his people before the final victory. The idea is confined to Palestinian Judaism, and it is difficult to know how widely it was held.

The most that we can gather from this evidence is that the dying and rising Messiah had a precedent in late Judaism, and so was within the possible range of thought. It cannot be allowed to contradict the evidence of the New Testament itself that the Passion was held to be an objection to the Church's claims about Jesus, and had to be strenuously defended. It must be remembered that the rejection of the Lord's Messiah *by his own people* was a wholly new constituent in the picture, even where the death of the Messiah was visualized. Moreover it was a very uncongenial idea to the Jewish rulers, for they could not concede it without condemning themselves. Also the *manner* of death by crucifixion was very different from the heroic death in battle which might have been expected, and had the unfortunate effect of placing the sufferer under the curse of Deut. 21.23.[2] It will be interesting to observe the various traces of arguments dealing with this point in our scriptural material. It is also this very same fact which in the end makes possible Christianity's greatest advance, when it is perceived that the limitations of the old Law have been broken.

[1] *Op. cit.*, pp. 66-71. For a different view, cf. William Manson, *Jesus the Messiah*, 1943, pp. 168ff.
[2] Zimmerli and Jeremias, *op. cit.* p. 76, n. 331.

The development of doctrine is often the consequence of reply-
ing to objections. We shall therefore expect to find that analysis of
the Passion apologetic illustrates the history of the doctrine of the
Atonement. From this point of view it is significant that the quotations used in this apologetic are drawn from a narrow range of
scripture, i.e. the fifty-third chapter of Isaiah, certain psalms, and
the prophecy of Zechariah.[1] The Prophets and Psalms were largely
interpreted in an eschatological sense in late Judaism, as also by
the Qumran Covenanters. They contain the chief passages generally recognized to be messianic.[2] In fact the messianic hope is only
one element (and outside Christianity a comparatively unimportant
element) in the apocalyptic eschatological frame of thought. This
is also the home of the earliest attempts at forming an atonement
doctrine. It is only at a slightly later stage that the Pentateuch is
used in formulating the doctrine in terms of the legal prescriptions
of sacrifice. The thought of the early Church was rooted in eschatological expectations, and this is where the doctrine of the Atonement originally belongs. This means that, although the Passion
apologetic is a catalyst to bring the doctrine to positive expression,
there is no clean break between the thought of the first Christians
and that of Jesus himself.

### 1. ISAIAH 53

Although actual quotations from this famous chapter are not
specially numerous in the New Testament, allusions to it are em-
bedded so deeply in the work of all the principal writers that it is
certain that it belongs to the earliest thought of the primitive
Church.[3] It is highly probable that it was inherited from Jesus
himself, and that it exercised a decisive influence on his mind.
The Passion predictions indicate a deliberate choice of a course of

[1] Cf. Dodd, *Acc. Scrip.* pp. 64-67.
[2] E.g. Isa. 7.14, 9.1ff., 11.1ff., 42.1, 61.1; Ps. 2.7, 110.1; Zech. 9.9, etc.
[3] This is the generally accepted view. Since these pages were written
there has appeared a drastic reappraisal of the influence of Isa. 53 by
Morna D. Hooker, *Jesus and the Servant*, 1959. Her main target is the
impression, often given in recent works of biblical theology, that the figure
of the Servant of the Lord can be differentiated from the known figures of
messianic expectation in late Judaism and early Christianity. Her stric-
tures (in some ways much needed) do not seem to affect the argument of
the present work. She does, of course, take a minimizing view of the
implications of literary allusions to Isa. 53, in contrast to the view here
expressed.

action leading to certain death, and this may well have been founded on the belief that it was his destiny to fulfil the deep insights of this prophecy. It is true that Jesus is not recorded as having used the title Servant of the Lord with reference to himself.[1] But the enigmatic Son of Man seems to include this idea in certain contexts.[2] His instruction to the disciples about his coming Passion is likely to have made use of this prophecy at least sufficiently to give it a secure place in their thought. When a Passion apologetic was required, it was there ready-made in the teaching which they had received.

It is thus to be expected that the Church's earliest use of this prophecy is identical with our Lord's own teaching from it. This makes it virtually impossible to distinguish genuine dominical sayings from church-formations in the Gospel tradition, unless some other factor is present to decide the matter. Thus it is possible to argue both ways about δοῦναι τὴν ψυχὴν αὐτοῦ λύτρον ἀντὶ πολλῶν in Mark 10.45 (cf. Isa. 53.11f.), and there is no need to feel bound to exclude it because it turns up again as ὁ δοὺς ἑαυτὸν ἀντίλυτρον ὑπὲρ πάντων in I Tim. 2.6.[3] The same applies to the Marcan version of the words spoken by our Lord over the cup at the Last Supper. It might be thought that τὸ ἐκχυννόμενον ὑπὲρ πολλῶν is an addition to the original words, but J. Jeremias has shown that it is at the basis of all the versions of the words, even Paul's in I Cor. 11.25.[4]

This brings us to the starting-point for the history of the Christian use of Isa. 53. Full weight must be given to the fact that both the *verba Christi* in the Marcan tradition (Mark 10.45 and 14.24) are allusions to Isa. 53.11f., differing from each other and from the

[1] The nearest we get to it is Luke 22.27, closely parallel to Mark 10.45, but originally separate from it.
[2] Mark 9.12, 10.45.
[3] So also Titus 2.14, where other scriptural allusions have been combined with the expression. The thought of Isa. 53.11f. is echoed by a number of different NT phrases. (a) Where the giving of life includes the idea of the sin-offering: Rom. 4.25, 8.3; I Cor. 15.3; II Cor. 5.21; Gal. 1.4; Heb. 10.12; I Peter 3.18; I John 2.2, 4.10. (b) The giving of life on behalf of someone: ἐκχυννόμενον, Matt. 26.28 = Mark 14.24 = Luke 22.20; παραδοῦναι, Rom. 8.32, Gal. 2.20, Eph. 5.2, 25, cf. Acts 15.26; δοῦναι, Gal. 1.4; παθεῖν, I Peter 2.21, cf. Acts 9.16; τίθεναι, John 10.11, 15, 13.37f., 15.13, I John 3.16; ἀποθανεῖν and similar expressions, John 11.50f., 18.14, Rom. 5.6-8, 14.15, I Cor. 1.13, II Cor. 5.15, I Thess. 5.10, Heb. 2.9, cf. Acts 21.13.
[4] *The Eucharistic Words of Jesus*, ET 1953, pp. 113f.

Septuagint. Other allusions to the same verses exhibit further
varieties of expression. The giving of his life for many, for the
remission of their sins, is a way of speaking about the death of
Jesus which gives it *positive* significance. It is the beginning of a
doctrine of the Atonement. The wide variety of non-Septuagintal
phrases indicates that the biblical work has been done at the earliest
possible period, very probably by Jesus himself. The results have
entered into normal Christian speech, and there is no need to
adduce the specific text. In other words, we have here another
case of a biblical passage providing a theologumenon of the early
Church. It is neatly expressed in the *paradosis* of I Cor. 15.3, 'that
Christ died for our sins according to the scriptures'.

So far we are not necessarily in the realm of the Passion apologetic. The very primitive allusions which we have just noticed to
the leading idea of the prophecy indicate that the whole passage
Isa. 52.13 - 53.12 was accepted by the first Christians as a prophetic account of what had happened to Jesus, his sufferings, death
and exaltation. It is all ready to answer the question, when posed
by hostile critics, Why did God allow Jesus to die, if he is the
Lord's Christ? It is because he was foreordained to fulfil the mission of the Servant. Such an answer, relying on the relevance of
the passage as a whole, is consistent with the earliest phase of the
Church's thought, when there is still uncertainty in what sense
Jesus can be spoken of as the Messiah. There is a hint of it in the
speeches where this hesitation still shows through in Acts 3 and 4.[1]
The title παῖς in Acts 3.13, 26; 4.27, 30 is probably due to this and
other Isaiah passages. The title ὁ δίκαιος in Acts 3.14 and 7.52 may
well be an actual reference to Isa. 53.11 (cf. p. 20, n. 2). The
phrase ἐδόξασεν τὸν παῖδα αὐτοῦ in Acts 3.13 not only alludes to
Isa. 52.13,[2] but also implies a complete explanation of the events
of redemption in terms of the whole chapter, as it is logically the
final stage in the history of the παῖς. This use of the prophecy is
consistent with the idea that the Passion is the work of the Servant/
Son of Man, who has subsequently been declared Messiah at his
Resurrection.

On the other hand we have seen traces of a messianic interpretation of Isa. 53 itself. The question is bound to be asked, If Jesus
fulfilled that prophecy, was it as the Christ that he suffered? The

---

[1] Cf. J. A. T. Robinson, 'The Most Primitive Christology of all?'
[2] Zimmerli and Jeremias, *op. cit.*, p. 86, n. 380.

Church's enemies deny this interpretation, but the mere fact that the Christians appeal to this passage raises the presumption that they themselves adhere to it. We have already seen in connection with Ps. 110.1 that the Church soon decided that the risen Jesus was the *Messias revelatus* rather than *designatus*. This means that it was as Messiah that he suffered. The value of the prophecy now is that it reveals a predetermined divine plan. We thus reach the classic position of the Passion apologetic, the scriptural proof of the theoretical point *that the Messiah should suffer*, repeated in the anti-Judaic literature with unfailing regularity.[1] The original position, closely connected with the rudimentary Atonement doctrine, had been that Jesus, who is the Messiah, had in his atoning death fulfilled the mission of the Servant of the Lord. The later position shows a greater christological interest, that Jesus is the Christ because it was prophesied that the Messiah should suffer; or, *vice versa*, that Jesus suffered because he is the Christ, and the Christ must suffer.

This general Passion apologetic is indicated when emphasis is placed on the scriptural warrant, that 'Christ died for our sins κατὰ τὰς γραφάς' (I Cor. 15.3). It is also implied in the many instances where ὡς γέγραπται and κατὰ τὸ ὡρισμένον are used.[2] It is a favourite idea in the Lucan literature.[3]

The same motive is the foundation of a word used with peculiarly evocative overtones, παραδίδοναι, which is to be connected with Isa. 53.12.[4] It sums up the story of Jesus' sufferings from the point of view of the necessity of the atoning death of the Servant. Jesus was 'delivered up' because it was God's plan of salvation. It belongs to the earliest stratum of thought without necessarily conveying a messianic colouring, but takes this on when there is an apologetic motive. Thus it is used in two of the Passion predictions (Mark 9.31 and 10.34, parr.) to give positive meaning to the death;

---

[1] Justin, *Dial.* 39; Tertullian, *Adv. Jud.* 10; Cyprian, *Ad Quirinum: Test adv. Jud.* II.15; Lactantius, *Inst.* IV 16.

[2] Zimmerli and Jeremias, *op. cit.*, pp. 90ff. Note 405 mentions: Mark 8.31, and par., 9.12, and par., 14.21, and par., 14.49, and par.; Matt. 26.54; *al.*

[3] *Ibid.*, nn. 405 and 414: Luke 9.31, 18.31, 22.22, 24.32, 44, 46; Acts 2.23, 3.18, 4.28, 7.52, 10.43, 13.27, 29, 17.2, 26.22f.

[4] *Ibid.*, pp. 90, 96. In the Gospels we find it in (*a*) the Passion predictions, (*b*) references to Judas (almost exclusively so in John). Paul exhibits it at Rom. 4.25, 8.32; Gal. 2.20; Eph. 5.2, 25. Is John 19.30 (παρέδωκεν τὸ πνεῦμα) intended to recall Isa. 53.12 (נפשׁ ... הערה = παρεδόθη ... ἡ ψυχὴ αὐτοῦ)?

but these predictions probably owe their preservation in the Gospel tradition at least partly to the apologetic position that the Christ should suffer. The word is also specially used to describe the act of Judas Iscariot, who was the unwitting agent of the fulfilment of Isa. 53.12. We may note particularly Mark 14.21, ὅτι ὁ μὲν υἱὸς τοῦ ἀνθρώπου ὑπάγει καθὼς γέγραπται περὶ αὐτοῦ· οὐαὶ δὲ τῷ ἀνθρώπῳ ἐκείνῳ δι' οὗ . . . παραδίδοται. The sense demands that ὑπάγει be regarded as an equivalent of παραδίδοται, i.e. 'is delivered up'; but it is avoided by Mark on account of the following use of the same word in the specialized meaning 'is betrayed'. This application to Judas has a further apologetic motive, the need to 'explain' his conduct. That also fitted into the predetermined plan. More elaborate items of the Passion apologetic in connection with Judas will appear when we study the Psalms and Zechariah.

The *Passion predictions* combine the positive doctrine of our Lord's death with the apologetic concerning it. They are probably dependent on the use of Isa. 53 for this purpose, though there are few actual verbal links. We have just mentioned the use of παραδίδοναι. There is probably also a hint of Isa. 53.5 in the use of μαστιγώσουσιν in the third prediction (Mark 10.34), though it is not found in the Septuagint of this verse. It is picked up by John in his account of the trial before Pilate (19.1). This third prediction shows by its greater fulness the need to find prophetic justification of the details of the Passion. Mark 9.12 belongs together with the Passion predictions, and this contains another vivid touch, ἐξουδενηθῇ. It is generally recognized to be a reference to Isa. 53.3 נִבְזֶה, though the Septuagint has ἠτιμάσθη. Aquila, Symmachus and Theodotion, however, have ἐξουδενώμενος, which probably represents an older Palestinian tradition. It is notable that the scope of the scripture is made to include John the Baptist as well as Jesus himself (v. 13), which means that it is being viewed simply as the appointed way of salvation in the pre-messianic sense.[1] The same word passed into the apologetic proper, proving that the rejection of Jesus is not inconsistent with the messianic claim. Jesus is the one 'set at nought' in the same sense as he is 'the rejected stone' which nevertheless has become 'the head of the corner' (Ps. 118.22). It is thus not surprising to find that this very verse of Ps. 118 is

---

[1] Cf. J. A. T. Robinson, 'Elijah, John and Jesus: an Essay in Detection', *NTS* 4, 1958, pp. 263-81, now reprinted in his *Twelve New Testament Studies*.

cited in Acts 4.11 with ἐξουθενηθείς instead of ἀποδοκιμασθείς. The later interest in the prophesying of exact details narrows down the application to the mocking of Jesus by Herod's soldiers (Luke 23.11 ἐξουθενήσας δὲ αὐτὸν ὁ Ἡρῴδης).

We have here evidence of a primary theological interest, to formulate a doctrine of the Atonement. There is secondly the apologetic issue of the Passion in relation to theoretical messianism. And at a third stage there is a tendency to use the prophecy for subsidiary purposes, such as the desire for vivid narrative details.

The *theological* use of Isa. 53 continues throughout the New Testament without losing any of its importance. Paul is able to refer to it with ease and freedom in expounding the Atonement in the early chapters of Romans. In 4.25 παρεδόθη διὰ τὰ παραπτώματα ἡμῶν evokes the whole chapter, using a non-Septuagint word. It underlies the entire argument of ch. 5. There is probably an allusion to Isa. 53.10 in 8.3, and to v. 12 in 8.32 and 34 (the intercession of the exalted Lord).[1] On the other hand both the actual quotations from Isa. 53 (Rom. 10.16 and 15.21) are examples of the shift of application, and so must be left out of consideration for the moment. The most sustained theological use of Isa. 53 is to be found in the famous christological passage, Phil. 2.5-11. It is poetical in character, and may have been taken over by Paul from a liturgical source.[2] The affinity to the prophecy lies not so much in the actual allusions as in the general thought of the passage. It is significant that the words which bear the closest resemblance to Isa. 53 all depend on the Hebrew text, not one being found in the Septuagint version of the chapter.[3]

Another sustained passage based on this prophecy occurs in I Peter 2.21-25. Words and phrases are drawn from at least vv. 4, 5, 6, 9 and 12 of Isa. 53. If I Peter is a Paschal homily,[4] the preacher is here presumably drawing on the liturgy itself at this point. The liturgy thus contained either Isa. 53 itself as one of the lections, or else a prayer based on it. In either case the inclusion of

---

[1] So Dodd, *Acc. Scrip.*, p. 94. The allusion is to the Hebrew.

[2] Cf. L. Cerfaux, 'L'hymne au Christ-Serviteur de Dieu', *Miscellanea historica in honorem Alberti de Meyer*, 1946, pp. 117-30.

[3] μορφῇ, cf. v. 2 תֹּאַר; ἐκένωσεν, cf. v. 12 הֶעֱרָה (=laid bare, but LXX παρεδόθη, Targum מְסַר, cf. ἐκχυννόμενον, Mark 14.24); δούλου; ἐταπείνωσεν, cf. v. 4 מְעֻנֶּה, but LXX, v. 8 ἐν τῇ ταπεινώσει; ἑαυτὸν . . . μέχρι θανάτου, cf. v. 12 לַמָּוֶת נַפְשׁוֹ; ὑπερύψωσεν, cf. 52.13, גָּבַהּ מְאֹד.

[4] Rather than a liturgy itself, as proposed by F. L. Cross, *I Peter: a Paschal Liturgy*, 1954.

it in the liturgy is in connection with the Atonement. This doctrine is also implied in another reference to Isa. 53.11f. at 3.18.

The Epistle to the Hebrews also presupposes this theology. At 2.9 the language of it is used in an exposition of Ps. 8.5-7. At 7.25 the intercession of the exalted Lord is mentioned in the same phrase as Paul used in Rom. 8.34, and the idea occurs again in different words in 9.28. The thought of 10.12, οὗτος δὲ μίαν ὑπὲρ ἁμαρτιῶν προσενέγκας θυσίαν εἰς τὸ διηνεκὲς ἐκάθισεν ἐν δεξιᾷ τοῦ θεοῦ, briefly summarizes the Christian interpretation of Isa. 53, and so suggests that the whole of this writer's exposition of the Atonement in terms of the sin-offering of Leviticus actually stems from this prophecy. The writer to the Hebrews does not actually quote from Isa. 53, but he takes it for granted and builds his own work upon it.

Similarly this theology has so deeply penetrated the mind of John, that he can concentrate the whole story of Isa. 53 into a single paradoxical idea, using ὑψοῦν, and especially δοξάζειν. This evokes Isa. 52.13, ὁ παῖς μου . . . ὑψωθήσεται καὶ δοξασθήσεται σφόδρα, a sentence which combines both the beginning and the end of the matter. The idea of the 'lifting up of the Son of Man', which is overtly connected with the brazen serpent in the wilderness, probably stems from this passage in the first instance.[1] Like Paul, when John actually quotes from this chapter it is for one of the subsidiary purposes, showing the shift of application. The fact that theological allusions to Isa. 53 are so frequent in the New Testament, while the shift of application has often taken place in actual quotations, is surely the most eloquent testimony to the extreme antiquity of the use of this prophecy in the early Church.

Actual quotations of Isa. 53 often show the *apologetic* connected with the Passion, though sometimes this has been overlaid by a subsidiary motive. The story of Philip and the Ethiopian eunuch fastens attention upon the interpretation of an extended quotation of Isa. 53.7-8a (Acts 8.32f.). The story itself probably comes from an old tradition. It is notable that it contains no express statement of the messiahship of Jesus, except in the spurious v. 37. But the quotation is (as usual in Acts) from the Septuagint, and it cannot be assumed that Luke has left the narrative material untouched. At any rate the precise words quoted are not intrinsically necessary to the argument, but stand for the whole prophecy. Any other

[1] See p. 236, *infra*.

significant part of it might equally well have been used. Luke himself was probably responsible for the choice of the particular verses to quote. The eunuch's question in v. 34 perhaps reflects the discussion with which the Passion apologetic was concerned. The applications which come to his mind (and so may be actual Jewish interpretations of the first century[1]) are the prophet himself or some other historical personage. We are then told that Philip 'beginning from this scripture preached unto him Jesus' (v. 35). It is unfortunate that the verse is so manifestly Lucan that it is impossible to get behind it to the original narrative. The study of the theology based on Isa. 53 which we have already made suggests that Philip showed the eunuch how the mission of the Servant had been achieved in Jesus' death and Resurrection. Luke himself, however, probably thinks of it along the lines of the Passion apologetic proper, that the prophecy is messianic, that Jesus has fulfilled it, and that therefore he is the Christ.[2] In short, this may be another case where Luke has drawn on the stock of apologetic biblical material to illustrate his history, as in the speech of Acts 2.

Further traces of this apologetic are preserved in St Luke's Gospel. First there is the saying about the 'strong man' in the Beelzeboul controversy, Luke 11.21f. The whole passage seems to have existed in two forms, Mark and Q, which were both available to Matthew and Luke. It is problematical whether the Q version followed by Matthew contained the strong man saying in the form in which we have it in Luke, because Matthew has clearly abandoned his source at this point in favour of Mark. At any rate the Marcan version is the simpler one, and presumably nearer to the original. It says that no one can rob a strong man of his goods unless he first bind the strong man.[3] Luke's version develops this general statement into a gnomic story, describing first a strong man in peaceful possession of his belongings, and then the arrival of a *stronger* man, who overpowers him and *divides his spoils*. The italic words are all significant for our purpose. The apparently

---

[1] Not taken as evidence for such by C. R. North, *The Suffering Servant in Deutero-Isaiah*, 1948/56, but used as the starting-point of enquiry by S. Mowinckel, *Der Knecht Jahwäs*, 1921, pp. 8f.

[2] The passage cannot, therefore, be classified as an example of the argument from literal fulfilment, as in the case of Ps. 110.1, which is only possible when the messianic interpretation is common ground between Christians and Jews.

[3] Held by most scholars to be based on Isa. 49.24f. For the Lucan version see W. Grundmann, art. ἰσχύω, *TWNT* III, p. 403.

ordinary ἰσχυρότερος takes on definite messianic colouring from its use in the preaching of the Baptist (Mark 1.7, parr.). Taken in conjunction with Luke 11.20 (ἄρα ἔφθασεν ἐφ' ὑμᾶς ἡ βασιλεία τοῦ θεοῦ), it is an unmistakable invitation to recognize that the Messiah is actually here. The Messiah conquers his foe and then celebrates his victory in the manner of the Servant by 'dividing the spoils of the strong',[1] Isa. 53.12a: τῶν ἰσχυρῶν μεριεῖ σκῦλα. The allusion in Luke 11.22, τὰ σκῦλα αὐτοῦ διαδίδωσιν, is based on the Greek text, the different verb perhaps deriving from a Palestinian recension. As Luke always follows the Alexandrian text, it is probable that this developed form of the saying already existed in his source.

The apologetic motive which lies behind this development must now be shown. A saying of Jesus has been given messianic application and linked to the 'plot' of Isa. 53. The Passion is not mentioned, but is assumed in the struggle with the strong man. This development coincides in time with the actual claims of the Church about Jesus, using this prophecy. From the apologetic point of view it is desirable to show that these claims go back into the remembered words of Jesus himself. This is an aspect of the primitive apologetic which we shall meet again later in other connections.

The other Lucan passage is the quotation of the phrase καὶ μετὰ ἀνόμων ἐλογίσθη with specific reference to the Passion in Luke 22.37. It occurs in the short paragraph about the two swords, which is only found in Luke, and which may be from a Zealot source.[2] The words are from Isa. 53.12c, again in a form differing from the Septuagint. The whole verse, Luke 22.37, breaks the sense of the paragraph, and probably is no true part of it. If the saying is genuine, it may well owe its preservation to the Passion apologetic. Otherwise it is a product of the needs of apologetic. It gives a scriptural warrant in answer to the objection that Jesus suffered a criminal's death (rather than some other way more appropriate to a dying Messiah). But of course it is tempting to understand it in a purely biographical way, describing how Jesus was actually crucified between two thieves; and so it is inserted into the Passion narrative of Mark (15.28) in some manuscripts.[3] This is another

---

[1] The Hebrew 'among the great . . . with the strong' means that the Servant receives the reward of a hero. No doubt the LXX was intended to convey the same meaning, but it is possible to take the genitive objectively, so that the Servant dispossesses the great and the strong.

[2] W. L. Knox, Sources of the Synoptic Gospels I: St Mark, p. 125.

[3] The verses about the two thieves (Mark 15.27 and 32b) are classified

example (post-canonical) of the later interest in prophetic anticipations of every detail of the narrative.

Further light on the apologetic is provided by the formula-
quotation of Isa. 53.4 in Matt. 8.17.

| Matt. 8.17 | Isa. 53.4 | |
|---|---|---|
| αὐτὸς τὰς ἀσθενείας | οὗτος τὰς ἁμαρτίας | אָכֵן חֲלָיֵנוּ |
| ἡμῶν ἔλαβεν καὶ | ἡμῶν φέρει καὶ | הוּא נָשָׂא |
| τὰς νόσους ἐβάστασεν. | περὶ ἡμῶν ὀδυνᾶται. | וּמַכְאֹבֵינוּ סְבָלָם |

It is evident that the Septuagint here is interpretative, correctly
piercing through the metaphor of sickness to the fact of sin.[1] The
*pesher* text adopted by Matthew takes it literally, so that he can
easily apply it to our Lord's healing miracles. It is not enough,
however, to see it merely as scriptural justification for the miracles,
for it comes from a chapter which describes the sufferings of the
Servant himself. The fundamental issue is that Jesus' own sufferings are redemptive—in reply to the objection that the physical
indignities that he suffered are inconsistent with the messianic claim.
The connection of this with the healing miracles may represent an
intermediate stage of interpretation, which explains why these
words were singled out as a select quotation before being incorporated by Matthew into his narrative. This will be shown in
greater detail in a later chapter.

The *subsidiary purposes* to which this prophecy may be put have
already appeared as we have looked at those quotations which preserve the primitive Passion apologetic. We need not refer again to
the desire to derive narrative details from the prophecy. There are
two other kinds of motive still to be taken into consideration.

The first is the question of the Jews' refusal to believe. This
appears in three citations, together comprising Isa. 52.15b - 53.1.

52.15b   For that which had not been told them shall they see;
        And that which they had not heard shall they understand.
53.1a   Who hath believed our report?
  b   And to whom hath the arm of the Lord been revealed?

as secondary material in the analysis of the Marcan Passion narrative by
Vincent Taylor (*The Gospel according to St Mark*, 1952, Additional
Note H). The possibility that this tradition was itself inspired by the
apologetic use of Isa. 53.12c is a further question which lies beyond the
scope of the present enquiry.
[1] So also the Targum.

These verses are not likely to have been interpreted in isolation
from the whole chapter in the first instance. They are singled out
because they explain how it is that so many refuse to believe the
Atonement theology which the Church finds in this prophecy.
Thereafter they can be applied to unbelief in general, and then to
several different specific issues. Their function is thus very similar
to that of Isa. 6.9f., already referred to.[1] It is not surprising to find
that Isa. 53.1 is cited in full in John 12.38 alongside Isa. 6.9f. This
shows what seems to be the first stage of development, the application not to the Church's teaching but to the signs which Jesus
did, regardless of the Passion context. The next stage is represented
by the quotation of Isa. 53.1a only, in Rom. 10.16. Here Paul is
arguing about the preaching to the Gentiles. He points out that
the present unbelief of the Gentiles is only due to the fact that
they have not yet had opportunity of hearing the Gospel, in contrast to the Jews, who have heard it and yet have refused to believe.
The quotation is one of a catena on this subject which forms the
structure of the argument. The application is thus to the unbelief
of the Jews, considered in relation to the Gentiles controversy.
Finally Isa. 52.15b is quoted in Rom. 15.21 as the justification of
Paul's policy of evangelizing completely untouched areas. Judging
by the other quotation, it is clear that this one was valued by Paul
as a warrant for preaching to the Gentiles in general. The application to his pioneer work is a further refinement. The proper
context of the verse has now been altogether forgotten.[2]

The other subsidiary motive is not a matter of apologetic, but
simply the moral needs of the internal life of the Church. There is
a natural tendency to use this fine Atonement chapter, fulfilled in
Jesus, as an example which all must follow. So the theological
hymn in Phil. 2.5-11 has been turned into homiletic by the introductory words 'Have this mind in you', which belong to the context of the chapter and may replace some other opening.[3] Similarly
we observed traces of the theology of Isa. 53 in I Peter, and here
also the purpose is entirely homiletic. It should be observed that
this moral usage stems directly from the theological, and is unaffected by the apologetic interests noticeable elsewhere.

[1] *Supra*, pp. 17f.
[2] This exegesis is continued by Justin, *Dial.* 42, who applies Isa. 53.1f.
to the preaching of the apostles and the reception accorded them.
[3] Note the use of φρονέω in Phil. 2.2 (twice). On the other hand ταπεινο-
φροσύνη in v. 3 may have been suggested by the hymn itself (v. 8).

It is an impressive fact that the great theological importance of Isa. 53 has to be deduced from the numerous allusions without the aid of actual quotations. There are only six proper citations (at Matt. 8.17; Luke 22.37; John 12.38; Acts 8.32f.; Rom. 10.16, 15.21), and all of these are concerned with apologetic issues. We notice also that five of these belong to connected groups of quotations. Matt. 8.17 is one of the formula-quotations which are a special feature of this Gospel. The same is true of John 12.38, which also has another member of the same group beside it in 12.40 (Isa. 6.9f.). The Romans quotations belong to a group of Gentiles texts. Luke 22.37 seems to stand apart, but can be classified with the formula-quotations of Matthew and John. On the other hand Acts 8.32f. is probably Luke's own choice of words from his general acquaintance with the use of this prophecy in apologetic. These factors will have to be taken into account in the final assessment of the New Testament quotations.

The general picture which emerges from all these references to Isa. 53 is of the Church, taking its lead from Jesus himself, using it to work out the meaning of the events which closed his life on earth. This is partly done under stress of opposition from the Jewish religious authorities. They raise the question whether the suffering and death of Jesus is consistent with the claim that he is the Messiah. And this leads on to more specific questions—why Jesus included the traitor Judas among his closest companions (Mark 14.21), why Jesus was 'set at nought' (Mark 9.12; Luke 23.11; Acts 4.11), why he suffered a criminal's death (Luke 22.37), why he was subjected to such physical maltreatment (Matt. 8.17, first stage), what basis has the Church's claim about these things in the teaching and work of Jesus himself (Luke 11.22; Matt. 8.17, second stage), and why, if it is true, it does not positively compel belief (John 12.38). There are also matters internal to the life of the Church, the preaching to the Gentiles and moral exhortation of the faithful.

## 2. PASSION PSALMS

The psalms to be considered are 22, 31, 34, 41, 69 and 109. The early Church's use of them follows largely the same pattern as we have seen in studying Isa. 53. It begins with a general application to the Passion apologetic, and proceeds to a number of miscel-

laneous issues, some of them quite unconnected with the Passion.
They will be taken in order, and at the end an attempt will be
made to synthesize the results.

## Psalm 22

This psalm is so familiar in descriptions of the Passion, that it
may come as a surprise that it actually yields little for our purpose
in digging beneath the New Testament quotations. It was from
the beginning the psalm of the righteous sufferer, and so it always
remained, with only rare exceptions.

The foundation of its use, both in narrative and in apologetic,
must be our Lord's cry of dereliction on the cross, Mark 15.34=
Matt. 27.46, the Aramaic version of the words 'My God, my God,
why hast thou forsaken me?' All the other citations and allusions
presuppose the Septuagint text, which is of course that of the translation in this instance too. The genuineness of this saying, as actually spoken by Jesus, can hardly be disputed.[1] It is in any case
impossible to find a motive for inventing it, if it is not genuine.
Besides this, the textual phenomena attest its antiquity in the
Gospel tradition. Even Luke is a witness to both these points, for
his silence may well be largely due to discomfort at the starkness
of the saying, and yet he preserves what appears to be a trace of it
in a different way, as will be shown in a moment. In Mark the
quotation of the Aramaic words is a sign of specially careful
accuracy.[2] But it was also necessary in this case to account for the
mention of Elijah in the next verse as a misunderstanding of it.
This pun is itself an aid to memory, although memory is liable to
be faulty about the exact form of words where Aramaic is not
spoken. Hence the great textual confusion.[3]

Two other punning versions of the saying are perhaps attempts
to explain it away. The first is the well-known version of the *Gospel*

---

[1] Some scholars (Loisy, Bacon, Bertram, Bultmann) have maintained
that the passage was supplied as the great cry of Mark 15.37.

[2] Such is the impression of the other Aramaic *verba Christi* (5.41, 7.34,
14.36). κορβᾶν (7.11) is a technical term. Liturgical usage may have been
a factor in some cases.

[3] The Hebrew text represented by D is a comparatively late correction,
characteristic of this MS. This is indicated by comparison with the Itala,
which retains the Aramaic in the best authorities of Mark, but largely
follows D's correction of Matthew. Mark dropped out of use in the West
after the diffusion of Matthew.

of Peter 5.19: ἡ δύναμίς μου, ἡ δύναμίς μου, κατέλειψάς με. The opening words may be due to actual confusion between אֵלִי and חֵילִי.[1] The second is the addition of τοῦ ἡλίου ἐκλιπόντος to the Marcan words about the darkness in Luke 23.45. Although this is a perfectly natural additional explanation, falls in line with the tendency to multiply portents,[2] and exactly fulfils eschatological prophecies,[3] the words occupy the position of the great cry in Mark and invite comparison with it. It is the proper Greek expression for an eclipse, but not a biblical one (the Old Testament always has the idea of the sun's being darkened). Moreover the verb can be both transitive and intransitive. It is thus conceivable that the cry in the darkness was taken to mean that the *sun* had forsaken Jesus (rather than God).[4]

These testimonies to actual memory, with its inevitable vagaries, are bound to place this psalm in the oldest class of Passion material. Nevertheless they are also precisely the reason why it does not appear specifically in the apologetic. It is an integral part of what has got to be explained. The apologetic motive is evident in the *Gospel of Peter* and in Luke, where attempts are made to get rid of it without actually denying its existence in the tradition.

On the other hand, the rest of the psalm as a whole provides the answer to the scandal of the opening words. It is a poem of the righteous sufferer, and leads up to a promise of vindication. In this way it is suitable for the general apologetic position, that the sufferings of Jesus fit into a predetermined plan. So when it is said that Christ suffered 'according to the scriptures', it is possible that Psalm 22 is one of those scriptures, besides the fundamentally important Isa. 53.

From this point of view it becomes a quarry for pictorial detail in writing the story of the Passion. Every detail of the tradition has its counterpart in prophecy, and so it cannot be objected that anything falls outside the divinely ordered scheme of redemption. Psalm 22 thus provides phrases for describing the distribution of

---

[1] It has been suggested by Dibelius that this was a correction derived from Ps. 22.16, ἐξηράνθη . . . ἡ ἰσχύς μου (in *Abhandlungen zur semitischen Religionskunde und Sprachwissenschaft*, BZAW 33, 1918, p. 145).

[2] Matt. 27.51ff.; *Ev. Petri* 5.15-17.

[3] Joel 2.31 (3.4), cf. Acts 2.19; Amos 8.9. The reading ἐσκοτίσθη ὁ ἥλιος of the Koine and Caesarean texts has been influenced by this consideration.

[4] For the aspirate in חֵילִי and ἥλιος, cf. Mark 15.34 it.: *heli heli*.

the clothes of Jesus,[1] the attitude of the onlookers,[2] and their jeers.[3] None of these are essential items in the story, and so could easily have been worked up from the text of the psalm without any basis in fact. On the other hand they may well be genuine memories, but couched in the language of the psalm in reply to the taunts of the unbelieving Jews. This seems to be true of the distribution of the clothes, which has received special elaboration in John 19.23f. All four gospels at this point quote Ps. 22.19, about dividing the clothes and casting lots on them. It has been pointed out that whereas Mark correctly understands the poetic parallelism of the verse, taking the two halves to be equivalents, John has taken them separately, in much the same way as Matt. 21.2 supposes that Zech. 9.9 requires Jesus to ride on *two* beasts at his triumphal entry. In the latter case, Stendahl has argued that there was an actual tradition of two animals, which lies behind the form of the text quoted; it is thus not a matter of making the facts fit the text, but the form of the text has itself been adapted to the factual tradition.[4] Although it is doubtful whether we can really postulate a tradition of two animals, Stendahl is undoubtedly right in saying that the textual phenomena do not support the generally accepted idea that Matthew has been simply guilty of a naive deduction from the Zechariah quotation.[5] Similarly John must not be held to be ignorant of the most constant characteristic of Hebrew poetry. John knew that Ps. 22.19 meant what the Synoptists made of it (whether he had a copy of one of them in front of him or not), but *purposely* chose to take it literally.[6] This was because of his interest in the seamless robe, to which he attached symbolical significance. The fact that the scripture said that they cast lots for an item of clothing proves that Jesus' χιτών was seamless. And that means that he wore a garment appropriate to the high priest.[7] This reflects the controversy about our Lord's high-priesthood which is more

---

[1] Matt. 27.35 = Mark 15.24 = Luke 23.34, cf. John 19.23f.

[2] Matt. 27.39 = Mark 15.29; Luke 23.35.

[3] Matt. 27.43. This quotation of Ps. 22.9 has been adapted from the LXX for its present context, no doubt suggested by the allusion to Ps. 22.8 in 27.39, which was found in Mark.

[4] *SSM*, p. 200.

[5] See *infra*, p. 114.

[6] Cf. *Ev. Petri* 4.12, where the verse is interpreted of two successive actions: *first* the soldiers divided the clothes into heaps, *then* they cast lots for them—Dibelius, *op. cit.*, pp. 133f.

[7] Josephus, *Ant.* III 161.

clearly seen in the Epistle to the Hebrews. It does not belong to the primitive period, but is one facet of developing christology.[1]

But the really surprising thing to the reader familiar with the English versions of Psalm 22 is that the New Testament does not mention v. 17 (RV 'they pierced my hands and my feet'). It would have been valuable to explain the scandal of death by the method of crucifixion. We shall see that this question was indeed raised, but answered in another way.[2] The reason is that the Hebrew is corrupt, and gives nothing like this sense as it stands. The Septuagint ὤρυξαν[3] means, in the context, that the bystanders made 'digs' at the sufferer's hands and feet.[4] Other versions thought of them as trying to *bind* his hands and feet,[5] which is still further removed from the Christian interpretation. Nevertheless the Church's understanding of the psalm as prophetic of the Crucifixion was bound to suggest it in the end, though not without some difficulty.[6]

As with Isa. 53, so a phrase from this psalm can suggest the whole Passion story. There is an allusion of this kind in Heb. 5.7, δεήσεις . . . μετὰ κραυγῆς (cf. Ps. 22.25, δεήσει . . . ἐν τῷ κεκραγέναι).

[1] *Infra*, p. 142.
[2] See the analysis of Zech. 12.10, pp. 124f.
[3] Reading כָּארוּ for MT כָּארִי, 'like a lion'.
[4] As 'dogs' they *bite* him. The parallel shows that the maltreatment affects all the sufferer's bones (limbs?). Or perhaps the LXX means that they *punch* him like boxers, cf. Aristophanes, *Pax* 898.
[5] The Syro-Hexapla gives 'as seeking to bind' as the reading of Symmachus. This derives from an error in the Greek manuscript tradition, and BH[3] is wrong to cite ὡς ζητοῦντες δῆσαι (Field's retranslation of Syro-Hexapla). The true reading of Sym. is ὡς λέων =MT, published by C. Taylor, *Hebrew-Greek Cairo Genizah Palimpsests from the Taylor-Schechter Collection*, as long ago as 1900. The origin of the error is the misreading of ΩΣΛΕΩΝΤΑΣΧΕΙΡΑΣ as ΩΣΔΕΟΝΤΕΣΧΕΙΡΑΣ. The Syro-Hexapla thus has a double translation of δέοντες =(1) need, (2) bind. It is possible that the same error has inspired ἐπέδησαν and συνεπόδισαν (both attributed to Aquila), and *vinxerunt*, the reading given by Jerome as *juxta Hebraeos*. If so, another reading ascribed to Aquila, ἤσχυναν (=כָּאבוּ?), may be genuine, and the case for an early interpretation in the sense 'bind' disappears. ἤσχυναν at least supports the plural verb. The true reading is thus probably כָּארוּ. This seems more likely than the suggestion of W. E. Barnes (*JTS* 37, 1936, pp. 385f.) that כָּארִי ='as a hearth', i.e. burnt up with fever.
[6] *Ep. Barn.* 5.13 has the composite text καθήλωσόν μου τὰς σάρκας, ὅτι πονηρευομένων συναγωγαὶ ἐπανέστησάν μοι.. Here words from Ps. 119.120 have replaced ὤρυξαν etc., to prove that it refers to the nailing—perhaps originally a separate comment. (The translator did not know סָמַר ='bristle up', though it is correctly rendered ἔφριξαν in Job 4.15, the only other occurrence of this word.)

In Rom. 5.5 ἐλπὶς οὐ καταισχύνει (cf. Ps. 22.6 ἤλπισαν καὶ οὐ κατῃσχύνθησαν), the application has been transferred to the Christians themselves in their imitation of Christ, a homiletic usage. This happens again even more clearly in II Tim. 4.17, where the Apostle speaks of his own sufferings in terms of Ps. 22.22 (ἐκ στόματος λέοντος). For a real shift of application, after the whole psalm has been generally accepted christologically, there is the possibility of a link between μονογενῆς in John 1.18 and in Ps. 22.21,[1] but there is no hint of the Passion.

Finally there is a quotation showing the shift of application in Heb. 2.12 = Ps. 22.23: 'I will declare thy name unto my brethren, in the midst of the congregation will I sing thy praise.' These words belong to the 'vindication' part of the psalm, and so originally would have been applied to the Resurrection. There is a trace of this in the narrative of the women at the sepulchre, Matt. 28.10, and especially in John's version of it (John 20.17, πρὸς τοὺς ἀδελφούς μου). The application to the Resurrection has also been preserved in Justin, Dial. 106. But in Hebrews the connection with the Resurrection is presupposed, and the passage can be adduced simply to prove the Christians' participation in that victory. The quotation is followed by two others, Isa. 8.17(?) and 18. We shall come across Isa. 8 again in the primitive apologetic, with a similar shift of application to that of Ps. 22.[2] The psalm has here ceased to be a proof 'that the Christ should suffer' and 'that he should rise again'. All the emphasis is on the one word 'brethren'. By that means it has become the proof that Jesus is 'the representative Head of a redeemed mankind'.[3] Exactly the same shift of application with regard to this verse has happened in Ep. Barn. 6.16.

In these ways Psalm 22 was found to be useful as christology developed. But the application of it to the Passion, both in general and in detail, has always remained paramount.

## Psalm 31

The use of this psalm in the primitive apologetic is less certain. It seems to have been specially connected with the persecution of the Church by the unbelieving Jews rather than with the question of the sufferings of Jesus. The chief interest in it is v. 6, 'Into thine

---

[1] Cf. Dodd, Acc. Scrip., p. 97.
[2] Infra, p. 176.
[3] The phrase is Dodd's, Acc. Scrip., p. 20 (referring to this passage).

hand I commend my spirit', quoted in Luke 23.46. Besides this, words from v. 14 are used by Matthew when rewriting the Marcan account of the Sanhedrin's plot against Jesus (Matt. 26.3f. = Mark 14.1): 'They took counsel together (ἐπισυναχθῆναι) against me, they devised (ἐβουλεύσαντο) to take away my life.' The reminiscence of these words probably reflects the growing bitterness of the Church at the persecution which it has received. The use of this psalm is thus internal to the life of the Church, encouraging the Christians who share the sufferings of the righteous Christ.

Verse 6, 'Into thine hand (LXX hands) I commend my spirit', has its proper Christian application in this context, especially when there is imminent danger of death. There appear to be two independent allusions to this verse in precisely this sense in Acts 7.59 (the death of Stephen) and I Peter 4.19 (a persecution context).

It is natural to assume that the actual quotation of this verse in Luke 23.46 is derived from the same devotional practice of the Church. Although Luke uses a largely non-Marcan Passion narrative, at 23.44 he is in touch with Mark's account, rewriting it and abbreviating it. In doing so, he alters the sequence of events to create a different impression. Mark 15.33-38 describes the portent of the darkness, then the cry of dereliction with the suggestion that this refers to Elijah, then the sip of vinegar, next a great cry and the death of Jesus, and finally the portent of the rent veil of the temple. The two portents are linked to the emotions of the events with great effect. Luke has a different kind of artistry. He has already mentioned the vinegar in 23.36, and in vv. 44-46 he summarizes the rest of Mark's material in such a way as to make the moment of death the climax. First he mentions the portent of darkness, to which he adds the genitive absolute τοῦ ἡλίου ἐκλιπόντος. This may represent a variant tradition of the cry of dereliction, as we have seen, but here it has become an alternative way of expressing the darkness. Then the other portent of the rent veil follows immediately. Next Jesus makes a great cry, as in Mark, but Luke has inserted the appropriate words, i.e. Ps. 31.6. By this means the emotions aroused by the impressiveness of the portents are hushed, and the last breath of Jesus, using the same word ἐξέπνευσεν as Mark, is a separate short sentence, pointing the pathos of the moment of death.

Although the quotation occurs in the place of the *second* cry in the Marcan account, Luke's omission of Ps. 22.1 made it necessary

to specify the actual words at this point. In favour of the genuineness of the saying is the plain vocative πάτερ (without μου or ἡμῶν)
which precedes the quotation, cf. ἀββᾶ ὁ πατήρ in Mark. 14.36;
Gal. 4.6; and Rom. 8.15. But its presence here need only be due
to Luke's knowledge of this characteristic, which is found in Luke
10.21, 11.2 and 22.42. The possibility must be left open that he
has supplied it from its Christian use, as the most suitable way of
understanding the great cry mentioned by Mark. It has been suggested that our Lord's prayer in Gethsemane followed the pattern
of the Jewish prayer for one at the point of death, which may even
then have included this quotation, as it still does today.[1] This
would be another way of accounting for its presence in Luke. And
we are still not in the realm of the Passion apologetic.

### Psalm 34

There is an important contribution to the Passion apologetic in
John 19.36, ὀστοῦν οὐ συντριβήσεται αὐτοῦ. This is given after the
full formula, 'For these things came to pass, that the scripture
might be fulfilled.' In John, just as in Matthew, the introductory
formula is normally an indicator of the *pesher* quotation used in
apologetic. If there are difficulties in the text, they are essential to
the exegesis. In this case a progressive exegesis is indicated by the
form of the text.

The words of the quotation are derived from the Septuagint,
but the quotation could have been derived from more than one
passage. There is first the prescription for the Passover, Ex. 12.46
and Num. 9.12 (also Ex. 12.10 in LXX): ὀστοῦν οὐ συντρίψετε
(-ουσιν) ἀπ᾽ αὐτοῦ. But there is also Ps. 34.21: . . . πάντα τὰ ὀστᾶ
αὐτῶν, ἓν ἐξ αὐτῶν οὐ συντριβήσεται. Obviously John's words are
closer to those of Exodus. On the other hand the Psalter was from
the beginning a source-book for the Church's theology, as the
numerous quotations testify, so that it is desirable on general
grounds to regard the psalm as the real source here.

The one textual factor that can help us to decide is that John
has the verb in the passive in common with the psalm, whereas
Exodus has the active. If Exodus is the source, there seems no
reason why he should make this change. The context gives suitable
persons to whom 'they' (as in Num. 9.12) could apply, and this

---

[1] *Authorised Daily Prayer Book*, 24th edn, p. 317. See D. Daube, 'A
Prayer Pattern in Judaism', in *Studia Evangelica*, pp. 539-45.

would be far more natural in view of the following quotation of Zech. 12.10, where the subject 'they' has been left untouched. This suggests that the psalm was the original text, but it has been subsequently conformed to Exodus, possibly by John himself. This represents the introduction of a new interest.

For the stages of interpretation, we note first that the psalm describes the divine providence watching over the righteous in general, but then in vv. 20f. the singular is used.[1] The Septuagint here rightly understands it as collective and translates it by the plural. But the early Christian exegete had a liking for the letter of scripture, and here the use of the singular is clearly an invitation to take 'the Righteous' as a messianic title, as in Acts 3.14 and 7.52. This means that the psalm can be given a messianic interpretation. Thus in answer to the question, Why did God allow the Messiah to die?, it can be pointed out that the Resurrection proves that the Lord does not desert the Righteous, just as this psalm has promised in general. If then it is further objected, Why was he crucified rather than gloriously slain in battle (or some other way)?, it can be answered that even this was providential, fitting into God's determined plan, because it left his body perfect (apart from the wounds of the nails) for the Resurrection, exactly as Ps. 34.21 has specifically promised. Jesus rose from the dead intact. From this fact it may be deduced that the practice of breaking the legs to hasten death was not done in his case. We can see here an apologetic concerning the possibility of the claim that the Lord's Christ was the very same man as had been crucified.

John is aware of this apologetic, but his interest is in the theological implications of the fact which has been deduced from it—that Jesus' legs were not broken. In his presentation of the Passion as a whole he has linked the death of Jesus to the Passover, adopting a tradition of the date which differs from that of Mark. Consequently he is alive to the reference to the Passover ceremonial contained in this text, which gives sacrificial significance to our Lord's death. He gives the text in its briefest form, just like the ceremonial directions in Exodus. John so frequently writes with a double meaning that it is surely probable that he is aware of the previous apologetic use of this text, to which he now gives a typological twist.[2]

[1] צדיק ... עצמותיו

[2] The companion testimony, Zech. 12.10, similarly belongs in the first

It is interesting to note how the application of this psalm of divine protection to our Lord's death draws attention to the question whether the breaking of the legs had been done or not. It is then used to support the theory that this was not done, a theory which perhaps rests (as has been indicated) on a reasonable inference from the traditions concerning our Lord's risen body rather than on precise factual memory of this specific point. The scriptural text thus fills out the tradition by a logical deduction which coincides with a narrowing down of its application. It then becomes a basis for further theological construction, which is reached in John's handling of it.

Before leaving Psalm 34, we must look at the quotations and allusions in I Peter. Here we find it in the homiletic tradition, but it is linked to the Passion apologetic by the liturgical context of the Christian Pasch.[1] So there is first a passing reference to Ps. 34.9 in I Peter 2.3, ἐγεύσασθε ὅτι χρηστὸς ὁ κύριος. This may be an allusion to the rite of baptism, which has just been performed. The context implies that ὁ κύριος is Jesus himself, and uses the complex 'Stone' theme, which (as we shall see in the next chapter) has great importance in the early apologetic. There seems to be another allusion to the same verse, also in a baptismal context, in Heb. 6.4f., especially καλὸν γευσαμένους θεοῦ ῥῆμα, where the predicative position of καλόν strengthens the impression that the words are based on this verse.

Besides this, there is a full quotation of Ps. 34.13-17 in I Peter 3.10-12, following the Septuagint exactly, except for the necessary change from second to third person throughout. It is a purely hortatory passage, giving the moral grounds on which divine protection may be expected. This time also there is a hint of the same words in Heb. 12.14, where εἰρήνην διώκετε is an allusion to Ps. 34.15.

The psalm thus seems to belong to the early catechetical use of scriptures, and we may well ask whether its use in the Passion apologetic is not perhaps due to the value of referring to the example of Jesus in the catechesis. This would be the reverse of what we saw in the case of Isa. 53. But it means that it enters the

place to a more general apologetic, and is narrowed down to the piercing of our Lord's side, as will be shown. For the transformation of Passion apologetic into Passover typology compare the phrase ὁ ἀμνὸς τοῦ θεοῦ in John 1.29, 36, which is probably based primarily on Isa. 53.7.

[1] F. L. Cross, *I Peter : a Paschal Liturgy*.

Passion apologetic at a rather later stage, which accounts for the
Septuagint form in John's *pesher* quotation.[1]

## Psalm 41

This psalm brings us to a special element of the Passion apologetic, the conduct of Judas Iscariot. We have already had a hint of
it in connection with Isa. 53. The action of Judas must have been
a severe blow to the followers of Jesus. Confidence in the messianic
claim about him might be shaken by his apparent error of judgment in including Judas in the number of the Twelve. Both within
and without the Church it was necessary to explain his behaviour.
The classic passages dealing with this question are Matt. 27.3-10,
using Zechariah, and Acts 1.15-20, using Pss. 69 and 109.

In the Fourth Gospel the treachery of Judas is a recurring
theme, making a heightened dramatic effect in the presentation of
the Passion. At 13.18 John cites Ps. 41.10b with introductory
formula: ὁ τρώγων μου (v.l. μετ᾽ ἐμοῦ) τὸν ἄρτον ἐπῆρεν ἐπ᾽ ἐμὲ
τὴν πτέρναν αὐτοῦ. It introduces the episode at the Last Supper
which makes the climax to the previous references to the traitor,
and sets the note of pathos which is sustained throughout. The
use of an introductory formula, and the notable differences from
the Septuagint, mark this as a *pesher* text already established in the
apologetic. The psalm as a whole speaks of suffering at the hands
of enemies, who are foiled by God in his mercy. The general application would be to the death and Resurrection of Jesus, showing
that the treatment he received was already revealed in prophecy.
The selection of a single verse at an early date shows that the
question of Judas has been raised, and demands a special application of this general position.

There is an allusion to the same verse in the words ὁ ἐσθίων
μετ᾽ ἐμοῦ in Mark 14.18. The omission of them in the parallel
narrative of Matt. 26.21 raises the probability that they are not
part of the original text of Mark, although they are present in some
form in all manuscripts.[2] Matthew is following Mark very closely
at this point, so that if these words were in the text he was using,
he must have missed the reference, and so regarded them as re-

---

[1] John's quotations are normally fairly close to the LXX, but several,
which can claim to be early apologetic material, have notable non-LXX
features, viz. the quotations at 12.15, 40, 13.18, 19.38.

[2] The words are placed before παραδώσει με by syr^sin pe sa bo; and the
reading is τῶν ἐσθιόντων μετ᾽ ἐμοῦ in B 330 sa bo.

dundant. This is not impossible as μετ' ἐμοῦ (for ἄρτους μου) is not found either in the original Hebrew or in the Septuagint. It is a variant reading in John's citation. If it is original there, it is to be regarded as a deliberate licence in translation to bring out the full enormity of the breach of table-fellowship. But its presence in Mark is presumably due to ὁ ἐμβαπτόμενος μετ' ἐμοῦ εἰς τὸ ἓν τρύβλιον in v. 20. This suggests that even if the words are an added gloss the thought of Ps. 41.10 was already present in the context, and is one of the scriptures implied in the next verse (καθὼς γέγραπται). The addition is independent of John's version. The fact that in the Marcan original the whole episode remains in general terms, without specific mention of Judas, shows that the primary motive was to explain why Jesus allowed himself to be betrayed.[1] Matthew's rewriting of Mark, John's use of the *pesher* text, and the hint of the same quotation added to Mark 14.18, all exhibit this in the form of a real Judas-apologetic. It will be found as a rule that these Judas passages are not only an element of the Passion apologetic, but are all based on it as a secondary development.[2]

## Psalm 69

The largest contribution to the Passion apologetic comes from Psalm 69, which is undoubtedly the most important of these psalms. It is quoted or alluded to by several writers in a variety of interesting ways. It is clear that it was found useful *as a whole* by the early Christians. It is thus rightly regarded by Dodd as one of the chief proofs of his theory about the primitive scriptural theology.[3] We have already had occasion to mention it in connection with John's account of the cleansing of the temple.[4] This must be

---

[1] Ps. 41.10 is alluded to in connection with slanderers in a quite general way in 1QH 5.23.

[2] Pss. 42-43 are also quarried for Passion references in both Mark and John. The refrain of Pss. 42.6, 12, 43.5 lies behind our Lord's words at Gethsemane (Mark 14.34 = Matt. 26.38): ἵνα τί περίλυπος εἶ, ψυχή; Ps. 42.7 seems to lie behind the Johannine version of his inner struggle (John 12.27): ἡ ψυχή μου ἐταράχθη. The same words, however, also occur in Ps. 6.4, which is more likely to be the intended source because of the following σῶσόν με, cf. Ps. 6.5. The literary influence of 'righteous sufferer' psalms is certain, but it would be hazardous to use this coincidence in Mark's and John's choice of them as evidence for the early apologetic.

[3] *Acc. Scrip.*, pp. 57-59.

[4] *Supra*, pp. 67f.

further elaborated after other passages where it is used have been examined.

To begin with, we have to assume a general application of the psalm to the Passion, for which the whole tenor of it is obviously appropriate. But it has left only one trace in the Passion narratives. This is the note in Mark 15.36 that, immediately after the cry of dereliction, someone offered vinegar to Jesus to drink. It is described in words drawn from Ps. 69.22b. Modern readers are likely to think of this as an act of compassion to our Lord, like the spiced wine provided by the soldiers as they crucified him (Mark 15.23). But the overt allusion to the psalm makes it more probable that it was done with a hostile motive, or at least taken as such by Mark when he included it in his narrative at this point.[1] Similarly Luke has an allusion to the same verse in his account of the mocking of Jesus by the soldiers (Luke 23.36f.). The reason for this is the use of the psalm in the Passion apologetic. It goes into considerable detail about the hostility shown to the righteous sufferer. From the apologetic point of view it is desirable to show how all the foreordained cruelties have been fulfilled in the treatment of Jesus. The sponge of vinegar corresponds to one of these details, and so, even if it was actually intended as a kindness, it comes into the narrative as an act of cruelty.

It is instructive to see what the other evangelists do with this. John 19.28-30 considerably elaborates the allusion, just as he did in the case of the dividing of the clothes. Ps. 69.22 reads

$$\kappa a i \ \ddot{\epsilon}\delta\omega\kappa a\nu \ \epsilon i s \ \tau \grave{o} \ \beta\rho\hat{\omega}\mu \acute{a} \ \mu ou \ \chi o\lambda\grave{\eta}\nu,$$
$$\kappa a i \ \epsilon i s \ \tau \grave{\eta}\nu \ \delta \acute{\iota}\psi a\nu \ \mu ou \ \dot{\epsilon}\pi \acute{o}\tau\iota\sigma \acute{a}\nu \ \mu\epsilon \ \ddot{o}\xi os.$$

John presumably means this when he says $\emph{ἵνα} \ \tau \epsilon \lambda \epsilon \iota \omega \theta \hat{\eta} \ \dot{\eta} \ \gamma\rho a\phi \acute{\eta}$, $\lambda \acute{\epsilon} \gamma \epsilon \iota \cdot \ \delta\iota\psi\hat{\omega}$. This is the only case where the verb $\tau \epsilon \lambda \epsilon \iota \omega \theta \hat{\eta}$ is used in an introductory formula instead of $\pi \lambda \eta \rho \omega \theta \hat{\eta}$. It shows the theological interest, evinced by the use of the same verb earlier in the verse. The apologetic interest disappears. The thirst of Jesus is an essential item, as John sees it, in the revelation of divine glory through the Incarnation. This was already adumbrated in the discourse at Jacob's well in ch. 4. It is now the reason for working up

[1] See the commentaries for the grave difficulties of Mark 15.35f. Wellhausen may well be right to regard v. 36a as a separate tradition. The fact that the offer of vinegar is meant in a hostile sense is shown by its close connection with the taunt about Elijah, as it now stands. Luke 23.36 is certainly hostile.

the detail about the vinegar in the Passion narrative. Moreover John says that the vinegar was offered to Jesus ὑσσώπῳ, an impossible substitute for Mark's καλάμῳ. This, if it is the true reading,[1] is prompted not by tradition, nor by probability, but by the motif of the Passover, which we have already noticed in John's handling of the themes of the Passion apologetic. These things are superimposed on the original observation that a striking incident shortly before the death of Jesus proved him to be the righteous sufferer of the Psalms.

There may perhaps be influence of John in the corresponding passage in the *Gospel of Peter* 5.16f.: καί τις αὐτῶν εἶπεν· ποτίσατε αὐτὸν χολὴν μετὰ ὄξους· καὶ κεράσαντες ἐπότισαν. καὶ ἐπλήρωσαν πάντα καὶ ἐτελείωσαν κατὰ τῆς κεφαλῆς αὐτῶν τὰ ἁμαρτήματα. But it is clear that reference has been made to the actual text of Ps. 69.22. The gall of the first half of the verse has been mingled with the vinegar. This not only improves the allusion from the point of view of the prophetic fulfilment, but also precludes any idea that this might have been an act of kindness rather than of hostility. It is thus in line with the main motive of this item in the Passion apologetic. There is no trace of further theologizing here.

Matthew's version is specially interesting, for he is dependent on no other source than Mark at this point. He also has taken note of the first half of the verse, but finds a separate fulfilment of it. So at 27.48 (= Mark 15.36) he leaves Mark almost untouched, containing the words ὄξους . . . ἐπότιζεν from Ps. 69.22b. But earlier in the narrative, where the soldiers offer the spiced wine, he has changed ἐσμυρνισμένον οἶνον of Mark 15.23 to οἶνον μετὰ χολῆς μεμιγμένον (Matt. 27.34). This change has been inspired by Ps. 69.22a. So this is another case of taking the *parallelismus membrorum* separately and literally,[2] and it is specially illuminating, because this time there can be no doubt that the two incidents are genuinely distinct in Matthew's source. It cannot be asserted that he has doubled one incident by a false inference from the psalm verse. In fact we can see the actual process at work. For Mark had simply recorded the usual offer of spiced wine without any scriptural motif, and only introduced the allusion when he mentioned the

---

[1] It has been conjectured that it is an early error for ὑσσῷ = 'spear', which actually appears in the first hand of one minuscule. But in any case ὑσσώπῳ is to be preferred as the *lectio difficilior*.

[2] Cf. Matt. 21.7; John 19.23f.

vinegar later on. Matthew, knowing the reference in the second occasion, has decided that the former one corresponds to the first stichos of the psalm verse, and so has modified the text accordingly. If we had not got Mark to compare with Matthew, we might suppose that the two offers of drink were doublets, because Luke and John only mention one. As it is, we see a real incident affected by the desire to conform the events to the prophecy, but not in the least created *ex nihilo*.

The apologetic value of Psalm 69 is enhanced by the fact that, after describing the cruelty of the wicked, it proceeds to give some terrible warnings of the consequence of their actions. From the Christian point of view they refer to the unbelieving Jews, who take the part of those who crucified Jesus.[1] This has survived in Rom. 11.9f., quoting the curses of Ps. 69.23f. But there is a shift of application in his use of it. The interest is fastened on the *blindness* of the Jews, yet not as something inflicted on them as a punishment for their wickedness, but as the *cause* of their tragic failure to grasp the salvation that has been offered to them. It is a blindness ordained by the inscrutable wisdom of God.[2] To rake up biblical curses against the enemies of the Church is a naive, but perfectly natural, apologetic procedure. Paul's depth of mind is too great for this, and he transforms them to serve the needs of his most fundamental religious problem.

The Book of Revelation also refers to these warnings, but broadens their application to include the whole world arrayed against the Church (i.e. the pagan Roman Empire).[3]

The same warnings, taken in their proper sense of divine punishment, can be used for the special apologetic in connection with Judas Iscariot. Ps. 69.26 is quoted from the Septuagint, but with significant variations, in Acts 1.20.

| Ps. 69.26 | Acts 1.20 |
|---|---|
| γενηθήτω ἡ ἔπαυλις | γενηθήτω ἡ ἔπαυλις |
| αὐτῶν ἠρημωμένη, | αὐτοῦ ἔρημος |
| καὶ ἐν τοῖς σκηνώμασιν αὐτῶν | καὶ |
| μὴ ἔστω ὁ κατοικῶν | μὴ ἔστω ὁ κατοικῶν ἐν αὐτῇ. |

The change of αὐτῶν to αὐτοῦ marks the application of the verse

---

[1] So the warning of Hab. 1.5 is quoted in just this way in Acts 13.41.
[2] It is blindness in the sense of *porosis*, cf. pp. 159-67 *infra*, on Isa. 6.9f.
[3] Ps. 69.25 is one of the literary influences behind the Seven Last Plagues, cf. especially Rev. 16.1. Ps. 69.29 lies behind Rev. 3.5, 13.8, 17.8, 20.12, 15, 21.27.

to Judas in particular. The other changes emphasize the vacancy
in the number of the Twelve that must now be filled. The deserted
dwelling is not simply the due punishment of the traitor, but the
technical grounds for electing a new Apostle. This is the motive
for the inclusion of this passage in its present context. There is
thus a progressive exegesis here. First the conduct and subsequent
fate of Judas is explained by the quotation; he had ranged himself
with the enemies of Jesus, and so his death is the first example of
these prophetic warnings coming true. Then secondly it can be
applied to the practical matter of the need for scriptural warrant
for the election. So the 'Judas legend' grows in the cradle of the
Passion apologetic.

There are two examples of the characteristic tendency to use
the apologetic material at a later date for homiletic instruction.
One of these is John 15.25, where ἐμίσησάν με δωρεάν may be a
reference to Ps. 69.5.[1] The full introductory formula, and the
possibility of previous textual history, indicate that the words have
been taken over from a more direct apologetic usage, to assert the
innocence of the Sufferer. Here they are introduced to prepare the
disciples for their share in the same sufferings, for the persecution
of the Church is, in the Johannine theology, an extension of the
Passion.

The other example is interesting because it contains an element
of biblical theory. It is Ps. 69.10b, quoted in Rom. 15.3, 'The
reproaches of them that reproach thee are fallen upon me.' This
occurs in an exhortation to patient and thoughtful behaviour after
the example of Christ. There is no mention of the Passion, though
that is obviously the supreme example of his patience, and is also
the proper Christian application of the words quoted. The basis
of the apologetic use of Scripture is the need to prove that all that
happened to Jesus followed a predetermined plan. It seems that
Paul's thought has run on from this to see how the life of the
Church also corresponds to scriptural expectations, inasmuch as
the life of the Church *is* the life of Christ. A single thread runs
right through.[2] From the apologetic point of view, this verse (and

---

[1] οἱ μισοῦντές με δωρεάν. Other possible references are Ps. 35.19 (identical
text), Ps. 109.3 (ἐπολέμησάν με δωρεάν), and *Ps. Sol.* 7.1 (οἱ ἐμίσησαν ἡμᾶς
δωρεάν). It has been suggested that more than one of these are the background of a memory-quotation, cf. Bent Noack, *Zur johanneischen Tradition*, 1954, p. 75.

[2] Verse 4 means that the Scriptures, which were fulfilled in Christ, have

also its parallel, Ps. 69.10a, quoted in John 2.17) proves that the Passion was due to resistance to a genuine zeal for God. It is not a very good choice for Paul's argument in Rom. 15, but was presumably dictated by familiarity with it in another connection (i.e. apologetic). It is possible that we also have echoes of this verse in ὀνειδισμόν in Heb. 11.26 and 13.13, where the same apologetic motive is presupposed, though again it is in a homiletic application.

Finally we return to the citation of Ps. 69.10a, 'The zeal of thine house hath eaten me up', quoted (with change of the verb to the future 'shall eat') in John 2.17. It is the other half of the verse quoted by Paul in Rom. 15.3, serving the same purpose in the apologetic. That is in itself a striking fact, but the manner in which it is employed in the episode of the cleansing of the temple, John 2.13-22, is even more remarkable. Unlike the Synoptic tradition of the cleansing, John does not place the biblical quotation on the lips of Jesus himself. But the disciples *remember* that this was written in the Scriptures. They also *remember*, after the Resurrection, that Jesus had promised to rebuild the temple in three days, meaning the temple of his Body. There have been several indications in the course of this study of the testimonies that John was in touch with the Church's early apologetic, even though writing at a later date with very different aims. In the light of this, it is tempting to see this passage as an actual description of the apologetic in the making. It shows the process of reflection on the events of the Gospel, and then linking them to significant passages of Scripture. Moreover the whole 'plot' of the psalm is brought into play by the temple incident, not merely the line which is actually cited. This means that it is in close touch with the original general use of the psalm in the Passion apologetic, before it is dismembered for secondary applications. Thus we may well be at the source of the use of this psalm by the early Church.

A quick analysis of the psalm will make this plain. Verses 1-22 are the sufferer's complaint, seeking for divine aid, and describing the treatment he has received at the hands of his enemies. In the course of it—at v. 10—he claims that the reason for their hostility

moral value for those who belong to Christ. It is perhaps worth noting that historical typology springs from this appreciation of the Scriptures, cf. Irenaeus, *Adv. Haer.* IV 34.4: 'These things were acted beforehand in Abel, and also previously declared by the prophets, but were accomplished in the Lord's person: and the same is still true with regard to us, the body following the example of the head.'

was his 'zeal for thine house', that is, his championing of the cause of God himself. Then vv. 23-29 are a series of curses, of which almost every line is quoted or alluded to in the New Testament. After this the psalm closes with a long prayer and the final assurance of vindication and of the rebuilding of the cities of Judah when Zion is saved.

In the primitive apologetic the first part applies to the Passion in general. We need hardly suppose that the Church had to wait until the time of John before perceiving that the sufferings of Christ were due to an unjust estimate of his 'zeal for the house of God', both metaphorically and literally. It was true that he had provoked the hostility of the Jewish authorities, but that was because he bore the reproach of God. This could be said of the work of Jesus as a whole—hence the quotation of v. 10a, preserved by Paul in Rom. 15.3. But to connect v. 10b with the cleansing of the temple, especially in its Synoptic position immediately before the betrayal and Crucifixion, gives it a literal application which is particularly congenial to the early defenders of the faith. The first three Gospels probably give more accurate traditions of the actual episode, and their dating of it is to be preferred to John's. But John, whose dating is governed by theological considerations, has not invented his version out of his own head, but uses the apologetic presentation of it, in which it is interpreted in terms of Psalm 69.

It follows that the whole has been thought through in this way before it came to John, probably well before the fall of Jerusalem and the destruction of the temple in A.D. 70. The final verses, which speak of rebuilding, cannot have then been applied to a literal reconstruction of the temple, even though it was known that Jesus had prophesied its downfall. In fact they must have been taken metaphorically from the first, in line with the general interpretation of the whole psalm. They would thus have referred to the Resurrection of Jesus, the Sufferer, and to the resulting spread of the Church. There would be no difficulty in this, as the eschatological interpretation of the Psalms, necessarily involving much use of metaphor, belongs to pre-Christian Judaism.[1] This brings us to the point where the thought turns to the promise of revival in three days, already examined in ch. II. In spite of the cruel results of

[1] Cf. Jacques Guillet, *Thêmes Bibliques*, 1951, p. 16. The process can be seen in the allusions to psalm verses in a new application in *Pss. Sol.* 11 and 17, etc.

'the zeal of thine house', the spiritual renewal which Jesus proclaimed would be speedily achieved. And by his Resurrection it actually was achieved, at any rate in his own person, in 'the temple of his Body'. So the first Christians worked it out when pressed to account for the hostility and cruelty shown to Jesus, and perhaps the 'scripture' connected with the 'word' of Jesus referred to in John 2.22 was the final verses of this psalm. In this way, as was suggested in the last chapter, the equivalence of temple and Body has been reached in apologetic material which may be older than the work of Paul, and in any case is independent of it. And already there is implicit the beginning of the doctrine of the supersession of the temple and its cultus.

The psalm and the cleansing of the temple thus stand together in the Passion apologetic, but they are not indispensable to one another. The temple incident was valued by the Church for more than one reason,[1] but its apologetic usefulness was a decisive influence in the pre-Marcan stage. Psalm 69 is demonstrably the most widely used psalm in the Passion apologetic. At some point —and probably fairly early on—the psalm and the incident were in use together, the one forming a commentary on the other, in much the same way as John has described. The alleged saying about rebuilding the temple in three days seems to have arisen in the process. The value of this apologetic may be estimated by picturing the plight of the Church in the early days. The Church had to discover its own beliefs and to defend them in controversy at one and the same time. The temple incident was important for understanding Jesus, because it epitomized his ministry in a vivid way. But, besides being a sign (John 2.18) in this way, it had provoked the high priest and his party to their final decision to take action against him (Mark 11.18, parr.). The high priest appeared to gain his ends, but in fact the stand taken by Jesus was vindicated, albeit in an unexpected fashion. It is the unexpectedness of what happened which both demands careful constructive thought on the part of the Church, and also makes it necessary to claim warrant from Scripture to prove that it was all nonetheless divinely ordered. In this situation Psalm 69 just happened to fit from every point of view. It is sufficiently personal in character to account for the

---

[1] As Gospel tradition it no doubt had its place in the Christian lectionary, cf. G. D. Kilpatrick, *The Origins of the Gospel according to St Matthew*, 1946, pp. 94f.

sufferings of Jesus as an individual,[1] it explains the action in the
temple which precipitated his arrest, it contains a number of curses
which show how this frightful deed will inevitably bring down the
wrath of God, and it includes the Church's triumphant assertion
that the Righteous Sufferer has been vindicated and his claim
fulfilled.

John presents this incident with its commentary as it appears in
the apologetic. It suits his purpose to do so, as he wishes to give a
single episode as a sign of the whole teaching of Jesus, and its
consequences in the Passion, at the outset of his narrative. He
selects the most telling line from the psalm, and of course has to
change the tense of the verb, as the Passion is still a future event
from the point of view of the narrative.

The Marcan narrative (Mark 11.15-19) shows the influence of
the Passion apologetic first and foremost by its structural position.
It is the principal cause of the plot to arrest Jesus. There is no
interweaving of Psalm 69. The texts placed on the lips of our Lord
have their foundation in the Passion apologetic, but have acquired
a new interest. In the first, Isa. 56.7, Jesus speaks in the character
of the Servant, who is the presumed speaker right through the later
chapters of Isaiah.[2] As so often when these scriptures are quoted,
the motive is the Gentiles controversy. As the full text in Mark
11.17 shows, Jesus is staking a claim, not for a temple suitably
quiet for the purpose of praying, but for the inclusion of the Gentiles in its worship. Matthew and Luke have missed the point and
shortened the text, though apparently independently of one another.[3] Secondly the clean sweep of the paraphernalia of sacrifiical
cultus is justified by an allusion to Jer. 7.11, which puts onto Jesus
the character of the most persecuted prophet of the Old Testament.
This also has a further interest, complementary to the inclusion
of the Gentiles, the idea that the old sacrifices are superseded in
the new kingdom of God. The purveyors of cult animals are not
'thieves' in the literal sense, but are robbing God of his due by

---

[1] The sufferings of the Messiah ben Joseph would be the wounds of
battle alongside his friends. There was no real precedent for what had
actually happened to Jesus.

[2] Dodd, Acc. Scrip., p. 94.

[3] It cannot be argued that the short text as found in Matt. 21.13 is the
common original, because the slightly different short form of Luke 19.46
can only have been reached in an effort to abbreviate a longer form, as
Mark's.

perpetuating an obsolete form of worship and depriving the Gentiles of their place in the coming theocracy. The Marcan account of the temple cleansing has thus been taken a stage further than the strict Passion apologetic to aid the Church in tackling the burning issues of the period of expansion outside Palestine. The development is strictly parallel to what was discovered in Mark's version of the closely associated saying about rebuilding (Mark 14.58).

We are bound to ask whether Mark or John has given in their respective accounts anything approaching a genuine record of this important episode, or whether the apologetic motives have smothered it beyond recovery. It can be said at once that there is nothing in the Marcan story which is impossible in a purely Jewish setting, in spite of the implied attitude to the cultus.[1] On the other hand it is tempting to see the incident as a dramatization of Mal. 3.1, and if so it belongs to a period much earlier in the ministry of our Lord, when the expected return of Elijah was a dominant factor.[2] In that case the Johannine dating might even rest on a genuine tradition. But although Mal. 3.1 is quoted more than once by the Synoptists, none of the accounts of the cleansing contain any hint of it. The Passion apologetic, and subsidiary interests, have taken control. Nevertheless, whether it was a fulfilling of Malachi, or was more like the record of Mark or John, in either case it remains true that it showed most dramatically Jesus' 'zeal of thine house'.[3]

---

[1] An attitude shared by the Essenes and the Qumran Covenanters, cf. O. Cullmann, 'The Significance of the Qumran texts for Research into the Beginnings of Christianity', *JBL* 74, 1955, pp. 213-26 (see p. 142, n. 2); A. F. J. Klijn, 'Stephen's Speech—Acts 7.2-53', *NTS* 4, 1957, pp. 25-31.

[2] J. A. T. Robinson, 'Elijah, John and Jesus'.

[3] There are also in the context of this episode hints of the Zechariah Passion prophecy. These are two allusions to the final chapter, which tells of the future restored temple. The first is ἐμπορίου, John 2.16, which is a reference to Zech. 14.21 (MT), understanding כנעני in the sense of 'trader'; the fact that it is from MT is another sign that early apologetic material has been preserved in this *pericope*. The second is more doubtful. The 'mountain' in Mark 11.23 may be an allusion to Zech. 14.4 (cf. William Manson, *Jesus the Messiah*, pp. 29f., 39f.). The difficulty is that this is probably a floating saying attached to the withered fig-tree, which itself was not necessarily a component of the temple episode in the pre-Marcan stage. On the other hand—quite apart from the cleansing of the temple—our Lord may have used the idea of removing the mountain as a vivid way of expressing his work of renewal. Mark 11.23 would then have a definite application before it became generalized into a 'whosoever'

## Psalm 109

The last of the Passion Psalms is so similar in style and motive to Psalm 69 that one would expect it to be used equally widely. On the contrary allusions to it are few. Its only certain function in the Passion apologetic is in connection with the special issue of Judas Iscariot. Ps. 109.8b, καὶ τὴν ἐπισκοπὴν αὐτοῦ λάβοι ἕτερος, is quoted without significant change in Acts 1.20. It immediately follows Ps. 69.26, which we have just examined. Whereas the latter proved that such a vacancy in the number of the Twelve *could* occur, this verse from Ps. 109 provides for the election of a new Apostle to fill it.[1] We noticed before that this technical matter marked a shift of application from a more general usage, and the same may well be true here again. For the larger context is once more a string of bitter curses, applicable first to those who crucified Jesus and then to Judas in particular. Then this phrase is selected for the special matter of the apostolic election. If the narrative of Acts at this point is a reasonably accurate account of what happened, these shifts of application may be an indication that the election did not really take place quite so early as Luke makes out. He may have been influenced by his desire to regularize the apostolic band *before* the experience of Pentecost, which is so important in the presentation of his narrative. But we shall see in another connection that the incident has undeniably legendary features.

The application of these cursing psalms (whether 69 or 109) to Judas points to the apologetic necessity of explaining the defection of one of the closest friends of Jesus. There is a further refinement of this in John 17.12. It has to be shown that Jesus' 'mistake' in choosing Judas was not due to ignorance of his real character, but was intentional, so that 'the scripture might be fulfilled'. There can be little doubt that these psalms are the scripture referred to, though it is not possible to be sure about the exact verse intended.

There is a verbal allusion to Ps. 109.16c, κατανενυγμένον τῇ καρδίᾳ, in Acts 2.37.[2] This belongs to Luke's editing of speeches based, as we have seen, on apologetic material. It was probably suggested by his use of this psalm in 1.20. This raises the possi-

saying in the course of transmission. It is in any case quite distinct from the rather similar Q saying preserved in Luke 17.6. They have been conflated to form one saying in Matt. 17.20.

[1] Dodd, *Acc. Scrip.*, p. 58 n. 1.
[2] E. Haenchen, *Die Apostelgeschichte*, 1956, *ad loc.*

bility that he was responsible for the selection of the quotation in
1.20, and so for its 'technical' application, choosing it again from
his stock of apologetic scriptures. But the verdict must be left
open.

It should also be noted that Ps. 109.25 is another possible source
for 'wagging their heads' (Matt. 27.39 = Mark 15.29), besides
Ps. 22.8. The same verse also contains ὄνειδος, which needs to be
taken in conjunction with Ps. 69.10. In all these features Psalm
109 seems to be a secondary and additional source.

In this survey of the Passion Psalms it has been possible to trace
development from a general use to explain our Lord's sufferings
and death to a variety of secondary purposes, often concerned with
specific features of the scandal of the cross. There has been the
need for scriptural warrant for various items of the Passion traditions, sometimes with a theological motive overlaying it (Pss. 22
and 69); the question why crucifixion was the method of death, if
death was the divine plan for the Messiah (Ps. 34); the scandal
that Jesus (who should have known better) had table-fellowship
with the traitor (Pss. 41, 69 and 109); the scandal that Jesus should
be allowed to suffer if he was really innocent (Ps. 69.5), and that
the Lord's Christ should be exposed to such a 'reproach' (Ps.
69.10); and above all the need to account for the collapse of the
whole final demonstration of Jesus, from the cleansing of the temple
to the death on the cross (Ps. 69). The pattern is similar to that
which was shown in the study of Isa. 53. Ps. 31 stands outside the
strictly apologetic development, but links up with some of its later
phases, i.e. homiletic usage and literary allusion. The whole effect
of the Passion psalms is to leave in the mind a fuller picture of the
emotions and stress and conflict which necessarily accompanied
the early Christians' attempt to establish their position. We must
seek further details from the evidence of the equally important
material from the prophecy of Zechariah.

### 3. ZECHARIAH

The later chapters of this book contribute a number of quotations and allusions to the New Testament, most frequently in
apocalyptic contexts. It seems that its obscure and colourful eschatological character had already secured the attention of the apoca-
lyptists of late Judaism. It can be expected that the early Christians

will find it congenial from the start, so that they turn to it and
work through it in the attempt to fit the events in which they have
so lately been concerned into eschatological expectations. We need
not consider in detail the many allusions to this prophecy in strictly
apocalyptic contexts,[1] for these belong to the conventional imagery
used by Christian and Jew alike. So our attention will be directed
to the four principal passages where the primitive apologetic can
be detected. These are our Lord's entry into Jerusalem on Palm
Sunday (Zech. 9.9), the treachery of Judas (11.12f.), the quotation
of 'whom they pierced' (12.10), and the scattering of the sheep
(13.7). We shall also have to take into account the mention of 'the
blood of the covenant' (9.11); and we recall the references to
6.11-13 and to the fourteenth chapter already observed.[2]

## The Entry into Jerusalem

The Palm Sunday story contains, in varying measure in the four
Gospels, quotations and allusions to Zech. 9.9 and to Ps. 118.25f.
It is quite clear that the motive is to give definite messianic significance to it. It is not directly concerned with the problem posed by
the Passion. But its structural position in the narratives inevitably
makes it the opening of the account of the Passion itself. A glance
at the list of Zechariah passages shows that the quotation of 9.9 is
the opening of a series concerned with the Passion in various ways.
This correlation points to the following conclusion: it was a necessary part of the Passion apologetic to show that Jesus suffered
*as the Messiah*, and this was proved both by investing the entry
with messianic significance and by linking it to the messianic quotation which opens the Zechariah 'Passion commentary'.

The quotations are thus to be seen as interpretative accretions
to the original story. The Marcan account (Mark 11.1-10) is told
in such a way as to emphasize two points, the newness of the ass
and the reaction of the crowd. The fact that the ass had not been
used for riding before suggests a religious motive (cf. I Sam. 6.7).
The cry of the people (literally 'Blessed the coming kingdom of our
father David') implies that Jesus inaugurates the kingdom, but

---

[1] Matt. 24.31, par. (Zech. 2.10), 25.31 (14.5); Luke 21.24 (12.3); I Cor.
15.52 (9.14); I Thess. 3.13 (14.5), 4.16 (9.14); Rev. 5.6 (4.10), 6.2 (6.1-3),
7.1 (6.5), 10.7 (1.6), 11.2 (12.3), 11.4 (4.11-14), 11.18 (1.6), 12.9 = 20.2 (3.1),
21.3 (2.14), 21.6 (14.8), 21.7 (8.8), 21.25 (14.7), 22.1 (14.8), 22.17 (14.8).
[2] *Supra*, pp. 69-71, 108 n. 3.

need not be anything more than forerunner and prophet.[1] There is no reference to Zech. 9.9, though it is hardly possible to suppose that it is not in the background of thought. It seems from this that the action of Jesus was not so much making a claim concerning himself as giving a sign of the immediate fulfilment of his preaching about the kingdom of God. It is not the coming of the Messiah, but the inauguration of the kingdom in peace. The King, then, will soon be revealed, but Jesus does not overtly claim to be the King himself. The shout of *Hosanna* thus has the religious significance familiar in the liturgy of the Feast of Tabernacles,[2] and does not necessarily mean that the people hail him as Messiah. Our argument prompts the suggestion that the quotation from Ps. 118 in Mark 11.9f. is a composite production. ὡσαννά (instead of LXX σῶσον δή) is from liturgical usage. It was originally followed by the substance of v. 10, i.e. 'Blessed the coming kingdom', etc. But this has been put into the Septuagint language of Ps. 118.26 which has also been inserted in v. 9 before it. The insertion of this doublet helps to imply the messianic interpretation desired by those who use this story. The whole complex shows the need to give greater precision to the reference to Ps. 118, so as to characterize the incident as a messianic claim. This will be analysed more fully when we consider the use of this psalm in the next chapter.[3]

Similarly—and what concerns us now—the allusion to Zech. 9.9 receives greater emphasis to bring out the messianic interpretation of the event. It is duly quoted by Matthew and John in differing forms, which illustrate the Church's *midrash pesher*. The fact that the quotation is introduced *after* the first currency of the *pericope* is a sign that it is in use in the Church's teaching and apologetic about Jesus. The disciples have thought about the event, and *remember* that Zech. 9.9 foretold the coming of the King riding on a colt. This is what is actually described in John 12.16. John gives the text in its shortest and most pointed form, and then mentions the Church's process of reflection on the event and linking it to a messianic text. Some commentators object that the disciples could not possibly have failed to understand what our Lord was doing, when all the people were hailing him as the Messiah.[4] But, as in the similar case of 2.22, it was a matter of a lack of *scriptural*

---

[1] Such is the view of Dalman, J. Weiss, and A. Schweitzer.
[2] *Sukkah* 3.9.          [3] *Infra*, p. 169.
[4] Cf. C. K. Barrett, *The Gospel according to St John*, 1955, *ad loc.*

understanding. It was only after the Resurrection that they could see that this event, fulfilling messianic prophecy, defined the Passion which came after it. In other words, the entry into Jerusalem proves that Jesus *suffered as the Messiah*—which is precisely the original motive which we have postulated for both *pericope* and Zechariah quotation in the primitive apologetic.

For this reason we are disposed to give John priority over Matthew. Here again, as in the cleansing of the temple, we have a glimpse into the Church's apologetic in the making. This brings us to the point where we must note the forms of text employed.

| Zech. 9.9 | Matt. 21.5 | John 12.15 |
|---|---|---|
| χαῖρε σφόδρα, θύγατερ Σιών· κήρυσσε, θύγατερ Ἰερουσαλήμ· ἰδοὺ ὁ βασιλεύς σου ἔρχεταί σοι δίκαιος καὶ σῴζων αὐτός, πραῢς καὶ ἐπιβεβηκὼς ἐπὶ ὑποζύγιον καὶ πῶλον νέον. | εἴπατε τῇ θυγατρὶ Σιών· ἰδοὺ ὁ βασιλεύς σου ἔρχεταί σοι πραῢς καὶ ἐπιβεβηκὼς ἐπὶ ὄνον καὶ ἐπὶ πῶλον υἱὸν ὑποζυγίου. | μὴ φοβοῦ, θύγατερ Σιών· ἰδοὺ ὁ βασιλεύς σου ἔρχεται καθήμενος ἐπὶ πῶλον ὄνου. |
| גִּילִי מְאֹד בַּת־צִיּוֹן הָרִיעִי בַּת יְרוּשָׁלַ‍ם הִנֵּה מַלְכֵּךְ יָבוֹא לָךְ צַדִּיק וְנוֹשָׁע הוּא עָנִי וְרֹכֵב עַל־חֲמוֹר וְעַל־עַיִר בֶּן־אֲתֹנוֹת: | Isa. 62.11 εἴπατε τῇ θυγατρὶ Σιών, ἰδού σοι ὁ σωτὴρ παραγίνεται . . . | Zeph. 3.16f. θάρσει Σιών . . . κύριος ὁ θεός σου ἐν σοί, δυνατὸς σώσει σε . . . אַל־תִּירְאִי צִיּוֹן |

The short form of text in John is not accidental. It can be presupposed that the King, when he comes, will be 'just and having salvation'. The other passages which replace the opening words (Isa. 62.11 in Matthew and probably Zeph. 3.16 MT in John) can say as much. But the point is that Jesus was riding on a colt never put to this use before. This can be expressed by reducing the parallel phrases to the simple πῶλον ὄνου. The often quoted saying of Rabbi Joshua ben Levi[1] confirms that the apologetic interest of this text is mainly directed to this one fact. It is true that Jesus came to Jerusalem as Messiah, but he was innocent of the charge

[1] SB I, p. 843.

of sedition against the Romans, for he came in peace. The Passion prophecy of Zech. 9-13 begins with the arrival of the King to bring peace to the war-stricken people.

John's abbreviated text has been achieved by cutting out all repetitive words and phrases. The text in Matthew begins to restore them by reference to the Septuagint version. Matthew is not working directly on the form of text which has been preserved by John, though John's form seems to be nearer to the original *pesher* text. However the variant openings show independent development. In John's circle the prophecy of Zephaniah has been used as a commentary on it, in Matthew's the 'new Jerusalem' passage of Isa. 62. But the chief motive in Matthew's version is again to draw attention to the freshness of the colt. This time it is done, not by abbreviating, but by a fuller and more literal rendering of the Hebrew. This is also the reason why Matthew's narrative mentions the ass in addition to the colt (Matt. 21.2, 7). It is a refinement of exegesis, whereby the two members of the parallel have been used to say virtually the same thing as Mark 11.2. For it goes without saying that a colt 'whereon no man ever yet sat' has not yet been parted from its mother. This is thus not a case of ignorantly misunderstanding the nature of Hebraic parallelism, but a way of correlating the text more closely to the facts for the sake of greater cogency. We have already come across the same feature in the use of Pss. 22.19 and 69.22. This does not mean that there was a tradition (unknown to any other evangelist) that there were actually two animals involved, but simply that Matthew had good reason to assume it on account of the newness of the colt. Why he writes in v. 7 in such a way as to suggest that our Lord was riding on two beasts at once is a mystery on any showing. Presumably it is confused writing rather than anything else.[1]

The influence of Zech. 9.9, suggesting the desired messianic interpretation, may also be discerned in Luke's editing. He follows Mark closely, but at 19.35 he substitutes ἐπεβίβασαν (cf. LXX ἐπιβεβηκώς) for ἐκάθισεν. Then he abbreviates the cry of the crowd by omitting the barbarous ὡσαννά and rewriting the rest. The chief feature of this is that Mark's βασιλεία is incorporated

---

[1] Stendahl, *SSM*, p. 200, thinks that Matthew knew a tradition of two animals, and mentions the newness of the foal only as 'a secondary reason' for the resulting form of the quotation. This fails to do justice to the subtlety of exegesis which the actual form of the quotation exhibits.

into the text of Ps. 118.26 as ὁ βασιλεύς, i.e. of Zech. 9.9. Thus Luke knows that this text is the key to the episode, though the importance of the colt has disappeared from view.

References to this text in the writings of Justin Martyr enable us to trace further developments of exegesis. In *I Apol.* 35 he quotes it at the end of a long series of prophecies of the life of Christ. He is familiar with Matthew, and follows his version of the text, and correctly draws attention to the essential point that our Lord rode on a foal. But in two ways he shows his dependence on the work of the exegetes with whom John had contact. He first ascribes the quotation to Zephaniah, and then restores the Septuagint opening of the verse. Now these words are in the Septuagint identical with Zeph. 3.14. We have already seen that John's opening is probably to be connected with Zeph. 3.16. Justin's mistaken attribution is thus due to the influence of the exegetical work of correlating these 'salvation' texts, which was also known to John.

When Justin cites the passage again in *Dial.* 53, he has taken care to look it up and get both author and form of text right.[1] The interpretation of the text has been enriched by linking a new passage to it, Gen. 49.11 ('Binding his foal unto the vine, and his ass's colt unto the choice vine', etc.). This takes up the points to which all the previous exegetical work had pointed. It is a messianic context[2] and visualizes the inclusion of the Gentiles.[3] It permits the distinction between the ass and the colt, thus preserving the importance of this element in the story. Justin does, however, give a novel explanation of this feature. The ass is a symbol of the Jews yoked to the Law, the colt of the unharnessed Gentiles. This shows the anti-Judaic motive at work, which is otherwise foreign to the Palm Sunday story. Finally the connection with the Passion is enhanced by the second half of the verse ('He hath washed his garments in wine, and his vesture in the blood of grapes').

[1] Not absolutely identical with the standard Alexandrian text. It is impossible to say whether the slight differences are due to characteristic carelessness on the part of Justin or to the actual text available to him.

[2] See Gen. 49.10 (LXX). A fragment from Qumran gives a messianic commentary on this verse. See J. M. Allegro, 'Further Messianic References in Qumran Literature', *JBL* 75, 1956, pp. 174-87, document I: 4Q*Patriarchal Blessings*.

[3] This had perhaps been implied by the allusion to Isa. 62.11 in the opening of Matthew's version of Zech. 9.9.

## The Treachery of Judas

In our examination of the Passion Psalms we observed that the
fate of Judas is a special element of the Passion apologetic. Although the importance of the issue belongs to a comparatively
early phase of the Church's history, it is secondary from the point
of view of logical sequence. Pss. 69 and 109, which are concerned
with it, had a prior use in connection with the Passion of Jesus. It
will now be argued that this is also true of the original use of
Zech. 11.13, which is the basis of the legend of the fate of Judas,
and the kernel of the most elaborate product of the Church's
*midrash pesher* to be found in the New Testament.

The main task is to unravel the complex narrative and quotation
in Matt. 27.3-10. But first we must notice that Matthew has already
made an allusion to Zech. 11.12 (ἔστησαν . . . τριάκοντα ἀργύρια)
at 26.15. These words form his rewriting of the statement of Mark
14.11 that Jesus was betrayed by Judas for a sum of money. It is
clear that Matthew has been prompted to do this by his Judas
*pericope*, with its Zechariah quotation, which he will include later
in his narrative. But it reveals the starting-point of the whole complex—the need to explain why Jesus was sold for money. It is a
thing which was obviously well known to the priests, who are the
very people to whom the serious biblical apologetic is directed.
It would be very easy for them to object that it is unworthy of one
who is said to be the Messiah, that he should be the dupe of such
a scheme. If he had really been the Lord's Messiah, he would
never have allowed that sort of thing to happen almost under his
very eyes! This can be countered by adducing Zech. 11.12f., which
shows that what happened was already preordained in prophecy.
This is the use of this passage in the Passion apologetic proper.

Parallel to this defence of the messiahship of Jesus, there is another argument. Although Jesus was sold for money, God showed
his innocence by the fate of the recipient of it. The money is 'the
price of blood', and the sudden death of Judas is the result of the
divine displeasure at the condemnation of the Chosen of God. It
appears that this money was used to buy some land called (from
its use as a cemetery) the Field of Blood. Such a coincidence is
bound to appeal to the superstitious mind. The actual name of the
land proclaims the divine judgment on the traitor. No further
argument is needed to prove that the behaviour of Judas is no
count against the Church's claims about Jesus.

We now have, besides the biblical argument in connection with the money, a popular argument based on Judas' bad end. This is attested independently of Matthew in Acts 1.18f., which we may usefully pause to consider briefly. The details of the story vary considerably from Matt. 27.3-10. The agreement consists in the suddenness of the death of Judas, the purchase of land with the money, and the name of the land. There is perhaps an allusion to Zech. 11.12 in the occurrence of μισθοῦ (v. 18), but the reappearance of the whole phrase μισθοῦ τῆς ἀδικίας in II Peter 2.13, 15 in a quite different connection makes this unlikely. The fact that the story goes behind St Luke is shown by the Aramaic name Aceldama, which has to be translated to make its point (notice the choice of χωρίον instead of Matthew's ἀγρός). This also shows the independence from Matthew. Now the three facts noted as common to Acts and to Matthew are all that need be held as the firm nucleus of the legend, the rest of the story being deduced from them. The idea that Judas had himself bought the field is a perfectly natural assumption. The description of the sudden death depends on the meaning of the name, i.e. the Field of Blood. The note that it was this occasion which first made people adopt this name for the land is due to the desire to get the most out of the few known facts. The whole legend is 'an aetiological story around the name'.[1]

The development of the legend shows a growing interest in the fate of Judas quite apart from the necessity of explaining his part in the Passion. The quotation of Zech. 11.13, which at first was culled from the Zechariah Passion prophecy to account for the particular point of the betrayal for money, now becomes the centre of another form of the legend. It is possible to trace successive stages in the correlation between what was known (or supposed) to have happened and scriptural testimony. These stages coincide with changes of language. The text is first studied in the original Hebrew, then a Palestinian Greek recension is used, and finally it is brought into line with the standard Septuagint text. We shall see this happening both in the narrative of Matt. 27.3-8, where Matthew is writing up older material, and also in the composite quotation in vv. 9f. The analysis will also explain the false attribution of the quotation to Jeremiah. It will be helpful if the Hebrew and Greek texts of Zech. 11.13 are now set out in parallel for reference as we examine Matthew's text in detail.

[1] Stendahl, *SSM*, p. 197.

ויאמר יהוה אלי
השליכהו אל־היוצר
אדר היקר
אשר יקרתי מעליהם
ואקחה שלשים
הכסף ואשליך אתו
בית יהוה אל־היוצר:

καὶ εἶπεν κύριος πρός με
Κάθες αὐτοὺς εἰς τὸ χωνευτήριον,
καὶ σκέψαι εἰ δόκιμόν ἐστιν,
ὃν τρόπον ἐδοκιμάσθην ὑπὲρ αὐτῶν.
καὶ ἔλαβον τοὺς τριάκοντα
ἀργυροῦς καὶ ἐνέβαλον αὐτοὺς εἰς
τὸν οἶκον κυρίου εἰς τὸ χωνευτήριον.

The first allusion to the Zechariah text is τὰ τριάκοντα ἀργύρια in Matt. 27.3. Then in v. 5 there is the phrase ῥίψας τὰ ἀργύρια εἰς τὸν ναόν, describing Judas' return of the money to the priests. This represents the final words of the Hebrew text, but the verb is that used by Aquila.[1] It is thus possible that this phrase belongs to the stage when a Palestinian Greek recension is being used by the exegetes. It marks a step forward in the development of the legend from the biblical text. It is *known*, as in the Acts version, that Judas died suddenly and that the money was used to buy land, but it is *assumed* that the money was first thrown into the house of the Lord, because the prophecy says so.

Next in v. 6 we have βαλεῖν αὐτὰ εἰς τὸν κορβανᾶν. This appears to be a doublet of the same phrase. The verb, however, is probably derived from the Septuagint by the final editor, and the rest is the *continuation* of the previous phrase. It means that Judas returned the money to the temple for the treasury. The Aramaic κορβανᾶν is a sign that the writer was aware of the interpretation of יוצר in Zech. 11.13 as אוצר, if indeed it was not actually so written in the Hebrew text which he was using.[2] It has been treated separately from the rest of the phrase, describing the return of the money by Judas, because the writer knows that the money, being 'the price of blood', could not really have been put into the treasury without causing defilement. This helps the transition to the traditional fact that it was used to buy land. This was of course the Field of Blood, which derived its name, not from the death of Judas there (as in Acts), but from its actual function as a burying-ground for Gentiles.

In v. 8 this land is described as τὸν ἀγρὸν τοῦ κεραμέως. The

---

[1] Aquila and Symmachus: καὶ εἶπε κύριος πρὸς μέ· ῥῖψον αὐτὸ πρὸς τὸν πλάστην (Sym. εἰς τὸ χωνευτήριον)· ὑπερμεγέθης ἡ τιμή, ἣν ἐτιμήθην ὑπὲρ αὐτῶν. καὶ ἔρριψα αὐτὸ ἐν οἴκῳ (Sym. εἰς τὸν οἶκον) κυρίου πρὸς τὸν πλάστην (Sym. εἰς τὸ χωνευτήριον).

[2] The possibility that such a text existed is indicated by the OT Peshitta (*bēth gazzā'*), but is denied by C. C. Torrey, *Documents of the Primitive Church*, 1941, pp. 87f.

phrase is drawn from the composite quotation in vv. 9f. But it serves no function in the legend. Matthew might just as well say 'a certain piece of land'. He is only concerned to report that the land acquired the name of the Field of Blood. It follows that in writing up the legend Matthew has not used all the biblical material at his disposal. He is summarizing a more elaborate exegesis, which contains details of which we would know nothing if it had not been for the fact that he chose to quote the *pesher* text in its final form. We shall see that the final form is the work of an exegete who used the Septuagint version, but was also familiar with the Hebrew. He drew his material about the potter from the prophecy of Jeremiah. Consequently it is to him that we must attribute the erroneous ascription of the quotation (Jeremiah for Zechariah) rather than to Matthew, who had no interest in the connection with Jeremiah. Matthew knew that the nucleus of the text came from Zechariah, for he had already made his own (Septuagint) allusion to Zech. 11.12 at 26.15, and has perhaps alluded to the same version of v. 13 in his use of $\beta\alpha\lambda\epsilon\hat{\imath}\nu$.[1] But, seeing that the text and commentary which he has available for writing up the Judas legend differ so markedly from what he found in Zechariah, he may perhaps be forgiven for leaving the false attribution untouched. We must now trace the formation of the composite quotation through its various stages.

To begin with, the text is chosen out of the Passion prophecy, and *abbreviated* to draw attention solely to the point at issue in the Passion apologetic. This was the need to explain the betrayal of the Messiah for money. So the two sentences of the one verse are telescoped as follows:

ואקחה שלשים הכסף אדר היקר אשר יקרתי מעליהם ואשליך
אתו בית יהוה אל־היוצר:

The next stage is to apply it to the fate of Judas. This seems to coincide with the translation of the text into Greek, independently of the Septuagint. Now the 'I' becomes Judas himself, and the details of the verse are taken seriously. This means that 'the goodly price that I was priced at' has to be put into the third person to show that it refers to Jesus. This is done so elaborately that it is probably intended to be understood messianically, the original motive of the choice of the text. This yields the following version:

[1] In retaining $\kappa o\rho\beta\alpha\nu\hat{\alpha}\nu$ from the earlier work he may have thought of it as a true equivalent of LXX $\chi\omega\nu\epsilon\upsilon\tau\acute{\eta}\rho\iota o\nu$ ( = 'foundry', i.e. the temple mint).

καὶ ἔλαβον τὰ τριάκοντα ἀργύρια, τὴν τιμὴν τοῦ τετιμημένου ὃν
ἐτιμήσαντο ἀπὸ υἱῶν Ἰσραήλ, καὶ ἔρριψα αὐτὰ εἰς τὸν ναὸν εἰς τὸν
κορβανᾶν.

In this form the text shows how the behaviour of Judas was
already known in the secrets of Scripture. He received money, but
brought it back to the temple treasury. But it is already a fixed
element in the tradition that the money was used for the purchase
of land. It is the achievement of the final exegete to complete the
biblical warrants for what happened by observing a connection
between the Zechariah text and a transaction for the purchase of
land in Jeremiah.

This is done by reference to the Hebrew text. The exegete takes
היוצר in its normal meaning of 'potter' (cf. Aquila's πλάστην).
Now Jer. 32(39).6-14 describes the purchase of land, and at the
end the title-deeds are stored in a clay vessel (ἀγγεῖον ὀστράκινον)
until such time as Jeremiah can resume ownership. Although by
no stretch of the imagination can the placing of papers in a pot be
made equivalent to the paying of money to a potter, the coincidence
of a potter in Zech. 11.13 and pottery in this passage seems to have
suggested the use of it to give the necessary scriptural warrant for
the purchase of the land which the Zechariah passage lacked. Obviously the pot must have been made by a potter, and Jeremiah had
gone down εἰς τὸν οἶκον τοῦ κεραμέως and seen him making an
ἀγγεῖον in Jer. 18.3f. So various passages are correlated to obtain
the desired result. It may be that the use of ἀγρός for the name of
the land in Matt. 27.8, instead of Acts 1.18 χωρίον, is due to its
occurrence in Jer. 32(39).7f.[1]

With these thoughts in mind our exegete writes a comment on
the last line of the Greek form of the *pesher* text that he has before
him (καὶ ἔρριψα, etc.): καὶ ἔδωκαν (v.l. ἔδωκα) αὐτὰ εἰς τὸν ἀγρὸν
τοῦ κεραμέως. Because this is given as the *meaning* of the line,
Matthew has used it in the quotation, treating the line which it
replaces as if it were the comment, which he can incorporate into
his narrative. Thus text and comment change places. The use of
ἔδωκαν is not altogether happy, for if it means 'gave' it requires
expression of the indirect object, as is implied by the Hebrew
אל־היוצר, and if it means 'put' the noun following εἰς should

---

[1] χωρίον is perhaps a better translation of חקל (by metathesis for חלק),
though the usual LXX rendering is μερίς. ἀγρός nearly always represents
שדה, as here.

be the clay vessel used for the purpose. It is quite possible that it
has been suggested by Jer. 32(39).12, 14, where Jeremiah *gave*
(ἔδωκα, וָאֶתֵּן) the title-deeds to Baruch, and then commanded
(συνέταξα) him to *put* (θήσεις, וּנְתַתָּם) them into a clay pot.[1] As
it is, ἔδωκαν . . . εἰς has yet another meaning, i.e. 'they gave it *for*
the potter's field', which very briefly summarizes Jeremiah's transaction.

The Jeremiah verse just referred to also accounts for the final
phrase of the *pesher* text, καθὰ συνέταξέν μοι κύριος. The actual
words (without μοι) are found in Ex. 9.12, in connection with the
hardening of Pharaoh's heart after the plague of boils. The link
between this and the rest of the exegesis is to be found in the
Septuagint χωνευτήριον at the end of Zech. 11.13, which is yet
another interpretation of יוֹצֵר. Evidently this ingenious final
exegete connected this 'foundry' in his mind with the furnace from
which Moses obtained the dust to produce the boils. So he expresses the idea of the divine command, suggested to him by Jer.
32(39).14, in the phrase found in the Exodus passage.

The reason for these elaborations of textual work is the desire
to show that every detail of the known history of Judas was pre-
figured in Scripture, so that the whole falls into the divine plan.
From this point of view the final phrase is vitally important, even
though it has been arrived at in a very roundabout way. It is the
complete answer to the problem of Judas Iscariot. It is worth
noting that the Fourth Gospel finds it necessary to combat any
suggestion that Jesus did not see into the mind of Judas from the
beginning (John 6.70f.; 13.18, 27).

The developments which we have traced not only coincide
with changes of language, but also show different hermeneutical
methods. The original choice of a particular passage from the
Passion prophecy of Zechariah (the Hebrew stage) is a straightforward matter. The cryptic character of the prophecy makes it
easy to believe that the Passion of Jesus is precisely what it refers
to. The second (Palestinian Greek) stage is concerned with the
correlation of the details of the passage and the known facts about
the fate of Judas. The method at this stage is to draw out the fullest
implications of the text itself. The final exegete (using the Septuagint, but paying careful attention to the original Hebrew) intro-

---

[1] It has to be remembered that this exegete is careful to compare both
the Septuagint and Hebrew texts.

duces an allegorical element by seeing an equivalence, a mysterious identity, of Zechariah's prophecy and Jeremiah's transaction—not to mention the plague of boils. There is still a fourth stage. Matthew himself disregards the work of the final exegete, because he is only interested in the *pesher* text and its commentary from the point of view of his narrative. It is the *second* layer of exegesis which provides him with the information which he wants.

The question arises how much of the narrative in Matt. 27.3-8 can be accepted as accurate. The analysis has suggested that the only fixed points of the tradition are the sudden death of Judas and the purchase of land bearing the remarkable name the Field of Blood. If we have to choose between what Matthew and Acts make of these facts, we are bound to feel that the suicide of Judas, after returning the money to the priests, is intrinsically the more probable. The motive of remorse is psychologically acceptable. It follows from this that the decision of the priests to buy the land is also to be regarded as founded on fact, and again the motivation seems entirely credible. Stendahl maintains that it was actually a potter's field, but this is not really likely, as this information is more probably an assumption from the *pesher* text itself. If this is granted, then there is no reason to suppose that the land had not always been called the Field of Blood. The name is not derived from the death of Judas (Acts), nor from its subsequent use for the burial of foreign visitors (Matthew). Presumably it was already a burial-ground, though in private hands before this date. Thus Matt. 27.8 shares with Acts 1.19 the aetiological motive.[1] It may be deduced from the way in which the whole material is handled that, though the story is not created out of the text, the text may be freely used to fill up the gaps in the story. This seems to the early Christian exegetes a perfectly legitimate hermeneutical procedure.

### Whom They Pierced

There are allusions to Zech. 12.10 in Matt. 24.30, John 19.37, and Rev. 1.7. The relations between them are too complicated for them to be set out in parallel columns, so that it is better to arrange them successively in sense-lines.

---

[1] It was suggested by A. Klostermann, *Probleme in Aposteltexte neu erörtet*, 1883, pp. 1-8, that Ἀκελδαμαχ (Acts 1.19) is really a transliteration of חקל־דמך = 'place of sleep', i.e. cemetery. It has been treated as if it were חקל־דמא, an ironical pun, in the earliest phase of the Judas legend.

Zech. 12.10-14 (LXX<sup>B</sup>)

... καὶ ἐπιβλέψονται πρός με ἀνθ᾽ ὧν κατωρχήσαντο, καὶ κόψονται
ἐπ᾽ αὐτὸν κοπετὸν ὡς ἐπ᾽ ἀγαπητῷ,
καὶ ὀδυνηθήσονται ὀδύνην ὡς ἐπὶ τῷ πρωτοτόκῳ ... καὶ κόψεται
ἡ γῆ κατὰ φυλὰς φυλάς ...
πᾶσαι αἱ ὑπολελειμμέναι φυλαί ...

Matt. 24.30

καὶ τότε φανήσεται τὸ σημεῖον τ. υἱοῦ τ. ἀνθρώπου ἐν οὐρανῷ,
καὶ τότε κόψονται πᾶσαι αἱ φυλαὶ τῆς γῆς
καὶ ὄψονται τ. υἱὸν τ. ἀνθρώπου ἐρχόμενον ἐπὶ τῶν νεφελῶν τ.
οὐρανοῦ ...

Rev. 1.7

ἰδοὺ ἔρχεται μετὰ τῶν νεφελῶν,
καὶ ὄψεται αὐτὸν πᾶς ὀφθαλμὸς καὶ οἵτινες αὐτὸν ἐξεκέντησαν,
καὶ κόψονται ἐπ᾽ αὐτὸν πᾶσαι αἱ φυλαὶ τῆς γῆς.

John 19.37

ὄψονται εἰς ὃν ἐξεκέντησαν.

Two striking agreements will be noticed at once. Both Matthew
and Revelation conflate the passage with the famous Parousia text,
Dan. 7.13. Both John and Revelation use the non-Septuagintal
ἐξεκέντησαν, which is closer to the Hebrew, and found also in
Aquila and Theodotion.[1] These are surely more than coincidences,
and indicate that here is another text selected for a special purpose
in the Passion apologetic.[2]

The conflation with Dan. 7.13 is not surprising, seeing it occurs
in apocalyptic contexts. But it has obscured the text underlying
the final form preserved in Matt. 24.30. Considering its relationship to Rev. 1.7, it is probable that at an earlier stage it included
the same characteristic word which Revelation shares with John.
It is thus possible to trace behind all three passages a common
original text, not quite the same as the standard Septuagint text,

[1] Aquila: σὺν ᾧ ἐξεκέντησαν; Symmachus: ἔμπροσθεν ἐπεξεκέντησαν; Theodotion: ὃν ἐξεκέντησαν (cod. 86: Syh. εἰς ὅν); Lucian: εἰς ὃν ἐξεκέντησαν.
[2] It is not usually possible to press the exact form of text in apocalyptic
writings, because of the great freedom which these writers habitually
employ. Recognition of this helps us in the present instance to see a
common original variously quoted.

abbreviated for its apologetic purpose before its later employment in Christian apocalyptic. This was as follows:

$$\kappa\alpha\grave{\iota}\ \emph{ὄψονται}\ \emph{εἰς}\ \emph{ὃν}\ \emph{ἐξεκέντησαν}$$
$$\kappa\alpha\grave{\iota}\ \emph{κόψονται}\ \emph{ἐπ'}\ \emph{αὐτὸν}\ \emph{πᾶσαι}\ \emph{αἱ}\ \emph{φυλαὶ}\ \emph{τῆς}\ \emph{γῆς}.$$

John only quotes the first clause, which alone is relevant to his immediate purpose. Revelation puts it alongside words from Dan. 7.13 (the one passage being a commentary on the other), and then slightly expands the first line in order to have two subjects, πᾶς ὀφθαλμός and οἵτινες, which necessitate some further minor changes. We shall see that this has been done deliberately. It seems that Matthew also knew the text with Dan. 7.13 beside it. Finding ὄψονται at the opening of an unmistakable allusion to Dan. 7.13 in the Marcan apocalypse which he was rewriting (Mark 13.26), he took it to be the first word of the Zechariah testimony. As he wished (presumably for the sake of the sequence of the narrative) to transpose it to follow the mourning of the tribes, it was necessary to omit ἐπ' αὐτόν after κόψονται. Thus the whole testimony is represented, though the first clause has been replaced by the already existing Daniel text. But the idea of the first clause retains its place at the beginning by the introduction of another Son of Man saying in v. 30a, φανήσεται etc., so that it is represented twice over. The repetition of καὶ τότε shows the sutures of the patchwork text, as frequently in Matthew.

We must now try to find the motives of these forms of the citation, and first of all that of the postulated common original. It is an abbreviation of the Zechariah passage, in order to free it from matter foreign to its purpose. The precise meaning of the whole context is impossible to determine. At any rate, it describes the restoration of Jerusalem after devastating warfare, and then, when the new life of the city begins, the inhabitants are expected to 'look upon me whom they have pierced'. The sight will be such as to make them mourn as at a family funeral, and they will do this arranged in liturgical order. Of course the very obscurity is the apologist's opportunity to secure the desired interpretation, as in the Dead Sea *Habakkuk Commentary*. Thus attention is sure to be drawn to the mysterious 'piercing', which is seen by the people just at the moment of victory and of the outpouring of the spirit of grace (v. 10a). The motive of referring to this now becomes obvious. The Church, exulting in the victory of Jesus and the outpouring of the Spirit, can assert that the Messiah was bound to be 'pierced' in the task of achieving this, for it is already so determined in Scripture. It is, then, a Passion apologetic accounting for the death of Jesus by crucifixion (rather than any other way). Here is the question and its answer, which we felt was bound to be asked when we were studying the use of Ps. 22, but which was not (as might have been expected) answered with the aid of Ps. 22.17.

In itself the idea of piercing might not be considered sufficient to indicate death rather than a grievous wound, though in fact the word seems to be always used to denote a wound with intent to kill, as the context normally indicates. In Zech. 12.10 the fatal effect of the wound is implied by the mourning of the tribes, as if for an 'only son' or for a 'firstborn'. From the point of view of developing christology it might be thought that these words would be retained in the citation.[1] Their disappearance may thus be a sign of early date in the selection of this text for apologetic use. As it is, our abbreviated quotation includes the mourning of the tribes only to emphasize the basic motive, i.e. scriptural warrant for the death of the Messiah by crucifixion. Now we noticed in considering Ps. 69 that the Passion apologetic of the early days contained an element of dire warning to those who refuse the Gospel message.[2] Similarly the mourning may have been thought of as the remorse of those who, having refused to believe, find themselves cut off from the blessings of the restored Jerusalem when they realize too late that the Church's claim has been vindicated.

From this interpretation it is easy to see how the brief form of the quotation came into the Christian apocalyptic tradition. The moment of vindication and judgment is the Parousia, when the Son of Man is revealed. Then the wounds caused by the nails will be seen, and the unbelievers will have good cause to mourn.[3] This is the motive in Rev. 1.7. We have observed that this version of the text contains a deliberate modification, so as to distinguish between the whole of humanity who see the sight and the smaller group within the whole who had pierced the Son of Man. This modification is due to the desire to apply the passage to the apocalyp-

---

[1] MT יחיד and בכור; LXX ἀγαπητός and πρωτότοκος.
[2] *Supra*, p. 102.
[3] Thus the already existing Passion text, Zech. 12.10, is used as a comment on Dan. 7.13.

tic programme. For the coming of the Son of Man in judgment entails the vindication of the righteous and the condemnation of the wicked simultaneously; and the wicked are those who crucified him.

There seems to be much the same motive in Matt. 24.30, but limited simply to the terrifying effect of the sudden appearance of the Son of Man. If the 'sign' in the first line of the verse (in spite of being originally a separate item of tradition) was intended by Matthew to mean the sight of 'him whom they pierced', then perhaps the old patristic idea that it is the cross may be right after all.[1] But it cannot be regarded as Matthew's purpose to call attention to this, seeing that he has obscured it so successfully. In fact he has allowed the apocalyptic interest to take complete control, so that the primary connection of this testimony with the Passion apologetic has disappeared from view.

John shows an interesting development of a quite different kind. He uses only the words about the piercing, and retains the strict reference to the Passion. It is notable that the original meaning, accounting for the piercing of the hands and feet of Jesus with nails, comes very close to that of Ps. 34.21 (a bone shall not be broken) from the point of view of apologetic. John quotes these together in 19.37f., and characteristically gives them both a new interpretation for the sake of his theology. So in this case he transfers the application of the testimony from the nailing of our Lord to the cross (i.e. punishment by crucifixion) to the wounding of his side with a spear. This incident is unknown to the Synoptists,[2] but may be based on genuine historical tradition. However, the controlling factor is the symbolism of the blood and water. The testimony thereby acquires a new purpose, to combat the incipient heresy of docetism.

The original application of the passage to the Crucifixion may perhaps be an example of the argument from literal interpretation. In the rabbinic tradition we find this verse used messianically of

---

[1] First in Cyril of Jerusalem, *Cat.* 15.22, cf. his *Letter to Constantius* 4, and Eusebius, *Life of Constantine* I 28. The idea was presumably already current in popular expectation, cf. *Didache* 16.6: σημεῖον ἐκπετάσεως ἐν οὐρανῷ, explicitly referring to Matt. 24.30; W. Telfer, *Cyril of Jerusalem and Nemesius of Emesa* (Library of Christian Classics IV), 1955, p. 163 n. 97.

[2] Matt. 27.49b = John 19.34 is rejected by most modern authorities, though it is found in the most ancient MSS (hence its inclusion in RVm).

the (mortal) Messiah ben Joseph.[1] If this goes back into the first century, it might have been an exegetical point agreed by both sides. The precise form of 'piercing' remains obscure, and the Church can assert that crucifixion is the literal fulfilment of it. This clinches the argument in favour of the messianic claim about Jesus.

If it is right to postulate one common non-Septuagint text underlying the three New Testament allusions, it is bound to raise the possibility of a written Testimony-Book in the early days of the Church. It is to avoid this conclusion that Stendahl (*SSM*, p. 213) goes too far in minimizing the verbal agreements between the three versions. It is probably better to imagine a living apologetic tradition, oral rather than written, in which the practical usefulness of the abbreviated text helps to preserve its identity. It is possible that its two clauses were sometimes used in reverse order. This is implied by Matt. 24.30 ($\kappa \acute{o} \psi o \nu \tau a \iota \ldots \, \acute{o} \psi o \nu \tau a \iota$), and occurs again in the very free précis of Zech. 12 in Justin's *First Apology*.[2] The false ascription of this passage to Hosea, when he alludes to it in *Dial.* 14.8, is another sign that it belongs to living tradition. These considerations weaken the case for a Testimony-Book, though the matter must be left for further treatment in the last chapter.

## The Scattering of the Sheep

Our Lord's forecast of Peter's denials is introduced in Matt. 26.31 = Mark 14.27 with words from Zech. 13.7, 'I will smite the shepherd, and the sheep (of the flock) shall be scattered abroad.' This must be studied in relation to the shepherd and sheep theme in general.

In the New Testament this theme can be classified under two heads, pastoral and redemptive. The *pastoral* references naturally belong to the 'church order' type of context, and are derived from the normal Old Testament use of the theme. There, shepherds are often mentioned as a metaphor for government, sometimes refer-

---

[1] *B. Sukkah* 52a.
[2] 52.11. If Justin derived his text from the NT, then it is an amalgam of all three passages, Matt. 24.30, John 19.37 and Rev. 1.7. The idea of acquaintance with a living tradition from the common original is surely more plausible. The application to the Parousia occurs in *Dial.* 14.8, 32.2, 64.7 and 118.1, all using ἐκκεντέω.

ring to Moses[1] or to David,[2] or else to the rulers in general.[3] This
is continued in the New Testament. Our Lord's parables in which
this theme is used are pastoral in tone, and do not include christological implications. These are the simile introduced by Matthew
into a Marcan story of healing (Matt. 12.11), the parable of the
lost sheep (Matt. 18.12-14 = Luke 15.3-7), the simile used for the
setting of the Great Assize, which can be regarded as detachable
material (Matt. 25.32b-33), and the parable of the sheepfold which
forms the nucleus of John's Good Shepherd allegory (John 10.1-5).[4]
It is unlikely that anything more than the pastoral theme is contained in the phrase 'little flock' in Luke 12.32. Paul's farewell
speech at Miletus in Acts 20 is an excellent specimen of the theme
in a 'church order' context. The Johannine appendix (John 21.
15-17) falls into the same class.

The *redemptive* use of the theme has an importance for us,
because it seems always to be possible to trace the phrases back to
Isa. 53 and Zech. 9-13. This was specially clear when we examined
I Peter 2.21-25, which has many words from Isa. 53. We find a
rather similar idea in the words 'the lost sheep of the house of
Israel', which occur twice in Matthew (10.6, 15.24). There seems
no reason to doubt the authenticity of this *logion* in one or other of
its forms. Its anti-Gentilic character marks it out as belonging to
the most primitive tradition, unaltered by subsequent apologetic.
It seems to be derived from Jer. 50(27).6, though this may be due
to Septuagint allusion on the part of Matthew himself. But the
*meaning* of the phrase is more closely akin to the thought of Isa.
53.6. It is for this reason that it becomes possible to classify it as
a redemptive usage. It is not a matter of gathering up the Jews of
the Diaspora, but a tender pastoral concern on the part of the
Servant of the Lord, who will bear their sins by his sacrificial
death.

The Passion apologetic is much clearer in the case of the quota-

---

[1] Ps. 77.21. In a Qumran fragment (published by D. Barthélemy and
J. T. Milik, *Qumran Cave I*, 1955, no. 34 ii, p. 154) a 'faithful shepherd'
is expected, who is evidently to be a new Moses.
[2] E.g. Micah 5.1 = Matt. 2.6.
[3] Notably Ezek. 34, which is the source of Matt. 9.36 = Mark 6.34; also
*Enoch* 89-90. In CD 13.10 the *mebaqqer* is spoken of as a shepherd. For the
actual quotation of Zech. 13.7 in CD 19.8 (recension B), see *infra*, p. 279.
[4] See J. A. T. Robinson, 'The Parable of John 10.1-5', *ZNW* 46, 1955,
pp. 233-40, now reprinted in his *Twelve New Testament Studies*. He regards these verses as a fusion of two genuine parables.

tion of Zech. 13.7, which is our proper concern now, and an important item of the redemptive class. The text in Matthew and Mark is fairly close to that of Septuagint A, itself closer to the Hebrew than to the interpretative Septuagint B. Fortunately the intricate textual problems do not much affect the analysis for our purpose.[1] The one really significant difference is the first person indicative πατάξω of the verb against the imperative of the Hebrew, Targum, Old Testament Peshitta, and almost all Septuagint texts. This is the more notable in that there seems to be no reason in the context for the change, and it actually makes the sense more difficult. For the subject of the next verb προάξω is Jesus himself, so that it is by no means easy to make God the subject of πατάξω as the meaning requires. If Jesus is the subject of this verb also, then presumably Peter is the shepherd. But there is no hint that Peter is to be 'smitten', merely that he will fail in his witness. It is interesting that the Fayyum Fragment considerably eases the narrative by omitting Mark 14.28 ('I will go before you into Galilee') altogether. Thus Peter's assertion that he would not be offended follows on our Lord's prophecy that all would be offended. As the Fragment is in any case abbreviating considerably, it is difficult to know whether the omission was the work of the editor or actually a feature of the text of Mark before him.

But it is very tempting to take this lead and go a step further, bracketing not only v. 28 but also v. 27b (i.e. the Zechariah quotation introduced by ὅτι γέγραπται). For Peter's reply takes no notice of either of these statements. The insertion of them (by Mark) can then be accounted for by the needs of the narrative-plot. At Mark 14.49 Jesus refers to the fulfilment of scriptures (i.e. specific texts), and in the next verse comes the flight of the disciples. This was as much a 'scandal' as St Peter's denials, and Zech. 13.7 was probably used to account for it. By inserting the text at v. 27b Mark has prepared the way for the flight of the disciples, although the scandal mentioned in v. 27a really only referred to Peter at that point. Similarly v. 28 is the forecast required by 16.7 ('into Galilee . . . as he said unto you'). The artificiality of this verse is evident from the plain and unadorned way in which Jesus is represented as saying μετὰ τὸ ἐγερθῆναί με as if there were nothing unusual or

---

[1] LXX<sup>A</sup> διασκορπισθήσονται = Mark 14.27; LXX<sup>B</sup> ἐκσπάσατε. That the reading of LXX<sup>A</sup> is independent of NT, being more probably a correction by reference to MT, is shown by Stendahl, *SSM*, pp. 81f.

unexpected about it at all. The insertion of this verse here is probably due to the underlying idea of the shepherd and sheep, for after his Resurrection Jesus will gather up the scattered disciples in Galilee (cf. John 21). However, we are not concerned with this, but with the fact that both 27b and 28 can be detached from the paragraph and be held to have had independent existence separate from each other.[1] The testimony in 27b can now be viewed in isolation, but with the flight of the disciples as its probable context (cf. John 16.32 σκορπισθῆτε).

The flight of the disciples is not, however, the original application of the passage. It implies specific identification of the shepherd with Jesus and the sheep with the disciples which is only possible when the verse has been torn from its context. The passage as a whole reproduces much of the thought of the preceding chapter, and we may notice particularly the similarity of 13.6 ('those wounds between thine hands') to 12.10 ('me whom they have pierced').[2] It is not easy to tell whether the shepherd is a good ruler or a wicked one. The uncertainty of modern commentators on this point seems to have been shared by the Septuagint translators. Where the plural 'shepherds' has been used (BS*W), taking the Hebrew as a collective, it implies that they are smitten for their bad handling of the flock. This is part of the refining process out of which the remnant will be saved (v. 8).[3] In other texts where the singular of the Hebrew has been retained it is possible that there is a Palestinian tradition, quite apart from the influence of Matthew and Mark on the manuscript tradition, in which a single shepherd is intended. In this case he is probably a good guide of the people. His removal, though instigated by the 'sword of the Lord', is one of the acts of the wicked rulers which will prove to be their undoing in the ensuing chaos. And out of this chaos the remnant will emerge refined like precious metal.

[1] Hence it is probably wrong to suppose that προάξω in Mark 14.28 is an intentional link with ἐπάξω in Zech. 13.7. There is no connection of meaning.

[2] Not used in the early Christian literature. In *Ep. Barn.* 5.12 τὴν πληγὴν τῆς σαρκός may be an allusion to this verse. It is immediately followed by a quotation of Zech. 13.7, differing from all other versions. The use of ἀπολεῖται for διασκορπισθήσονται (but *v.l.* σκορπισθήσεται) may be due to the influence of John 10.28 (cf. v. 12). There is a parallel to this in *Ep. Barn.* 11.10, where a quotation of Ezek. 47.1, 7, 12 (much abbreviated) seems to be influenced by John 6.51.

[3] These MSS thus have ἐκσπάσατε = 'save'.

Which of these interpretations was really intended in the original prophecy we cannot tell. But it is evident that the second one, which is implied by the Greek text which translates it most literally, is highly suitable for the Church's needs. Comparison of 13.6 with 12.10 would suggest the application of the whole passage to the sufferings of Jesus. This invites the identification of him with the shepherd in 13.7 who is the victim of the sword. The shepherd, being a good ruler of the house of David (12.10a), can be regarded as a messianic figure. The primary interpretation of the verse in its context is thus the death of the Messiah.

It is characteristic of the *pesher* quotations that they are selected to deal with particular issues within the general apologetic. The use of this passage on its own answers the question, Why did the friends of Jesus desert him in his hour of need, if they believed he was the Messiah, or if the death of the Messiah was part of the divine plan, as they now claim? The answer may perhaps contain something of the penitence of Peter: It is indeed bitterly true that they deserted him—but even this was foreknown by God and ordained in prophecy. No wonder that the Gospel is primarily a proclamation of forgiveness!

It is when the quotation is detached from its context that the change of the verb from imperative to πατάξω is likely to take place, simply for the purpose of an abbreviated text. The subject of the imperative is the sword of the Lord,[1] and so is virtually God himself. The first person verb gives the impression of God speaking directly through the prophet, and so helps to show how the flight of the disciples is part of the divine plan.

But the original application of Zech. 13.7 was, as we have seen, to the Crucifixion, though it consists of words containing the usual Old Testament metaphor of rulers as shepherds. It is comparable with the use of Isa. 53.6, already noted. These show the extension of the shepherd and sheep theme from pastoral to redemptive application by way of the Passion apologetic.

This is true also of the description of our Lord in Heb. 13.20: ὁ ἀναγαγὼν ἐκ νεκρῶν τὸν ποιμένα τῶν προβάτων τὸν μέγαν ἐν αἵματι διαθήκης αἰωνίου. There is a direct reference here to Isa. 63.11 (LXX), alluding to Moses.[2] The covenant, however, is Davidic-

---

[1] In spite of the change of gender, cf. Gesenius-Kautzsch[2], §§110*k*, 144*a*.
[2] The ideas of the shepherd and of the Servant of the Lord, who intercedes for the people and bears their sins, come together in the figure of

Messianic (Isa. 55.3), and certainly includes a reminiscence of 'the blood of the covenant' in Zech. 9.11. The shepherd and the blood of the covenant are ideas which have not been previously combined in the figure of Moses, but owe their combination here to the existing Christian apologetic tradition, using the Zechariah Passion prophecy. In this case other texts from the later chapters of Isaiah have been used to fill out the meaning. The figure of Moses as such does not come into it. It is entirely a product of the redemptive use of the shepherd theme.

We can see the same development in John 10.7-18. These verses draw on the whole treasury of Old Testament shepherd and sheep material. But the argument turns on the redemptive use of it. Jesus claims to be the shepherd who is smitten, whose sacrifice saves the sheep (vv. 15-18). The allegory has already contrasted the hireling, who flees when the wolf comes (v. 12). The result is that the sheep are not only seized by the wolf, but also scattered (σκορπίζει). The Good Shepherd does not flee, but is in his turn the prey of the wolf. It is natural to suppose that, as he has failed, the sheep are just as likely to be scattered by the wolf as when the hireling fled! But it is implied that this sacrifice actually saves the sheep, in spite of, or rather because of, its fatal consequence. In allegory it is not right to expect logical consistency, but we should rather expect illustration of the underlying ideas. In this example it is clear that it is an allegory of the divine necessity of the death of Jesus for the work of redemption, including a side-glance at the flight of the disciples. This occurs again in John 16.32. It is in fact the same issue as produced the Marcan citation of Zech. 13.7. First the question, If Jesus was the Messiah, why did he allow himself to be put to death? Then the objection, If this was God's plan, predetermined in Scripture, why did his followers desert him?

### The Blood of the Covenant

A further word is needed on this subject, because the phrase is not only found in Zech. 9.11 but also in Ex. 24.8. Hebrews has in fact correlated the various 'covenant' passages. Ex. 24.8 is actually quoted in Heb. 9.20, and alluded to in 10.29; and Jer. 31.33 (the new covenant) is cited in 10.16. The reason for thinking that Zech. 9.11 is nevertheless the primary scriptural passage is that the whole verse, in its context, is redemptive in motive in an eschatological Moses in late Judaism, cf. J. Jeremias, art. Μωυσῆς, *TWNT* IV, p. 857.

passage. The Exodus context, on the other hand, is the description of the actual ceremonial of the covenant, and demands the kind of typology for its Christian application that the writer to the Hebrews actually employs. Zech. 9.11 is a reminiscence of the escape from Egypt, and probably means by the blood of the covenant that which was put on the lintels of the doors (Ex. 12.22). This is more in accord with the requirements of a primitive theology of redemption. We cannot really decide the matter from the evidence of Hebrews, because it represents a comparatively advanced theology and use of Scripture.

More light can be gained from the Words of Institution at the Last Supper. It is probable that the original words over the cup were τοῦτό ἐστιν τὸ αἷμά μου τὸ ἐκχυννόμενον ὑπὲρ πολλῶν and that τῆς διαθήκης has been subsequently inserted into it.[1] Even so, this has been developed still further to refer to the *new* covenant already in our *earliest* documentary source (I Cor. 11.25). Without the specific mention of the covenant, the words have sacrificial significance in terms of Isa. 53.12. The addition of it is a consequence of the growing awareness of the implications of Christ's sacrificial death. This coincides with the apologetic task of upholding the Passion against the objections of the unbelieving Jews, and so with the use of the Zechariah Passion prophecy. Greater precision is achieved by allusion to the ceremonial of the first covenant (Ex. 24.8, cf. Heb. 10.29) or to the prophecy of a new covenant (Jer. 31.33, cf. I Cor. 11.25). The actual use of the term διαθήκη does not necessarily entail precise allusion to any of the three passages; but its occurrence in Zech. 9.11 comes closest to what the early Church meant by it. The use of the other passages represents a secondary (but pre-Pauline) stage of thought. Similarly the explanation of the Last Supper in terms of the Passover is a sign of developing thought about the Eucharist.[2]

[1] J. Jeremias, *The Eucharistic Words of Jesus*, p. 133, is wrong, however, in saying that the phrase τὸ αἷμά μου τῆς διαθήκης is 'impossible in Aramaic'; see the note on this expression by J. A. Emerton, *JTS*, NS 6, 1955, pp. 238-40. This does not affect his argument that on exegetical grounds τῆς διαθήκης is not likely to belong to the oldest form of the words. That Jesus acted as he did at the Last Supper with the thought of the new covenant in mind is not denied.

[2] This is comparable to the way in which John applies older apologetic material to a theology based on the Passover. We have observed this in connection with 'the lamb of God' (1.29, 36); the hyssop (19.29); and Ps. 34.21 (19.36). For the secondary character of the explanation of the

In all the passages from Zech. 9-13 which we have examined, it has been possible to see how they were selected for particular purposes from the general usage of these chapters as a Passion prophecy. This had to be assumed in the case of Zech. 9.9, in order to explain how this verse has been taken up into the warp and woof of the Palm Sunday story. The story shows that our Lord's sufferings followed on a definite messianic claim, subsequently vindicated by his Resurrection. So the fact that the *messianic* Zech. 9.9 comes from a *Passion* prophecy underlies the whole argument. So also Zech. 11.13 was used to account for the treatment of Jesus before being narrowed down to the story of Judas. The earliest version of the citation of Zech. 12.10 was concerned with the method of death by crucifixion. Zech. 13.7 was also probably used to explain the death of Jesus before being applied to the flight of the disciples. Allusion to 'the blood of the covenant' arises from Zech. 9.11 before the more precise correlation of other passages.

### 4. THE PASSION APOLOGETIC AND ATONEMENT DOCTRINE

The Gospel of Redemption was proclaimed side by side with the apologetic in response to hostile criticism. Atonement theology and Passion apologetic are worked out together, and naturally the same scriptures are used for both. It may be useful to give indications of this in the form of a brief summing up of this chapter.

The Resurrection is the starting-point, and the death of our Lord might be held to have no intrinsic value, except as the necessary prelude to this event. The Epistles to the Thessalonians give just this impression. But ideas of the redemption and reconciliation and atonement tend to give positive value to the death. This is implied as a matter of course in Gal. 1.4. It would be absurd to suppose that there has been such a radical development in the brief interval between the writing of these Epistles. It is in fact already present in the *paradosis* which Paul had received (I Cor. 15.3). For the purposes of a positive theory of the Atonement it is desirable to say that 'Christ died . . . according to the scriptures'. It is equally necessary so as to reply to the objection that, if Jesus is the designated Messiah, he ought not to have been put to death as an

Last Supper in terms of the Passover, cf. K. G. Kuhn, 'The Lord's Supper and the Communal Meal at Qumran', in K. Stendahl (ed.), *The Scrolls and the New Testament*, 1958, pp. 91f.

object of divine displeasure. The Passion scriptures, especially
Isa. 53, are the sources of the Church's attempts to deal with both
these matters.

The two motives are closely joined in the basic interpretation of
these scriptures. It is the *story* of Isa. 52.13 - 53.12 that counts.
The description of sufferings shows that Jesus' Passion was divinely
ordered; the idea of an atoning result applies to the efficacy of
Jesus' death. A more apocalyptic version of the story is found in
Zechariah, where the true shepherd is stricken before the restoration of the Davidic kingdom; and then a cleansing fountain will
flow (Zech. 13.1). The description of sufferings, with resulting
benefits, is also found in Pss. 22 and 69, the most important of the
Passion Psalms. Ps. 34 puts the matter in a rather different way.
The providence of God did not fail the Righteous, so that his
sufferings were all part of the divine plan.

Specific objections also play their part in the process of doctrinal thought. Some of these fasten on the Roman method of death
by crucifixion. It is the punishment for sedition (Luke 22.37 =
Isa. 53.12), without military glory (Ps. 34.21), and not properly
authorized in Scripture (Zech. 12.10). This is an aspect of another
controversy, that the method of crucifixion rendered Jesus subject
to the curse of the law of Deut. 21.23 (Gal. 3.13). This will be
considered further in a later chapter, when reason will be given
for holding the view that Paul is handling material already in use
in the Church's apologetic. The point to notice here is that the
objection to crucifixion (hanging on a tree) comes to have positive
value for deepening the doctrine of the Atonement. For it is in
bearing the curse of the Law in this way that Jesus removes the
curse of the Law in a much wider and deeper sense (Gal. 3.10-13).
It cannot have been easy to reach such a position. The first Christians must have felt the force of these objections acutely. The
answers given by quoting phrases from Isa. 53.12, Ps. 34.21, and
Zech. 12.10, taken by themselves, are mere palliatives, simply
showing that the objections are overruled in Scripture itself. The
acceptance of the same objections as elements of a much deeper
positive doctrine might well have to wait until further reflection
pointed the way.

Another range of objections pours scorn on the humiliations to
which Jesus was subjected. The shame of the whole proceeding is
a 'reproach' (Ps. 69.10), which must be shared manfully by the

Christians, but cannot be left unanswered. Psalm 69 gave two types of answer, the positive one that it was actually the reproach of God which Jesus bore, and the negative one that a whole heap of curses is in store for those who make such objections! This issue can be viewed in a legal way, and so enters into the groundwork of the controversy of the curse of the Law. But it can also be taken with more specific complaints, that Jesus allowed himself to be publicly humiliated and 'set at nought' (Isa. 53.3), to be disfigured physically (Isa. 53.4), to be plied with vinegar (Ps. 69.22), and to suffer various other indignities (Ps. 22). To these may be added the scandal of being sold for money (Zech. 11.13). All these charges may be adequately answered from the Passion scriptures, including the general assertion that, whatever humiliations Jesus has had to suffer, he was in fact innocent (Ps. 69.5). But, as before, it is precisely in accepting the objections that the doctrine is fruitfully advanced. For the worse the humiliations, the greater the *moral* value of the example of Christ's sacrifice. This is specially emphasized in the poem of Phil. 2.5-11, in Hebrews, and in I Peter.

The conduct of Judas was a special element of the Passion apologetic. The main defence is the double meaning of the notion of 'delivering up' ($\pi\alpha\rho\alpha\delta\iota\delta\acute{o}\nu\alpha\iota$), drawn from Isa. 53.6, 12. This word had considerable emphasis in Atonement theory, for it epitomizes the divine initiative which was always behind the human forces that brought Jesus to his death (Rom. 8.32). The special application to Judas is not something different from this doctrinal development, but actually enhances it. Moreover, it is part of the reproach against Jesus that he had had table-fellowship with such a man (Ps. 41.10) and was apparently ignorant of his true character (John 17.12). The answer to these objections is that the curses of Pss. 69 and 109 have already fallen upon him. To make this point clearer the popular legend of the death of Judas and the Field of Blood are put on a biblical basis (Zech. 11.13). These are special developments which do not affect Atonement theory; but they are paralleled by the great emphasis on the wrath of God against evildoers which is specially characteristic of the apocalyptic tradition (Zech. 12.10).

Other interests have been observed which are either less central or later in date. The Church soon had to reply to the taunt that its proclamation had failed to win universal assent. From the point of view of Atonement doctrine this can be explained as one of the ways in which the Church shares the humiliation of its Master (Isa. 52.15, 53.1). Another taunt is the flight of the disciples, leaving Jesus to face his accusers alone (Zech. 13.7). Corresponding to this we find Paul speaking of the 'one man' in the Atonement argument of Rom. 5. There was, too, an apologetic need to show a basis for the redemptive value of the death of Jesus in the traditions concerning his life. This appears in the use of Passion material in the Palm Sunday story (Zech. 9.9), the introduction of words from Isa. 53.12 into the Lucan version of the Strong Man (Luke 11.22), and of course in the Passion predictions. In the use of older apologetic material in the Fourth Gospel, we have observed an explicit Passover typology (Ps. 34.21, influenced by Ex. 12.46, etc.). This shows the interest in the question *how* the death of Jesus is redemptive. There is also the need to uphold the reality of the death of Jesus against docetic tendencies (Zech. 12.10). Finally, the sacrificial phrase 'the blood of the covenant' has connections with the Passion apologetic through the use of Zechariah as an apocalyptic prophecy (Zech. 9.11). So the liturgical act in which the early Christians celebrated the Redemption had as its aim to 'show the Lord's death till he come' (I Cor. 11.26). This means—to put the matter in Johannine terms—that the Church, which first preached the glory of the Resurrection, had learnt with the aid of the Passion apologetic to discern that glory already in the moment of ignominious death.

# IV

## CHRISTUS REVELATUS

IN the second chapter of this book it was shown that the
Church's initial proclamation was supported by presenting the
Resurrection in terms of important biblical texts. There was
a startling correspondence between the plainest literal meaning of
the texts and what had actually happened. Nevertheless the Messiahship of Jesus was immediately challenged on the score of the
Crucifixion. We thus had to turn our attention to the Passion
apologetic. But of course the work of finding further scriptural
support for the Church's messianic interpretation of the Resurrection continued alongside the biblical labours involved in the
Passion apologetic. So we now have a rather miscellaneous group
of important testimonies to consider, which can be regarded as
witnesses to apologetic developments parallel to the Passion apologetic which we have just studied.

The chief characteristic of this group of texts is that they show
a tendency to be applied to events in the life of our Lord *before*
the Passion. This is in every case a secondary development. The
Church's claims about Jesus begin with the Resurrection. Whatever may have been the teaching of Jesus about himself, he scarcely
fitted into a recognizably messianic pattern. Although the disciples
came to believe that he was indeed the Messiah, their conviction
was shattered by the Crucifixion. Then the Resurrection reversed
this once more. Hence the earliest proclamation was of Jesus as
*Christus designatus* at his Resurrection. This conception was quickly
interpreted as *Christus revelatus* with power and glory.[1] There is
then a motive for working backwards, to account for all that had
gone before the Resurrection in the light of this new understanding
of it. Such work could include an assertion of the pre-existence of

---

[1] See the concluding section of ch. II above.

Jesus in the counsels of God,[1] and an explanation, first of the Crucifixion, then of various known episodes of his life and ministry, as the work of the *Messias incognitus* in preparation for his manifestation.[2] Thus just as a redemptive efficacy was immediately realized in the death of Jesus, so positive value was soon felt to belong to the preparatory work. That was also a messianic act, though not openly declared to be so. This is to see Wrede's theory of the 'messianic secret' as a stage in the Church's apologetic. The next logical step is to say that the life of Jesus should all along have been recognized as messianic. The failure of so many to see this is due, not to any intention of secrecy on the part of our Lord, but to their own blindness and hardness of heart. Once this is asserted, then the moment of manifestation is no longer the Resurrection, but must be pushed back to the very beginning of the ministry, to the Baptism of our Lord by John at the Jordan. This step has already been taken in the traditions which underlie all four Gospels.

## I. THE BAPTISMAL TEXTS

It is generally assumed that the words of the divine voice at our Lord's Baptism (Mark 1.11, par.) are a conflation of Ps. 2.7 and Isa. 42.1:

| Ps. 2.7 | Mark 1.11 | Isa. 42.1, as given in Matt. 12.18 |
|---|---|---|
| υἱός μου εἶ σύ, ἐγὼ σήμερον | σὺ εἶ ὁ υἱός μου ὁ ἀγαπητός, | ἰδοὺ ὁ παῖς μου ὃν ᾑρέτισα, ὁ ἀγαπητός μου |
| γεγέννηκά σε. | ἐν σοὶ εὐδόκησα. | ὃν εὐδόκησεν ἡ ψυχή μου. |

The influence of other passages (e.g. Gen. 22.2, ἀγαπητός) has also been suggested. Recently J. Jeremias has taken up the argument of Dalman and Bousset that the supposed allusion to Ps. 2.7 is only apparent, because it depends on the presence of υἱός in the text, which goes back in reality to עבדי of Isa. 42.1.[3] This theory envisages an intermediary Greek stage, in which παῖς has been

---

[1] Cf. John Knox, *Christ the Lord*, 1945 (=the second part of *Jesus, Lord and Christ*, 1958), ch. V. The matter will be dealt with in the next chapter.

[2] Cf. E. Stauffer, 'Die Eschatologie des vierten Evangeliums', in Davies and Daube, *The Background of the NT . . .*, pp. 287-91.

[3] Zimmerli and Jeremias, *The Servant of God*, p. 81 n. 350, where references are given.

used, before being altered to υἱός for greater christological precision, in a non-Jewish setting where the other would give the
wrong impression. This contention would carry more conviction
if other examples of υἱός replacing an original παῖς = עֶבֶד could
be found (the change of ὁ ἐκλεκτός to ὁ υἱός in the manuscript
history of John 1.34, though similar, is not strictly parallel, as it
has not been necessitated by a semantic problem in the word
itself).

The strongest argument in favour of this theory is the non-
Septuagint form of Isa. 42.1 given in Matt. 12.18. But if that represents the original form of the baptismal text, then it is not a case of
a mere substitution of υἱός for παῖς in a Greek setting. It is more
likely that the moment when this change might have happened is
the moment when an original version consisting of words from
Isa. 42.1 only is conflated with words from Ps. 2.7. In other words,
the christological development implied by the change of παῖς to
υἱός was more consciously contrived by the addition of another
messianic text, replacing the opening phrase.[1] We are thus saved
from having to assume that the similarity of the resultant opening
to Ps. 2.7 is pure coincidence. The early Fathers did not think so,
as can be seen from the Western Text of Luke 3.22 and from
patristic references to the Baptism, which quote Ps. 2.7 alone.[2]

It seems, then, that Ps. 2.7 did not originally belong to the text
of the Baptism. We must look elsewhere for its primary application.
It is quoted in Acts 13.33, and in Heb. 1.5, 5.5, 7.28 (allusion).
These references use this verse in relation to the Resurrection.

Although Paul's speech in Acts 13 has the marks of being a
Lucan composition, it is probably based on stock examples of
Christian apologetic, some of which are of considerable antiquity.[3]
Notice the way in which Ps. 16.10, with its argument from literal
fulfilment, is repeated from the material used in Acts 2. The speech
begins convincingly with a brief summary of Israelite history, leading up to a simple statement of the fulfilment of the promise to

[1] Compare the variant openings in the citations of Zech. 9.9.
[2] D *a b c ff² l r* Justin *Dial.* 88; 103; Clem. Alex. *Paed.* I 6.25; Meth.
*Symp.* VIII 9; *Didascalia* 9; *Apost. Const.* II 32; Lact. *Inst.* IV 15; and
other later writers. The process can be seen in *Ev. Ebion.* (Epiph. *Haer.*
XXX 13), where καὶ πάλιν· ἐγὼ σήμερον γεγέννηκά σε has been added after the
full text as given in Matt. 3.17.
[3] The speech has been analysed by Otto Glombitza, *NTS* 5, 1959,
pp. 306-17.

David in the person of Jesus (v. 23). The next two verses, describing John the Baptist, are drawn from Gospel tradition, and may be modelled by Luke on his own version of it (Luke 3.3-16). It is remarkable that he stops short without mentioning the Baptism of Jesus. Then vv. 26-31 are a typical Lucan exposition of the trial and death and Resurrection of Jesus as an unwitting fulfilment of Scripture (cf. Luke 24.25-27). This has moved the thought to the Resurrection, which is now made the starting-point for the detailed proof of the messiahship of Jesus. It is here that Ps. 2.7 is introduced: 'God hath fulfilled the promise unto our children; as also it is written in the second psalm, Thou art my Son, this day have I begotten thee.'

This use of Ps. 2.7 is legitimate according to the proper meaning of the psalm. It was probably a coronation ode in the ancient New Year Festival.[1] The verse about God's 'begetting' of his son is equivalent to v. 6, being a poetic metaphor for the religious significance of the act of enthronement. In later days, when all such psalms were interpreted eschatologically, this became a truly messianic psalm in the strict sense, and a grasp of its poetry would suggest that this verse should be connected with the moment of revelation of the Messiah, rather than literally with the time of his physical birth (for which the thought of God's begetting would be felt to be inappropriate and distasteful, if not blasphemous). To the early Church the Resurrection, and its special aspect of Heavenly Session, was precisely the moment of this expected revelation. Granted that Ps. 2.7 is a metaphor of enthronement, then it can be claimed that the expectation embodied in the whole psalm has been fulfilled in Jesus. The argument is very close to that of Ps. 110.1.

We may thus feel fairly confident that Luke is here reproducing the original application of this psalm. This is all the more probable, seeing that he has refrained from introducing this messianic motif in connection with the work of John the Baptist (contrast Acts 10.37f., where the Baptism unmistakably implies messianic anointing). There is also no hint here that our Lord is 'Son of God' in any other sense than the messianic psalm itself means by the expression.

It is from this Resurrection usage that the references to Ps. 2.7 in Hebrews are derived. It is true that the quotation of it in 1.5

---

[1] S. Mowinckel, *Psalmenstudien* III, 1923, pp. 80-88; A. Bentzen, *King and Messiah*, ET 1955, ch. II.

follows a statement of the pre-existence and eternal sonship of Jesus in the opening verses. But the thought which dominates the whole chapter, and makes the climax to the exordium, is his unique position now at the right hand of God (expressed in terms of Ps. 110.1). Then in v. 5 there is a series of messianic testimonies, beginning with Ps. 2.7. These serve to bring out the implications of the Heavenly Session. They are skilfully concluded by the second half of Ps. 110.1, bringing the catena to its full circle. Consequently the quotation retains its original connection with the Resurrection, though probably including metaphysical implications not present in the earlier period.

In Heb. 5.5 it is quoted purely and simply as a messianic text, along with Ps. 110.4, 'Thou art a priest for ever after the order of Melchizedek'. The argument of the Epistle at this point gains new importance from the messianic expectations of the Qumran Covenanters.[1] They preserved strictly the idea that the proper government of the People of God should be (and would be) by both a priestly and a secular Messiah, the high priest taking precedence over the other. This sharply differentiates their view from that of the early Church, which in other respects shows remarkable parallels.[2] From this point of view the Christian polity was defective. To meet such a criticism as this may well be one of the chief apologetic motives of Hebrews.[3] The argument of Heb. 5.5f. exactly corresponds to this situation, and could be paraphrased as follows: So also the Messiah did not arrogate to himself the dignity of high priest; but he who spoke one classic messianic text (i.e. Ps. 2.7) said also in the same way in another (i.e. Ps. 110), 'Thou art a priest', etc. Hence one man fulfils the roles of both Messiahs. It is clear that the use of Ps. 2.7 here is entirely devoid of any interest in the idea of the eternal generation of the Son, but is confined to the messianic implications, agreed by all sides. In 7.28 the phrase 'a Son, perfected for evermore' succinctly combines both testimonies and links them to the Heavenly Session.

The use of the whole psalm in connection with Christ's victory

---

[1] Cf. K. G. Kuhn, 'The Two Messiahs of Aaron and Israel', in *The Scrolls and The New Testament*, pp. 54–64.

[2] These are collected by O. Cullmann, 'The Significance of the Qumran Texts for Research into the Beginnings of Christianity', in the same volume, pp. 18–32 (reprinted from *JBL* 74, 1955).

[3] Cf. R. E. Brown, 'The Qumran Scrolls and the Johannine Gospel and Epistles', in the same volume, p. 290 n. 111.

is continued in Revelation, though the seventh verse is not actually cited.[1] The only place where a suspicion of further interpretation appears is 12.5, which reads: καὶ ἔτεκεν υἱὸν ἄρσεν, ὃς μέλλει ποιμαίνειν πάντα τὰ ἔθνη ἐν ῥάβδῳ σιδηρᾷ. The reading ἄρσεν (A C) for ἄρσενα is probably original, being derived from ἔτεκεν ἄρσεν in Isa. 66.7. So υἱόν has been inserted ungrammatically, and the other textual authorities have felt bound to adjust the adjectival agreement. In view of the following words from Ps. 2.9, and the fact that υἱόν is otiose, there may here be an allusion to Ps. 2.7. This means that the metaphor of birth has been concretized to express the idea of *Messias designatus* at his birth, rather than *revelatus*. It is doubtful whether any metaphysical implications are present.

The evidence for the application of Ps. 2.7 to the Resurrection gives probability to the suggestion that it is this testimony that Paul is referring to in Rom. 1.4. Here Jesus is described as τοῦ ὁρισθέντος υἱοῦ θεοῦ ἐν δυνάμει κατὰ πνεῦμα ἁγιωσύνης ἐξ ἀναστάσεως νεκρῶν. This is a clear instance of the messianic sonship of Jesus in terms of the *Messias revelatus* at his Resurrection. The whole phrase aptly summarizes our argument about the use of this passage in the primitive apologetic.

On the other hand the citation of Ps. 2.1f. in the prayer of Acts 4.24-30, in spite of the archaic δέσποτα and τὸν ἅγιον παῖδά σου, is probably due to Luke's own composition.[2] The 'plot' of the psalm has been fitted to the events of the Passion in a way that appears to be dependent on Luke's own Passion narrative, and the messianic anointing in this case must be referred to the Baptism, as in 10.38. The implication is that, by the time this was written, Ps. 2.7 has already become well established in connection with the Baptism, although Luke uses the older application in Acts 13, as we have seen. It is interesting that Justin Martyr, who twice cites this verse as the baptismal *vox Dei*,[3] similarly traces the plot of the psalm in relation to the hostility of the Jewish and imperial rulers when he writes out Pss. 1 and 2 in full, and thereby implies that v. 7 is fulfilled in the Resurrection without mention of the Baptism.[4] So the original application lingers on.

---

[1] Allusions to Ps. 2 occur in Rev. 2.26 (vv. 8f.), 6.15 (2), 11.15 (2), 11.18 (1, 5, 12), 12.5 (9), 17.18 (2), 19.15 (9), 19.19 (2).
[2] J. A. T. Robinson, 'The Most Primitive Christology of all?', p. 179.
[3] *Dial.* 88; 103.
[4] *I Apol.* 40. This continuous citation of the first two psalms as one

The reason for linking this verse to Isa. 42.1 in the baptismal saying is precisely its function of expressing (poetically) the moment when the Messiah is revealed. It is probable that the original form of the saying was something similar to the version of Isa. 42.1 found in Matt. 12.18, which lays all the emphasis on the element of the divine choice. When the needs of apologetic demand that this experience be adduced as the divine manifestation of Jesus as the Messiah, the opening words of the text are adapted in the *pesher* manner to suggest Ps. 2.7, which has now become a classic text of the *Messias revelatus*. Alternatively we cannot be sure that Isa. 42.1 was at first applied to the Baptism. It too may have been used with reference to the Resurrection. In that case, the conflation of the two texts could have happened before the whole is used to interpret the Baptism. At any rate, the use of the resultant text in the Baptism narrative serves the purpose of defining it as a messianic manifestation. Matt. 3.17 takes this a stage further by putting the words in the third person, to make it a declaration to the crowd, not just to Jesus himself.

The same motive accounts for the use of this conflate text again in the Transfiguration (Mark 9.7 and par.). Here further modification shows the desire to identify Jesus with the Prophet of Deut. 18.15 (ἀκούετε αὐτοῦ for ἐν σοὶ εὐδόκησα). The general tenor of the episode, as a prevision of the vindication of Jesus as the Son of Man of Dan. 7.13,[1] links it with the Resurrection rather than with the Baptism. It is possible, then, that the conflate text, as a testimony of Jesus' messianic manifestation, has been transferred back from the Resurrection to the Transfiguration and to the Baptism independently. In each case it is to secure the messianic character of his work before the Passion.

### Isaiah 42.1

The other baptismal text is not clearly referred to apart from the Baptism and Transfiguration, except in the long quotation of Isa. 42.1-4 in Matt. 12.18-21. The introductory formula marks it out as a *pesher* quotation, presumably developed in response to the needs of apologetic. Comparison of the form of the text with the

psalm may be connected with the strange reading τῷ πρώτῳ of D *gig* Origen at Acts 13.33, cf. Westcott and Hort, *The NT in Greek* II, 1882, Appendix p. 95.
[1] J. A. T. Robinson, *Jesus and His Coming*, p. 133.

Hebrew and the Versions shows that this development has been extremely complex.[1]

Before we examine Matthew's version, it will be well to consider Isa. 42.1-4 just as it stands. These four verses are complete in themselves, but after an impressive new announcement (v. 5) are repeated in a different form in vv. 6f. The theme is God's choice of the Servant to establish the new reign of justice, which will include the Gentiles in its scope. It is a plausible assumption that this is how the earliest Christians interpreted this passage. The opening words, 'Behold, my servant', seem to imply the moment of revealing, which is in the first instance the Resurrection. That is the moment when Jesus is designated as the Lord's Servant; his new life shows him to be filled with the Spirit, and so constitutes the anointing to his task; and his work of preaching proceeds by peaceful means, and is destined to cover the whole world. This is a general interpretation of the whole passage, in line with the original affirmation of the Resurrection faith, which does not presuppose any intentional deviations from the Hebrew.

A striking parallel to this hypothetical interpretation is to be found in the poetical kerygmatic summary of I Tim. 3.16: 'He who was manifested in the flesh, justified in the spirit, seen of angels, preached among the nations, believed on in the world, received up in glory.' Here, although the first phrase refers to the Incarnation of the pre-existent Son of God, 'justified in the spirit' means the Easter victory, which reveals the hidden plan of redemption which even the angels had not previously known (I Peter 1.12). The preaching to the Gentiles until all the world is evangelized is the earthly counterpart to the glory which has now been manifested. The value of this comparison is that we have here the Resurrection as the real moment of revelation, when God's initiative in the Incarnation is at last seen to be vindicated, and we also find the preaching to the Gentiles as an essential element of the redemptive work.

From the general interpretation we can trace selective use of the passage for specific purposes. The first verse ('Behold my servant, whom I uphold; my chosen, in whom my soul delighteth: I have

---

[1] To Stendahl (*SSM*, pp. 107-15), who gives this text an exhaustive examination, the complex history makes it a valuable witness to his theory of the exegetical work of the local Matthean 'school'. It will be shown, however, that the process of adaptation was motivated by apologetic considerations, and that the resulting text owes nothing to its present context.

put my spirit upon him') can be used to express the messianic
anointing. As has been suggested, this need not have been in the
first place anything else than one way of looking at the Resurrection
itself. The conflation with Ps. 2.7 helps to show that it is truly the
*messianic* anointing. However, we do not find it so used, but only
in the Baptism and Transfiguration narratives, probably independently. In the latter case, the idea of anointing has been omitted
altogether, so that the allusion to Isa. 42.1 is confined to the element of the divine *choice*. This appears in the version of Luke 9.35,
where ἐκλελεγμένος may be original, Mark's ἀγαπητός being due to
the Baptism narrative.[1] All the emphasis thus goes on the idea of
the messianic choice, which accords well with the motive of the
Transfiguration as an anticipation of the Resurrection. The addition of an allusion to Deut. 18.15 only adds further detail to the
christology, as will be shown in the next chapter.

The Baptism, unlike the Transfiguration, is not an anticipation
of the future revealing, but has become itself the moment of revelation. The story has been written up around Isa. 42.1. The descent
of the Spirit has been identified with the endowment mentioned
in this verse. The divine words, both by their extreme brevity and
by the conflation with Ps. 2.7, are directed solely to proclaiming
the christological importance of the occasion.[2] The use of Isa. 42.1
in the presentation of the Baptism story is also implicit in the
Fourth Gospel. If ἐκλεκτός[3] is the true reading at John 1.34, we
have independent evidence that this text is in mind.

---

[1] Luke is following Mark, but appears to have access to non-Marcan
material.

[2] The use of ἀγαπητός to represent בְּחִירִי shows a weakening of interest
in the element of *choice* in favour of the motif of messianic *manifestation*.
The idea of choice would not have been out of place here, as the reading
at John 1.34 testifies. It has been suggested by D. Plooij, 'The Baptism of
Jesus' in H. G. Wood (ed.), *Amicitiae Corolla* (Essays presented to J. R.
Harris), 1933, p. 247, that ἀγαπητός is to be taken as part of the quotation
of Ps. 2.7 by way of the Targum: 'Beloved as a son to his father thou art
to me.' This was accepted by T. W. Manson ('The OT in the Teaching
of Jesus', *Bulletin of the John Rylands Library* 34, 1951-2, p. 324). But it
is doubtful if this is a pre-Christian comment. It seems rather to be motivated by the desire to avoid metaphysical implications (cf. Dalman, *The
Words of Jesus*, ET 1902, p. 271). It is of course possible that it is due to
the influence of an additional OT text, i.e. Gen. 22.2.

[3] In Luke 23.35 this word is used as a messianic title by the enemies of
Jesus. It does not refer here specifically to Isa. 42.1, but is an accepted
messianic title, just as in Ethiopian *Enoch* 39.6, etc. Nevertheless it is
probably derived ultimately from Isa. 42.1.

We have now passed from the use of this passage to provide messianic interpretation of the Resurrection to its use to give this significance to the Baptism, at the outset of the ministry. The next step is to reinterpret the rest of the passage to explain Jesus' work. If his preaching and healing activity had been simply that of a religious leader or rabbi, the question would not have arisen in the same way. But once the revaluation of him as the Messiah has been pushed back to the Baptism, it is necessary to answer the objection that this work did not follow a recognizably messianic pattern. It is to deal with this question that the *pesher* version of Isa. 42.1-4 has been evolved, before being incorporated into Matt. 12.18-21. The significance of the modifications can be appreciated most readily, if the passage is examined verse by verse.

| Matt. 12.18 | Isa. 42.1 | |
|---|---|---|
| ἰδοὺ ὁ παῖς μου | Ἰακὼβ ὁ παῖς μου, | הן עבדי |
| ὃν ᾑρέτισα, | ἀντιλήμψομαι αὐτοῦ· | אתמך בו |
| ὁ ἀγαπητός μου | Ἰσραὴλ ὁ ἐκλεκτός μου, | בחירי |
| ὃν εὐδόκησεν | προσεδέξατο αὐτὸν | רצתה |
| ἡ ψυχή μου· θήσω | ἡ ψυχή μου· ἔδωκα | נפשי נתתי |
| τὸ πνεῦμά μου ἐπ' | τὸ πνεῦμά μου ἐπ' | רוחי עליו |
| αὐτόν, καὶ κρίσιν τοῖς | αὐτόν, κρίσιν τοῖς | משפט |
| ἔθνεσιν ἀπαγγελεῖ. | ἔθνεσιν ἐξοίσει. | לגוים יוציא: |

The quotation begins with characteristics which concern the earlier use of the text. The idea of choice is already reached in the use of ᾑρέτισα for אתמך בו.[1] ἀγαπητός (if not simply due to the Baptism narrative) is a possible translation of בחירי, because the idea of choice has already been included in the verb, and has been adopted to aid the messianic interpretation.[2] The verb θήσω places the anointing within the future work, now fulfilled, of course, in Jesus. So far no modification for a new application has been introduced. This begins with the last word of the verse, where ἀπαγγελεῖ (cf. the Targum יגלי) changes the idea of 'bringing forth judgment' from acting decisively to the work of preaching.

[1] The translator has taken it to mean 'grasp', 'lay hold of', cf. Prov· 3.18 MT.
[2] The next phrase, ὃν εὐδόκησεν, is a Palestinian rendering, also preserved by Theodotion and Symmachus.

| Matt. 12.19 | Isa. 42.2 | |
|---|---|---|
| οὐκ ἐρίσει οὐδὲ | οὐ κεκράξεται οὐδὲ | לא יצעק ולא |
| κραυγάσει, οὐδὲ | ἀνήσει, οὐδὲ | ישא ולא |
| ἀκούσει τις ἐν ταῖς | ἀκουσθήσεται | ישמיע |
| πλατείαις τὴν φωνὴν | ἔξω ἡ φωνὴ | בחוץ קולו: |
| αὐτοῦ. | αὐτοῦ. | |

It has long been recognised that ἐρίσει represents a mistranslation of *naribh* of the Syriac Peshitta version of Isa. 42.2. This means 'cry aloud', and exactly corresponds to the *second* verb in the Hebrew text.[1] But the same root in Hebrew has the meaning 'strive' or 'plead'. Stendahl (*SSM*, pp. 111f.) maintains that this is not a mistake due to ignorance of the language, but represents the deliberate choice of a reading presumably already current in an Aramaic Targum. This has been done with the licence exemplified in the double meanings of the *Habakkuk Commentary*.[2] The transposition of this verb to the first place in the sentence is designed to make it more emphatic.

According to Stendahl, the reason for this modification is to be found in the actual Matthean context. The text has been adapted to illustrate Jesus' withdrawal from controversy with the Pharisees (v. 15). On the contrary, we have already seen enough of Matthew's *pesher* quotations to feel fairly confident that the process of adaptation is complete before they are incorporated into the Gospel.[3] Following the normal procedure of Form Criticism, we must interpret the passage out of itself without regard to its present context. The most probable motive that springs to mind is the patient and silent suffering of Jesus which is a feature of the Passion apologetic. For the purpose of proving that the whole ministry of Jesus is a messianic act, this feature is shown to be a consistent characteristic of it, and the chosen text from Isaiah is modified accordingly. Matthew's context narrows this down to a specific instance for the

---

[1] It should properly have the object 'his voice' expressed, as in Num. 14.1 Pesh., but omits it here in common with the Hebrew. The Peshitta version of Isa. 42.2 reads: *la' neq'e' wla' naribh wla' nashma' qaleh*, and this has been followed by the Old Syriac at Matt. 12.19, apparently unconcerned by Matthew's exceptional text; but Matt. 12.19 Pesh. translates the Greek without using the word: *la' nethchre' wla' neq'e'*.

[2] E.g. 1QpHab. on Hab. 1.9, where MT קְדִימָה ( = towards the east) has been read as קָדִים in order to permit an interpretation based on the meaning 'east wind'.

[3] *Supra*, pp. 117-22

sake of the narrative. At the end of the verse the active verb ἀκούσει
τις, and the concrete phrase ἐν ταῖς πλατείαις (for the adverbial
בחוץ) help to impress the quietness of our Lord's ministry.

| Matt. 12.20f. | Isa. 42.3f. | |
|---|---|---|
| κάλαμον συντετριμ- | κάλαμον (συν)τεθλασ- | קנה רצוץ |
| μένον οὐ κατεάξει | μένον οὐ συντρίψει | לא ישבור |
| καὶ λίνον τυφό- | καὶ λίνον καπνιζό- | ופשתה כהה |
| μενον οὐ σβέσει, | μενον οὐ σβέσει, | לא יכבנה |
| | ἀλλὰ εἰς ἀλήθειαν | לאמת |
| | ἐξοίσει κρίσιν. | יוציא משפט: |
| | 4 ἀναλάμψει | לא יכהה |
| | καὶ οὐ θραυσθήσεται | ולא ירוץ |
| ἕως ἂν ἐκβάλῃ εἰς | ἕως ἂν θῇ ἐπὶ | עד ישים |
| νῖκος τὴν κρίσιν. | τῆς γῆς κρίσιν· | בארץ משפט |
| 21 καὶ τῷ ὀνόματι | καὶ ἐπὶ τῷ ὀνόματι | ולתורתו |
| αὐτοῦ ἔθνη ἐλπιοῦσιν. | αὐτοῦ ἔθνη ἐλπιοῦσιν. | איים ייחלו: |

Just as in v. 18 the notion of 'bringing forth judgment' had to be
softened, so in this verse the same phrase is omitted altogether.
The next words, 'he shall not burn dimly nor be bruised', militate
against the desired interpretation of a peaceful ministry ending in
the apparent failure of the cross. The effect of these omissions is to
telescope the two closely similar phrases about judgment.[1]

When the translator continues the quotation, however, he alters
it considerably, apparently under the influence of Hab. 1.4.[2] This
verse begins the surviving text of the *Habakkuk Commentary*, and
the comment is fragmentary, but appears to apply it to the persecution of the Teacher of Righteousness and his successors. So also
Jesus only succeeded in 'bringing forth judgment' after persecution
and the cross. The allusion to Hab. 1.4 here may carry a hint of
this idea, thus forming another link between the development of
this quotation and the Passion apologetic. It is highly significant
that ideas of active and decisive methods have been carefully suppressed until this climax is reached, where εἰς νῖκος suggests the

---

[1] Compare the telescoping of equivalent phrases in the *pesher* quotation
of Zech. 11.13 in Matt. 27.9f.

[2] ἕως ἂν ἐκβάλῃ εἰς νῖκος τὴν κρίσιν represents עד־יוציא לנצח משפט,
cf. Hab. 1.4 ולא־יצא לנצח משפט. The supposition of, O. Bauernfeind
(*TWNT* IV, p. 944) that εἰς νῖκος translates לאמת in the lines omitted
from Isa. 42.3 is less likely.

Resurrection victory.[1] The idea of non-violence is maintained to the end,[2] which suggests the apologetic motive that the political charge against Jesus was false. The climax is important, for it renders the quotation suitable for the desired interpretation, in which the Resurrection is the open proof that the quiet work of teaching (and the subsequent patient suffering) was a proper messianic ministry. It is true that he acted as *Messias incognitus*, but his work nonetheless conformed to the canons of messianic prophecy.

For the final words of the quotation, Matt. 12.21 has the version of the Septuagint, which differs markedly from the Hebrew. This is sufficiently unexpected to suggest that the verse is an interpolation, though it is found in all manuscripts except one minuscule. But the verse so well rounds off the oracle of Isa. 42.1-4 (in fact it only represents three words in the Hebrew text), that it is unlikely that it should not be included in the quotation in some form. These words in the original—'the isles shall wait for his law'—are consistent with the general interpretation in terms of the Resurrection. Both the 'land' and the 'isles' (Palestine and the Diaspora?) are to receive the benefits of the inauguration of the messianic kingdom. They are equally consonant with the reinterpretation in terms of the quiet messianic ministry culminating in the Resurrection and subsequent proclamation. If they dropped out when the text was modified for this purpose, it was not because they were unsuitable, but because the alteration in the preceding phrase under the influence of Hab. 1.4 had virtually entailed the abandonment of strict citation of the passage already. On the other hand it is more likely that these words were retained, but in a form closer to the Hebrew.

It is not difficult to see why the words were finally conformed to the Septuagint. As the Church spread beyond Judaea, the question of the admission of the Gentiles became increasingly important.

---

[1] The Hebrew meaning of נצח = 'everlastingness' and the Aramaic 'victory', come from a common root meaning 'to shine', cf. S. R. Driver, *Notes on the Hebrew Text of the Books of Samuel*[2], 1913, pp. 128f. Aquila adopted εἰς νῖκος as the regular translation of the phrase (A. Rahlfs, 'Über Theodotion-Lesarten im Neuen Testament und Aquila-Lesarten bei Justin', *ZNW* 20, 1921, pp. 186-9). This may have been partly due to the desire for a rendering distinct from that chosen for עולם, and partly due to assonance (like שכן and σκηνόω in John 1.14). That it did not originate with Aquila is proved by I Cor. 15.54. It is an interpretation which would be congenial to the early Christians, though not found elsewhere in the NT.

[2] The verb ἐκβάλλω does not necessarily involve violence, unless the context requires it. Contrast v. 35 with vv. 24-28.

The later chapters of Isaiah are specially useful in dealing with this matter, and the Septuagint version frequently favours universalism by comparison with the Hebrew.[1] In this case the changes involved serve two purposes. The possible limitation of scope to the Jewish Diaspora only is avoided, and the messianic work is saved from confusion with the extension of the Mosaic Law. For the use of Septuagint texts in this way, we may compare St Paul's catena in Rom. 15.9-12. This seems to represent a stage of development after the adaptation of the text for its main purpose with regard to Christ's work is complete. But even so, it must surely have been done *before* Matthew adopted the quotation, because it plays no part in the functioning of the quotation in the context he has chosen for it.

The analysis of the whole passage as it stands in Matthew has shown traces of four successive phases of application—the Resurrection, the Baptism, the gentle ministry, and the Gentile mission. There remains the question why Matthew has inserted it into its present context. In the preceding verses (Matt. 12.15f.) he is rapidly summarizing Mark 3.7-12. He dispenses with almost all the information given in his source, and consequently throws one point into greater prominence, the charge of secrecy. This is the application of Isa. 42.1-4 as he sees it, and the reason why he now inserts it. He is probably quite unaware of the real point of the adaptation of the text, to prove that the gentleness of Christ's methods is consistent with the Church's claim about him. On the contrary he has simply drawn *from Mark* the idea of a 'messianic secret'. The passage in its modified form suits this idea admirably. But this is an individual application, produced by the one writer's dependence on the other, and so tells us nothing further about the apologetic use of Isa. 42.1-4. Nor can it be taken as evidence of an apologetic in terms of the 'messianic secret' as this idea is usually understood, i.e. that Jesus himself was both claiming to be the Messiah and hiding the fact at the same time. That seems to be a Marcan construction upon the Gospel traditions.[2] The reality to which this idea testifies is the fact that, though Jesus was actually the Messiah, he avoided a recognizably messianic programme. As

---

[1] I. L. Seeligmann, *The Septuagint Version of Isaiah*, Leiden, 1948, pp. 110ff., has shown that the translator intended exactly the opposite. But the frequent use of σωτηρία gives this impression.

[2] Cf. Vincent Taylor, *St Mark*, pp. 122-4.

we have seen, the pre-Matthean development of Isa. 42.1-4 was precisely directed to coping with this problem.[1]

## Isaiah 61.1

Before leaving this section on the baptismal texts, a word must be said about Isa. 61.1, which includes the important word ἔχρισεν. This invites the use of this passage in connection with the moment of messianic manifestation. It is possible that, like the other texts which we have studied in this section, it was first used of the Resurrection in this sense, but there is no evidence for this. It is applied to the Baptism as the messianic anointing in Acts 4.27, 10.38. On this basis it becomes possible to use phrases from the same verse to show the messianic character of our Lord's ministry. This is found in the Q material Matt. 5.3 = Luke 6.20 and Matt. 11.5 = Luke 7.22. Finally the verse is quoted in full in Luke 4.18f. to show the work as the direct consequence of the messianic anointing at the Baptism. The use of this passage thus shows a similarity to the development noted in Isa. 42.1-4. Accordingly it must be pronounced an insecure basis for speculations concerning our Lord's 'messianic consciousness'.

## 2. CHRIST'S HIDDEN WORK

The analysis of Isa. 42.1-4 has brought us to the problem of the discrepancy between our Lord's ministry and what might be expected of a messianic claimant. This question occupies an important place in the primitive apologetic. It was finally resolved by a

---

[1] The distinction is an important one, though not easy to grasp. The idea of the 'messianic secret' presupposes that Jesus was conscious of being the Messiah in the traditional sense, but that he deliberately held the fact in reserve. This is one way of solving the discrepancy between the facts about Jesus and the popular notions about messiahship. Our apologetic furnishes a different solution. It maintains that the popular idea is inadequate, and that a proper appreciation of messianic scriptures proves that there is no real discrepancy at all. Neither of these explanations is likely to be historically correct. In so far as he was conscious of being the Messiah at all, he was creating a new definition of messiahship. And in spite of the protestations to the contrary, this was soon turned into christology in the hands of the early Christians. The problem is similar to the classic dilemma of dogmatic theologians, viz. how to explain the discrepancy between the doctrine found in the NT and traditional orthodox belief. See Owen Chadwick, *From Bossuet to Newman: the Idea of Doctrinal Development*, 1957, esp. pp. 153f.

natural evolution, in which the work of Jesus, as remembered and interpreted by the Church, itself became the definition of Messiah's function. The various Scripture passages adduced for apologetic purposes naturally hold key-places in this transformation.

Two passages from Isa. 53 have already been shown to have been used in this connection.[1] The first of these is Isa. 53.1, quoted in Rom. 10.16 and John 12.38. This was selected from the Passion chapter to deal with the problem of the unbelief of the Jews. Whereas Paul in Romans retains the general application to unbelief of the Gospel message, though now relating it specially to the Gentiles controversy, John applies it to the Jews' refusal to accept the evidence of our Lord's miracles. This shows the transference of interest to the messianic import of the ministry of Jesus. The rather artificial way in which his 'signs' are constantly argued about in the Fourth Gospel is probably the result of looking at him through the prism of this early apologetic. It is obviously to the advantage of the Church to emphasize the miracles in face of this problem, and this may be one motive for the collection of them in the Gospel tradition.

The other text is Isa. 53.4, quoted in Matt. 8.17 in the form 'Himself took our infirmities and bare our diseases'. The significance of the non-Septuagint form of the text has already been discussed on p. 86. Something further must now be said about the introduction of this quotation into its present context. Matt. 8.16 is a summary of our Lord's work of healing and exorcism, manifestly based on Mark 1.32-34, though greatly abbreviating it. This is exactly parallel to Matthew's procedure which we have just noticed in connection with Isa. 42.1-4. It is very interesting that he has these *pesher* quotations, and cannot find any way of including them in his narrative, except to take the opportunity afforded by nondescript general statements. We noticed in the other case (Matt. 12.15f. = Mark 3.7-12) that he reduced his source in such a way as to concentrate attention upon the one point (the charge of secrecy) which the quotation could illustrate. The same thing happens here also. In v. 16b he transposes the Marcan phrases, so that the exorcisms come first, and the healings second. The command to secrecy is omitted altogether. This throws all the emphasis on the healings, and brings them into direct relation with the quotation of Isa. 53.4, which he now inserts. At the same time we can

[1] *Supra*, pp. 86f.

now see that he is saving up the command to secrecy in order to bring in his citation of Isa. 42.1-4 at a later stage.

It follows that the application of the one passage to the healing miracles is likely to be as arbitrary and unprecedented as the application of the other to the 'messianic secret'. In fact the application of Isa. 53.4 to healing miracles is not really appropriate. It only becomes possible if the verbs have the meaning 'take away',[1] which is certainly not the meaning of the Hebrew they translate, and contrary to the intention of the original context. It does not mean that Jesus cured diseases, but that he bore them himself. We have previously decided that the proper Christian understanding of this verse is the atoning efficacy of the Passion. But because it is a literal translation of the Hebrew, it is necessary to see a real reference to the diseases of the people who came to Jesus, when the verse is selected for a particular purpose in isolation from the whole context. As such, it may have been used to relate Christ's healing miracles to his total work of redemption. It thus widens the scope of the great Passion prophecy from the strict Passion apologetic to the whole of our Lord's ministry. The healings are as much a part of his messianic work as the Passion itself. It was prophesied that the Lord's Servant would bear our diseases, and Jesus both removed men's diseases by his miracles and himself suffered their pains on the cross. These were not the acts of a wonder-worker, but should have been recognized as the proper work of the Christ, even if he was only *Messias incognitus*.

When Matthew incorporates this quotation in its present context, he loses sight of the connection with the cross. All that he is interested in is the fact that the work of healing can receive warrant from Scripture. The purpose is pictorial rather than apologetic. The details of the life of Jesus are already present in the revelation given to the prophets. But Matthew scarcely realizes that his use of the verse accords ill with its real meaning.

### Our Lord's Use of Parables

The effect of the two quotations which we have so far studied in this section is to prove that when Jesus did acts of healing he

---

[1] Arndt and Gingrich, *Lexicon of the NT* (ET of Bauer's *Wörterbuch*), 1957, mention Galen as using βαστάζω in the sense of removing disease. But there is no NT parallel. Ignatius, *Polyc.* 1.3, alludes to Matt. 8.17, but appears to apply the verse to sympathetic pastoral ministry to the sick.

was acting as the Messiah. This raises the question whether people can be held culpable for failing to recognize this. This aspect of the matter appears in a further pair of texts which are concerned with our Lord's use of parables. The analysis will show that the early Church not unnaturally adopted the position that failure to see the messianic character of his work was really caused by the people's own blindness. There was a fundamental refusal to understand and to believe.

We begin by observing how Matthew precisely repeats with regard to the parables the procedure he had used for healings and exorcisms. He takes two virtually equivalent Marcan summaries, abbreviates them to make one point each, and adds what he thinks to be the appropriate testimony in each case.[1] The matter is further complicated, however, by the fact that the earlier passage about parables already contains the quotation material (i.e. Isa. 6.9f.) in the Marcan original; and this is a quotation which has wide ramifications throughout the New Testament.

The first summary is Mark 4.10-12. It is a short paragraph on the reason for parables, largely based on Isa. 6.9f., which Mark has inserted here to 'mark time' between the parable of the sower and its interpretation. Matthew does not add a new quotation, but on the other hand abbreviates the Marcan version still further, when he rewrites this in Matt. 13.10-16.[2] His improvements consist in (a) the insertion of the proverbial saying about 'Whosoever hath, to him shall be given', etc., from Mark 4.25; and (b) the addition of a Q saying about the blessedness of the disciples, which has a closely similar vocabulary to that of the Isaiah allusion. These improvements have the sole motive of enhancing the superiority of the disciples, who have the secret knowledge which others fail to perceive. The inserted verse properly denotes a warning against

[1] For similar treatment of Q material in Matthew, see V. Taylor, 'The original order of Q', in A. J. B. Higgins (ed.), *New Testament Essays: Studies in memory of T. W. Manson*, 1959, pp. 250f., 255.

[2] Matt. 13.14f. contains the full citation of Isa. 6.9f., with an unusual version of the introductory formula. Although these verses are found in all our MS authorities, they cannot be accepted as part of the true text. Unlike all the other formula-quotations, this follows the LXX exactly. The variation of the formula is due to the partial citation of the text itself in the preceding verse. It is quite uncharacteristic for Matthew to insert the quotation suggested by the words of Jesus. He always uses testimonies which can give messianic warrant to the actions of Jesus. On the other hand, any reader of this Gospel would feel tempted to insert the quotation obviously implied, seeing that the book is so rich in warrants from Scripture.

taking spiritual privilege for granted. It retains this in its Marcan context (Mark 4.21-5, otherwise omitted by Matthew), and even more clearly in its Q version at the end of the parable of the talents (Matt. 25.29 = Luke 19.26). But here it actually increases the sense of privilege, which directly contradicts our Lord's intention! The added Q saying on the blessedness of the disciples is really concerned with the blessedness of the *present generation*, when the kingdom of God is breaking in, by contrast with the unfulfilled hopes of previous generations. But Matthew has made it underline the good fortune of the disciples as a privileged *élite*.

The second summary is Mark's conclusion to the chapter (Mark 4.33f.).[1] In Matt. 13.34 Matthew takes over the first of these two verses, which says that Jesus gave all his teaching in the form of parables. But he suppresses the other, which tells how Jesus afterwards interpreted them to the disciples privately. Instead he inserts from his own stock the formula-quotation of Ps. 78.2: 'I will open my mouth in parables; I will utter things hidden from the foundation [of the world].' These changes thus cut out any further mention of the privilege of the disciples, which had been specifically developed in the former summary, and place the emphasis solely on the intentional obscurity of Jesus' public teaching. We shall see that in both cases Matthew's interpretation of the material is the end of a process which reflects changing conditions in the Church. As the second is much the simpler one of the two, it will be best to consider it first.

| Matt. 13.35 | Ps. 78.2 | |
|---|---|---|
| ἀνοίξω ἐν παραβολαῖς τὸ στόμα μου, | ἀνοίξω ἐν παραβολαῖς τὸ στόμα μου, | אפתחה במשל פי |
| ἐρεύξομαι κεκρυμμένα ἀπὸ καταβολῆς. | φθέγξομαι προβλήματα ἀπ' ἀρχῆς. | אביעה חידות מני קדם: |

The keyword for Matthew is ἐν παραβολαῖς. As the whole of the first line is identical with the Septuagint, it probably represents the final stage of the adaptation of the text. This is to make it specifically applicable to the use of parables. For earlier stages we have to look at the second line, which is an independent rendering of the Hebrew text. This was not necessarily concerned with para-

---

[1] Matthew (who has his own conclusion in 13.51f.) uses this Marcan material as the 'sandwich filling' between his parable of the tares and its interpretation.

bles at all. The most notable feature of it is the translation κεκρυμ-μένα ( =things kept hidden) for חידות ( =riddles).[1] This directly contradicts what is said in Ps. 78.3f., that these things have been handed down from the fathers, and 'we will not hide them'[2] from succeeding generations. Thus this version disregards the context, presumably intentionally.

Nevertheless there is evidence that this psalm was used by at any rate one circle in the Church with closer attention to its meaning. In John 6.31 our Lord's opponents quote v. 24: 'He gave them bread out of heaven to eat.'[3] The objection is that Jesus' claim to be the Messiah is invalidated by his failure to repeat the miracle of the manna. It is evident that the feeding of the multitude is held by John to be a proper repetition of this miracle. But the teaching shows that the miracle is fulfilled more truly at a much deeper level. This implies an interpretation of the whole psalm in terms of our Lord's redeeming work. The psalm is a poetical narrative of the acts of God in redemption. The elaborate opening verses, speaking darkly of a mystery from the foundation of the world, are intended to show that such acts are always true of God. The whole thing is thus an expression of faith, that he who acted in this way can do so again. In the same way, those who try to figure out eschatological programmes can expect the same acts to be repeated. This was perhaps too naively imagined by some. But if the Jews objected that Jesus had failed to perform the repetition of acts of redemption expected in the eschatological programme, the Church could reply that he had indeed fulfilled it, though in a mystery. This is an apologetic motive for the feeding miracles.[4] And it also shows how Jesus was truly acting as the Messiah in the time *before* his Crucifixion.

We have now arrived at an intelligible reason for κεκρυμμένα as a rendering of חידות. These 'riddles' are the righteous acts of God in redemption, as the psalm itself implies. The works of Jesus —primarily his atoning death, but also, at this stage in the apolo-

---

[1] Aquila: αἰνίγματα; Symmachus προβλήματα ( =LXX).

[2] LXX: οὐκ ἐκρύβη.

[3] Neh. 9.15 might be the source of this quotation, but the balance is in favour of Ps. 78.24 on account of the word φαγεῖν. See Barrett *ad loc*.

[4] This is of course only a very subsidiary reason for the preservation of these miracles. Their importance in the Gospels is due primarily to the obvious connection with the Eucharist, and also to their relation to the whole theme of the eschatological banquet.

getic, the rest of the ministry—are the final expression of these acts
of redemption. But if it be objected that his works bore little relation to the way in which this was expected, then it invited the
apologist to place the emphasis on the *hiddenness* of God's ways.
To say that Jesus' works were genuinely messianic, but took the
form of חידות, so that they could only be perceived as such by
the elect, solves the whole problem.

Such is the application of Ps. 78 considered as a whole. The
selection of v. 2 as a *pesher* quotation narrows the application to
the *teaching* of Jesus. It is the full and final revelation (cf. Heb.
1.2a). In the first line במשל has a roughly equivalent meaning to
חידות in the second. To apply it to the *parabolic method* is a
further refinement, effected with the aid of the Septuagint rendering. Finally Matthew inserts the resultant text into his parables
chapter for its 'pictorial' value, just as he used Isa. 53.4 at 8.17.

These stages of development reflect the Church's changing outlook. To begin with, the Resurrection is held to be the revelation
of the mystery of redemption, the open demonstration of God's
saving activity to which all previous sacred history has been leading. This idea is commonly met with in the Pauline Epistles, e.g.
I Cor. 2.7, where it characteristically refers principally to the cross.
Secondly the teaching of Jesus is held to be an essential part of
the revelation, though its true significance was known only to the
'elect'. Thus the construction put upon the teaching in the light of
the Resurrection faith is read back as if that was its recognized
meaning all along. This is exactly parallel to the attitude adopted
to the healing miracles.[1] It was a natural position to take, once the
Teacher himself had withdrawn. It is similar to the position of the
Qumran Covenanters, who preserved a tradition of biblical exegesis, derived from their founder, which they regarded as a secret
revealed to the *élite*.[2] The third and final stage is the claim that
this method was a deliberate policy on the part of Jesus, to prevent
the mystery from being revealed to any but the few who are chosen.
It is probable that this idea of a policy of concealment on the part
of our Lord corresponds with an actual impression given by his
anxiety to prevent his own radical reinterpretation of the kingdom
of God from being confused with popular expectations. The special
Marcan nuance in connection with this is the impression that even
the inner group of disciples were themselves equally mystified by

---

[1] *Supra*, p. 154.                    [2] 1QS 5.9; 1QpHab. 2.8.

the parabolic method (Mark 8.17). A concomitant of the final stage is the sect-type doctrine of the Church. The Church is a privileged *élite*, having access to knowledge denied to those outside its ranks.

## Isaiah 6.9f.

We now turn to the earlier paragraph on parables, and look first at the material as it stands in Mark 4.10-13. It is clear that we have here an original saying built on Isa. 6.9f., sandwiched between Marcan editorial matter which considerably alters the sense of it.[1] The nucleus consists of vv. 11f., which is a perfect expression of the doctrine of the *élite*. The mystery of the kingdom is given to the disciples, but to outsiders all things are 'in parables'. The purpose is to sift the people, for (it is assumed) the elect perceive the mystery, but the rejected are blind to it. If ἐν παραβολαῖς represents במשל (collective), as it actually does in the Septuagint of Ps. 78.2, then the original saying was probably more general in intention, and it is Mark who has narrowed it down to parables in the technical sense. Verses 10 and 13 are a typical expression of the disciples' inability to understand them, and, as Knox has pointed out,[2] really amount to a refusal to give an interpretation.

So vv. 11f. must be considered quite apart from the particular question of parables. They are concerned with belief in the message of Jesus, or rather the Church's claim about him. All the emphasis is thrown on the blindness of the outsiders. The passage thus accounts for the *unbelief of the Jews*. Isa. 6.9f. is in fact the classic passage to explain unbelief, and is frequently alluded to in the New Testament. As the doctrine of the *élite* belongs to a secondary stage in the apologetic development, we must look elsewhere for the beginnings of the use of this testimony. It had already undergone development before it reached Mark.

The antiquity of its use may be deduced from the keyword πωρόω or πώρωσις.[3] This is not found in the Septuagint version of the text, but occurs in the form of it cited in John 12.40. We find this word used in a way that evokes this testimony in Mark 3.5, 6.52, 8.17; Eph. 4.18 (all with καρδία); II Cor. 3.14 (with νοήματα, cf. 4.4); Rom. 11.7, 25. For this reason it seems likely that John

---

[1] Briefly explained above in ch. I, p. 18.
[2] W. L. Knox, *Sources of the Synoptic Gospels* I: St Mark, p. 36, regarding the formation of these verses as entirely pre-Marcan.
[3] Cf. Dodd, *Acc. Scrip.*, pp. 36-39.

preserves one of the forms in which the text was current at an early time. It is instructive to compare the three ways in which it is cited in the New Testament.

| Mark 4.12 | John 12.40 | Acts 28.25-27<br>( =Matt. 13.14f. =LXX) |
|---|---|---|
| ἵνα βλέποντες<br>βλέπωσιν καὶ<br>μὴ ἴδωσιν, | [John 9.39: ἵνα οἱ<br>μὴ βλέποντες<br>βλέπωσιν . . .] | ἀκοῇ<br>ἀκούσετε καὶ<br>οὐ μὴ συνῆτε, |
| καὶ ἀκούοντες<br>ἀκούωσιν καὶ<br>μὴ συνιῶσιν, | | καὶ βλέποντες<br>βλέψετε καὶ<br>οὐ μὴ ἴδητε· |
| | τετύφλωκεν<br>αὐτῶν τοὺς<br>ὀφθαλμούς, | ἐπαχύνθη γὰρ<br>ἡ καρδία τοῦ<br>λαοῦ τούτου, |
| | καὶ ἐπώρωσεν<br>αὐτῶν τὴν<br>καρδίαν, | καὶ τοῖς ὠσὶν<br>αὐτῶν βαρέως<br>ἤκουσαν |
| | | καὶ τοὺς ὀφθαλμοὺς<br>αὐτῶν ἐκάμμυσαν, |
| μήποτε | ἵνα μὴ ἴδωσιν<br>τοῖς ὀφθαλμοῖς | μήποτε ἴδωσιν<br>τοῖς ὀφθαλμοῖς<br>καὶ τοῖς ὠσὶν<br>ἀκούσωσιν |
| | καὶ νοήσωσιν<br>τῇ καρδίᾳ | καὶ τῇ καρδίᾳ<br>συνῶσιν, |
| ἐπιστρέψωσιν<br>καὶ ἀφεθῇ αὐτοῖς. | καὶ στραφῶσιν<br>καὶ ἰάσομαι αὐτούς. | καὶ ἐπιστρέψωσιν<br>καὶ ἰάσομαι αὐτούς. |

It will be seen that both Mark and John agree in mentioning the eyes first, spoiling the characteristic chiasmus structure of the original. All the *words* in Mark are derived from the Septuagint, except the final phrase, but the *form* of the quotation is roughly equivalent to John. On the other hand John owes little or nothing to the Septuagint except the final phrase. It is tempting to suppose that Mark has preserved the original ending which John has altered, but there is no possibility of proving it. At any rate, the abbreviation of the text in both cases, and the unexpectedness of the endings, give us a few significant facts from which the process of interpretation may be deduced.

John's form is notable for its brevity, a sign of the desire to use it for one specific purpose. The inversion of clauses, and omission of the phrases about hearing, show an interest in the fundamental disposition to believe. First the text mentions the means of perception, then it goes behind that to the heart, which is the seat of intelligence and the will. The text thus implies that, in spite of God's self-disclosure in Christ, the Jews were blinded by a fatal obstinacy, such as God always gives to the rebellious. This prevented them from accepting the proffered salvation, so that they cut themselves off wilfully. This apologetic is concerned with the response to the Church's message in general.

At the next stage, when the messianic claim has been pushed back to cover our Lord's ministry, it answers a different objection. If the work of Jesus was genuinely messianic, why was it not recognized as such? The answer is that it was so recognized—by those who had eyes to see. This again might have been concerned with the ministry in general to begin with. But when John inserts it at 12.40, he narrows down the application still further. The proper conclusion was not drawn from the evidence of the healing miracles. It is at this point, the third stage of application, that the Septuagint form of the final phrase becomes ironically appropriate. It is thus possible that the words were adapted in this way only at this stage, replacing another form such as Mark's.

The progressive shift of application is parallel to what we found in the case of the companion testimony on unbelief (John 12.38 = Isa. 53.1). That text gave a scriptural warrant for the phenomenon of unbelief. Now the second text has given the scriptural explanation of *how* such a thing could happen. It is significant that both these testimonies are alluded to by Paul in his argument on the rejection of the Jews in Rom. 10.16 (Isa. 53.1) and 11.7 ($\epsilon\pi\omega\rho\acute{\omega}$-$\theta\eta\sigma\alpha\nu$ = Isa. 6.10, John's version).

At the first stage, when the application is to the lack of response to the Church's kerygma, the motive is practical. There is no suggestion of 'vessels of wrath and vessels of honour'. But at the second stage, when this situation is predicated of the ministry of Jesus, it necessarily implies the doctrine of the *élite*. Those whose eyes were open could see all along that Jesus acted as the Messiah. The failure of many to believe, so far from being a count against the Church's later claims, was merely a wilful refusal on their part.

It is at this second stage that Isa. 6.9f. has been used in the pre-Marcan matter of Mark 4.11f. Our Lord's audience consisted of two classes of people, those to whom the mystery of the kingdom is given, and those to whom it remains an insoluble riddle. The work of inaugurating the kingdom in a mystery was deliberate and necessary on account of the innate rebelliousness of men's hearts, just as the blinding of their eyes was in the days of Isaiah.

On the other hand, the final ἀφεθῇ αὐτοῖς of the Marcan form may well go back to the original use of the testimony in the early apologetic. It represents the normal interpretation of ורפא לו in first-century Judaism,[1] and accords with the basic gospel message of the forgiveness of sins.[2] It would indeed have been strange that the Gospel of forgiveness should be so easily refused, if God had not already revealed it through his prophet. Presumably, when Mark incorporated these verses into his parables chapter, he approximated the scriptural words to the Septuagint as far as possible (this seems to be his normal practice), but felt that the last phrase was too different to be altered. It is perfectly suitable for his own use of the testimony for the question about parables.

Mark also contains the verb πωρόω, which has survived in John's version of Isa. 6.10, but not in Mark's. In Mark 3.5 the noun πώρωσις is used to express our Lord's displeasure at the rigidity of the Pharisees about the sabbath. This may reflect something of the hostility towards the Church later on, which first called forth the use of this testimony. The verb appears in 6.52 and 8.17 actually applied to the disciples themselves. They are blind to the messianic implications of the miracles of Jesus. It is possible, of course, that the doctrine of the élite had been challenged—not even the disciples themselves really knew that Jesus was acting as the Messiah during his lifetime. To this it must be replied that they, too, shared the obtuseness of 'this generation', until brought to repentance and belief. But this may be no more than the impression of Mark's method of presentation, with his characteristic 'messianic secret'. It is interesting that 8.17 is followed by words very similar to Isa. 6.9, though in fact much closer to Jer. 5.21 and Ezek. 12.2. This illustrates the tendency of a well-established testimony to attract other related passages to cluster round it.

John's version also seems to lie behind the allusions in II Cor. 3.14, ἐπωρώθη τὰ νοήματα αὐτῶν, and 4.4, ὁ θεὸς τοῦ αἰῶνος τούτου ἐτύφλωσεν τὰ νοήματα τῶν ἀπίστων. In this Epistle the question of unbelief has been transferred to the Judaistic controversy. In ch. 3

---

[1] Targum וישתבקין להון, i.e. reading ורפה לו, an interpretative rather than a mistaken rendering.
[2] Mark 1.4, 2.5; Acts 2.38, 3.19, 10.43, etc.

Paul is saying that the Jews were guilty of *porosis* even in the time of Moses, and that this persists even now when they cling to the old Law. It is thus implied that the mystery which has now been made known in Christ was also known to Moses, but the people failed to recognize it from the very start. We are thus in a very different field of thought from the kind of approach which we found in the Gospels, whether Mark or John. Paul's argument is in fact characteristic of the Hellenistic element in early Christianity, and has much in common with the classic example of it given in Stephen's speech (Acts 7). According to this way of thinking, the failure of the Jews to recognize Jesus as the Christ was due to their failure to perceive the real meaning of the Law from the very beginning. Hence the unbelief of the Jews is a very strong argument against the Judaizers.

But this argument is double-edged. After all, many Gentiles also fail to believe. So in 4.4 Paul uses the same text with regard to the Gentiles. The unbelieving Gentiles are also blind, because they are under the domination of 'the god of this aeon'. Just as the Jews must be freed from the letter of the Law in order to perceive the truth revealed in Jesus, so the Gentiles must be freed in their turn from their own brand of spiritual bondage. The way in which this is expressed is frankly dualistic, and is probably an application of the late Jewish doctrine of the two spirits in man.[1] In these developments Paul is working on the primary use of Isa. 6.9f., i.e. the problem of unbelief in the Gospel message as a whole. There is no suggestion of moving the application backwards to include the messianic interpretation of the earthly ministry of Jesus. Nevertheless this passage about the Gentiles shows how the use of this text tends to lead to the doctrine of the *élite*, distinguishing between those who are blinded and those who are receptive.

We now have two parallel but distinct developments. In the pre-Marcan unit of Mark 4.11f. and in John we have the kind of questioning liable to happen in Palestine, where memories of the impact of the personality of Jesus are still fairly clear, and the claims of the Church about him may be checked by enquiry on the spot.

[1] The importance of this doctrine for Pauline theology is now being more widely recognized as a result of the notable expression of it in the *Manual of Discipline* (1QS 3.15-21), cf. K. G. Kuhn, 'New Light on Temptation, Sin, and Flesh in the NT', in *The Scrolls and the NT*, pp. 94-113.

Paul's usage, on the other hand, reflects the situation which would arise in the course of his missionary work, where there is likely to be a more pragmatic approach. This *porosis* of the Gentiles is mentioned again in Eph. 4.18.

What I have called the doctrine of the *élite* should not be confused with the doctrine of election, which appears when Isa. 6.9f. is referred to yet again in Rom. 11.7, 25. The doctrine of the *élite* only claims that unbelief on the part of some shows up the superiority of the privileged few, which turns the tables on those who say that unbelief is an objection to Christianity. But the doctrine of election makes this a dogmatic theory, that the unbelief of many was actually *necessary* to the working out of redemption. For (it is argued) the old distinction between Jew and Gentile, which was the old criterion of election, had to be abolished, so that a new line of demarcation might be drawn—between believers and unbelievers, whether Gentiles or Jews. The *porosis* of the Jews at large is the reverse side of the idea of the faithful remnant, which is the positive aspect of the doctrine of election (Rom. 11.7). After the verbal allusion to Isa. 6.9f. (ἐπωρώθησαν), Paul adds closely similar scriptural warrant in the form of a conflated adaptation of Isa. 29.10 and Deut. 29.3 (v. 8).

How deeply Paul had thought about this question may be seen from this conflate quotation, which is not merely a matter of catchwords. Deut. 29.3 refers to the Israelites' inability to perceive the meaning of the revelation given to Moses (this time not the Law, but the 'signs and wonders' which accompanied the Exodus). Isa. 29.10 occurs in a context much used in connection with the rejection of the Jews.[1] The necessity of the blindness of the Jews until the evangelization of the Gentiles is complete is a thesis which is to be regarded as a Pauline development, taking the matter a stage further than he had left it in II Corinthians. It is succinctly summarized in Rom. 11.25, where πώρωσις occurs.

There still remains for consideration the full citation of Isa. 6.9f. in Acts 28.26f. Although it is simple enough in itself, the way it is introduced shows some interesting cross-connections with texts of rejection. From the literary point of view Luke has been saving up this quotation as the climax to the repeated theme that Paul was opposed by the Jews, but found a better hearing amongst the

[1] Isa. 28.11 is cited in I Cor. 14.21; Isa. 28.16 in Rom. 9.33, I Peter 2.6; Isa. 29.13 in Mark 7.6f. par.; Isa. 29.14 in I Cor. 1.19.

Gentiles.[1] He has saved *this* text for the purpose, because it is by now the classic passage for the rejection of the Jews.

The quotation is introduced by the following phrase (v. 25b): καλῶς τὸ πνεῦμα τὸ ἅγιον ἐλάλησεν διὰ Ἡσαΐου τοῦ προφήτου πρὸς τοὺς πατέρας ὑμῶν λέγων. This bears a close similarity to the way in which St Mark has introduced another quotation which is very relevant to the same issue (Mark 7.6): καλῶς ἐπροφήτευσεν Ἡσαΐας περὶ ὑμῶν . . . ὡς γέγραπται. . . . The quotation that follows is Isa. 29.13, following the Septuagint, which differs importantly from the Hebrew[2]: 'This people honoureth me with their lips, but their heart is far from me. But in vain do they worship me, teaching as their doctrines the precepts of men.'

Three things may be observed about this. In the first place it is clear that the argument of the whole passage turns on the Septuagint form of the text.[3] Consequently the citation cannot be part of the genuine Gospel tradition. It is probable that our Lord's indictment of the scribes and Pharisees was valued by the Church for use in the Judaistic controversy, and the quotation may have been added to it in the course of it. So it is not surprising to find an allusion to Isa. 29.13 for this purpose in Col. 2.22.[4]

Secondly, although the verse differs from Isa. 6.9f., it belongs

---

[1] This has been well brought out by J. Dupont, 'Le Salut des Gentils et la signification théologique du Livre des Actes', *NTS* 6, 1960, pp. 132-55.

[2]    Mark 7.7                              Isa. 29.13

μάτην δὲ σέβονταί με          μάτην δὲ σέβονταί με          וְתְּהִי יִרְאָתָם
διδάσκοντες διδασκαλίας      διδάσκοντες ἐντάλματα        אֹתִי מִצְוַת
ἐντάλματα ἀνθρώπων.          ἀνθρώπων καὶ διδασκαλίας.    אֲנָשִׁים מְלֻמָּדָה׃

The very slight difference between Mark and LXX contributes to the intention of applying the text to the scribal tradition rather than to formalism.

[3] The passage is clearly composite. The question in v. 5 about washing hands is not actually answered. But the mention of the tradition of the elders has suggested two additions, (*a*) the Isaiah testimony in vv. 6f., and (*b*) a detached saying about *Korban* in vv. 10-12. The remaining verses (8, 9, 13) form the connections, mostly in words taken from vv. 5-8. The first few words of v. 14 are editorial, with πάλιν characteristically marking the transition to new material. This view is shared by Dibelius (*From Tradition to Gospel*, ET 1934, pp. 220-2) and A. Meyer (in *Festgabe für A. Jülicher*, 1927, p. 39), but it must be confessed that there is considerable divergence of opinion among critics concerning these verses.

[4] The phrase ἐντάλματα καὶ διδασκαλίας τῶν ἀνθρώπων shows yet another slight variation from LXX.

to the same polemic. We have already seen this in the use of Isa.
29.10 in Rom. 11.8.[1]

Thirdly, it is not without significance that this is a section of
Mark which Luke has omitted from his Gospel. For there are
several instances of his use of material omitted from the Gospel
in the composition of Acts.[2] This fact probably applies in this case
too. The similarity between Acts 28.25b and Mark 7.6a is thus not
accidental. Luke omitted a large slice of Mark (6.45 - 8.26), presumably because it contains a good deal of reduplication (the feeding of the multitude, for example). But he no doubt saw the point
of the Marcan narrative. It is dominated by the hardened blindness both of the scribes and Pharisees and of the disciples themselves. It ends with the healing of a blind man. Then, where Luke
takes up the Marcan tale once more, the disciples' eyes are opened,
and Peter confesses that Jesus is the Christ (Mark 8.29 = Luke
9.20). Luke saves this up for the end of Acts. Here we find Paul
giving a similar indictment against the Jews. The classic text of
blindness is quoted. It is left to the reader to open his eyes and
confess that Jesus is Christ.

This discussion of the use of Isa. 6.9f. has necessarily been
diffuse, and it may help to give a brief summary of the results.
The original purpose was to explain why certain Jews failed to
accept the Christian message. This was followed by two parallel
developments. On the one hand it was used to explain why the
earthly ministry of Jesus was not universally perceived to be messianic. This usage has left traces in the Gospel tradition. In John
the application is narrowed down to the significance of the healing
miracles. In Mark it is extended to the response of the disciples as
well as of unbelievers. On the other hand it had a special usefulness
in the expansion of Christianity as a weapon to justify preaching to
Gentiles rather than to Jews. Paul takes this even further by using
it both to rebut the claims of the Judaizers and to explain a failure

---

[1] In a more generalized way the 'wisdom' quotation of Isa. 29.14b by
Paul in I Cor. 1.19 is concerned with the issue of response. It is interesting
that Paul has changed κρύψω of LXX ( =MT) into ἀθετήσω. This may be
his own deliberate adaptation.

[2] E.g. in Luke 8.54 the Aramaic words *tlitha' qoumy* are omitted from
Mark, but in Acts 9.40 Luke writes ταβιθά, ἀνάστηθι (Syr. pesh. *tbhitha'
qoumy*); Acts 10.14 ('nothing common or unclean') recalls Mark 7.15, part
of the long section omitted by Luke. See L. S. Thornton, *The Dominion
of Christ*, 1952, p. 24 n. 1, and the references there to Lake and Cadbury,
*The Beginnings of Christianity* I. IV, pp. 8, 69, 111, 134.

of response on the part of the Gentiles. Of course the Judaistic controversy was settled and gradually passed out of mind, so that it was the anti-Judaic application which finally continued into the patristic tradition. The beginning of this must be seen in the last chapter of Acts. It is then found in Justin's *Dialogue with Trypho*.[1] A further patristic development is to be found in Irenaeus. He uses the text to answer the famous difficulty raised by Marcion about the morals of a God who 'hardened Pharaoh's heart',[2] and it is in connection with this question that it passes into Origen.[3]

### 'Out of the mouth of babes'

In this section on Christ's hidden work we have been concerned to show an apologetic which seeks to prove the messianic character of our Lord's miracles and parables, and to account for the lack of response. It was also suggested in a previous chapter that the form of the Palm Sunday story has been influenced by the same motive, whatever may have been the real purpose in the mind of Jesus. This may be a suitable place to add a footnote to that analysis by commenting on Matthew's use of words from Ps. 8.3 (Matt. 21.16): 'Yea, did ye never read, Out of the mouth of babes and sucklings thou hast perfected praise?'

This is a purely Septuagint quotation in a context which has an artificial appearance. The point of the citation depends on the one feature which distinguishes the Septuagint from the Hebrew text (αἶνον for עֹז). Even if it be maintained with Lagrange that this is a correct understanding of the Hebrew in this context,[4] it is much more likely that this text first came into use for the shouts of the people who applauded Jesus in a Greek milieu. In fact Matt. 21.15f., detached from its context, seems to be part of the description of the entry into Jerusalem, rather than the cleansing of the temple (cf. Luke 19.39f.). Its apologetic purpose is to support the

---

[1] *Dial.* 12.2, where words similar to Isa. 6.10 are ascribed to Jeremiah. It is possible that Jer. 5.21 is intended, which seems to lie behind the wording of Mark 8.17. This confusion supports the idea that Justin is drawing on traditional apologetic material.          [2] *Adv. Haer.* IV 29.1.

[3] *De Principiis* III 1.7, cf. *Comm. in Ex.* 10.27.

[4] M.-J. Lagrange, *Évangile selon Saint Matthieu*[3], 1927, p. cxix. The LXX rendering depends on the idea of strength as a theme in an ascription of praise, cf. Ps. 29.1, כָּבוֹד וָעֹז (LXX δόξαν καὶ τιμήν). The argument is, then, that a similar rendering is equally possible in the Aramaic underlying Matthew at this point, so that direct influence from the LXX is not inevitable. But this scarcely carries conviction.

messianic interpretation of the entry. Though the Jewish authorities refused to acknowledge the kingship of Jesus, the 'babes' celebrated his arrival in accordance with prophecy. The acclamation of the common people is taken as evidence of the rightness of the Church's claim about Jesus, because it is they whom the psalm specially mentions as destined to acclaim the Christ.

Now this testimony of the simple is another expression of the doctrine of the *élite*. The 'babes' can be singled out as a privileged class, receptive to the revelation of God in Christ, in contrast with the 'wise and prudent' who are blinded and hardened. We find this in Matt. 11.25, where νηπίοις occurs, and may well be an allusion to Ps. 8.3.[1] But the verse as a whole is largely modelled on Isa. 29.14b, which we have seen is actually cited by St Paul in this range of apologetic in I Cor. 1.19. Whatever be the provenance of Matt. 11.25ff., the passage has clearly been preserved with the apologetic motive which produced the doctrine of the *élite*. It is probably safe to say that the original use of Ps. 8.3 also belongs to this apologetic. It was applied to the triumphal entry because the shouts of the crowd were a well-known feature of the story, and with the aid of this text could be made to enhance the messianic character of it. But we may suspect that Matthew, whose editorial work is evident in transferring this verse to the cleansing of the temple was thinking mainly of its pictorial value, and so he mentions the children in v. 15. This pictorial motive is typical of Matthew.[2]

The matter cannot, however, be left there, for Ps. 8 has important christological use elsewhere. We have already referred to this at the conclusion of the analysis of Ps. 110.1. There we found that the psalm as a whole, and particularly v. 7, is used by three New Testament writers to express the implications of the lordship of the risen Christ.[3] The special value of this psalm is that it enabled early Christian thinkers to express the concept of the risen Lord as the 'inclusive representative'[4] of redeemed humanity. It is a

---

[1] Closer literary parallels are provided by Pss. 19.8 (σοφίζουσα νήπια) and 119.130 (συνετιεῖ νηπίους), cf. A. H. McNeile, *The Gospel according to St Matthew*, 1915, *ad loc.* There is no *specific* allusion here, but a common background of thought to which the use of 'babes' in both passages belongs.

[2] This has already been noted in our analysis of 8.17 and 13.35.

[3] I Cor. 15.27; Eph. 1.22; Phil. 3.21; Heb. 2.6-9; I Peter 3.22.

[4] The phrase is from Dodd, *Acc. Scrip.*, whose treatment of this christological development is a specially notable feature of the book. See pp. 116-23, 131.

psalm of praise for man's redemption in and through the person of Jesus, crucified and risen. It is not properly a messianic psalm, like Pss. 2 and 110, but acquires this character through its usefulness to fill out the meaning of the christology formulated by means of these psalms.

Once the christological interpretation has been secured, it is easy to apply v. 3 to the members of the Church. And so begins the process which has led to the inclusion of this verse in Matt. 21.16. The original christological use of the psalm (always with Ps. 110) seems to belong to the early teaching work of the Church, whether in kerygma or catechesis, and is taken up by St Paul and by the authors of Hebrews and I Peter. The use of a single text (v. 3) belongs to the apologetic in connection with the problem of the messianic nature of our Lord's earthly ministry, and survives only in the Gospel tradition preserved by Matthew.

### 3. THE REJECTED STONE

In this chapter we are concerned with the apologetic of response. The christological aspect of this is the assertion that there is scriptural warrant for a failure to recognize the Messiah. We now have further light on this theme from a group of texts in which there is mention of a stone, or rock. These are Ps. 118.22; Isa. 8.14; 28.16; and Dan. 2.34. The connections between them are intricate and illuminating. The tendency to group these texts together, or to conflate them, is one of the clearest examples of catchword technique in the New Testament, and the theme of the rejected stone proved attractive and persistent, so that it continued into the patristic tradition. The 'stone' texts thus figured largely in Rendel Harris's theory of the Testimony-Book. However, the New Testament evidence is better interpreted along the lines of progressive *pesher* formation. New applications may be traced at each stage.

### Psalm 118.22

The verse with which we are specially concerned is the fruit of an imaginative flash of poetic feeling in the course of a hymn of victory. It may have been originally connected with an Enthronement festival, in which the anointed Priest-King takes his place as Yahweh's vicegerent.[1] At any rate, the victor enters the temple in

---

[1] A. Bentzen, *King and Messiah*, ch. II.

triumph (vv. 19-21). As he mounts the steps of the throne, it is as if a new and highly decorative coping stone has been added to the cornice, which the builders had failed to beautify completely: 'The stone which the builders rejected is become the head of the corner.' Only when the King is on the throne is the temple complete in its glory.

The whole tenor of the psalm suits well the sense of relief and triumph of the disciples after the Resurrection. The idea of the rejected stone is specially appropriate. In fact it has the appeal of *literal fulfilment*. The fact that the Resurrection followed rejection by the Jews is proof of his messiahship, for he literally fulfils this striking element of this messianic psalm.

It is possible that Ps. 118 was in use quite early from this point of view, though it has left few traces. However, precisely this literal fulfilment of v. 22 appears in Acts 4.11. The context is a dialogue which is probably a Lucan composition. But we have seen already that Luke draws on stock examples of scriptural exegesis, in which the original application has sometimes persisted.

The Resurrection is the Christian interpretation of the psalm as a whole. The fact that it is this particular verse which is quoted indicates that the thought has already moved from the basic announcement of victory to the Passion apologetic. The emphasis falls on the element of *rejection*. This motive seems to have left a trace in the actual form of text in Acts 4.11. All the words of the allusion are from the Septuagint, except that $\dot{a}\pi\epsilon\delta o\kappa i\mu a\sigma a\nu$, correctly translating the Hebrew, has been changed to $\dot{\epsilon}\xi o\upsilon\theta\epsilon\nu\eta\theta\epsilon i s$. In our study of Isa. 53 we saw reason to believe that in some contexts of the Passion apologetic this word represents נבזה of Isa. 53.3.[1] It thus seems probable that the use of this word in Acts 4.11 is due to the influence of this element of the Passion apologetic. So although the verse is the best example to illustrate the primary use of Ps. 118, it also shows what is logically the second stage.

Another example of the use of this same verse in the Passion apologetic occurs in the first prediction of the Passion, Mark 8.31, parr. Here Jesus says that 'the Son of man must suffer many things $\kappa a i$ $\dot{a}\pi o\delta o\kappa\iota\mu a\sigma\theta\hat{\eta}\nu a\iota$ by the elders', etc. The significant word can be omitted without spoiling the sense, and accordingly $\kappa a i$ $\dot{a}\pi o\delta.$ is missing from Matt. 16.21. It is thus possible that it is an addition to the text of Mark at a very early stage, but not found in the copy

---

[1] *Supra*, p. 81.

available to Matthew.[1] On the other hand it is included in Luke
9.22, and he has repeated it with only the slightest stylistic variation in an apocalyptic passage, Luke 17.25. The motive here is to
identify the Parousia with the Resurrection.

There are one or two other traces of the original application of
Ps. 118. In Acts 2.33 and 5.31 the use of the verb ὑψόω may be an
allusion to Ps. 118.16. When we studied these texts in ch. II, we
saw that the immediate background of the whole phrase in each
case was provided by other psalm verses more relevant to the context (Pss. 16.11, 68.19, 110.1). But the literary influence of Ps.
118.16 cannot be altogether excluded. Luke was working on established traditions of biblical exegesis. He was no doubt familiar
with the use of the whole psalm in connection with the Resurrection victory. To him 'the right hand of the Lord hath exalted me'
refers to the Ascension as a separable event, whereas originally it
was probably a way of describing the meaning of the Resurrection.
We also see another trace of the use of this psalm in the Passion
apologetic in John 10.24, where ἐκύκλωσαν may be a literary
allusion to Ps. 118.10ff.[2]

The next stage in apologetic development is to take the messianic scripture, and move it back from the Resurrection to the
ministry of our Lord. Ps. 118.26a, 'Blessed be he that cometh in
the name of the Lord', twice occurs in the Gospel tradition for
this purpose.

The first of these to consider is the Palm Sunday story. In all
four Gospels the greeting of the crowd is expressed in words from
Ps. 118.25f. In the last chapter it was shown that this quotation
came into the narrative to define the entry into Jerusalem as a
messianic act, the King coming to claim his own. Mark 11.9f. contains the *hosanna* of Ps. 118.25 untranslated, and then 26a twice
over in the language of the Septuagint. It was argued that ὡσαννά
and the *second* version of 26a ('Blessed [be] the coming kingdom
of our father David') are likely to be original. They agree with the
religious usage of the psalm in late Judaism as a prayer for the
restoration of the Davidic kingdom (now thought to be imminent).[3]

From the standpoint of the disciples after the Resurrection, the

[1] Cf. Matt. 26.21, where Mark's words from Ps. 41.10 have been
omitted.
[2] Dodd, *Acc. Scrip.*, p. 99.
[3] So both Targum and Midrash, cf. SB I, p. 850.

incident is a remarkable anticipation of the truth now revealed (that Jesus is *Messias designatus*). From the apologetic point of view it acquires a new importance to show that Jesus was the Messiah all along—only they were too blind to see it. While the authorities refused to believe, the simple people, who are close to God, were already aware of the truth. They are inspired to welcome him in terms of messianic prophecy (compare the use of Ps. 8.3 in Matt. 21.16). The insertion of the actual words of Ps. 118.26a in Mark helps to make this explicit in two ways: (*a*) it more effectively evokes the psalm as a whole, which is by now established as a proof of the messiahship of Jesus; (*b*) it includes the word ὁ ἐρχόμενος, which seems to have had some currency as a messianic title in early Christianity.[1] Thereafter it is the person of the King, rather than the idea of the coming kingdom, which gives point to the story. So the other three Gospels have the Septuagint version of Ps. 118.26a without the Marcan doublet. John and Luke bring out the messianism by the use of the word βασιλεύς, no doubt influenced by Zech. 9.9. Matthew retains the idea of Davidic kingship by placing τῷ υἱῷ Δαυίδ after the first ὡσαννά.

The other instance of Ps. 118.26a in the Gospels is in the lament over Jerusalem, which is preserved in almost identical form in Matt. 23.37-39 and Luke 13.34f. As it stands in both Gospels, Jesus laments the rejection of the long line of prophets, including himself. It is implied that he is the last, and even he will not be seen again until the saying, 'Blessed is he that cometh', etc., comes true. Suspicion attaches to this interpretation of the saying, because the period of waiting for the fulfilment of the prophecy is so short as to reduce the whole thing to bathos. Matthew implies that it will only be the short time to the Resurrection. Luke inescapably invites his readers to see the fulfilment in the entry of Jesus on Palm Sunday, though the preceding verses (13.31-34) suggest that he intended to mean the Resurrection.

But the textual evidence shows that this is not the real interpretation of the saying. The quotation of Ps. 118.26a is introduced, according to the true text,[2] with these words: οὐ μὴ ἴδητέ με ἕως

---

[1] Vincent Taylor, *St Mark, ad loc.* The question appears not to be considered by Mowinckel in his great study of messianism, *He that Cometh*, although the phrase alone gives the title to the book.

[2] This reading alone explains the variants. Some MSS follow the expedient of the parallel in Matt. 23.39, and omit ἥξει. The Curetonian Old Syriac, and some Old Latin MSS, insert 'the day' as subject of it.

ἥξει ὅτε εἴπητε. This means that ὁ ἐρχόμενος is a different person from the speaker. As an isolated unit it seems to be a prophecy in which the speaker is God himself (speaking through Jesus). It is a heart-broken final appeal, couched in terms reminiscent of Jer. 22.5. The last of the prophets has been rejected, and now the temple ('your house') will be deprived of the presence of God until the restoration in the coming kingdom.

Here again, then, the proper eschatological meaning of the psalm, as it prevailed in late Judaism, seems to be the original meaning. It owes its preservation to its fulfilment in the Resurrection. Interpreted as a saying about Jesus himself, it fits in well with the idea of the rejected stone, prominent in the same psalm. The Jewish rulers, true to past history, committed the final apostasy in condemning the Lord's Christ, thereby driving the divine presence out of their midst. But God raised him up, and in the act of Resurrection his messiahship is revealed. From the apologetic point of view, the preservation of such a saying, which can be interpreted in this way, shows that our Lord knew himself to be the Messiah all along. The rulers, too, would have known it, if they had not been hardened in enmity against God.

And so we come back to the apologetic of response. The messianic touches in the traditions about our Lord's life refute the objection that Jesus cannot have been the Messiah, because he was not accepted as such by those best qualified to judge. On the contrary, their refusal to believe is their own condemnation. The verse about the rejected stone (Ps. 118.22) can be used very effectively to make this point. We have already seen it as a testimony of the meaning of the Resurrection, and also as an argument in the Passion apologetic. We now turn to a Gospel passage in which it is used in the apologetic of response. The implication is that those who rejected Jesus are themselves rejected by God.

Accordingly Ps. 118.22f. (in Luke v. 22 only) is quoted at the conclusion of the parable of the wicked husbandmen (Mark 12.1-12 and parr.). The motive of the parable is very similar to the lament over Jerusalem, which we have just studied. The Jewish rulers have always refused God's messengers, and can be expected to do the same again at the final reckoning. The parable is complete at this point, and so may have ended at Mark 12.8.[1] J. Jeremias, however, includes the next verse in the original parable by interpreting

[1] Dodd, *The Parables of the Kingdom*, 1935, pp. 126f.

the 'others', to whom the vineyard is to be given, as the 'poor' to whom the good news of the coming kingdom is preached.[1]

When the parable is allegorized in terms of the death and Resurrection of Jesus, the final verse (whether original or only now added) clearly implies the rejection of the unbelieving Jews (not, of course, the Jewish nation as a whole); for the kingdom is now given to 'others'. This interpretation of the parable is actually presupposed by the addition of Ps. 118.22f. For the quotation lays stress on the exalted position of the stone which had been rejected, whereas the parable itself makes no reference to this. On the other hand it does not press home the real point of the parable, that the wicked husbandmen are themselves rejected, though it can be presumed that it is intended to imply this. Matthew and Luke both feel the need to make up this deficiency. Matthew goes the whole length of writing an explanation of Mark 12.9 in terms of a new nation ($\ell\theta\nu\epsilon\iota$, Matt. 21.43).[2] This presumably means the Gentiles, and it exactly corresponds to what we should expect in the development of the apologetic of response. When a text has come into use to prove the rejection of the Jews, it automatically becomes available to prove the acceptance of the Gentiles. Luke on the other hand introduces an obscure saying about the destructive effect of the stone. It belongs to further developments of this theme, and will be considered later in this chapter.

The synoptic parallels thus show the continuation of an apologetic tendency in handling this parable, which has already begun before Mark, and of which the introduction of Ps. 118.22f. represents one stage. This citation is in process of becoming a classic passage, though in itself it hardly warrants it, for a theory first of the rejection of unbelieving Jews, and then of the rejection of the whole nation.

There is one more instance of this apologetic use of this verse in the New Testament, and that is the important cluster of 'stone' texts in I Peter 2.1-10. This includes Isa. 8.14 and 28.16, and so discussion of it must be held over until we have considered each of these texts separately.

---

[1] *The Parables of Jesus*, ET 1954, p. 60.
[2] Matt. 21.44 is equivalent to Luke 20.18, and can hardly be supposed to be original in Matthew, in spite of considerable MS support. It has probably crept in from Luke on account of the importance of the anti-Judaic issue. The text of Mark has escaped the addition, because it largely fell out of use after the diffusion of Matthew and Luke.

### The Precious Corner Stone

It has already been shown that Isa. 29 was drawn into the apologetic of response which grew around Isa. 6.9f. It seems that the preceding chapter was also used for this purpose to some extent. The principal theme of Isa. 28 is the rejection of the prevailing ungodly government and the promise of a divine ordering of society. The latter idea is contained in v. 16 in the memorable image of the precious corner stone. The judgment on the disobedient rulers is also expressed in a lively image: the word of the Lord, which should have been their guide to action, will be to them as incomprehensible as their own drunken speech (vv. 7-13). This certainly was used in the apologetic, for v. 11 and the last phrase of v. 12 are quoted (in a form very different from the Septuagint) in I Cor. 14.21. Here St Paul claims that this prophecy is fulfilled in the effect of glossolalia on unbelievers. There is also a possible allusion to the 'rest' (v. 12a) promised to the remnant in our Lord's great invitation, Matt. 11.29.

Now the use of Isa. 28.16 (the precious corner stone) was probably always as a commentary on other 'stone' passages. But it was brought into service just at the time when the greater interest in the whole problem of response to the Gospel, and its effect in the rejection of the Jews, was compelling the Church to examine appropriate scriptures with great care, and so the purview was extended to include Isa. 28 as well as 29. It is presumably on account of this kind of exegetical work that Isa. 28.16 enters the early Christian literature in a form slightly different from the Septuagint. In I Peter 2.6 it is quoted alongside Isa. 8.14, and in Rom. 9.33 the same two texts are conflated. In both cases the verb is $\tau i\theta\eta\mu\iota$, instead of the Septuagint $\dot{\epsilon}\mu\beta\alpha\lambda\hat{\omega}$, and the fact that the stone is laid 'for a foundation' is omitted.

### The Stone of Stumbling

The same is true of Isa. 8.14. The chapter as a whole is a message of confidence in the support of the divine presence. But, just as in Isa. 28, the grounds of confidence are equally an assurance of destruction to those who are disobedient. God is at one and the same time a sanctuary for those who trust in him (v. 14a—no doubt referring to the rock on which the temple is built), and a stumbling-stone to the others.

In the apologetic of response, this confidence is not simply adherence to God, but primarily belief in Christ. That is the issue at stake. It is notable that it is from this point of view that this chapter is employed several times in the New Testament. Verses 8 and 10 contain the phrase 'Immanuel', not simply as a symbolic name, but in a meaningful context. This seems to have influenced not only Matt. 1.23, but also Rom. 8.31 and Rev. 21.3, expressing the presence of God through the redeeming work of Christ. Verses 12f. are alluded to in I Peter itself, at 3.14f. It is a homiletic passage, and the Christians are exhorted to sanctify the Lord *Christ* in their hearts. Then we have quotations of words from vv. 17f. in Heb. 2.13. The astonishing thing about this is that, although the words are consecutive in Isa. 8, they are quoted as if they are two distinct citations: 'I will put my trust in him; *and again*, Behold, I and the children whom the Lord hath given me.' It is true that the words of the first quotation occur also in II Sam. 22.3 and Isa. 12.2. But even if these passages are in the writer's mind, he can hardly have been unaware that he is quoting words which actually precede his next quotation without a break. The probable explanation is that he intentionally divides them in order to make two distinct points, both concerned with the unity of Christ with the believers. The first proves that he, like them, was in the human position of needing to trust God. The second draws a parallel between the relation of the prophet to his band of disciples (who are the true remnant of Israel) and that of Christ to those whom he has redeemed.[1] So there has been a shift of application. The chapter at first showed the consequences of trust in the risen Lord, with its opposite of 'scandal' to the unbelievers. Now it can be used for a christological assertion of the unity of redeemed mankind in the one Lord by faith.[2]

Isa. 8 is thus chiefly concerned with confidence, properly belonging to the apologetic of response, though capable of christological development. Only the words in v. 14 about 'the stone of stumbling and rock of offence' are concerned with lack of faith. The verse is singled out because of its vivid imagery of the stone,

---

[1] This is the view of Westcott, *Hebrews*[3], 1903, *ad loc.* C. Spicq, *L'Épitre aux Hébreux*, 1952/3, decides in favour of 'un florilège', which correlates the passage with the identical Isa. 12.2 and II Sam. 22.3. Against this see Dodd, *Acc. Scrip.*, p. 82.

[2] The accompanying words from Ps. 22.23 also show the shift of application. See above, p. 93.

to be used with Isa. 28.16. That this happened early is clear from
the fact that once again Rom. 9.33 and I Peter 2.6 agree together
in their choice of Greek words against the Septuagint.[1]

It is reasonable to expect that the pattern seen in the analysis
of Isa. 8 as a whole will be true also of these 'stone' texts when
used in combination. The stone is first of all an article of belief,
belief in Christ, the crucial test between belonging to the New
Israel or being rejected from it. Only afterwards does the stone
become a symbol of Christ himself and his Church.

### Romans 9.33

To appreciate the implications of the conflate text in Rom. 9.33,
it is necessary to see it in relation both to the Septuagint and to
the version in I Peter of the two passages concerned.

| Isa. 28.16 (LXXA) | I Peter 2.6 | Rom. 9.33 |
|---|---|---|
| ἰδοὺ ἐγὼ ἐμβαλῶ | ἰδού, τίθημι | ἰδού, τίθημι |
| εἰς τὰ θεμέλια Σιὼν | ἐν Σιὼν | ἐν Σιὼν |
| λίθον πολυτελῆ ἐκλεκτὸν | λίθον ἐκλεκτὸν | λίθον προσκόμματος |
| ἀκρογωνιαῖον ἔντιμον | ἀκρογωνιαῖον ἔντιμον, | καὶ πέτραν σκανδάλου, |
| εἰς τὰ θεμέλια αὐτῆς, | | |
| καὶ ὁ πιστεύων ἐπ' | καὶ ὁ πιστεύων ἐπ' | καὶ ὁ πιστεύων ἐπ' |
| αὐτῷ | αὐτῷ | αὐτῷ |
| οὐ μὴ καταισχυνθῇ. | οὐ μὴ καταισχυνθῇ. | οὐ καταισχυνθήσεται. |

| Isa. 8.14 | I Peter 2.8 |
|---|---|
| . . . καὶ οὐχ ὡς | . . καὶ |
| λίθου προσκόμματι | λίθος προσκόμματος |
| συναντήσεσθε αὐτῷ | |
| οὐδὲ ὡς πέτρας πτώματι. | καὶ πέτρα σκανδάλου. |

The way in which St Paul introduces this quotation in v. 32b
very strongly gives the impression that he expects his readers to
be familiar with it already. 'They stumbled at *the* stone of stumbling', the stone which you know from the well-known quotation.
He shows no sign of being conscious that it is not an exact quotation at all. It is highly probable that the conflation was already
current. That the two texts were in use together we know from
I Peter. To have quoted them both, one after the other, as I Peter
does, would have suited his purpose sufficiently well. But he has
adopted this version, which had already undergone a process of
abbreviation and adaptation for the needs of apologetic. So we

---

[1] See the next section.

must first examine the resultant text as it stands, apart from the context in Romans.

The primary form is the unconflated version in I Peter. Both I Peter 2.6 and Rom. 9.33 present a *pesher* text of Isa. 28.16. The change of verb and the omission of 'the foundations' are both due to the same interpretative motive. The exegete wishes to avoid the idea of casting the stone into the foundations, i.e. below ground level. This stone is placed on the ground, where it can be seen—or else becomes a stumbling-block to the unwary. This interpretation would be valueless unless it were used in conjunction with the idea of the stone of stumbling found in Isa. 8.14. Consequently it is certain that the phrases from the latter text were always used in conjunction with the *pesher* text of Isa. 28.16. The stone is precious to those who believe, but a cause of stumbling to those who do not.

The conflated form in Rom. 9.33 makes exactly the same double point. The stone is no longer said to be precious, but is first and foremost a stone of stumbling. But nevertheless those who believe are safe.

The original application of this text was surely the same as that of Isa. 6.9f., the question of response in general. The stone is not a symbol of Christ, but a vivid poetic image. The consequence of belief in Christ, or of unbelief, is *like* a precious stone in your way. If you see it and take hold of it, you have got something of real value. If you are blind, it trips you up.

Paul in Romans has applied this to the controversy between Jew and Gentile. The Jews as a whole stumble, because they trust in the works of the Law. The Gentiles make the response of faith, and so gain the prize. Then in the next chapter he takes this a stage further still. Having narrowed down the issue to the contrast between Jew and Gentile, Paul widens it once more to show that this racial distinction is obsolete. The real distinction is between believer and unbeliever, whether he be Jew or Gentile. So it is not surprising that he quotes the end of Isa. 28.16 again in 10.11 with the significant addition of πᾶς: '*Everyone* that believeth . . . '. It is an argument which he had already adumbrated in Rom. 2.[1]

These two 'stone' texts from Isaiah had first been selected to deal with the question of unbelief. How can the Christian claim of

[1] Rom. 2.9-11. There is probably an allusion to Isa. 8.22 in the words θλῖψις καὶ στενοχωρία (Dodd, *Acc. Scrip.*, p. 79).

universal salvation be true, if it is not universally believed? By the time that Paul uses this material the issue is bound up with the Judaistic controversy. It is now an argument for the rejection of the Jews. In Paul's hands it becomes the means of transcending the racial question altogether.

## I Peter 2.1-10

The homiletic purpose of the Epistle governs the use of the two Isaiah texts, and of Ps. 118.22 which is now included with them. The passage which we now examine is addressed to the newly baptized. They have been initiated into Christ, and therefore are under obligation to imitate his moral perfection (2.1-3). Their relation to Christ is expressed in the figure of a building. They are joined[1] to him as to λίθον ζῶντα, ὑπὸ ἀνθρώπων μὲν ἀποδεδοκιμασ-μένον παρὰ δὲ θεῷ ἐκλεκτὸν ἔντιμον. The meaning of the word ζῶντα is that Jesus communicates the life of the Spirit, which the people have just received in their baptism (cf. John 4.14). He can do this because he is himself risen from death to new life. The paschal setting of the Epistle makes this an important element of thought. The author carefully introduces a text which expresses it in terms of his metaphor of a building. The death of Christ can be put in terms of the rejected stone, i.e. Ps. 118.22, represented here by ὑπὸ . . . ἀποδεδοκιμασμένον. The Resurrection can be put in terms of placing the stone at the head of the corner, for this is the vital place to ensure the stability of the walls that lead away from it at right angles, so that a specially well-squared and massive stone is needed for this position. We should expect the author to make this point by using the phrase εἰς κεφαλὴν γωνίας from the same quotation. But instead he chooses to use another phrase, ἐκλεκτὸν ἔντιμον, from Isa. 28.16. It is less appropriate from the point of view of the metaphor, but perhaps more personal and appealing. It prepares the way for v. 5, where the neophytes are to be built up into Christ as 'God's true temple'.[2] At this point the fuller implications of Isa. 28.16, as a poetical expression of stability of the new temple (i.e. divine government), are present to the mind. And so this verse is quoted in v. 6.[3]

[1] For the meaning of προσερχόμενοι see E. G. Selwyn, *The First Epistle of St Peter*, 1946, *ad loc.*, quoting Hort's suggestion that the verb has been chosen in allusion to Ps. 34.6.

[2] So Selwyn translates οἶκος πνευματικός, *op. cit.*, pp. 160, 286-91.

[3] Selwyn (p. 163) argues that the anarthrous γραφῇ of v. 6 indicates a

Several points are worth noting in the verses we have just considered. The foundation of the whole metaphor is the idea that Christ is a stone, and this depends on Ps. 118.22, which is already in use in connection with the death and Resurrection. It follows that Isa. 28.16 is adopted by the writer as a comment upon it. It gives a fuller description of the second half of the verse. Ps. 118.22b merely said that the stone reached 'the head of the corner'. Isa. 28.16 defines this 'corner stone' as 'elect, precious' and worthy of 'belief'. The catchword connection between them is, then, not λίθον but ἀκρογωνιαῖον. Such a connection is only possible if the stone is above ground. So it is essential to the functioning of the quotation that the idea of the foundations should be omitted. We have seen that this had already been made necessary in the earlier usage of the text in the apologetic of response.

The *pesher* text of Isa. 28.16 used here naturally comes with the words from Isa. 8.14 as its comment (though not conflated with it as in Rom. 9.33). The writer is glad to work this in, too, because it is a good way of warning his readers against apostasy. We should expect v. 7 therefore to read like this: 'The stone is "precious" to you who believe; but to those who disbelieve it is "a stone of stumbling and a rock of offence".' But instead we have the whole of Ps. 118.22 before Isa. 8.14 is quoted. The inevitable conclusion is that the writer is familiar with Ps. 118.22 as a proof of the rejection of the Jews, just as it is found in the parable of the wicked husbandmen. For the purposes of homiletic he is generalizing an argument which belongs to the controversy between Jew and Gentile.

This passage in I Peter seems to be the first place where the stone is identified with the person of Christ. It has been effected with the aid of Ps. 118.22. This means that the attractive imagery of Isa. 28.16, released from its connection with Isa. 8.14, is available to form a commentary on the temple as a metaphor for the Body of Christ.[1] Then the foundations can be included in the range of symbolism. There is an allusion to Isa. 28.16 in this way in Eph. 2.20. At this stage yet another chapter of Isaiah can be

written but *non-biblical* source, such as a testimony-book or hymn. Some prior written work is in any case indicated by the identical non-LXX opening to the quotation here and in Rom. 9.33.

[1] In ch. II §5 reason was given for seeing the beginnings of this theme in the apologetic use of Ps. 69. See also the discussion of this psalm in ch. III.

adduced to improve the picture, the idea of the new Jerusalem in Isa. 54.11f. This is alluded to in Rev. 21.19.[1]

## Tu es Petrus

From the facts which we have reviewed it is evident that the two Isaiah texts had a fairly wide currency, and had been selected before Paul wrote Romans. It is therefore not unreasonable to suppose that they have been influential in the formation of the Petrine passage of Matt. 16.17-19, 23. In v. 18 the rock on which the Church is to be built is possibly an allusion to Isa. 28.16. This may not appear probable at first sight, but is suggested by the more overt allusion to Isa. 8.14 in v. 23.[2]

To take the latter first. In Mark 8.33 Jesus rebukes Peter with the words, 'Get thee behind me, Satan: for thou mindest not the things of God, but the things of men.' Matthew reproduces this exactly, copying Mark word for word, except that after 'Satan' he inserts σκάνδαλον εἶ ἐμοῦ.[3] In the non-Septuagint version of Isa. 8.14 common to both Rom. 9.33 and I Peter 2.8 we read πέτρα σκανδάλου. In Matt. 16.18 we have the feminine form πέτρα as a play on the name Πέτρος. It can hardly be denied that this insertion into the Marcan text which Matthew is following so faithfully has been prompted by the current pair of Isaiah testimonies. Peter himself is the 'stone of stumbling and rock of offence'.

As we have seen, this phrase from Isa. 8.14 is used as a commentary on Isa. 28.16. We have no evidence of its use apart from the other. We are bound to search for Isa. 28.16 in a context where Isa. 8.14 occurs. Quite clearly Matt. 16.18 has the right *meaning*, the placing of a stone as the beginning of a new temple ( = divine

[1] These references may be due to traditional messianic interpretation of the passage, cf. the Targum: 'Therefore thus saith the Lord, Behold, I will appoint in Zion a king, a strong king, powerful and terrible' (J. Stenning, *The Targum of Isaiah*, 1949). This makes it all the more interesting that the *pesher* text of this verse in Romans and I Peter shows no sign of this interpretation.

[2] It is astonishing that this classic pair of 'stone' testimonies receives no mention at all in O. Cullmann's *Peter* (ET 1953). There is also no note of the significance of the addition in Matt. 16.23. Lagrange in his commentary recognizes the possibility of references to both these texts, but does not follow them up.

[3] Most of the variants are not significant. But the genitive is awkward, and εἰ ἐμοί in D and the Versions is an attempt to get over the difficulty. Abbott's suggestion of σκάνδαλον εἰμί σοι (W. C. Allen, *Matthew* (ICC), 1907, *ad loc.*) has not found favour with recent commentators.

government). The choice of words is governed by other factors. πέτρα can be substituted for λίθος with the aid of Isa. 8.14, for the sake of the word-play. οἰκοδομήσω may be due to a typology based on Zech. 6.12.[1] It might be supposed that the Church was to be built on the rock as the *foundations* of the building. But the text does not say so. This accords with the *pesher* version of Isa. 28.16, from which the idea of the foundations has been carefully expunged. Peter, then, is the precious corner stone of the new temple, i.e. the new Israel (ἐκκλησία = *qāhāl*).

We now have to ask how this 'stone' material became associated with our Lord's saying to St Peter. Matt. 16.17-19 is not found in Mark, but is likely to be early material on account of the Semitisms.[2] Our texts from Isaiah, in spite of their differences from the Septuagint, have obviously not been selected independently from it, but are actually adaptations of it. Consequently they belong to a Greek milieu. Thus they have been influential on the Petrine material at a later stage. The original *pericope*, which in any case does not belong to the confession at Caesaraea Philippi, may have been evoked by a similar profession of faith either at the Last Supper or after the Resurrection.[3] In either case it is more than an act of faith. It includes the scandal of unbelief as well—if not the prediction of the Passion of Mark 8.31f., then at least the three denials (Luke 22.31-34, cf. John 21.15-17). It would not be difficult to attach the two Isaiah texts to this, seeing that they are precisely concerned with belief and unbelief. Moreover in this case they appeal to a taste for a play on words.[4]

The two texts are concerned with faith in Christ, as in Rom. 9.33. But they show a development which diverges from both Romans and I Peter. Here we do not see them transferred to the Judaistic controversy and the rejection of the Jews. Nor is there any hint of the typology in which Christ is the stone. It is more like what might be expected in a Jewish-Christian setting, where the original concern with believers and unbelievers in general would remain, without the complications introduced by the Gentile question. The interest moves along the line of developing ecclesiastical institu-

---

[1] Cf. *supra*, p. 70.    [2] Cullmann, *op. cit.*, p. 166.

[3] Cullmann, 'L'apôtre Pierre instrument du diable et instrument de Dieu: la place de Matt. 16.16-19 dans la tradition primitive', in *NT Essays*, pp. 94-105.

[4] The connections are very easy in Aramaic, as כֵּיפָא does duty for λίθος, πέτρα and Πέτρος.

tions. It becomes not so much a matter of belief or unbelief in Jesus the Messiah as of adherence or opposition to the true congregation of the people of God. This means that the two texts are employed in this setting in connection with the formulation of the doctrine of the Church.[1]

It seems, then, that a confession of faith by Peter has been amplified with the 'stone' texts which are concerned with the church. We may suppose that the motive is aetiological. The nickname Peter was undoubtedly given by our Lord himself.[2] The earliest record gives no explanation.[3] Presumably it was not unconnected with the choice of *Boanerges* for the sons of Zebedee.[4]

The original saying concerned the formation of the *qahal* in the coming kingdom. Properly speaking, this could not be *built*, for it is a gathering of persons rather than the place of meeting. Metaphorically it might be spoken of as the true temple.[5] To begin with it might have been expressed in terms of the 'little flock'.[6] This means that only the words ἐπὶ ταύτῃ τῇ πέτρᾳ οἰκοδομήσω need be regarded as later development. They show the point where the metaphor of the temple was introduced, probably with the aid of Isa. 28.16, and they mark the adaptation of the saying for its aetiological purpose.[7]

### Daniel 2.34

There is still one more development of the theme of the rejected stone, and that is the complex allusion in Luke 20.18. This is the end of the parable of the wicked husbandmen. We have already

---

[1] In connection with this we may note that the *Manual of Discipline* requires twelve men and three priests to maintain the purity of observance of the Law by the members of the Qumran community; by this arrangement the members will be the 'precious cornerstone' of Isa. 28.16 (1QS 8.1-8). Cf. also 1QH 6.26, where God's truth (i.e. faithfulness to his revealed purposes) is spoken of in the imagery of a building, perhaps referring to this passage.

[2] Cullmann, *Peter*, p. 20.  [3] I.e. Mark 3.16.

[4] Various views on this name are summarized in V. Taylor, *St Mark*, pp. 231f.

[5] I Peter 2.5, and cf. p. 179 n. 2.  [6] Luke 12.32.

[7] The above discussion is not intended to be a new solution of the perplexing problems of these important verses, still less of the ecclesiology connected with them. But it does seem probable that the two 'stone' texts, which imaginatively show response to and rejection of Christ as the obverse and reverse of one coin, have prompted Matthew to insert special material into the Marcan account of Peter's confession and subsequent rebuke.

seen that Mark quotes Ps. 118.22-23 as an anti-Judaic testimony.
Luke, however, cites only v. 22 of the psalm. Then he continues:
πᾶς ὁ πεσὼν ἐπ' ἐκεῖνον τὸν λίθον συνθλασθήσεται· ἐφ' ὃν δ'ἂν
πέσῃ λικμήσει αὐτόν.
The first line is composed of words from the context of a text
with which we are already familiar, Isa. 8.14, the stone of stumbling. The next verse reads διὰ τοῦτο ἀδυνατήσουσιν ἐν αὐτοῖς
πολλοὶ καὶ πεσοῦνται καὶ συντριβήσονται.[1] It makes the same point
as I Peter 2.8, where the stone of stumbling is used in conjunction
with Ps. 118.22—the destructive effect of the stone on the unbelievers (in this case the Jews). It thus strongly emphasizes the
threat already implied in the Marcan text.

The second line is reminiscent of Dan. 2.34, 44f. in the recension of Theodotion: ἐτμήθη λίθος ἐξ ὄρους ἄνευ χειρῶν . . . (v. 44)
. . . ἀναστήσει ὁ θεὸς τοῦ οὐρανοῦ βασιλείαν, . . . λεπτυνεῖ καὶ
λικμήσει πάσας τὰς βασιλείας . . . (v. 45) ὃν τρόπον εἶδες ὅτι ἀπὸ
ὄρους ἐτμήθη λίθος ἄνευ χειρῶν καὶ ἐλέπτυνεν τὸ ὄστρακον. The
fact that Theodotion's text provides the closest parallel to what
we have in Luke is a sign that he is taking his material from a
previous exegetical tradition. The connection with the first line is
not simply the catchword 'stone', but a real similarity of thought.
In the vision of Dan. 2 the stone represents the Jewish nation,
whose kingdom will be permanently established after the pagan
empires have been crushed and 'scattered as dust' (λικμήσει). The
Christian exegetes have transferred it to the Church as the new
People of God. Now it is the unbelieving Jews who take the place
of the pagan nations. Thus the addition of this allusion goes beyond
anything we have yet had in the anti-Judaic apologetic of the rejected stone. It implies the rejection of the whole nation. It belongs
to the same Hellenistic milieu as the prophecy of rebuilding the
temple 'without hands' (ἀχειροποίητον) in Mark 14.58, which is
probably an allusion to ἄνευ χειρῶν in Dan. 2.34, 45.[2] In this
Hellenistic development the stone has become the Church.

This strange couplet conveys the strongest possible interpretation of the stone of stumbling. It is a commentary on Isa. 8.14,

[1] In the text of Luke συνθλασθήσεται is ἅπ. λεγ. in the NT. It is found a
few times in the LXX, sometimes alongside συντρίβω, and sometimes as a
variant of other synonyms. In the present instance the allusion is by way
of meaning rather than words, so that the use of this word has no special
significance.

[2] Cf. supra, pp. 68f.

but here attached to Ps. 118.22. By the time that Luke was writing (after Paul, and probably after I Peter) the stone theme had grown, and become an accepted part of anti-Judaic propaganda. The parable of the wicked husbandmen obviously served this purpose. But the quotation from Ps. 118 added by Mark did not bring it out sharply enough. In Luke's set of Gentile Christians this testimony was no doubt regularly supplemented with the other stone texts. When he inserted them into his rewriting of Mark, he presumably felt that this was where they originally belonged in the teaching of Jesus.

The theme of the rejected stone has been traced from a general use of Ps. 118 to prove the messianic significance of our Lord's Resurrection. Amid all the developments which sprang from it, this original application has always remained in the thought of the Church. Not unnaturally it sometimes occurs in homiletic passages in a purely hortatory way. The underlying argument is that those who have been baptized into Christ's death may expect to share the benefits of his Resurrection. So v. 6, expressing confidence in time of persecution, is quoted in Heb. 13.6. There may be an allusion to v. 18 in II Cor. 6.9 (joy in persecution). The same verse is also quoted by Clement in ch. 56, characteristically reducing the idea to the spiritual value of discipline. He also quotes vv. 19f. ('Open me the gates of righteousness', etc.) a little earlier, in ch. 48, to impress on his readers that righteousness is the only way to overcome the situation of internal strife in the church at Corinth.

The identification of the stone with Christ was put to a novel purpose by the writer of the *Epistle of Barnabas* 6.2-4. Here it means his *flesh*. Isa. 28.16 is first quoted in such a way as to suggest that the laying of the foundation stone is the Incarnation. Then comes Isa. 50.7 ('I set my face as a hard rock') to introduce the Passion. And then Ps. 118.22-24 means the Resurrection in the flesh.

In the anti-Judaic literature the whole argument arising from these texts can be summed up in the contention 'that Christ is called a Stone' without further explanation. We find in Justin's *Dialogue* 36 that Trypho the Jew is willing to concede this point, although the actual texts have not been previously referred to. In fact 'the Stone' is listed as one of the messianic titles.[1]

[1] *Ibid.* 100. In the same list 'the Day' is probably a reference to Ps.

We have noticed that the inclusion of the stone of Dan. 2 in this apologetic marked the strongest anti-Judaic tendency. The identification of the stone with the risen Christ became so much taken for granted that even this could be bent to other purposes. So Justin makes out that the fact the stone was 'cut without hands' is a proof that the Messiah would be born of a virgin without human generation (*Dial.* 76).

## 4. THE LIFE OF CHRIST AND THE APOLOGETIC OF RESPONSE

The principal purpose of this chapter has been to show how testimonies, which were originally applied to the Resurrection, were transferred to events in our Lord's life and ministry, in order to show its messianic character. We found that this was true of the baptismal texts, Ps. 2.7 and Isa. 42.1. It is possible that this applied also to Isa. 61.1, though sufficient evidence is lacking. This means that Jesus is declared to be the Messiah from the outset. So the most notable features of his ministry had to be interpreted in this way. The *pesher* text of Isa. 42.1-4 was used to explain the healing work of Jesus and the gentleness of his methods. Verses from the Passion prophecy, Isa. 53.1 and 4, were also turned to this purpose. Similarly the recorded teaching of Jesus had to be shown to be messianic revelation, although given in a mystery (Ps. 78.2; Isa. 6.9f.).

In this connection the entry into Jerusalem on Palm Sunday is specially important. It is the link between the Passion apologetic and previous ministry. So we find the great Resurrection Psalm 118 incorporated to give it definite messianic significance. In Matthew there is a quotation from the christological Psalm 8. Ps. 118.26 in our Lord's lament over Jerusalem seems to have a similar motive.

The treatment of Gospel episodes in this way, before the writing of Mark, shows a double process, each part of which is complementary to the other. It proves that the life of Jesus was genuinely messianic, in spite of appearances to the contrary, and at the same time it creates a new definition of what messianic work really is. When Mark opens his Gospel with the words 'The beginning of the gospel of Jesus Christ', he is not setting out to draw a picture of the figure expected in late Judaism. He is describing the life of an historical Person which has come to be understood messianically

118.24. Cyprian, *Ad Quirinum: Test. adv. Jud.* II 16f., has a list of testimonies under the heading *That Christ is called the Stone.*

because of certain significant aspects of it. Consequently the teaching of Jesus about the coming kingdom is both preserved and distorted. It tends to be cramped into the strait-jacket of contemporary ideas, but at the same time it profoundly modifies them. If the original idea that Jesus was revealed as the Messiah at his Resurrection had remained unchanged, two fatal results would have followed. On the one hand there would have been no check on theories of his function purely derived from apocalyptic speculation, because the records of his life would not have exercised strong enough control. And on the other, this record of his life (as prophet or rabbi) would have remained largely unintegrated into the Church's understanding of the nature of salvation. By pushing the moment of revelation back to the Baptism, it was possible for the Church to break through conventional ideas and to appreciate the unique importance of our Lord's work and teaching. What this could mean to a perceptive mind, seeking to pierce to the heart of religion, is demonstrated in the Gospel according to St John.

The messianic interpretation of the ministry of Jesus was bound up with the question of belief and unbelief. To the mind of the early Christians the truth which they proclaimed was self-evident. Not to accept it is a sign of culpable obduracy. This attitude may seem to us shallow and unreasonable, but it is the natural reaction in face of the first opposition to the apostolic preaching. It has the effect of producing a sect-type doctrine of the Church. This was observed in our discussion of the texts used in connection with the parables (Ps. 78.2, and especially Isa. 6.9f.). They are a mystery accessible only to the disciples. It can hardly be supposed that this was intended by Jesus himself. The saying in Luke 22.30, in which the Twelve are given formal positions in relation to the Twelve Tribes of Israel, suggests a mission to the whole nation, gradual perhaps, but not eclectic.[1] In the first chapter of Acts this formal constitution of the Twelve appears as a curious survival. It preserves the original 'doctrine of the Church', before the actual course of events changed it into the sectarian idea so natural in first-century Judaism (e.g. the Pharisees and the Qumran Sect).

It is in consequence of this tendency that the two Isaiah 'stone' texts (8.14 and 28.16) are first brought together. Like Isa. 6.9f., they are transferred to the Judaistic controversy, give the grounds for a theory of the rejection of the Jews, and finally raise the whole

[1] Cf. also Matt. 10.23b.

conflict to the level of acceptance or rejection of the Gospel by all, whether Jews or Gentiles. On the way they pick up Ps. 118.22 as a text of rejection, and Dan. 2.34, 44f. is also tacked on. On the positive side they may be referred either to the *object of belief*, that is, the risen Christ himself, or to the *believers*, that is, the Church and specifically St Peter. The net result of these developments is that the Jewish categories of thought are released from their exclusively national application to become the groundwork of the doctrine of the Church Catholic and Apostolic, built upon Jesus Christ.

# V

## BETHLEHEM OR NAZARETH?

IT has long been recognized that the Gospels preserve traces
of a conflict concerning the origins of Jesus. It was known that
he was a Galilean, and that he came from Nazareth. But if he
was the Messiah, then popular sentiment required that he should
come from Bethlehem as the son of David.[1] This might constitute
a very serious objection to the Church's teaching.

The conflict arises from the discrepancy between the known
facts and the preconceived notions of what they ought to be. It has
been noticed in previous chapters that the actual facts frequently
modify the traditional expectations profoundly. In this case it is
different. By attention to the textual form of certain testimonies
it is possible to detect an initial attempt to assert that Galilean
origin is not inconsistent with the messianic claim. But this position
is not sustained, and by the time that the earliest books of the New
Testament were written it is conceded that a connection with
David is necessary, at least in some sense.

So in Rom. 1.3 Jesus is said to be 'born of the seed of David
according to the flesh'. It is significant that in the following verse
there is the contrasting statement that he was 'declared (ὁρισθέντος)
to be the Son of God with power, according to the spirit of holi-
ness, by the resurrection of the dead'. This latter verse retains the
original perspective. Jesus is known to be the Messiah, not because
of any traditions about his birth, but by the divine act of the
Resurrection. The Semitism πνεῦμα ἁγιωσύνης suggests that υἱοῦ
θεοῦ is also a Semitism, and so to be understood primarily as an

---

[1] Dodd can speak of 'a certain distaste for the whole conception of
the Davidic Messiah' (*Acc. Scrip.*, p. 81 n. 2). Cf. J. Knox, *Christ the
Lord*, pp. 13-16; R. Bultmann, *Theology of the New Testament* I, ET, 1952,
p. 28.

expression for the Messiah (cf. Ps. 2.7).[1] This does not, however, mean an 'adoptionist' christology, for he who is revealed at the Resurrection has been designated for this function from the very beginning. Paul takes it for granted that birth from the seed of David suits this position. This does not of itself imply that Jesus acts as Messiah all through his life, but simply that Davidic descent makes him the proper candidate when the time of his manifestation arrives. Without it the claim would be spurious.

When this point has been settled, it is to be expected that there will be a tendency to push the moment of messianic manifestation further back, from the Baptism of Jesus to his birth at Bethlehem. This is the logical development of the process observed in the last chapter. It has not affected the New Testament very much, apart from the infancy narratives in Matthew and Luke. Nevertheless it is a factor of great importance in the history of christology. Just as the second phase (Christ revealed at the Baptism) forced the Church to reappraise the work and teaching of Jesus in a way which brought to light the deeper meaning of it, so it may be felt that the logical conclusion of the process (Christ revealed at birth) alone makes it possible to do justice to the significance of his unique divine-human personality.

But another question must also be faced. If it is true that Jesus' Galilean origin was not questioned when it was first claimed that he was the Messiah, can we be sure that even that was the first stage? In Matt. 21.11 he is described as 'the prophet from Nazareth of Galilee'. It may thus be argued that the messianic claim has been added later, and that Jesus was originally regarded as a prophet. This complicates matters, because the Prophet of Deut. 18.15 also entered into first-century messianic expectations. If this particular identification was not at first intended by the use of the title, it inevitably happened later on.

It has often been held that expectation of the Prophet is not characteristic of Judaism, but belongs properly to Samaritan ideas.

---

[1] This is not to suggest that 'Son of God' was a normal appellation of the Messiah in late Judaism. Thus S. Mowinckel says, 'In the rabbinic literature the term "Son of God" is used of the Messiah only in citations of Ps. 2 and other similar passages which are interpreted messianically. It is never used as a personal name for the Messiah' (*He that Cometh*, pp. 293f.). He points out that the use of the expression in the Latin II (4) Esdras stands alone in Jewish literature, and may be due to the Christian translator.

This is certainly true of later times, but it has been recognized by many scholars that the New Testament itself provides evidence for it in the first century. The appearance of 'the prophet and the messiah(s) of Aaron and Israel' in the *Manual of Discipline*,[1] and the actual citation of Deut. 18.18f. along with messianic texts in another Qumran fragment,[2] now proves that this was an important element in at least one Jewish school of thought in the period of Christian origins.

As a figure distinct from the Messiah, the Prophet has the task of preparation for the coming kingdom (cf. Mal. 3.22-24). If Jesus is called the Prophet, it means a different estimate of him from the prevailing view of Davidic messiahship.[3] On the other hand the Samaritans only thought in terms of one messianic person, called the *Taheb*, who was the Prophet of Deut. 18.[4] This is correctly understood by John in his account of our Lord's conversation with the Samaritan woman, who mentions teaching as the sole function of the Messiah (John 4.25). Something rather similar to this seems to have been the attitude of the Ebionites to Jesus himself, whom they regarded as the 'true prophet'.[5] Whether they derived this from a living tradition within Jewish Christianity, or even from such influences as the Qumran Sect, cannot be decided with any certainty, because of the very scanty evidence.

The question of Jesus' origins is thus closely bound up with the question who he is. Recollection of the controversy, presented as a Gospel episode, survives in John 7.40-42.[6] Some say that Jesus is ὁ προφήτης, others that he is ὁ Χριστός. Against the latter it is objected that he came from Galilee, whereas this claim requires descent from David and birth at Bethlehem. There the matter is left, without drawing the obvious conclusion that no objection has been made against the claim that he is the Prophet. The reason is

---

[1] 1QS 9.11. The Prophet here is clearly a distinct person. It is disputed whether two Messiahs are meant, or whether one person fulfils both roles.

[2] 4QTestimonia (published by J. M. Allegro, *JBL* 75, 1956, pp. 182-87).

[3] Cf. J. A. T. Robinson, 'Elijah, John and Jesus'.

[4] J. A. Montgomery, *The Samaritans*, 1907, pp. 243-9. Cf. M. Simon, *St Stephen and the Hellenists in the Primitive Church*, 1958, pp. 38, 61.

[5] H. J. Schoeps, *Theologie und Geschichte des Judenchristentums*, 1949, pp. 87-98; J. A. Fitzmyer, 'The Qumran Scrolls, the Ebionites, and their Literature', *The Scrolls and the NT*, pp. 208-31.

[6] This raises the question of the historical worth of the other questionings, John 1.19-22; Mark 8.27-29, par. It is probable that even in the latter case the tradition reflects subsequent controversy.

that, by the time John was writing, this is no longer to be reckoned with as a serious possibility, at least in the milieu to which this Gospel belongs.

In this chapter we shall first survey the evidence of the quotations for the Davidic controversy. We shall then try to discover how far the idea of the Prophet of Deut. 18 has influenced the estimate of Jesus, who in any case was regarded as *a* prophet in his lifetime. Finally we shall consider the place of certain quotations in the development of a metaphysical christology.

### I. THE CONTROVERSY

| Matt. 2.6 | Micah 5.1(2) LXX[B] | |
|---|---|---|
| καὶ σὺ Βηθλέεμ, | καὶ σύ, Βηθλέεμ | ואתה בית־לחם |
| γῆ 'Ιούδα, οὐδαμῶς | οἶκος 'Εφραθά, | אפרתה |
| ἐλαχίστη εἶ | ὀλιγοστὸς εἶ τοῦ | צעיר להיות |
| ἐν τοῖς ἡγεμόσιν | εἶναι ἐν χιλιάσιν | באלפי |
| 'Ιούδα· ἐκ σοῦ γὰρ | 'Ιούδα· ἐκ σοῦ μοι | יהודה ממך |
| ἐξελεύσεται ἡγούμενος | ἐξελεύσεται τοῦ | לי יצא |
| ὅστις ποιμανεῖ τὸν | εἶναι εἰς ἄρχοντα | להיות מושל |
| λαόν μου τὸν 'Ισραήλ. | τοῦ 'Ισραήλ. | בישראל: |

ἐκ σοῦ] ἐξ οὗ  B*C
ἐξελεύσ.] + ἡγούμενος  A

Although this quotation forms part of St Matthew's narrative, it is generally reckoned with his formula-quotations, and in fact is a typical example of *pesher* adaptation. All the variations from the Hebrew and Septuagint contribute to a specific interpretation.

The passage in Micah is a promise that after the time of captivity a strong ruler will arise, who will beat off the national foes. The poet remembers how the great ruler David came from a small and unimportant place. So also, when his successor appears, the remnant will be small, but will nonetheless hold up its head among the nations (vv. 6ff.). It is implied that this ruler will be a descendant of David, and in that sense it can be said that he will 'come out of' Bethlehem.

In the text of Matthew we notice first that 'land of Judah' has replaced 'Ephratha'. This may be simply due to the desire to give an easier map-indication, but gains significance from the repetition of Judah later on. We must think of Judah personally, the ancestor of the tribe to which David belonged. The Messiah must, then, come from the tribe of Judah.

Then comes the most substantial alteration of the sense. The strong negative οὐδαμῶς has been added for the sake of the interpretation, without authority of either the Hebrew or the Septuagint.[1] It throws into relief the choice of ἐλαχίστη to translate צָעִיר (= inferior; contrast LXX ὀλιγοστός = few in number). This completely changes the meaning. The original gives the sense, 'Though thou art little, yet out of thee shall come a ruler'. But Matthew's text has to insert γάρ into the second clause to make it intelligible: 'Thou art not at all the most inferior; *for indeed* out of thee shall come a ruler.'

Another alteration is 'princes' (ἡγεμόσιν) for 'thousands'.[2] This calls attention to the possibility of rival dynasties. Only the dynasty that springs from Bethlehem accords with God's will made known through his prophets. Finally the last clause has been conflated with words from II Sam. 5.2.[3] This clinches the identification of the ruler with David's family.

The force of these changes is to make Bethlehem the place of messianic origin, presumably in contrast to another possible Judaean city. The obvious one would be Jerusalem, the royal seat. Moreover the Messiah must be a member of the tribe of Judah, and actually of the house of David. All these points could be held against the Hasmoneans and the Herods. There was certainly a body of opinion opposed to these dynasties precisely on these grounds.[4] It is probable that some held that the failure of these kings to establish the messianic kingdom was due to this defect. The hated Hellenizing policy which they pursued (from another point of view the real cause of the failure) was only to be

---

[1] Interrogative μὴ is found before ὀλιγοστός in one minuscule, some MSS of the Lucianic recension and of the Catenas, some of the Versions, and several patristic writers. It does not alter the sense in the manner of Matt. 2.6.

[2] Perhaps there is influence of Ps. 68.28, ἐκεῖ Βενιαμὶν νεώτερος ἐν ἐκστάσει, ἄρχοντες Ἰούδα ἡγεμόνες αὐτῶν (רגמתם). The translation ἡγεμόνες may be due to assonance with the unknown Hebrew word. If this really did influence the text, it belongs to a second stage of adaptation, working with the Greek text.

[3] II Sam. (II Kdms.) 5.2, σὺ ποιμανεῖς τὸν λαόν μου τὸν Ἰσραήλ, καὶ σὺ ἔσει εἰς ἡγούμενον. This also belongs to a stage when the Greek text is in use for comparison. Stendahl, *SSM*, p. 100, seems to disregard the fact that it is this text which has provided ἡγούμενος for מושל.

[4] This is a chief motive of the *Psalms of Solomon*, especially 8 and 17. Cf. E. Schürer, *A History of the Jewish People in the Time of Jesus Christ* II iii, ET 1886, pp. 18-20; E. Bevan, *Jerusalem under the High-Priests*, 1904, pp. 143f.

expected of those whose messianic claim was in any case spurious.

Thus the *pesher* text of Micah 5.1 gives the proper credentials for messiahship. It is even possible to imagine the formation of it simply to voice this point of view, without specific reference to Jesus himself. But it is more probable that it arose in a Christian setting, so as to make it absolutely clear that Jesus *does* pass the test for Davidic messiahship. The various nuances need not have been introduced all at one time. The Church accepted the challenge contained in the text, and no doubt the use of such testimonies was the starting-point for research into the origins of Jesus, which resulted in the collection of the infancy narratives. The use of this text in controversy is attested by John 7.42, where there is clear allusion to it in the words ἀπὸ Βηθλέεμ . . . ἔρχεται. Other Davidic texts (II Sam. 7.12; Ps. 89.4f.) are also referred to in this verse.

### Matthew 2.23: Ναζωραῖος κληθήσεται

We have seen how the need for descent from David was expressed, and how the Church capitulated to it. From the first our Lord was probably known generally as Jesus of Nazareth. At some stage prior to the acceptance of the implications of Micah 5.1(2), there seems to have been an attempt to make out a case for Nazareth as a proper place of messianic origin, duly warranted in Scripture. A trace of this survives in the enigmatic words of Matt. 2.23. Ναζωραῖος does not occur in the Old Testament. In the Gospels and Acts it is found several times as a descriptive adjective of Jesus, 'the Nazarene', and once denotes the Church (τῆς τῶν Ναζωραίων αἱρέσεως, Acts 24.5). At a later stage the Jewish Christians were known as the Ναζωραῖοι, but this is not significant for the present text. More to our purpose is the fact that according to Epiphanius there was a pre-Christian Jewish sect known as the Νασαραῖοι.[1]

A variety of possibilities come to mind. The name may have meant a Nazirite.[2] Or it may have been transferred from the Νασα-

---

[1] *Haer.* 18. In the introductory *anakephalaiosis* to the volume, Epiphanius translates the name ἀφηνιασταί (unbridled). This indicates that he was transliterating a formation of the root נסר or נשר = 'fall off, become apostate'. This hardly seems likely to be a self-chosen title of the Sect, but is rather another example of a pun *in malam partem*. Possibly the original name was נצרים.

[2] Judg. 13.5, 7. This seems the least likely alternative, because it is appropriate neither to our Lord nor to the early Church, and suggests a Samson typology for which there is no other evidence at this date.

ραῖοι, if such existed, in which case it probably meant נצרים, i.e.
'observants'. Or it might have been a messianic description derived
from נצר, the 'Branch', Isa. 11.1. In every case the choice of the
word involves a deliberate pun on the name Nazareth.

The words in Matt. 2.23 are introduced by the usual formula,
albeit rather vaguely, and this indicates that it comes from Matthew's stock of *pesher* quotations. This at once predisposes us in
favour of the derivation from Isa. 11.1, for the purpose of these
texts is to prove the messiahship of Jesus. Moreover they are the
product of a careful biblical exegesis. This suggests that serious
consideration should be given to the proposal of G. H. Box that
Ναζωραῖος represents נצירי of Isa. 49.6.[1] This is traditionally
vocalized as a passive participle,[2] 'to restore the *preserved* of Israel',
but could be read as an adjective from נצר of Isa. 11.1, or even
as a patronymic, i.e. 'a Nazarene'.[3] If so, the sentence would run:
'It is a light thing for thee to be to me a servant to raise up the
tribes of Jacob, and a Nazarene to restore Israel.' Of course this is
not what anyone really thought that the verse meant. It is a punning interpretation, taking advantage of the licence furnished by
the consonantal text, such as occurs in the *Habakkuk Commentary*.[4]
This sort of thing is only done for dogmatic reasons, to win a
debating-point. It ingeniously correlates the Nazarene with the
Branch of Isa. 11.1. Hence it can be claimed that the Branch of
Jesse was due to spring from Nazareth.

In the nature of things it is impossible to be more than speculative about this testimony. But further support for the connection
with Isa. 49.6 can be found in the second word of the testimony,
κληθήσεται. It is not represented in the Hebrew text, but occurs
in the Septuagint translation: μέγα σοί ἐστιν τοῦ κληθῆναί σε παῖδά
μου . . . . This marks a further stage of exegesis. The deliberate
misreading of the Hebrew text gains the point that the Messiah

---

[1] *St Matthew* (The Century Bible), 1922, *ad loc*. See also his article,
'The Value and Significance of the OT in relation to the New', in A. S.
Peake (ed.), *The People and the Book*, 1925, pp. 433-67.

[2] Qri נצורי.

[3] The most probable restoration of the original text is נצרי = *branches*
*of* Israel, cf. the parallel *tribes* (lit. *stems*) of Judah. But the confusion is
older than the LXX (διασποράν).

[4] This is the seventh of the hermeneutical principles listed by W. H.
Brownlee, 'Biblical Interpretation among the Sectaries of the Dead Sea
Scrolls', *The Biblical Archaeologist* 14, 1951, pp. 54-76, where examples
are given.

should come from Nazareth. The use of this interpretation with the Greek text asserts that the Messiah should actually be known as the Nazarene. As Box has observed, the patronymic, which was originally applied contemptuously, thereby becomes equivalent to a messianic title.[1]

We have already noticed that these testimonies are often abbreviated, so as to make the one point required for their apologetic use. In this case the quotation seems to have been so fragmentary that Matthew did not know its source.[2] He may well have abbreviated it still further when he incorporated it into his narrative. For his interest in it is confined to geographical explanation. The implied subject of $\kappa\lambda\eta\theta\acute{\eta}\sigma\epsilon\tau\alpha\iota$ is in fact Joseph rather than Jesus. It is another instance of Matthew's 'pictorial' applications of proof-texts.

Contempt for our Lord's origin at Nazareth is voiced in John 1.45f. Whatever may be felt about the historicity of John's narrative at this point, it is certainly evidence for the kind of question which the early Christian apologists had to face. Philip is perhaps rash to say, 'We have found him, of whom Moses in the law, and the prophets, did write, Jesus of Nazareth', because anyone so learned as Nathanael is sure to know that no such privilege attaches to Nazareth in the canonical scriptures. He has yet to learn the subtlety that lies behind Matt. 2.23.[3]

| Matt. 4.15f. | LXX[B] | Isa. 8.23 - 9.1 (9.1f.) |
|---|---|---|
|  | τοῦτο πρῶτον πίε, ταχὺ | כעת הראשון הקל |
| γῆ Ζαβουλὼν | ποίει, χώρα Ζαβουλών, | ארצה זבלון |
| καὶ γῆ Νεφθαλίμ, | ἡ γῆ Νεφθαλὶμ καὶ | וארצה נפתלי |
|  | οἱ λοιποὶ οἱ τὴν | והאחרון הכביד |
| ὁδὸν θαλάσσης | παραλίαν καὶ | דרך הים |
| πέραν τοῦ Ἰορδάνου, | πέραν τοῦ Ἰορδάνου, | עבר הירדן |
| Γαλιλαία τῶν ἐθνῶν, | Γαλιλαία τῶν ἐθνῶν. | גליל הגוים: |

[1] It is similar to the variations in the name of the Jewish leader Bar Kokheba. This form (found as βαρχωχεβάς in Christian sources) is messianic, referring to Num. 24.17. The Talmud has the form בר כוזבא, i.e. 'the liar', evidently coined by his enemies. It is now known that his real name was neither of these. It has been found in fragments from Muraba'at in the Hebrew form בן כוסבה. See J. T. Milik, 'Une Lettre de Siméon bar Kokheba', *RB* 60, 1953, pp. 276-94.

[2] Of course τῶν προφήτων could perhaps refer to the *Liber XII Prophetarum*, but no likely text presents itself.

[3] The natural usage of Isa. 49.6 is to authorize the Gentile mission (see the next chapter).

| Matt. 4.15f. | LXX^B | Isa. 8.23 - 9.1 (9.1f.) |
|---|---|---|
| ὁ λαὸς ὁ καθήμενος | ὁ λαὸς ὁ πορευόμενος | העם ההלכים |
| ἐν σκοτίᾳ φῶς | ἐν σκότει ἴδετε | בחשך ראו |
| εἶδεν μέγα, καὶ τοῖς | φῶς μέγα· οἱ | אור גדול |
| καθημένοις ἐν χώρᾳ | κατοικοῦντες ἐν χώρᾳ | ישבי בארץ |
| καὶ σκιᾷ θανάτου | σκιᾷ θανάτου | צלמות |
| φῶς ἀνέτειλεν αὐτοῖς. | φῶς λάμψει ἐφ' ὑμᾶς. | אור נגה עליהם: |

The question of Messiah's origin does not in itself require distinction between the place of his birth and the area of his first ministerial activity. It is the latter idea which seems to be concerned in John 7.41, 'What, doth the Christ come out of Galilee?' But the next verse, with its mention of the seed of David, at once fastens attention on the place of birth. Eventually the Church succeeded in overcoming the difficulty by clarifying the distinction. Galilee remained the scene of the first preaching, but the traditions of the nativity were attached to Bethlehem.

The text of Isa. 8.23 - 9.1 (9.1-2) in Matt. 4.15f. is specially adapted to prove that Galilee was to be the place where the Messiah should first appear. It is mostly composed of words found in the Septuagint, but presupposes variants closer to the Hebrew text. The most important alteration is the omission of the verbs and temporal adverbs from 8.23. This makes the string of names, which had been their subject, equivalent to λαός in the next verse, and grammatically in apposition to it.[1] Also in 8.23 the Septuagint Γαλιλαία τῶν ἐθνῶν has been adopted, in order to make the Hebrew phrase into a proper name. This is of course the reason why the testimony was chosen for its present purpose. It may be objected that this is in any case what the Hebrew means, but Aquila and Symmachus did not think so.[2] It must then be allowed its full value as a selective reading to secure the desired interpretation.

There are two changes in the second verse. The use of καθη-

[1] There appears to be an exception in the case of ὁδὸν θαλάσσης, but it is really an adverbial accusative, 'towards the sea', correctly understanding the Hebrew—Blass-Debrunner, Grammatik⁹, 1954, §161, 1; Arndt and Gingrich s.v. ὁδός. It is a traditional variant (Aquila and Symmachus), and is found in LXX^A in addition to παραλίαν, though here it is hardly original, because it makes a double translation of דרך הים. Such a phenomenon is not, however, without precedent in the LXX of Isaiah (cf. Seeligmann, The LXX Version of Isaiah, p. 64; R. R. Ottley, The Book of Isaiah according to the Septuagint I, 1904, p. 35).

[2] Aquila: θῖνες (or θῖνας) τῶν ἐθνῶν; Sym.: ὅριον τῶν ἐθνῶν.

μένους for הלכים may have been suggested by Ps. 107.10,[1] but it is more likely that it depends on the following use of the same verb. As Stendahl says,[2] it stresses 'the local, geographical intention' of the interpretation. The other change is the use of ἀνέτειλεν, which refers to the *rise* of a luminary, rather than to its shining. Its normal Hebrew equivalent is זרח, and it occurs in Num. 24.17 (the star of Jacob) and Mal. 3.20 (4.2) (the sun of righteousness). It is possible that it is used here in allusion to one or other of these verses, to emphasize the messianic application.[3] But it serves a specific function in the *pesher* quotation. It means that the Messiah began his work, or even had his origin, in the region of Galilee. He did not merely arrive at some point during his ministry. It is not as if the light were already shining, and then turned its beam on the dark north, but the sun actually arose there, as the prophecy foretold.

These changes fasten attention on Galilee as the proper place for the origin of the Messiah. Moreover it becomes clear that it is intended to include not only the beginning of the ministry, but the birth as well. This follows naturally from the context of the passage in Isa. 9. It speaks of the birth of the Davidic king. It is probable that the passage was first chosen to prove that the son of David would spring from Galilee. The limitation of it to the first preaching belongs to a later stage, when Bethlehem has been accepted as the birthplace.

It is for this secondary purpose that Matthew has inserted the quotation into the narrative of Mark as a comment on the one word Galilee, Mark 1.14. In order to make it fit this situation exactly, he has first put in an editorial note to the effect that on returning to Galilee our Lord took up residence at Capernaum. It is given unusually precise map-indications: τὴν παραθαλασσίαν ἐν ὁρίοις Ζαβουλὼν καὶ Νεφθαλίμ. This is obviously constructed from the following citation. It shows once more that Matthew's interest is in the prophetic anticipation of pictorial details, rather than in the original apologetic usage.

There is a hint of the controversial use of Isa. 8.23-9.1 in John 7.52 and 8.12. We have already observed the objection to Galilee in 7.41. In v. 52 the chief priests and Pharisees confidently deny

---

[1] ישבי חשך צלמות = καθημένους ἐν σκότει καὶ σκιᾷ θανάτου, cf. Luke 1.79.
[2] *SSM*, p. 105.
[3] Cf. Matt. 2.2; Luke 1.78; Heb. 7.14.

that even a prophet[1] could arise from Galilee. The use of ἐγείρεται here exactly corresponds in meaning to Matthew's ἀνέτειλεν (cf. Matt. 11.11; Luke 7.16). By contrast Jesus immediately follows this by claiming to be 'the light of the world'.[2] Notice the use of φῶς, and also περιπατήσῃ ἐν τῇ σκοτίᾳ, which may be an independent translation (adapted) of הַהֹלְכִים בַּחֹשֶׁךְ. It is thus implied that those who are discerning can recognize in the man of Galilee the light promised in Isa. 8.23-9.1.

It seems odd that Isa. 9.5(6) is never quoted in the New Testament, seeing that it is an excellent messianic text. It may be that it was discredited because it was bound up with the untenable theory that the Messiah should be born in Galilee.[3] In the later literature, when the controversy has been settled, it can be referred to in connection with Bethlehem. Thus Luke 1.32f. contain clear echoes of Isa. 9.6(7). Verse 5(6) is then first quoted, with a secondary allegorizing of a single detail, by Justin Martyr (*I Apol.* 35), and occurs again in Irenaeus (e.g. *Epideixis* 56).

### The Son of David

Another aspect of the controversy is resistance to the idea that the Messiah must be descended from David. This has already been observed from the fact that Isa. 9.5 is not cited. Another piece of controversial material which gives evidence of this is the question about David's son (Mark 12.35-37, parr.). This has already been studied in relation to other citations of Ps. 110.1 in ch. II.[4] It was there shown that the argument depends on the distinction between 'my lord' and David himself. But this distinction had been first reached when the argument from literal fulfilment was applied to the Resurrection, as found in Acts 2.34. This proves the messiahship of Jesus independently of descent from David. When the question of descent comes up, it is only necessary to point to this verse in order to show that the messiahship of Jesus does not depend on such a consideration. The verse can even be used to ridicule such an idea. This is what we have in Mark 12.35ff. The Church, at this comparatively early stage, is content to follow Jesus himself in avoiding as far as possible the popular political messianic concepts.

---

[1] Or *the* Prophet, if the sole evidence of Papyrus Bodmer be accepted.
[2] John 7.53-8.11 must of course be disregarded, as no part of the original text.     [3] Dodd, *Acc. Scrip.*, p. 81.     [4] *Supra*, pp. 46f.

Within a short time the necessity for Davidic descent was accepted by the Church, presumably because of the kind of arguments which we have traced in the *pesher* text at Matt. 2.6. It then becomes an urgent matter to prove that Jesus actually was descended from David. As early as Rom. 1.3 St Paul assumes that it is true without question. The writer of II Tim. 2.8 can say 'Remember Jesus Christ, risen from the dead, of the seed of David, according to my Gospel', as if he is presenting two equally valid messianic proofs.

It is probable that the genealogies were compiled in order to provide the necessary proof. Both are independent of the nativity narratives. They trace our Lord's lineage through Joseph to the royal house of David, and then back to the origin of his family from Abraham (Matthew) or Adam (Luke). It is significant that Luke's genealogy comes into the midst of Marcan material, between the Baptism and Temptations. Like the formal opening before the description of John the Baptist in 3.1f., this is often taken as evidence that Luke originally planned the Gospel without the nativity stories. If this is correct, it means that the use of the genealogy belongs to the stage when the Baptism was held to be the moment of messianic revelation. It shows that the man who was then anointed with the Spirit was the Messiah Son of David. On the other hand Matthew's use of the genealogy as the introduction to the Gospel transfers the moment of revelation to the nativity (notice γένεσις in 1.1, 18). Both the messianic revelation and the descent from David are of course fundamental motives in the nativity narratives themselves in both Gospels.

At the same time the Davidic texts which had already been applied to Jesus' Resurrection can now be used again to support his descent from David. There are two cases of this in St Peter's speech in Acts 2. When this was examined in ch. II, we found that both Ps. 16 and Ps. 110.1 were used to prove the messiahship of Jesus from the fact of his Resurrection. But in both cases the argument depends on the contrast with David, the presumed speaker. It can be easily supposed (though the argument does not require it) that the Messiah to whom these texts refer is a scion of the house of David. And if he is a descendant, that in itself is a further messianic proof. So the argument comes full circle. It is probable that Luke himself thought of it in this way, seeing that Davidic descent was universally accepted by the time he was writing, and is to be found throughout Luke-Acts. The only exception is Acts 7.46, where David is mentioned without a trace of connection with Jesus. This is because the speech in this chapter is built on the arguments of the Hellenists, whose christology is based on the divine declaration (i.e. at the Resurrection) and is hostile to popular messianic ideas.[1]

Acts 13.17-23 gives the Davidic argument in its purest form. This is the speech ascribed to St Paul at Pisidian Antioch. We have already found traces of early scriptural exegesis in it.[2] The argument states that God had chosen David, and promised to raise up a ruler from his seed. Jesus is descended from him; therefore he is the expected ruler. But of course David has had numerous descendants, and so a more precise means of identifying the right one is required. This is done by drawing attention to our Lord's death and Resurrection. And so Luke makes his *real* messianic proof by reverting to the argument from the Resurrection, which goes behind the Davidic material to the earliest apologetic. The connection between the two has been helped by the use of Isa. 55.3 ('the sure mercies of David') as a comment on Ps. 16.10. It is specifically applied to the Resurrection. The clue to this is probably to be found in the words 'everlasting covenant', which immediately precede the parts of the verse quoted. The context of Isa. 55.3 shows that the reference is to the blessings that are to be showered upon Israel, and so it appears in the Christian eschatology.[3] This is how it became attached to Ps. 16.10. But Luke's purpose in including it here is presumably to link the psalm verses with the promise mentioned in v. 23. The character of this speech is such as to make it very doubtful whether any of it goes back to St Paul himself. But we must grant that the introduction of Davidic material is not inconsistent with Paul's own position, seeing that the argument from descent is already presupposed in Rom. 1.3. This makes it all the more interesting that it is possible to trace a pre-Davidic element in this chapter.

## The Root of Jesse

Before leaving this question, a word must be said about the 'root of Jesse', Isa. 11.1, 10. The whole passage makes an immediate

---

[1] Further on this speech in the next section.     [2] *Supra*, pp. 41f., 140f.
[3] John 7.37 (spiritualizing of eschatology); Heb. 13.20 (liturgical formula of blessing).

appeal as a messianic prophecy. It is thus surprising to find that it has had little influence on the New Testament. Professor Dodd notes this fact, but nevertheless includes the passage in his list of Primary Sources of Testimonies.[1] It is doubtful whether it can be rated so highly. The passage as a whole gives a picture of the times of the Messiah. It was understood messianically by both the Targum and the Talmud.[2] The description combines the characteristics of a vigorous earthly ruler with the fancifulness of a distant future. This makes it closer to futuristic apocalyptic than to the inaugurated eschatology of the Church's original proclamation. It was thus very different from the ideas of the earliest Christians concerning Jesus. And it is not surprising to find that it is in the realm of apocalyptic that it first enters the New Testament literature. There are allusions to Isa. 11.4 in II Thess. 2.8 and Rev. 19.15, in both cases referring to what Jesus will do at the Parousia.[3] Thus the use of this prophecy, which was not favoured to begin with, seems to have been encouraged by the apocalyptic interest of the period between Jesus and Paul.

Then there is a quotation of Isa. 11.10 in Rom. 15.12: 'There shall be the root of Jesse, and he that ariseth to rule over the Gentiles; on him shall the Gentiles hope.' In the context of the quotation the interest is not in the root of Jesse, but in the preaching to the Gentiles. It is the last of a short catena of testimonies on this subject. The Gentiles will share in the joyful praises of God, because they are under the same ruler, who is the object of their trust. This is rather different from the meaning of the Hebrew, which suggests that the root of Jesse will be the point to which the Gentiles will tend, i.e. conversion to Judaism. Paul thus makes his point by pressing home the implications of the Septuagint. It is not adduced as a messianic testimony, though of course Paul is not opposed to the idea of the son of David (Rom. 1.3). It is only used because of its application to the Gentiles. This must be seen in relation to the apocalyptic usage in II Thessalonians. The preaching to the Gentiles was part of the apocalyptic programme.[4] This

---

[1] *Acc. Scrip.*, pp. 83, 107.

[2] Stenning, *op. cit.*, p. 40; *Sanhedrin* 93b.

[3] The object of the Messiah's displeasure in this verse is 'the ungodly' (ἀσεβῆ), presumably intended as a collective singular. In II Thess. 2.8 has become the apocalyptic character ὁ ἄνομος. In Rev. 19.15 it is τὰ ἔθνη.

[4] This is presupposed in Rom. 10-11, especially 11.25. The most obvious text is Mark 13.10. G. D. Kilpatrick, however, has argued strenuously

will be shown to have had wider implications in the next chapter.[1]

It is only in the Fourth Gospel that we have an allusion which indicates the christological use of this passage.[2] In the account of the Baptism of Jesus the words ἐφ' ὃν ἂν ἴδῃς τὸ πνεῦμα καταβαῖνον καὶ μένον ἐπ' αὐτόν (1.33) are reminiscent of Isa. 11.2 ἀναπαύσεται ἐπ' αὐτὸν πνεῦμα τοῦ θεοῦ.[3] But of course even as early as Mark the presentation of the story presupposes that the Baptism is the moment of messianic revelation. The context is christological before the allusion to the root of Jesse has been introduced. So we cannot argue from it that Davidic descent was actually a formative influence in claiming that Jesus was the Messiah.

These few references to Isa. 11.1-10 have been instructive, because they have shown how even a great messianic prophecy was only reluctantly adopted by the Church to prove its faith. The first Christians, like their opponents, knew Jesus as the man of Galilee, and were not aware that he was a direct descendant from David, still less that he had been born in Bethlehem, the city of David. They believed that he was the Lord's Christ on account of the things that they had seen and heard, his life and teaching, his death and Resurrection, and the outpouring of the Spirit, and were not concerned to make him fit popular messianic ideas, which were often confused and mutually contradictory. In some respects, as the preceding chapters have shown, they were able to modify accepted messianic ideas profoundly in the light of what had actually happened. But in the matter of origins the stress of controversy forced them to investigate the early history of Jesus. The result was the assertion that Jesus was descended in the direct line from David through Joseph, and that he was born at Bethlehem. These may both be historically accurate, and it is not the purpose of this study to throw doubt upon them. But it is important to

that Mark intended a different punctuation, profoundly altering the sense, 'The Gentile Mission in Mark and Mark 13.9-11', in D. E. Nineham (ed.), *Studies in the Gospels: Essays in memory of R. H. Lightfoot*, 1955, pp. 145-58. On the whole subject see J. Jeremias, *Jesus' Promise to the Nations* ET (SBT 24), 1958, especially p. 71.

[1] Of course by the time of Revelation all the messianic and apocalyptic themes have been fused, so that we find the Root of Jesse as a title of Jesus in Rev. 5.5, 22.16.

[2] For the sake of completeness mention may be made of three other passages where there seem to be allusions to Isa. 11.1-10, viz. John 7.24, Eph. 6.14, I Peter 4.14. None of them is significant for our purpose.

[3] The text of John has influenced some MSS of Mark 1.11 to add καὶ μένον, perhaps specifically to introduce allusion to Isa. 11.2.

realize that they do not belong to the early proclamation, and only came to light in the subsequent controversy. This explains why they are presented in a legendary and tendentious way. The *theoretical* acceptance of the Davidic position is the first result of the controversy, and precedes the nativity stories. It is possible that Paul was writing at this intermediate stage of development.

## 2. THE PROPHET

It was only natural that during his lifetime Jesus should be popularly called a prophet. This followed from his declared function of preparing for the kingdom of God. In fact the various messianic claimants of the first century were generally regarded as prophets.[1] There are moments when Jesus likes to refer to himself as a prophet (Matt. 13.57, parr.; Luke 13.33). Of course these need be no more than acceptance of the popular estimate for the sake of an *argumentum ad hominem*. The idea is used for local colour in Matt. 21.11, 46; Luke 7.16, 39, 24.19-21. There is speculation whether Jesus is John the Baptist, Elijah *redivivus*, or the Prophet of Deut. 18 (Matt. 16.14, parr.). But the question we now have to ask concerns the claims about Jesus in the early days of the Church. Does the New Testament provide evidence that his life on earth was primarily explained in terms of the Prophet of Deuteronomy? On this view his work was that of the Prophet, and the Resurrection proves that he is ready as *Messias designatus* to return and claim the kingdom when the work of preparation which he has begun is complete. Put more simply, this view supposes that, when it is asked 'Who is Jesus?', the immediate answer is likely to be 'The Prophet like Moses, whose word must be obeyed'.

For the purposes of this study, what we have to do is to examine the quotations and allusions to Deut. 18.15, 19. There are no certain allusions in the Synoptic Gospels, except in the divine words in the account of the Transfiguration. The words are similar to those at the Baptism, consisting of the opening phrase of Isa. 42.1, probably also alluding to Ps. 2.7, but with the addition of ἀκούετε αὐτοῦ (Matt. 17.5; Mark 9.7) or αὐτοῦ ἀκούετε (Luke 9.35). One can only speculate whether this addition was originally meant to allude to Deut. 18.15 (αὐτοῦ ἀκούσεσθε). But the inversion of the words in Luke certainly looks like an intentional change for closer conformity with it. It was suggested in the last chapter that the

[1] Josephus, *Ant.* XX 97f., 169.

divine words may have come into the Transfiguration narrative direct from their use in connection with the Resurrection, and independently of the formation of the Baptism story. Isa. 42.1 and Ps. 2.7 were used by the early Christians to prove the messiahship of Jesus, and the Resurrection was the moment of messianic revelation. The Transfiguration anticipates this moment, but with the special additional features of the presence of Moses and Elijah. In the original divine saying the choice of scriptural words not only marked out Jesus as the Messiah, but also characterized him as *chosen* and *revealed* as such.[1] The additional words also serve a specific function in the adaptation of the quotation material, and it is reasonable to suppose that this is closely connected with the additional feature in the story. Jesus is not only the Messiah, already revealed, but also the Prophet, promised by Moses, and represented by Elijah (whose return at the End was indeed expected).[2] The additional words indicate that he is to be *heeded*. This is a third element in the progressive adaptation of the text.

The conclusion that these facts suggest is that the idea of the Prophet is a factor that has been added to the existing christology. It is not an alternative or a more primitive position, but the agglomeration of originally distinct concepts which naturally proceeds in the course of later reflection.

This conclusion is borne out by more general considerations. There are indications of a Moses typology in both Matthew and Luke, whereby the presentation of certain aspects of our Lord's saving work invites comparison with the events of the Exodus. We may instance the Q account of the Temptations, Matthew's setting of the Sermon on the Mount as a New Law, and Luke's elaboration of the Transfiguration itself. But this typology is not equivalent to a messianism in terms of the Prophet of Deut. 18. It is rather a consequence of a soteriology in terms of the Exodus. The idea of the New Exodus took a firm root in the Church's dogmatic tradition. The classic passage is I Cor. 10, but other references abound in the New Testament and early Fathers. But the accompanying Moses typology was never developed to any great extent. This is probably because the figure of Moses could not be easily separated from the idea of the Law. The rejection of

---

[1] *Supra*, p. 146.
[2] I Enoch 90.31 (the 'young ram'); II (4) Esd. 6.26; Targum of Jonathan on Ex. 40.10.

the Law, which was the centre of the Judaistic controversy and subsequent anti-Judaic polemic, effectively prevented it. It only creeps in later, when the Davidic messiahship of Jesus is so well established that it can be included in the gathering fulness of christological ideas.

In the Fourth Gospel the possibility that Jesus is the Prophet is mentioned several times.[1] This may be evidence of a primitive argument based on Deut. 18.15, but the text itself is not quoted. Alternatively it may be another example of the later use of this theme as christological ideas accumulated. In this connection it is interesting to compare the questioning of John the Baptist in John 1.19-22. It is clearly related to the questioning of our Lord in the Synoptic Gospels, but now 'one of the prophets' has become 'the Prophet'. In his replies, the Baptist refuses to be identified with any of the three personalities suggested. He is not the Messiah, nor Elijah *redivivus*, nor the Prophet. This contradicts the theory, common to Mark[2] and Q,[3] that he did in fact fulfil the Elijah expectation. This Synoptic tradition conveniently settles the question of the position of John the Baptist in relation to that of Jesus himself. If the Church preached that Jesus is the Christ it was necessary to decide about John, whose basic message was so similar.[4] It was natural to assign to him the role of the Forerunner. This is the logical sequence of events, and raises the presumption that, in rejecting the title to Elijah, the Fourth Gospel preserves the earlier tradition. We must respect the author's care to distinguish between the messianic expectations known to him and the record of the actual Christian claims. Just as he recognizes that the Baptist might have been Elijah, but refuses to say that he *was*, so he testifies to the fact that Jesus could have been the Prophet, but gives no sign that this was ever actually claimed.[5]

[1] John 4.19, 6.14, 7.40, 52, 9.17.　　　　[2] Mark 9.11-13.
[3] Matt. 11.2-19 = Luke 7.18-35.
[4] Cf. C. K. Barrett, 'The OT in the Fourth Gospel', *JTS* 48, 1947, pp. 155-69; C. H. Kraeling, *John the Baptist*, 1951, ch. V.
[5] I have not thought it necessary for the purposes of this study to go into the complicated question of the two testimonies on John the Baptist, Isa. 40.3 ( = Matt. 3.3 parr.) and Mal. 3.1 ( = Matt. 11.10, par.; Mark 1.2). The use of Isa. 40.3 is to define the Baptist's *function*, and the adoption of the LXX text makes it more relevant as *description*. Note that John 1.23 accurately represents this functional motive. The text of Mal. 3.1 has been conflated with that of Ex. 23.20, and uses words which do not occur in the LXX here. The conflation has probably happened through influence of the synagogue *haphtaroth* (Malachi being read in conjunction with

It is only in Acts that there are true quotations of Deut. 18.15. They occur in Acts 3.22f. and 7.37, both in contexts which differ importantly from the usual christology of Acts and are often held to be specially reliable. Jesus is not actually called the Prophet in either of these passages. But the quotations raise the presumption that this is intended. We must therefore observe carefully the function of the quotation in each case.

The argument of Acts 3.19-26 may be briefly summarized as follows. Repent, in order to be ready to receive the *Messias designatus* (τὸν προκεχειρισμένον ὑμῖν Χριστόν), Jesus. He will not act in this capacity until 'the restoration of all things', and in the meantime this opportunity of repentance is available. The time may be presumed to be short, and after it there will be no further chance to repent. The warning has already been given in the uncompromising threat of Deut. 18.19. On the other hand obedience entitles the hearers to the blessings promised to the seed of Abraham. Jesus was raised up precisely to fulfil this promise, and so the final issue—destruction or the promised inheritance—rests on response to his message.

The passage contains two quotations, one constituting the threat (Deut. 18.15-19) and the other the promise (Gen. 12.3). Although they both differ importantly from the Septuagint in their form, their vocabulary is derived from it almost entirely, so that it is best to regard them as *pesher* adaptations in a Septuagint milieu. Moreover they have influenced the vocabulary of the context in which they stand, and so must be considered in relation to it.

The form of the quotation of Deut. 18.15-19 has two major characteristics. The first is the very considerable abbreviation, largely achieved by telescoping the repetitions of vv. 15 and 18, and the omission of the intervening material. The second is the

Ex. 20). It has come into the Synoptic tradition in contexts concerned with the Baptist's *identity*, and carries with it the explicit identification with Elijah of Mal. 3.23 (4.5), cf. Luke 1.17, 76-79. In Matt. 11.7-11, par. the quotation may well have been added in the course of transmission to clarify this issue. But in fact it spoils the climax of the passage. It must still be considered a serious possibility that the presence of the quotation in Mark 1.2 is a very early interpolation; besides the difficulty of the ascription to Isaiah, its omission in Matt. and Luke has never been satisfactorily explained. For a discussion of the text, see Stendahl, *SSM*, pp. 47-53; for the influence of the *haphtaroth*, J. Mann, *The Bible as Read and Preached in the Old Synagogue* I, 1940, p. 479; and for the Church's use of the testimonies, Dodd, *Acc. Scrip.*, pp. 71f.

substitution of a very much stronger form of the threat at the end of v. 19 by using a fairly frequent Leviticus phrase, to which Lev. 23.29 offers the closest parallel. These two factors concentrate attention on one point, the solemnity of the threat.[1] The use of ἐλάλησαν in the verses immediately preceding and following the quotation is clearly derived from it, and puts the work of the other prophets in relation with it. They also testified to the divine displeasure at men's disobedience.

The quotation which attests the promise is primarily drawn from Gen. 12.3, with πατριαί for the more usual φυλαί. Gen. 22.18 (and the identical Gen. 26.4) does not provide such a close parallel, but seems to be the source of the phrase ἐν τῷ σπέρματί σου. The quotation is thus in a conventionalized form, and not to be interpreted by any single context. But it is worth noting that the opening words of Gen. 12.3 are very suitable to the argument in Acts 3, for God says, 'I will bless them that bless thee, and him that curseth thee will I curse.' In the following verse (Acts 3.26) εὐλογοῦντα is probably suggested by the quotation. Jesus, then, fulfils the promise to Abraham, and is the means of divine blessing.

The two quotations are the reverse sides of a single coin. Deut. 18.15-19 is a warning against failure to heed prophets, in particular a Prophet who is to come, and Jesus is that Prophet. Gen. 12.3 is a promise of blessing to the obedient, which will be fulfilled in the seed of Abraham, and Jesus is that seed. The latter argument is strikingly similar to St Paul's argument in Gal. 3. Here he quotes the same text from one or other of the Genesis passages, but with ἐν σοί (Gal. 3.8). A little later, in v. 16, he defines this by quoting the words καὶ τῷ σπέρματι, and argues that this is only truly fulfilled in the one person of Christ.

It must surely be evident from this that the two quotations belong in the primitive Christian apologetic to the issue of response. When Paul (who accepted our Lord's Davidic messiahship) argued from the promise to Abraham, he was not making out an Abrahamic christology. Similarly the implicit identification of Jesus with the Prophet in Acts does not mean a theory of christology in terms of this figure. The real difference between Acts and Galatians at this point is that Paul is concerned with the Judaistic

---

[1] It is interesting that in 4QTestimonia, which contains Deut. 18.15, the whole point of the document lies in a threat of punishment to the disobedient.

controversy, whereas Acts uses the same material for the question of response in general. This is something that was noted frequently in the last chapter.

The impression that we are left with is that the idea of the Prophet came into the gathering fulness of christology by way of the issue of response.[1] With this in mind, we may deal more briefly with the other quotation of Deut. 18.15 in Acts 7.37.

The speech of St Stephen includes a long series of reminiscences about Moses, designed to show how he was the saviour of Israel, but was constantly disobeyed. The climax of this section of the speech is the story of the giving of the Law at Sinai. Corresponding to it there is the climax of apostasy in the worship of the golden calf. The note that it was also Moses who promised the Prophet has been slipped in just before the giving of the Law. This is out of place in the sequence, for it properly belongs to the legislation ostensibly given much later on at Kadesh-Barnea. Presumably it has been placed earlier for the sake of the climax. The climax consists of the supreme revelation of God in the Law, the disobedience of the people, and the consequent divine punishment (v. 42). It is, then, a most terrible example of what happens when God's warning is not heeded. Now it becomes intelligible why Deut. 18.15 has been inserted prematurely. The *whole of the passage*, including the warning of v. 19, is implied by the argument. This means that the point of the quotation, as primarily concerned with response, is precisely the same as in Acts 3.

Closer examination of the text lends support to this interpretation. The quotation really comprises the same amalgam of Deut. 18.15 and 18 as Acts 3.22 as far as it goes, the text being identical (except for omission of $\kappa\acute{\upsilon}\rho\iota\upsilon s$). This suggests that the words quoted are just a pointer, to indicate the whole of the quotation given in the former passage. This is not impossible, because the function of this testimony in Stephen's speech differs from the majority of quotations, which are purely narrative material. This one is not part of the narrative, but is introduced to show the interpretation. The opening words are sufficient for this purpose, though the real point lies in the threat in the part that is omitted, as so often happens in the rabbinic literature.[2] Our conclusion must be that Deut. 18.15 here has no more significance for primitive christology

---

[1] The use of $\pi\alpha\hat{\iota}\delta\alpha$ in Acts 3.26 is derived from v. 13, alluding to Isa 52.13 (cf. *supra*, p. 79).    [2] E.g. *Pirqe Aboth* 3.3.

than in Acts 3. This is not the only example of Luke's capacity to use the same apologetic scriptural material in different speeches.[1]

It will be seen that this conclusion runs counter to much recent opinion among scholars that the figure of the Prophet in Deut. 18 was the main plank in a primitive christology. It is true that both the speeches where the quotation occurs exhibit very peculiar characteristics, which set them apart from the general development in the New Testament. But the analysis of the quotation has shown that it is hazardous to use *this* as the key to the problem.[2] And we should hesitate before seeing in it an anticipation of the Judaeo-Christian christology of the *Clementine Recognitions*. On the other hand, the use of the Deuteronomy passage in the apologetic of response brought the idea of the Prophet to the fore in Jewish and Christian discussion, and readily explains how the Judaeo-Christian position was reached.

### 3. THE PRE-EXISTENT CHRIST

We now return to the main stream of christological development to trace some further threads. The common starting-point of the lines of thought which have been examined is the revelation of the Messiah/Son of Man at the Resurrection of Jesus. Although the idea of the Messiah can and must be distinguished from the Son of Man for understanding some parts of the New Testament, they were already fused to a great extent in late Judaism, and this fusion is found in the New Testament tradition as well, in a variety of forms and emphases. It was concentration on strictly messianic elements which led to the demand for descent from David. But it is the Son of Man which is the basis of another idea, that Jesus will not only come again at the End of the Age, but was also preexistent in the counsels of God before his birth.

In the rabbinic literature the theory is expressed that the Law existed in the mind of God from the beginning of the creation, even though it was not revealed until God spoke to Moses on Sinai.[3] In late Judaism there is a similar theory that the Son of Man exists in the mind of God, but his manifestation awaits the End of the Age. Meanwhile, however, there may be special reve-

---

[1] Cf. the use of Ps. 16 in Acts 2 and 13.
[2] Such is the position of M. Simon, *St Stephen and the Hellenists in the Primitive Church*, pp. 59-63.
[3] SB II, pp. 334f.; IV, p. 435.

lations of what is already existent, though still awaiting its due time, by means of apocalypses to privileged individuals, such as Enoch or Salathiel. The fusion of the Messiah with the Son of Man means that he is also sometimes spoken of as pre-existent in this way.[1]

The identification of Jesus with the Messiah/Son of Man at a very early time would naturally carry with it some feeling at least that he, who had been manifested at the Resurrection, had existed previously for this very purpose in the mind of God.[2] Where links with direct memories of the life of Jesus were few, and so speculation could be comparatively unrestrained, the idea of pre-existence would gain great christological importance. Two passages in which this has happened are the opening of Hebrews and the first chapter of Colossians. In both of them there is a direct connection between the Resurrection and the manifestation of the pre-existent Son.

Thus in Heb. 1.5 there is a quotation of the messianic Ps. 2.7, which, as we have seen, was originally applied to the Resurrection. But here it is adduced to prove the prior metaphysical relationship with God, in contrast to the angels. A Davidic 'enthronement' text (II Sam. 7.14) is used in the same way in the same verse. It is presupposed that the whole life of Jesus partook of the character of divine sonship by virtue of the manifestation which came at its close. No earlier manifestation is mentioned, but in v. 6 it is assumed that the moment of birth is in some sense a revelation of sonship.[3] The use of $\pi\rho\omega\tau\acute{o}\tau o\kappa o\varsigma$ in this verse is derived ultimately from Ps. 89.28, which is interpreted messianically in the rabbinic literature,[4] and may well be in the author's mind in this context.

[1] S. Mowinckel, *He that Cometh*, pp. 334, 386-9.

[2] J. Knox, *Christ the Lord*, pp. 94f., shows that St Paul speaks in a way that presupposes the pre-existence of Jesus, as something that he simply takes for granted: Phil. 2.6; II Cor. 8.9; Rom. 15.3. Cf. Mark 1.38, 10.45.

[3] The quotation from Deut. 32.43, 'And let all the angels of God worship him', can be applied to the Messiah because of the change of subject. In the preceding verses God has been speaking in the first person, promising salvation. If God is still thought to be the speaker, then 'him' means the Messiah, who is to act on his behalf. Another line of this verse is quoted in a short catena of Gentiles quotations in Rom. 15.10. Both depend on the LXX for their interpretation. The words cited in Heb. 1.6 are not found in MT. Their precise form is that given in the *Odae* of LXX^A. It is interesting (but not actually relevant to the use of the text here) that the Hebrew of these words has appeared at Qumran. See P. W. Skehan, 'A Fragment of the "Song of Moses" (Deut. 32) from Qumran', *BASOR* 136, Dec. 1954, pp. 12-15.

[4] SB II, pp. 338, 426; III, p. 258.

In Col. 1.15-20 there is a formal balance between our Lord as the firstborn of creation and our Lord as the firstborn of the dead. The pre-existent Son was God's agent in creation; at his Resurrection he has become the agent of a new creation. It is probable that ἐν αὐτῷ ἐκτίσθη in v. 16 depends on an old *midrash* of Gen. 1.1.[1] This has been rewritten in vv. 19f. in terms of the Resurrection and its consequences. It may well be that the clue to this constructive thought has been the double meaning latent in πρωτό-τοκος. It was already a messianic term in virtue of its occurrence in Ps. 89, a psalm which was first applied to the Resurrection of Jesus. In Rom. 8.29 we find St Paul using πρωτότοκος of the inclusive nature of the Resurrection, but without the metaphysical connotation. We may conjecture that here Paul is nearer to the original Christian use of this term, and that Col. 1 represents a later development, whether his own or some other writer's.

From these examples it can be seen that the recognition of metaphysical implications in the revelation of the Messiah at the Resurrection inevitably draws the thought back to the moment of his birth. This now becomes the time of messianic manifestation. But the idea has been reached in a way that differs from the gradual movement from the Resurrection, back through the Passion and ministry to the Baptism, which was observed in the last chapter. There the motive was largely the need of the first Christians to show to their compatriots that the life and work of Jesus was truly messianic, even though it did not fit into conventional ideas. In this case the apologetic is directed towards men of the Hellenistic world, whether Jews or Gentiles, who are concerned with the metaphysical speculations which always attracted the Greek mind. That it is probable that from the very first pre-existence was implied in some way by the messianic claim, is itself a Hellenistic trait in Jewish speculation. Its development within Christianity did not happen at once, but only in a Greek-speaking milieu. This is shown by the fact that the Old Testament allusions in connection with this subject are always to the Greek Scriptures.

The speech ascribed to St Paul in Acts 17 aptly shows the sort of objections which helped to draw out this development. The speech begins with a theistic view of the universe, explicitly referring to Greek thought. It ends with the typically Jewish announce-

---

[1] I.e. Prov. 8.22, κύριος ἔκτισέν με ἀρχὴν (רֵאשִׁית) ὁδῶν αὐτοῦ. See C. F. Burney, 'Christ as the ΑΡΧΗ of Creation,' *JTS* 27, 1926, pp. 160-77.

ment of the coming Day of the Lord. The link between them is the Resurrection of Jesus. The doctrine of the pre-existence of Christ makes it possible to see the continuity of the creation, the Resurrection, and the coming judgment. The Christian teaching thus becomes more credible to people who have a basically cyclic view of time.

The connection between the pre-existence of Jesus and his manifestation at the moment of birth is stated with masterly brevity and evocative power in John 1.14, 'And the Word became flesh'. This combines the previous Jewish speculation about the pre-existent Law with the Logos of Greek philosophy, and equates both with the pre-existent Christ. Moreover it is probable that the words are intended to imply the virgin birth to instructed Christian readers.[1] It is in this context that we see how congenial the idea of virgin birth is to the thought of the manifestation of the pre-existent Son. It automatically links up the question of the origins of Jesus with a whole wealth of mythology and symbolism.

### Isaiah 7.14

Meanwhile the line of thought that is interested in descent from David has also tended to bring the moment of birth into prominence. It is likely to value any traditions about the birth which can be regarded as prophetic portents. So, in spite of tracing descent through Joseph, it is captured by the tradition of the virgin birth, when that comes to light. The confluence of these two traditions of the origins of Jesus appears in the use of the much debated text, Isa. 7.14: 'Behold, a virgin shall conceive, and bear a son, and shall call his name Immanuel.'

The importance of this text can be gauged by the fact that both Matthew and Luke have the combination of both the Davidic and pre-existence strands in the tradition of the virgin birth (though the Davidic strand *alone* is embarrassed by it), and that this testimony is the basis of the presentation of it in both Gospels. Thus the narrative of Matt. 1.18-23 contains the *pesher* citation of it at v. 23. But phrases from it occur in v. 18 (ἐν γαστρὶ ἔχουσα) and in v. 21 (τέξεται δὲ υἱόν, καὶ καλέσεις τὸ ὄνομα αὐτοῦ), which together make up almost the complete quotation. The latter part is repeated in v. 25. It is clear from the agreement of ἔχουσα in v. 18 with the

---

[1] Cf. E. C. Hoskyns and F. N. Davey, *The Fourth Gospel*[2], 1947, Detached Note 2, pp. 163-6.

particular variant ἕξει in the citation,[1] that the passage in its present form has been built around the quotation. It indicates pregnancy rather than conception. This is essential to the narrative of Joseph's perplexity.

Similarly Isa. 7.14 is the underlying motive in Luke 1.26-38, although it is a much more polished and allusive composition. It is suggested in v. 27 (παρθένον), and is quoted almost verbatim in v. 31, except for the necessary change of person in the verbs. This time the variant is συλλήμψῃ. This also is necessary for the narrative, which is concerned with the conception. Isa. 7.14 provides the phraseology again in Luke 2.21.

Comparison of both passages shows that in each case the quotation serves two functions, the virgin birth and the choice of the name Jesus. This is the more remarkable, because the text itself provides another name, Immanuel, which has been retained in Matthew's *pesher* citation.[2] The discrepancy is probably the reason for the modification of καλέσεις to καλέσουσιν, and the addition of the translation of it, μεθ' ἡμῶν ὁ θεός, from Isa. 8.8, 10.[3] This addition is only really necessary if there is a difficulty to be forestalled. Perhaps we should postulate an earlier use of this testimony in christological discussion. It is objected that it is not applicable to Jesus, because the name is wrong. The answer is that it is a title which corresponds to the truth about Jesus; his coming means that God is present to carry out his work of salvation. Such an explan-

---

[1] This is the majority LXX reading. LXX[B], a number of witnesses to the text of Origen, Lucian and the Catena recension, and also some of the Fathers, give λήμψεται. Aquila, Sym., and Theodotion have συλλαμβάνει. Cf. Luke 1.31.

[2] G. D. Kilpatrick, *The Origins of the Gospel according to St Matthew*, p. 53, has suggested that the quotation of Isa. 7.14 here does not belong to the story as Matthew originally planned it, and that the introductory formula has been transferred from v. 21b. The *pesher* text is thus αὐτὸς γὰρ σώσει τὸν λαὸν αὐτοῦ ἀπὸ τῶν ἁμαρτιῶν αὐτοῦ. This makes a much neater story, but is open to several objections. (*a*) The story is built around Isa. 7.14, which provides the real motive of it; the conventional explanation of the meaning of the name Jesus is a subsidiary interest (cf. Ecclus. 46.1). (*b*) Kilpatrick claims that v. 21b is an independent translation of Ps. 130.8, but both in MT and in LXX the essential point of comparison is wrong (פדה/λυτρώσεται for ישׁע/σώσει). (*c*) If it is not a *pesher* text, this verse can be regarded as a combination of conventional biblical phrases, especially Ps. 28.9 הושׁיעה את־עמך = σῶσον τὸν λαόν σου (notice ישׁועות משׁיחו in the preceding verse). The addition of ἀπὸ τῶν ἁμαρτιῶν αὐτοῦ may reflect the influence of Isa. 53.4, 8, 12, cf. I Cor. 15.4.

[3] Cf. Stendahl, *SSM*, p. 98.

ation represents the genuine meaning of the passage in Isaiah. If this was entailed in the original usage of this testimony in the primitive apologetic, it suggests that the choice of it was to support the messianic claim rather than the virgin birth. With the development of transcendental ideas about Jesus, it deepens christology by conveying the notion that in the person of Jesus God is 'with us' (Isa. 8.8). There are possible allusions to this phrase in John 1.14, Matt. 28.20, Rom. 8.31, and Rev. 21.3.

It is impossible to be more than speculative where possibilities are so tantalizing and actual evidence is so slight. But it may be worth while to follow these reflections a little further along the lines of the present enquiry. This means that we must postulate an original interpretation of the text consistent with the meaning of its proper context. The passage is a prophecy to the house of David to the effect that God's presence to save his people will be marked by the birth of a particular child. It is highly probable that Jewish as well as Christian exegetes held that this was the Messiah of the house of David.[1] The text thus has a legitimate use to assert the idea that the moment of birth is the manifestation of the Messiah.

The really significant thing about this is the fact that the translation 'virgin' (as opposed to 'young woman') does not enter into the matter at this stage at all. It could have been used in the original Hebrew without question of the tradition of exegesis reflected in the Septuagint translation παρθένος. However there is no evidence that it was so used. Rather the fact that the *pesher* text is exclusively based on the Septuagint, unlike the majority of Matthew's formula-quotations, indicates the contrary. What does seem probable is that, even though it was first used in the Christian apologetic in the Septuagint form, the interest lay in its usefulness as a testimony of messianic manifestation, rather than in the virgin birth as such.

Nevertheless the translation 'virgin' is there. Just as one objection, which we have seen in Matthew, lay in the wrong name, so another lay in the fact that the text is only applicable to Jesus if he is virgin-born. And here Justin may be right in his assertion that the Septuagint had genuine Jewish tradition behind it.[2] So it may

---

[1] Trypho's view that it refers to the birth of Hezekiah gives virtual support to this contention, Justin, *Dial.* 68.

[2] *Dial.* 71. It is an exegetical tradition in which the 'young woman' is interpreted symbolically as 'the virgin of Israel' (Jer. 31.4).

well have been agreed on all hands that such was required by the use of this text. It would follow from this that it was the need to meet this challenge which touched off the enquiry into the exact mode of the birth of our Lord, in addition to other predisposing factors noted earlier in this section. Consequently the only significant traditions of the virgin birth, i.e. the infancy narratives of Matthew and Luke, are couched in terms of Isa. 7.14, and this remains the final and classic application of the text.

### Infancy Legends

The acceptance of the birth as the moment of manifestation has the inevitable result of attracting further material to the infancy traditions. In the case of Luke it is possible that there was already similar legendary material ready to hand in connection with John the Baptist, to which he has added traditions concerning Jesus, and presumably rewritten the whole.[1] The rest of Matthew's stories, in ch. 2, are contrived around a series of testimonies, some of which have been used with a different motive at a previous stage of exegetical work.

In the story of the Magi the influence of Num. 24.17 and Isa. 60.1 is very clear, but the only text selected for citation is Micah 5.1(2). This is not because it is vitally important for the story, for it only supplies the one detail that Bethlehem is to be the birthplace, but because it has already assumed importance in the apologetic concerning the origins of Jesus, as we have seen. Similarly the enigmatic proof-text that 'he will be called a Nazarene' has a pictorial and biographical interest as it stands at the end of this group of episodes, whereas we have found reason to believe that its original apologetic purpose was something very different.

The other two quotations in this series present a far more difficult problem. The first is Matt. 2.15 = Hos. 11.1, 'Out of Egypt have I called my son'. The possibility that Matthew has taken this over from an apologetic use for a different purpose is suggested by the fact that his *text* is very close to the Hebrew,[2] whereas his

---

[1] C. H. Kraeling, *John the Baptist*, pp. 16, 195 n. 15.

[2] Matt. 2.15 ( =Aquila)            LXX                    Hos. 11.1

ἐξ (Aq. ἀπὸ) Αἰγύπτου          ἐξ Αἰγύπτου              מִמִּצְרַיִם

ἐκάλεσα τὸν                       μετεκάλεσα τὰ            קָרָאתִי

υἱόν μου.                          τέκνα αὐτοῦ.             לְבָנִי

The complete information of the Hexapla is provided at this point by

*interpretation* appears to be guided by the Septuagint of Num. 24.7f. This chapter has already supplied the idea of the star in the east, and it is well known that the prophecies of Balaam received messianic interpretation at an early date.[1] In Num. 24.7 the Septuagint plainly imports the messianic motive. The opening words of the Hebrew ('water shall flow from his buckets'), which are manifestly corrupt, are abandoned, and the passage reads ἐξελεύσεται ἄνθρωπος ἐκ τοῦ σπέρματος αὐτοῦ.[2] This means that the beginning of v. 8, θεὸς ὡδήγησεν αὐτὸν ἐξ Αἰγύπτου, which should refer to Jacob, could be understood to mean the Messiah. It is thus possible that Matthew interpreted the *pesher* text of Hos. 11.1 in the light of this passage, although it had been originally selected for a different purpose. What this was can only be guessed tentatively. It is tempting to think that this was one of the scriptures used to expound the redemptive significance of the death and Resurrection of Jesus, especially as the prophecy of Hosea was fairly widely used by the early Church. So Professor Dodd says, 'It would be quite understandable that the words of Hosea's prophecy should first have been held to be fulfilled in the deliverance of God's people "in Christ" (for the place where the Lord was crucified is "spiritually called Egypt", Rev. 11.8), and subsequently transferred to Christ himself.'[3]

The quotation of Jer. 31.15 in Matt. 2.18 is not easy to assess, because of its ambiguous relationship to the Septuagint.[4] Stendahl holds that it is an independent translation from the Hebrew, but without intentional changes.[5] The significant thing about it is the application which it receives in Matthew's narrative. In the original

LXX codex 86, and the scribe adds the comment that 'Matthew rendered it as the Hebrew plainly has it, and as Aquila interpreted it.'

[1] This is certainly true of Num. 24.17, cf. *Test. Levi* 18.3; *Test. Judah* 24.1; CD 7.19f.; 1QM 11.6f.; 4Q*Testimonia*. In the rabbinic literature Num. 24.7 is interpreted of the Torah, SB I, p. 780; III, p. 326.

[2] So also the Old Latin (*procedet homo de semine eius*). The Syriac Peshitta ('a mighty man shall proceed from his sons') and Targum Onkelos ('a king shall grow great, who shall be reared from his sons') appear to be independent of the LXX.

[3] *Acc. Scrip.*, p. 103.

[4] Most of Matthew's words are found in either LXX[A] or LXX[B]. Peculiar to Matthew are omission of θρῆνος (which is restored by some MSS), addition of πολύς, the verb κλαίουσα for ἀποκλαιομένη, and τὰ τέκνα αὐτῆς for ἐπὶ τῶν υἱῶν αὐτῆς. None of these differences bring the text closer to MT, in fact the reverse. They give the impression of unrevised recensional variants.

[5] *SSM*, pp. 102f.

context it is a prophecy of hope. Rachel can refrain from weeping, because she is to be provided with a new family. Matthew only thinks of the grief caused by the massacre of the Innocents. But it is probable that the early Church was aware of the proper meaning, so that the *pesher* text was in fact selected as a prophecy of the reversal of grief. The chapter (but not this verse) is quoted or alluded to elsewhere in the New Testament, always in a good sense.[1] It would seem then that the *pesher* text in this case is incomplete, and that the hopeful note of the next and following verses is intended. This would be another example of the rabbinic style in which the purpose of the quotation is to be found in the succeeding phrases to which the words actually quoted have been merely a pointer.[2]

It will be observed that, different as these two quotations are, the object for which they were originally selected is very similar, expressing the redemptive meaning of the salvation-event. Although they are both used in Matt. 2 with the evangelist's usual descriptive motive, they have not lost all connection with their original application. What has happened is that the oscillation between the people of God thought of as included in Christ, and the person of Christ himself who has redeemed them, has veered towards the latter with the growing interest in christology. 'My son' of Hos. 11.1 has been taken literally of Jesus, revealed as the Messiah/Son of God at his birth. The weeping of Rachel has been turned into joy because of the preservation of her true child, 'Jesus Christ, the son of David, the son of Abraham' (Matt. 1.1). Hence the transition from the original redemptive use of these quotations to their place in the nativity narratives is precisely the growing sense that the birth is the moment of messianic manifestation, which has been engaging our attention. From this point of view the whole series of incidents in Matt. 2 are portents presaging the great acts of redemption at the close of the Gospel. Jesus is treated as a king, yet rejected by Herod; he is thrust out to Egypt, the house of bondage and symbol of death; but Herod's evil intentions are defeated, so that Jesus is able to return and live in Galilee.

Finally, the new emphasis on the significance of the moment of birth was bound to affect the presentation of the Baptism of our Lord, which hitherto had been held to be the moment of reve-

---

[1] See Dodd, *Acc. Scrip.*, pp. 44-46, 85f.
[2] *Supra*, p. 209.

lation. It has forced Matthew to take notice of an objection (perhaps voiced at this time on other grounds as well) that the baptism of repentance is inappropriate to the sinless Son of God, if not virtually blasphemous. Matthew has placed this objection on the lips of John the Baptist with excellent imaginative feeling, so as to produce the answer, 'Thus it becometh us to fulfil all righteousness' (3.14f.). This is in keeping with the idea of Jesus as the 'inclusive representative of redeemed humanity'. The same difficulty has been felt by the author of the *Gospel to the Hebrews*, in which Jesus says to his mother and brethren: *Quid peccavi, ut vadam et baptizer ab eo? nisi forte hoc ipsum quod dixi, ignorantia est.*[1] Luke has not had the same sense of need, although his addition of προσευχομένου in describing the Baptism (Luke 3.21) creates the impression of an understanding between Jesus and his Father which is consistent with the story of Christ at twelve years old (2.49). This removes the impact of the Baptism as an inaugural experience, which it has in Mark.

### 4. THE ORIGINS OF JESUS AND THE GROWTH OF CHRISTOLOGY

There is a dogmatic motive at work in these modifications to the Baptism narrative, which shows through at many other points in the later strands of the New Testament. It is the question whether Jesus acts as a man or as a divine being. The Fourth Gospel is fully aware of it, and provides the classic answer in terms of a paradox transcending the dilemma of alternatives. The evidence of the quotation material reviewed in this chapter has shown that this was not the earliest question to compel the Church to investigate the origins of Jesus. The controversy was at first concerned with the theoretical issue of the proper messianic credentials. This was complicated by the variety of popular ideas about him, some regarding him as the son of David, others as a prophet. But gradually deeper understanding of the universal scope of his redeeming work fastened attention on the nature of the person of Christ. This is discussed in very different ways by St Paul in Romans and by the writer of Hebrews without mention of the virgin birth, but along lines of theology which necessitate the doctrine of pre-existence. First-century Christianity had no equipment to assert that Christ is the beginning of a new creation without it. Christo-

---

[1] Preserved in Jerome, *Adv. Pelag.* III.2.

logy is the response to the faith of the Resurrection, rather than a conviction arising from the impact of the life of Jesus.[1]

The controversy over the place of origin, Bethlehem or Nazareth, has left few traces, for the Davidic messiahship was quickly accepted and taken for granted, while resistance to nationalistic implications in it prevented much further interest along this line. It simply becomes an element in the Church's own composite christological picture.

The same is true of the idea of Jesus as a prophet. Theological interests follow this up by applying to him the idea of the Prophet of Deut. 18, but in the main stream of Christianity this is no more than one other feature of the portrait of Christ.

Naturally enough in view of the controversy, the stories of the nativity have been evolved in connection with the claim of descent from David. They are also centred upon the virgin birth, which is in some respects a response to the claim of pre-existence. This in its turn arises from reflection on the meaning of the redemption.

It has been interesting to note that, where a prior history of the use of a testimony can be postulated, it is often a question about the doctrine of redemption which seems to have been the starting-point. Thus there is a possibility that Matt. 2.23, 'He shall be called a Nazarene', was first used to prove that a Nazarene is the right person to accomplish the redeeming work of the Servant of the Lord. The use of Isa. 11.10 about the Root of Jesse, springs from the eschatological programme rather than from its value as a Davidic passage. The only certain citations of Deut. 18.15 lay stress on the danger of disobedience to God's chosen instrument of salvation, rather than on the figure of the Prophet himself. Even Isa. 7.14 shows more interest in the idea that the birth of Jesus is the time of messianic manifestation than on the fact of the virgin

---

[1] This must not be misunderstood as an expression of Bultmann's position, in which the 'historical Jesus' can be virtually dispensed with. Ultimately the Resurrection and the impact of the life of Jesus are a unity. The Person who rose from the dead is the Person who said and did such and such things. The Resurrection only has meaning in relation to the life that preceded it. But it seems clear from this study that the primitive scriptural apologetic was an attempt to defend the Church's interpretation of the Resurrection, and that this is the groundwork of the beginnings of christology. The New Testament knows nothing of theories derived from, e.g., our Lord's messianic self-consciousness. See J. M. Robinson, *A New Quest of the Historical Jesus* (SBT 25), 1959, and P. Althaus, *The So-Called Kerygma and the Historical Jesus* (ET 1959).

birth, for which it afterwards provided the classic formulation. The testimonies used with the flight into Egypt and the slaying of the innocents show in different ways that the death and Resurrection of Jesus have redemptive efficacy for the whole people of God.

This chapter has covered the history of various texts of christological significance. They furnish some idea of the process in which the doctrine of the person of Jesus was hammered out. They provide some of the components of the later christology of the Church. The New Testament itself does not give a single consistent picture. The major New Testament writers each give their own amalgam of the various elements available to them. All speak of the same *person* and of the same *event*, but each has his own implicit christology. Behind them there is the varied scene of the Church in different centres striving to understand its own message, preaching it to interested hearers, defending it against the objections of those who cannot or will not believe. The developments traced in this chapter have brought us to the level of the explicit positions of the New Testament writers themselves, and so to the limit of this line of research.

# VI

## QUOTATIONS IN ST PAUL

IN the course of this study it has been observed from time to time that St Paul's use of certain texts in the Judaistic controversy is taken over from their use in a slightly different context. This was pointed out with reference to the interpretation of Isa. 52.5 in Rom. 2.24, which was used in the first chapter of this book as a typical example of the shift of application.[1] It seems worth while to examine some of the Pauline Epistles a little further from this point of view.

It is not to be expected that the originality of Paul's thought will suffer as a result of this. When he made use of previous work he always strongly impressed it with his own creative ability. But it is in any case intrinsically probable that he should take whatever came to his hand for his own purposes. It is generally recognized that much of his specific teaching—the supersession of the Law and cultus, the spiritual temple of the Body of Christ, and the preaching to the Gentiles—was already held by Hellenistic Jewish elements in the Church, represented in Acts by St Stephen. It is in this milieu that lines of biblical exegesis were being followed, which could be of service to Paul in handling the acute difficulties encountered in his own apostolic labours. We can see the continuation of these in the scriptural arguments used by Paul in Galatians and Romans.

### I. THE USE OF SCRIPTURE IN GALATIANS

In his Epistles to the Thessalonians Paul does not argue from biblical texts. His Old Testament allusions are for the most part either apocalyptic references or hortatory phrases. These are too general in type to have an exclusively Christian character. In

_____
[1] *Supra*, pp. 22f.

Galatians the quotations and allusions are still comparatively few, but this time there has been close attention to the passages concerned.

### Isaiah 49

The first overt allusion occurs in Paul's description of his own conversion and vocation, Gal. 1.15f. Here he uses a phrase from Isa. 49.1, expressing a predestination long before his conversion, even 'from my mother's womb'. This was expressly to preach the Gospel to the Gentiles, just as it was for the Lord's Servant in the original context. We cannot fail, then, to see in v. 16 an implicit reference to Isa. 49.6. This verse is actually quoted to authorize the Gentile mission in Acts 13.47. It is alluded to in this sense in the *Nunc Dimittis* (Luke 2.32), a liturgical text older than Luke, possibly even pre-Christian. We have also seen a reference to it in the testimony of Matt. 2.23. The *Nunc Dimittis* is clearly messianic, and it seems that the principal Servant passages in Deutero-Isaiah also were so interpreted in Palestinian Judaism.[1] For this reason it was natural and inevitable that the early Christians should turn to this prophecy to explain our Lord's work.[2] It is thus probable that Isa. 49 was first applied to Jesus as the bringer of salvation. It would be left an open possibility that the inclusion of the Gentiles would be preceded by their entry into Judaism, as the Jews normally held. But it was clearly also possible to use the passage to support direct preaching to the Gentiles. It is this aspect of it which predominates later. Paul, accepting this, can even apply the prophecy to himself, designated for this purpose 'from my mother's womb'.

That this passage, already current in the Church in respect of Jesus and his saving work, had been deeply pondered by St Paul, and actually helped to formulate his own special apostolic vocation, may perhaps be deduced from the importance of it in this autobiographical section. For it seems to be in his mind all through the rest of the chapter. In v. 24 ἐδόξαζον ἐν ἐμοὶ τὸν θεόν echoes the divine words in Isa. 49.3, ἐν σοὶ δοξασθήσομαι. In fact it probably runs on into the next verses also, so that when the preaching to the Gentiles is again mentioned in 2.2 Paul can express his fear μή πως

---

[1] Zimmerli and Jeremias, *The Servant of God*, pp. 57, 77, 93.

[2] See the impressive list of allusions in the NT collected by Dodd, *Acc. Scrip.*, pp. 88-96.

εἰς κενὸν τρέχω. This is reminiscent of Isa. 49.4, κενῶς ἐκοπίασα καὶ εἰς μάταιον. Moreover this is a favourite phrase of St Paul's. He has already used it in I Thess. 3.5 in connection with his preaching work.[1] Already, then, before his *apologia* in Gal. 1, the prophecy of Isa. 49 was fundamental to his thought.

## Psalm 143.2

The next clear allusion is an adaptation of Ps. 143.2 in 2.16, οὐ δικαιωθήσεται πᾶσα σάρξ. The interesting thing about this is that Paul repeats himself exactly in Rom. 3.20, even using the same introductory words ἐξ ἔργων νόμου, which he has supplied, and the non-Septuagintal σάρξ.[2] The manner in which the allusion is introduced in Gal. 2.15f., first as a general statement known to all at the beginning of the sentence, then as a quasi-quotation to clinch the matter at the end of it, suggests that this verse, if not the whole psalm, is another passage which is already fundamental to Paul's thinking. Though it contains no mention of the Law, it can be applied to the question whether man may be justified by the works of the Law.[3] On the other hand, in the absence of any other New Testament allusions to it, there is this time no reason to doubt that Paul has picked out this text himself.

Gal. 3 works out the argument on the works of the Law and faith, which has been adumbrated by means of Ps. 143.2. This is done by means of two ranges of scriptural material, the story of Abraham and the curse of the Law. In both of these it is probable that Paul is making use of prior exegetical work. Both have links with Acts, the Fourth Gospel, and the Epistle of St James. Although the material in Acts was obviously written long after this Epistle, it appears to be parallel to, rather than derivative from, Paul's thought. The same may be said of the Fourth Gospel. The relation of James to Paul's writings is a controversial matter, but the balance of recent opinion seems to be on the side of a com-

---

[1] Also in I Cor. 15.58; Gal. 4.11; Phil. 2.16. There is a possible allusion in II Cor. 6.1, followed by quotation of Isa. 49.8 in the next verse.

[2] In the LXX πᾶσα σάρξ regularly translates כל־בשׂר. But it occurs for כל־חי in Gen. 6.19, 8.21, etc. In Ps. 143.2 the LXX reads πᾶς ζῶν.

[3] G. H. Rendall, *The Epistle of St James and Judaic Christianity*, 1927, p. 77, argues that the very natural use of ἔργα in James 2, and especially ἐξ ἔργων ἐδικαιώθη in 2.21, gave the expression to the Christian vocabulary. Then Paul has taken it over and inserted it into his quotations of Ps. 143.2 in a more specialized sense.

paratively early date and against a theory of direct connection with the Pauline epistles.[1]

## Abraham

The point of departure is the faith of Abraham, commended in the famous words of Gen. 15.6, 'Abraham believed God, and it was reckoned unto him for righteousness'. This is quoted by Paul in Gal. 3.6 and in Rom. 4.3, 9, 22, and it also occurs in James 2.23, all following the Septuagint. This was a text commonly used by first-century Judaism, both by Philo[2] and in the rabbinic literature.[3] James, whose manner of using it appears at first sight to be the exact opposite of Paul's, simply gives the usual Jewish view that faith is meritorious, if it is a quality of obedience leading to the performance of good works. Without such works it is impossible to know that faith exists.

Paul, on the other hand, has a more careful regard for the context. In Gen. 15.6 the faith of Abraham is acceptance of God's message without mention of any good works. From this he can go on to show that, as this promise was made not only to Abraham but also to the Gentiles, the justifying quality of faith applies to them too. He does this by citing Gen. 12.3 (Gal. 3.8), 'In thee shall all the nations be blessed'. Although these words are repeated at Gen. 18.18 and 22.18, the passage referred to must be 12.3, because the argument turns on the fact that the promise has already been made before 15.6. In the other passages it could be argued that Abraham has works to his credit, hospitality to strangers (Gen. 18),[4] and the sacrifice of Isaac (Gen. 22).[5] Paul's quotation differs from the Septuagint in one particular, the choice of ἔθνη for φυλαί, though the Septuagint has it at 18.18 and 22.18. This is a deliberate alteration, because φυλαί in Paul's vocabulary always refers to the tribes of Israel, whereas here he is bound to use the technical term for the Gentiles.

We have already seen that Gen. 12.3 was used in the speech of Peter in Acts 3.19-26, which may be based on fairly old material.

[1] Cf. H. Windisch, *Die Katholischen Briefe* (Handbuch zum NT 15) rev. H. Preisker, 1951, p. 19; L. E. Elliott-Binns, *Galilean Christianity* (SBT 16), 1956, pp. 46f.

[2] The principal references are collected in J. B. Lightfoot, *Galatians*[10], 1900, *ad loc.*

[3] SB III, pp. 186-201.

[4] Cf. *I Clem.* 10.                    [5] Cf. James 2.21.

In that case there was no question of the controversy about the Gentiles. The point at issue was belief or unbelief in the Gospel, the fulfilment of the promise to Abraham. Belief in Christ is an essential item of fidelity to the covenant. How this affects the value of fidelity to the works of the Law is not taken into consideration. The conclusion must be that, whereas James and Acts and *I Clement* use the idea of Abraham in ways familiar to the Jews of their time, in which faith is meritorious, Paul is adapting the texts for his own special purpose.

The question which Paul has so far left open is the time when the promise to Abraham should be fulfilled. He deduces that Christ is the fulfilment from the phrase 'and to thy seed', which occurs in various places in Genesis where the promise is given. We noticed that this had been introduced into the quotation of Gen. 12.3 in Acts 3.25 especially to mark the fulfilment in the person of Jesus. But there it is thought of not individually but inclusively, because Jesus is the culminating point of Jewish history, the climax of God's saving action. This is the Christian interpretation of what may be regarded as the normal meaning of 'seed' in this context, i.e. the people thought of collectively, just as we have it in the *Magnificat* (Luke 1.55). In Gal. 3.16, however, Paul disregards this in order to insist on interpretation of it as a particular person. If this is what it means, then the person intended is sure to be the future representative of the nation, the Messiah. It is tempting to take ὅ(ς) ἐστιν Χριστός in this sense, as an item of messianic theory rather than a direct reference to our Lord, but Paul so constantly uses the title simply as a variation for the name of Jesus that this is unlikely. He is not, then, arguing from a known messianic interpretation of the phrase. But another line of thought is possible. It is characteristic of Hebrew thought to see the whole contained in the beginning. Paul himself uses the idea of Adam as inclusive of the whole human race in Rom. 5. From this point of view the singular 'seed' refers to Isaac. The beginning of the fulfilment of the promise took place when Isaac was born contrary to natural expectation. But it could not be claimed that Abraham was 'the father of many nations' through Isaac, but only of the Jews and Edomites. The quasi-resurrection of Isaac does, however, point forward to the true factor for establishing the promise, the Resurrection of Jesus. Thus Isaac and his descendants are merely the figure of the promised seed, whereas the real reference is to Jesus and his members (Gal. 3.29). The argument is actually worked out along this line in Rom. 4.16-25.

Paul has used this argument in order to show that the Gentiles are included in the original scope of the promise, and need not become Jews first. But the argument is basically concerned with proving that it is Jesus who is the fulfilment of the promise by virtue of the Resurrection. It thus may well be that here again we have earlier exegetical work which Paul is adapting to his special purpose. The original function of the argument might have suggested precisely the opposite, as it would be an appeal to the Jews to accept the Christian way as the fulfilment of their own privileged position as God's people. Very conscious of being 'children of the stock of Abraham', they would be attracted by the claim that the promise made to Abraham had at last been fulfilled in the Resurrection of Jesus. It is not only the birth of Isaac that prefigures the Resurrection. The sacrifice on Mount Moriah is also adduced in this sense in Heb. 11.17-19.

The possibility of this earlier apologetic usage is supported by the independent discourse on Abraham in John 8. Without entering into a full analysis of this involved and obscure chapter, we may notice that the basis of the discussion is the Jews' claim that their descent from Abraham is sufficient guarantee of their salvation. Jesus replies that, whereas he himself has been sent by the Father whom Abraham obeyed, the Jews have forfeited their inheritance by rejecting him and serving the devil. But the climax of the argument comes in the twofold assertion that Jesus' word is the means of eternal life (v. 51) and that this is the substance of the faith of Abraham (v. 56). It is the common interpretation of the latter verse that the rejoicing of Abraham refers to the birth of Isaac (Gen. 17.17). Jesus can call it '*my* day' because it is mysteriously equivalent to his own Resurrection, which is the secret of the eternal life which he promises. Then the solemn words in v. 58, in which Jesus appears to be pre-existent and can appropriate the divine I AM, express the fact that he is in himself the fulfilment of the promise to Abraham, which was in the mind of God before he called him out of Ur of the Chaldees.

Here, then, worked into a chapter of much greater and deeper implications, is the presentation of the Christian message in terms of the definitive consummation of the promise to Abraham and his seed. The fact that much of this Johannine material, which is so different from anything in the Synoptic record, and which has been bent to the writer's theological purpose with such originality and creative skill, nevertheless faithfully reflects discussion between the Church and the unbelieving Jews at a fairly early period, is something which deserves greater attention than it has so far received. Ch. 8 is a specially good example.[1]

The keynote of this approach is very Jewish indeed. Jesus is the reality of Abraham's promise for Abraham's seed. It is likely to be valued where appeal to the Pentateuch is desirable. It does not in itself lay emphasis on the place of the Gentiles. It still remains tenable that inclusion of them in the scope of the promise requires their conversion to Judaism as a preliminary measure. The new element in Paul's handling of this material is his proof that the condition on which the promise is made, i.e. Abraham's faith, goes behind the Law, and behind even the rite of circumcision, which is not mentioned until Gen. 17.10. It is curious that the latter point is not made until Rom. 4. In Galatians it would have been a very useful observation, seeing that circumcision is the chief question at issue. But he deals with it as an essential element of the Law, not as something separate from it. Nevertheless the Bible asserts that Abraham himself practised circumcision. This may have been raised as an objection to the argument in the earlier epistle. Paul may be deliberately correcting it when he reproduces the same material with greater care in Romans.

## The Law

With the positive assertion of the blessing of Abraham, Paul has combined an argument on the curse of the Law. It is possible that this was originally distinct, as will be shown. The argument is contained in a short passage, Gal. 3.10-14, but even so it combines two separate issues. The first is the fact that any breach of the Law involves the curse attaching to the whole Law. The second is the fact that by his Crucifixion our Lord was himself rendered liable to that curse. These are proved by two quotations, Deut. 27.26 and 21.23.

The first can be regarded as a moral commonplace. It is mentioned in James 2.10 in order to prick the consciences of the readers

---

[1] See the penetrating study of this chapter by C. H. Dodd, 'À l'arrière-plan d'un dialogue johannique', *Revue d'Histoire et de la Philosophie Religieuses* 37, 1957, pp. 5-17.

and to rouse them to greater vigilance. Once it is realized that even
trivial offences constitute a breach of the whole Law, they will be
treated with suitable gravity. It is probable that James is simply
reproducing a normal Jewish point of view.[1]

Paul's purpose is completely different. He cites Deut. 27.26[2] in
order to show that the Law is not the means of salvation. Because
it is humanly impossible to keep it in its fulness, it only has the
effect of bringing a curse. He drives home his point by insisting
on the necessity of keeping every item of the Law, and to do so
adds another quotation, Lev. 18.5, 'which if a man do, he shall live
in (or by) them'. Perhaps again this is a normal text of rabbinic
argument.[3] At any rate it is clear that Paul has imposed upon it a
special interpretation for his own purpose. In the proper context
the word 'live' is roughly equivalent to 'be saved' or even 'be justified'. It has this meaning when it is alluded to in Luke 10.28.
But instead of referring to salvation-life it could be taken to mean
the manner of life adopted in order to obtain salvation. Paul has
forced the words to bear this meaning in order to make a complete
contrast with another manner of life, i.e. faith. This also has its
scriptural warrant, Hab. 2.4, 'The just shall live by faith'. In both
of these quotations in Gal. 3.12 the word ζήσεται has the nuance
of a manner of life which is the appropriate mode of response to
God. The argument is taken up again in Rom. 10.4-9. Paul says
that theoretically one could be justified by the Law,[4] but now that
God has given the greater salvation in the person of Christ, it is
necessary to adjust oneself to the new mode of response, which is
the act of faith. It is clear to us that faith could include obedience
to the Law, so that a Law-abiding Jew could still be placing his
hope of salvation in Christ by faith. But in Galatians Paul is anxious
to press the contrast to the limit, so as to win his point in favour of
the Gentiles. The best summary of the argument is to be found in
the Johannine tradition: 'This is the *work* of God, that ye *believe*
on him whom he hath sent' (John 6.29).

[1] Not only the LXX, but also the Samaritan and Palestinian *Sotah*
7, 21d, 6, attest the interpretation '*all* the words of the law'—SB III,
pp. 541f.

[2] Following LXX. The fuller phrase τοῖς γεγραμμένοις ἐν τῷ βιβλίῳ comes
from other cursing formulas, e.g. Deut. 29.19f., 30.10.

[3] SB III, pp. 277f.

[4] Note that in Rom. 10.5 Paul uses ζήσεται in the sense proper to the
context, not as in Gal. 3.12.

The Jews held that salvation-life could be won through the works of the Law (Lev. 18.5); in fact to keep the whole Law was indispensable (Deut. 27.26). Paul may well have taken both these texts from his opponents, but he has turned them against them by means of a text of his own, Hab. 2.4. He uses it again, almost as a slogan, and certainly as the key to his whole argument against the Law, in Rom. 1.17. His use of it in both Epistles is so specialized and technical that one is bound to ask how it was that he came across it. It is evidently fundamental to his thought, because it is this quotation that is responsible for the forced meaning of $\zeta\eta\sigma\epsilon\tau\alpha\iota$ when he cites Lev. 18.5. Fortunately we have two roughly contemporary comments on the same verse, the Qumran *Habakkuk Commentary*, which is Jewish and based on the Hebrew text, and the Epistle to the Hebrews, which is Christian and based on the Septuagint.

The *Habakkuk Commentary* applies the obscure words of the prophecy to the writer's own times and interests in the manner of an apocalypse. Then the promise of delay before the vision is fulfilled, which is contained in Hab. 2.3, serves the useful purpose of covering the writer's interpretation in case it is not fulfilled as soon as he has implied. After this v. 4 can be made to say that, during the indefinite period between the fulfilment of the main part of the prophecy and the final act, both the evil and the good will maintain the *status quo*. The evil will continue to pile up punishment, while the just will faithfully carry out the Law and so be assured of deliverance. This depends on the Hebrew reading, 'The just shall live by *his* faith'. This is the exact opposite of Paul's interpretation. The matter is further complicated by the fact that the faithfulness of the just not only includes fidelity to the Law, but also faith in the Teacher of Righteousness. This sounds like Paul's own teaching on faith in Christ. But of course there is a world of difference, for the Teacher is the *fons et origo* of the Sect's special tradition of the Law, whereas in his own person 'Christ is the end ($\tau\epsilon\lambda os$) of Law unto righteousness unto everyone that believeth' (Rom. 10.4, probably intentionally recalling Hab. 2.4). The likeness is, then, superficial, and the essential contrast remains.

The other comment is to be found in Heb. 10.36-39. Like the *Habakkuk Commentary*, the writer (who quotes Hab. 2.3f.) uses the text with awareness that it belongs to an apocalypse. He is writing an exhortation to his readers within a framework of conventional apocalyptic, having alluded to Isa. 26.11 in this sense in

v. 27. It is remarkable that Isa. 26.19, which prophesies the resurrection of the dead, appears not to be referred to in the New Testament. There has been nothing to remove it from its proper application to the final judgment. It is with this in mind that in v. 37 the writer begins his quotation of Hab. 2.3 with a phrase from Isa. 26.20, and so fixes the interpretation of the Habakkuk passage in an eschatological sense. He takes advantage of the Septuagint version of the verse to apply it to the coming of our Lord in judgment.[1] He then gives the two clauses of Hab. 2.4 in reverse order, so that ὁ δίκαιος becomes the subject of them both. This creates the desired contrast between 'shrinking back' and 'having faith', which are alternative modes of conduct open to 'my righteous one', i.e. the Christian reader, as v. 39 shows. The following chapter, with its panegyric of faithful men and women, leaves no further doubt that the writer thinks of faith primarily as a moral quality of obedience and stability. In order to interpret Hab. 2.4 in this way he has had to adopt the reading of LXX$^A$, which places μου before ἐκ πίστεως.[2] It can then be referred to the subject, viz. 'my righteous one', and leaves the way open for the assumption that he will live by *his own* faith. It is possible that this is a deliberate alteration on his part, and that LXX$^A$ is here influenced by this citation,[3] and that he actually had ἐκ πίστεώς μου of LXX$^B$ before him when he wrote. This is undoubtedly the true Septuagint text, following a Jewish tradition which is partially attested by Aquila.[4] This gives to faith the truly Hebraic sense of the steadfastness of God. But the alteration has the effect of bringing the meaning into closer accord with the original Hebrew. Paul, both in Galatians and Romans, tactfully omits the troublesome μου, leaving the text free for his own interpretation.

It cannot be claimed that the prophecy of Habakkuk was a great

[1] In the Hebrew it is the vision that is to come to pass quickly. But LXX retains the masculine pronouns in spite of the feminine ὅρασις. This probably denotes a messianic interpretation.

[2] The Western Text has it afterwards, like LXX$^B$, but such adjustments are typical, and there can be no question that the better attested reading is the correct one.

[3] On the vexed question of the possibility of the influence of NT citations on LXX$^A$, cf. Stendahl, *SSM*, pp. 169-82.

[4] This is perhaps a bold inference, but if incorrect does not spoil the argument on the text of Heb. 10.38. The facts are that in Hab. 2.4 the LXX translator read נפשי and באמונתי for שו־ and תו־. Aquila's text ἰδοὺ νωχελευομένου οὐκ εὐθεῖα ἡ ψυχή μου ἐν αὐτῷ καὶ δίκαιος ἐν πίστει αὐτοῦ ζήσεται attests נפשי but not באמונתי.

influence in early Christian thought. Where it does touch the tradition, it is treated in the manner of apocalyptic eschatology, like
the Qumran *Habakkuk Commentary*. So there is a warning sounded
at the end of Paul's speech at Pisidian Antioch in the words of
Hab. 1.5 (Acts 13.41), and Hab. 1.6 provides a phrase in Rev. 20.9.
It is pre-eminently a tract for a time of persecution, and if it had
any currency in Christian circles before Paul culled his favourite
text from it, it would be presumably in connection with the fears
that Christians had in common with Jews in the face of the Roman
authorities or the pagan mob.[1] Both Jew and Christian would be
agreed that at such a time the just would have to live by faith in
all its senses, a steadfastness based on trust in the steadfastness of
God, showing itself both in stability of mind (Hebrews) and fidelity
to religious obligations (Qumran). Paul also would have agreed
with this. We can imagine his use of the verse in this general way
in his mission preaching. But when the Judaistic controversy became a burning issue he finds himself asking in what does this
steadfastness of God consist, and what is the true form of fidelity
of conduct. The answer is the fact of salvation by Christ, to which
the act of faith corresponds. Hence steadfastness for the Gentile
need not, indeed must not, include fidelity to the Law, which is
inadequate to the new situation.

In this section on the Law we have so far been concerned with
the adequacy of the Law as such. Of the three quotations examined, two (Deut. 27.26 and Lev. 18.5) have probably been drawn
from current Jewish usage. The third (Hab. 2.4) may have been
present to Paul's mind through the apocalyptic interest of the
communities where he preached. His new application of it to the
controversy over the Law is thus due to his own creative handling.
We now turn to the second issue in this matter of the Law,
the fact that the Crucifixion of Jesus involved the curse of Deut.
21.23.

In his quotation of Deut. 21.23 in Gal. 3.13 Paul has conformed
the opening words to match the string of curses in Deut. 27, so
that instead of the factual statement that 'everyone is accursed who
hangs', etc., it becomes an anathema, 'cursed be he that hangs'.
This may perhaps be simply due to the preceding quotation of
Deut. 27.26. But it is also possible that it accurately represents the

---

[1] In 1QpHab. the Chaldeans of Hab. 1.6 are explained as the 'Kittiim',
i.e. the reigning imperial power (Seleucids?, Romans?).

sharpened form in which this text was already being used by the enemies of the Church. It is then possible to trace a shift of application, which shows how the Pauline position of the abrogation of the Law was reached. For there is an allusion to Deut. 21.23, without mention of the controversy about the Law, in the words of Peter in Acts 5.30, ' . . . whom ye slew, hanging him on a tree'. Of course the very condensed speech in which these words occur is no doubt mainly the work of Luke himself at a late date, but that does not alter the significance of the choice of phrase. The normal Greek word for crucifixion is avoided, and a phrase from Deut. 21.23 is employed, which in Hebrew (but not normally in Greek) came to have this meaning.[1] The use of the phrase is therefore likely to be an intentional allusion to the Old Testament passage.

We can thus start by postulating a Jewish objection that our Lord's death on the cross rendered him accursed of God. But a careful reading of the context in Deuteronomy, and comparison of the narrative of Josh. 10.26f., shows that the regulation was concerned not with the manner of execution, but with the practice of having a notable criminal strung up *after* he had been put to death. The man is not accursed because he has been hung, but hung because he is already accursed on account of his crime. It is for this reason that a rabbinic text says, 'None is hanged save the blasphemer and the idolater'.[2] When the text is applied to the Roman method of execution by crucifixion, the emphasis is still likely to be on the crime. Now Jesus was condemned for blasphemy, which (if true) necessarily involves the divine curse. The fact that the punishment was duly carried out clinches the fact that he is under the operation of the curse. On the contrary, the Resurrection immediately proved that God had not ratified the decision of the Sanhedrin and of Pilate, so that the curse was not actually operative. Although the bodies of those crucified had to be removed at sundown (cf. John 19.31), the body of Jesus would not have defiled the land, for he was not really accursed. This is the argument that is presupposed in Acts 5.30, where God's action in raising up Jesus is contrasted with the action of the Sanhedrin in condemning him. It is the simple first stage in this apologetic,

---

[1] κρεμάννυμι is used absolutely in this sense in Luke 23.39. Arndt and Gingrich cite one parallel from the Zenon Papyri (255 BC).

[2] *Sanhedrin* 6.4, where Deut. 21.23 is quoted and discussed. The interesting reference to this passage in 1QpNahum has no relevance to the NT material.

and it is obviously closely connected with the Passion apologetic which we have already studied.[1]

Luke uses the same phrase again in Acts 10.39, Peter's address to Cornelius. The context shows every sign of being a Lucan composition. As we have seen in other connections, Luke is not averse to using biblical material taken from the current apologetic more than once. It is possible that we should include also the use of τὸ ξύλον for the cross in Acts 13.29. This speech also appears to be based on typical Christian arguments for a Jewish audience. Here the Crucifixion is described in the words ὡς δὲ ἐτέλεσαν πάντα τὰ περὶ αὐτοῦ γεγραμμένα, after which Jesus is taken down ἀπὸ τοῦ ξύλου and buried. There can be little doubt that the principal scripture in mind is Isa. 53, the foundation text of the Passion apologetic. It is probable that 'lifted up' in Isa. 52.13 was referred to the cross (as it certainly is in the Fourth Gospel). As Deut. 21.23 was in any case applied to the Crucifixion, the bearing of the curse would be one of the indignities included in the whole idea that the sufferings of Jesus were according to the Scriptures. Thus it is part of the atoning work of Jesus that he should apparently bear the curse which is implied in this form of execution. This has advanced the matter a little nearer to the position of Gal. 3.13.

There may be another hint of this apologetic in I Peter 2.24, where the phrase ἐπὶ τὸ ξύλον occurs. This time the connection with Isa. 53 is explicit. It was observed when this passage was examined in ch. III that there has been a shift of application from the use of this material to formulate an Atonement doctrine, to the author's immediate purpose of paraenesis. If there is here a reference to Deut. 21.23, it indicates that this apologetic, which we find reflected in Galatians, had a wider currency. The emphasis in the passage as it stands is on the *act* of crucifixion.[2] The verse could almost be paraphrased thus: 'Who himself bore the curse which our disobedience brought on us (under the law of Deut. 27.26) by submitting his body to the curse involved in the act of crucifixion (by Deut. 21.23).' The same thought is expressed in very different terms in Col. 2.14.

The use of the Septuagint version has very likely assisted this

[1] For a primitive assertion that the curse has in fact fallen on those who did the deed, compare the remarks on Ps. 69.23-26, *supra*, pp. 102, 105.

[2] Cf. Selwyn, *ad loc.*, emphasizing the *activity* implied by ἐπί c. acc. In *Ep. Barn.* 5.13 ἐπὶ ξύλου πάθῃ simply means 'be crucified'.

development. For the explanatory 'cursed is the hanged man' of
the Hebrew places no emphasis on the phrase. It is merely one
word (תָּלוּי), simply meaning 'the culprit'. The Septuagint however is more descriptive, using the entire phrase ὁ κρεμάμενος ἐπὶ
ξύλου, and so helps the application of the curse to the act of crucifying.

When we return to consider Gal. 3.13, we find that Paul has
taken advantage of all these developments. The simple contrast
between the condemnation and the Resurrection, which we found
in Acts 5.30 and 10.39, has been turned into the contrast between
the curse of the Law as a whole and the blessing of Abraham. The
connection with Isa. 53, which makes it possible to use this text in
passages concerned with justification, is assumed by Paul, and even
taken a stage further. For Paul can speak of Christ as γενόμενος
ὑπὲρ ἡμῶν κατάρα. This shows knowledge of the Hebrew, where
the noun is used objectively, קִלְלַת אֱלֹהִים תָּלוּי. But he uses
it in the manner of the similar phrase in II Cor. 5.21, ὑπὲρ ἡμῶν
ἁμαρτίαν ἐποίησεν, which undoubtedly refers to the אָשָׁם of Isa.
53.10. The meaning is thus similar to the idea of the sin-offering,
and there is probably an intentional reference to the theory of
sacrifice. This overcomes the difficulty that only one curse has
been laid upon Jesus. Just as anyone who breaks one item of the
Law is guilty of the whole Law, so our Lord bears the curse in a
total sense. His atoning death removes the curse entirely. Thereafter, if men persist in adherence to the Law, they are liable to
incur fresh guilt; but if they adhere to Christ through faith, the
whole machinery of the Law and the curse ceases to be operative.
The issue of justification has been moved onto a new plane. Consequently there is no reason to lay the Law upon the Gentiles.

The above analysis has shown that Paul has brought together
two biblical arguments of early Christianity and given them a
fresh application to buttress his position in the Judaistic controversy. The blessing of Abraham was a statement of fulfilment in
Christ, not at first opposed to the obligations of the Law. The
curse of the Law was an aspect of the Passion apologetic, and
helped to produce the doctrines of Atonement and justification,
but was not at first advanced as a reason for regarding the Law as
cancelled. There the matter might be left, but it seems desirable
to add two other pieces of evidence about the curse of the Law
before closing this section.

There is in the first place interesting confirmation of the above
argument in the Fourth Gospel. It was noted in connection with
Acts 13.29 that in the Passion apologetic the 'lifting up' of Isa.
52.13 probably had a double meaning, both the raising of Jesus on
the cross and the glory of his subsequent Resurrection and Ascension. This is a favourite theme with John, who loves the theology
of paradox. Jesus was lifted up on the tree, apparently as a dreadful
warning of the curse, but really as the giver of life. John is the first
Christian writer to make use of the brazen serpent of Num. 21.9
as a type of the saving cross. In the Septuagint of this verse the
standard on which the serpent was hung is translated by the word
σημεῖον. It is known that the serpent round which this legend
evolved became an embarrassment to Israel's reformers (II Kings
18.4). Even the idea of it would be offensive to the later Jewish
conscience. In Wisd. 16.6 we can see how an Alexandrian writer
can take advantage of the Septuagint rendering to interpret it symbolically, and so he calls it σύμβολον σωτηρίας.

John stands in line with this tradition. In 3.14 he sees the
'symbol' fulfilled in the cross of Christ. He evidently found it so
useful to express the glory of the cross that the lifting up of the
Son of Man becomes a technical expression. So it recurs in 8.28
and 12.32, and is referred to in 18.32. But it is not a thing he can
take for granted with his readers, for the first use of it in 3.14
provides the type which underlies the expression.

The image of the brazen serpent on a standard caught the imagination of the church Fathers, who reproduce it with unfailing
regularity from *Barnabas* onwards. It is not found elsewhere in the
New Testament, and probably John thought of it himself. But
though it is new in John, it is simply his version of the earlier
apologetic which we saw illustrated in Acts 5.30. We notice, however, that Paul's use of the argument to prove that the Law is
abolished is not found here. It is an independent development
from the same starting-point.[1]

The second piece of evidence is in Justin, who combines the idea
of the curse of Deut. 21.23 with the brazen serpent of Num. 21.9.
It is probable that he knew both the Fourth Gospel and Galatians,

---

[1] It is interesting that *Ep. Barn.* 12.5-7, which refers to the brazen
serpent in a series of types of the Passion, continues the Alexandrian
tradition that, as the making of the serpent was a direct contravention of
the command against idols, it was intended symbolically from the first.
It always did mean Christ.

but he is not solely dependent on them. He continues the living tradition of the Church's apologetic to the Jews. In *Dial.* 32 Trypho objects that 'the last curse contained in the law of God fell on him, for he was crucified'. The last curse is Deut. 27.26, but one would expect Deut. 21.23 to be the one intended. It is perhaps due to the influence of Gal. 3, where Paul has conformed 21.23 to the style of 27.26, and cited it immediately after the latter. But it is more likely to be only a reference to 27.26, vaguely covering all eventualities. Justin does not follow up this objection, for his answer is a list of Passion prophecies, beginning of course with Isa. 53. At this point he is reflecting the first stage of the apologetic, in which the curse is treated as one aspect of the general position of the Passion apologetic.

But in *Dial.* 89f. Trypho takes up the point again. He is now ready to concede that the Christ must suffer, but distinguishes this from the curse involved in crucifixion. Justin's reply is to show that the cross itself was foreshadowed in various types, including the brazen serpent. He recounts this in a manner reminiscent of *Barnabas*, and makes the point that the curse was never ratified by God, though the Jews tried to place Jesus under it. In ch. 94 he tackles the matter afresh by saying that, just as God was blameless of the commandment against graven images because the serpent was always meant to be a sign of the cross, so also the curse of crucifixion does not apply to Jesus because it was the necessary way of salvation. In the next two chapters he actually cites both Deut. 27.26 and 21.23 to prove that Christ took upon himself the curse of the Gentiles, thus reproducing Paul's argument in Gal. 3.

The value of this evidence is not only that it shows a continuous tradition of apologetic, using the same arguments with greater elaboration and typological analogies. It also sets out the actual objections raised by the Jews, which we have felt to be necessitated by the history of the same material within the New Testament. It would be too much to say that the *Dialogue* can be used as a direct source book for Jewish objections to Christianity in the early period. But in this particular range of material it does seem to confirm the results of independent research.[1]

[1] In the above discussion on the blessing and the curse no reference has been made to Heb. 6.13f., where Gen. 22.16f. is quoted. If the danger which the writer sought to avert was a return to Jewish legalism, there might be a link here with Gal. 3. But the biblical background of the context is an allegory of the promised land, in which the land laid under a

### Other Quotations in Galatians

There only remain three more direct quotations, and they need not detain us long. The phrases from Gen. 21.10-12 in Gal. 4.30 are an essential part of the allegory of Sarah and Hagar. Although this has links with other passages in the New Testament (Heb. 12.22; Rev. 21), and although it may be derived from Alexandrian traditions of exegesis,[1] its interest lies in the apologetic method, and not in the re-application of material already used in the apologetic of the early Church. It is thus beyond the scope of the present enquiry. Within this allegory Paul includes a quotation of Isa. 54.1. This will be considered later in relation to other quotations from Deutero-Isaiah. The citation of Lev. 19.18 (the golden rule) belongs to the moral traditions of both Gospel and synagogue, but lies outside our terms of reference.

### 2. THE USE OF SCRIPTURE IN ROMANS

The argument in the Epistle to the Romans goes over much of the same ground as Galatians, but in a much more developed way. The origin of Paul's selection of testimonies is proportionately more complex. Besides his own previous use of Scripture, there are the influences of liturgical exposition and paraenesis within the Church, his own further study in controversy with his opponents, and the continuing tradition of earlier work, which he can exploit in his own way for new ends. The more important examples have already been noted in previous chapters, so that it will not be necessary to analyse the quotations in Romans with the same thoroughness as in the case of Galatians. It will be sufficient to select the texts and group them according to their earlier apologetic usage, indicating how further Old Testament passages have accumulated around them.

### (a) Justification

Paul has in Romans not only a citation (1.17) and an allusion (10.4) to the basic text Hab. 2.4 which he had used in Gal. 3.11,

---

curse in Gen. 3.17f. is contrasted with the fruitfulness of the land promised to Abraham. The latter, however, may be taken as further evidence for the Christian use of the blessing of Abraham as we have it in the other non-Pauline literature.

[1] Not directly from Philo, whose allegory of Sarah and Hagar is very different (discussed at length by J. B. Lightfoot *ad loc.*).

but also a reference to the related Ps. 143.2 in 3.20 (cf. Gal. 2.16). Along with the latter allusion he has drawn together a number of passages on the same theme from various places in the Psalter: Pss. 51.6, 14.1-3, 5.10, 140.4, 10.7 and 36.2. Between the last two he has inserted Isa. 59.7-8. This is drawn from the apocalyptic stock (*v. infra*). Ps. 32.1-2 in Rom. 4.7f. belongs to this group. The significant thing is that Paul's thought on justification has been deepened through study of the Psalter.

### (b) The Blessing of Abraham

The argument from the faith of Abraham is taken up in Rom. 4. As we have seen, the contrast is with his subsequent circumcision rather than with the institution of the Law. The key text Gen. 15.6 (Gal. 3.6) is referred to several times. Gen. 17.5, 1of., are also quoted. In Rom. 9 Paul brings up the matter again, this time taking up the matter of the promise, which he had worked out with the aid of the allegory of Sarah and Hagar in Gal. 4. The texts quoted are Gen. 21.12 and 18.10. He is able to introduce a further refinement into the argument by following the patriarchal history into the next generation. Both the sons of Isaac are of course 'children of the promise', but the older is made inferior to the younger. This suggests to Paul the temporary rejection of the Jews and their final reconciliation. The texts used are Gen. 25.23 and Mal. 1.2f.

### (c) The Inadequacy of the Law

The argument of Gal. 3 about the curse of the Law is not reproduced in Romans, but is replaced by the long and much more profound analysis of the inadequacy of the Law in Rom. 5-7. However Paul brings up the matter again in connection with the question of the rejection of the Jews in 10.1-11. He starts with an allusion to Lev. 18.5, as in Gal. 3.12, but he is able to simplify the argument considerably by producing an edited version of Deut. 30.12-14. The original is concerned with a hypothetical search for the Law, either above or below the earth, ending with the true place, which is in the heart. But the important thing is that this vivid fancy is set within an appeal to choose between the blessing and the curse. Obedience from the heart will alone secure the blessing. Although the passage is really concerned with the Law, it stands outside Paul's definition of it, which is primarily a matter of works as opposed to faith (Rom. 10.5). For him the passage *must* be concerned with Christ, who is the τέλος of the Law, for the conduct which it inculcates is precisely the attitude of faith. So the search for the Law becomes a search for Christ, who was sent from God and died and rose again. Paul has accordingly selected only such phrases as can be applied to Christ, replacing the idea of crossing the sea by words from Ps. 107.26, which are more readily applicable to resurrection from the grave. It thus presupposes the whole argument on faith and works, and seems to be a *pesher* text of Paul's own making.[1] In spite of this he can continue to inculcate the moral laws of the Pentateuch in Rom. 12.20 and 13.9 (as in Gal. 5.14).

## (d) The Passion Apologetic

That Paul was familiar with the general range of Passion scriptures was already indicated in our study of Gal. 3.13. We are thus not surprised to find clear allusions to Isa. 53.4-5, 12 in Rom. 4.25 (cf. I Cor. 15.3). It would seem that his love of the Psalter has led him to correlate Ps. 44.23 with the idea of the lamb led to the slaughter. In Rom. 8.36 it enables him to make a homiletic application of it to the members of the Church, as is done in I Peter (*supra*, p. 87). It is possible that Ps. 44 had already been attracted into the general stock of the Passion apologetic in this way before Paul used it, but other evidence is lacking.

Paul has two quotations from the prophecy of the Suffering Servant which receive new applications. These are Isa. 53.1 in Rom. 10.16 and Isa. 52.15 in Rom. 15.21. By this time these verses are already used more generally of acceptance and rejection of the Gospel, and the original setting in defence of the Passion has fallen into the background. They belong to the apologetic of response (see next section), and Paul can use them specifically of the unbelief of the Jews and the preaching to the Gentiles.[2]

There are also two quotations from the most important of the Passion Psalms. Ps. 69.23f., quoted in Rom. 11.9f., was originally a curse directed against those who did not repent of crucifying Jesus, but has now been applied to the fatal blindness of the Jews. It is thus another example of the apologetic of response. Ps. 69.10 in Rom. 15.3 is a case of the homiletic use of a Passion text.[3]

---

[1] There appears to be no linguistic connection with the allusion to Deut. 30.12-14 of Baruch 3.29f.
[2] For these quotations cf. pp. 86f. *supra*.          [3] *Supra*, pp. 102ff.

It is evident from this that Paul was not directly concerned with the Passion apologetic at all. The Passion does not need to be defended, but must be proclaimed. It is the essence of the Atonement and the example for all Christians to follow (Gal. 6.14). Nevertheless Paul is well aware that both Jew and Greek find objection to it (I Cor. 1.23).

### (e) The Apologetic of Response

In the fourth chapter of this book a number of testimonies were examined which are concerned with the question why the Gospel did not compel belief. It is a question which was bound to be raised in the missionary situation of the Church. For St Paul it is a matter of the greatest importance, as he finds increasing opposition on the part of his own countrymen, but a great measure of success among the Gentiles.

In Rom. 2.24 Paul cites Isa. 52.5 to show the scandal of the Jews' failure to keep the Law, even the precepts which meet universal approval. It was shown when this passage was considered in the first chapter that the real scandal implied by the context is their refusal to believe the salvation now offered. Paul has taken this from the apologetic of response for the purpose of undermining the argument of the Judaizers by showing that the Law is impossible even for the Jews themselves.

It is the second part of Romans which is chiefly concerned with response. When we studied the Stone series of testimonies, it was observed that Rom. 9.33 is a much abbreviated conflation of two complementary texts, Isa. 28.16 and 8.14, already applied to believers and unbelievers. It now becomes virtually equivalent to the contrast between the Jews and the Gentiles, but only to show that the whole issue transcends the politico-religious division altogether.

This suggests that the other citations about the remnant in the same chapter should be traced to previous usage. In our study of Isa. 6.9f. we saw that it tended to create a sect-type doctrine of the Church. In Rom. 11.8 Paul actually quotes one of the associated texts, Isa. 29.10, conflated with Deut. 29.3.[1] He transfers the distinction from believers and unbelievers within Judaism to the issue between Jews and Gentiles. The Jews are rejected totally, so that the remnant is the Gentiles. The doctrine of the remnant is correlative to the sect-type doctrine of the Church. It shows that,

---

[1] In 11.7 ἐπωρώθησαν is from the Church's *pesher* text of Isa. 6.10 itself.

whereas the fatal blindness of the Jews was foretold in Scripture, nevertheless the promises of God have not failed. The whole sacred history shows that there is always a faithful remnant in whom they can be fulfilled.

From the point of view of the rejection of unbelievers (applied to the Jews), Paul has attended to the whole context of Isa. 29, from which his quotation in 11.8 is taken. It may be that the link with Isa. 6.9f. has first drawn his attention to it. At all events his warrant for claiming that the Jews have been rejected in spite of being God's chosen people is a citation of Isa. 29.16 (Rom. 9.20). His wording has been influenced by Isa. 45.9, but it is ch. 29 which gives the proper context of thought. There is also an important citation of Isa. 29.14 in I Cor. 1.19.[1]

Another avenue along which he has reached this rejection theology has been his study of the patriarchal narratives in connection with the promise to Abraham, as we have seen in (b) above. So the doctrine of the *élite* associated with Isa. 6.9f. and the proclamation of the fulfilment of the blessing of Abraham—two aspects of the apologetic of response—have here converged in the working out of Paul's theory of rejection. In conjunction with these two lines of thought Paul has added the example of the hardening of Pharaoh's heart, quoting Ex. 33.19 and 9.16 (Rom. 9.15, 17). Then the quotations used to argue the doctrine of the remnant are Isa. 10.22f. and 1.9 in Rom. 9.27-29, and I Kings 19.10, 18 in Rom. 11.3f. Perhaps we need not look behind Paul himself for the choice of these passages, except the first, which is abbreviated and has slight differences from the standard Septuagint text. It may have been already in use, seeing that we have evidence of the study of Isa. 8 to 11 in the apologetic of response.[2]

But more important is the fact that the remnant series in Rom. 9 is introduced by a quotation which is not actually a remnant text, but demonstrably belongs to the more fundamental sect-type doctrine of the Church. This is Hos. 2.25 (EVV 2.23), 'I will call not-my-people my people', etc. In itself this passage guarantees the Christian claim to be the people of God without the necessity of proving continuity with the old Israel. If we think of the resurrection passage of Hos. 6.2 as the primary interest in the prophecy of Hosea, it is easy to see how the early Church, gradually becoming conscious of itself as the People of God in a special sense, and

---

[1] *Supra*, p. 166.    [2] *Supra*, pp. 176, 202.

yet at the same time aware of being 'not many mighty, not many noble', would value the opening chapters to show how those who respond to the Gospel's call to repentance are accepted as God's beloved people. The text as it stands in Rom. 9.25 evidently has gone through a process of adaptation. The order of clauses is inverted, and the whole seems to be an independent translation from the Hebrew.[1] Then part of Hos. 2.1 (1.10) has been added to it at a later stage, following the Septuagint exactly. This adds nothing new to the general sense, but emphasizes the idea of the Church as God's own People. But the *beginning* of Hos. 2.1, not quoted in 9.26, makes possible the transition to the idea of the remnant. For these words are very similar to the opening of Isa. 10.22, which Paul now proceeds to quote, to prove that 'it is the remnant that shall be saved', and in his quotation they have actually replaced it. Now the addition of Hos. 2.1 to 2.25 presents no problem, for it is the clustering of related scriptures characteristic of the living tradition of apologetic. It is also perfectly possible that the remnant text of Isa. 10.22f. should be added by means of the word-link to reinforce the doctrine of the Church as the true Israel. It is thus unnecessary to suppose that the shaping of this little group of texts is Paul's work at all. What is new is again his application of it to the Gentiles problem.[2]

This testimony, perhaps more than any other, demonstrates how Paul's attitude to the Gentiles is built upon the earlier doctrine of the Church. Brilliantly he extracts this doctrine from a too literal idea of the meaning of the chosen people. When Hos. 2.25 is used again in I Peter 2.10 the transformation is complete. The Church is all those who are joined to Christ by repentance and faith, regardless of whether they are Jews or Gentiles. Nor is it necessary to argue the rejection of the Jews; they are the People of God no longer.

So far we have been concerned with the rejection and remnant theories in Rom. 9 and 11. Between these two chapters there is a catena of quotations on faith, Rom. 10.11-21. This is still within the area of the apologetic of response. The section on the remnant in Rom. 9 led up to the brief conflate Stone citation at the end of the chapter. This sums up the whole argument so far in terms of belief

---

[1] This seems to me most probable, even though LXX[B] has ἀγαπήσω τὴν Οὐκ-ἠγαπημένην for LXX[A]'s ἐλεήσω, κτλ. In 1.6 both texts have Οὐκ-ἐλεημένη.
[2] Cf. Earle Ellis, *St Paul's Use of the OT*, p. 122 n. 6.

in, or stumbling at, the precious corner stone. It also sets the theme for the following chapter. So first of all Paul develops the thought of stumbling in 10.1-5, using some of his ideas from Gal. 3, as we saw in (c). Then the elaborate quotation of Deut. 30.12-14 makes a bridge to the thought of belief in Christ, which occupies the rest of the chapter. This is why he repeats Rom. 9.33b (= Isa. 28.16d) at 10.11, inserting πᾶς to emphasize the universal validity of the statement. *Everyone*, whether Jew or Gentile, shall not be put to shame. This verse has a close verbal similarity to a phrase repeated twice in Joel 2.26f. It is then not surprising that Paul cites yet another version of the same idea, Joel 3.5 (2.32). This, and the quotations which follow, can be classified under two heads, Preaching and Apocalyptic. The similar catena in Rom. 15.9-12 should be considered with them.

### (f) Preaching Testimonies

These are derived from two sources. In the first place there is the study of Deutero-Isaiah as a prophecy of salvation. This may have had its roots in the Passion apologetic. Compare Paul's use of Isa. 52.15 and 53.1 already noted in (d). By studying the context one quickly lights on the attractive words of Isa. 52.7. This and 53.1 itself give us the first two of Paul's preaching texts in Rom. 10.15f. At the end of the chapter Paul has selected two texts from the same prophecy, Isa. 65.1f., concerned with the response to preaching. We should also note his use of Isa. 52.5 in Rom. 2.24, and of Isa. 54.1 in Gal. 4.27.

The other source is the Psalter, which we have already found him using in (a). Here again the earliest use of the Psalms was for messianic texts and in the Passion apologetic. Now we find Paul studying them for his own urgent need to settle the Judaistic controversy. So he uses Ps. 19.5 in Rom. 10.18, and Pss. 18.50 and 117.1 in Rom. 15.9, 11. But his study of the Psalms must be regarded as extending also to the Song of Moses in Deut. 32. This is included in the *Odae* immediately after the Psalter in LXX[A], and although this collection has the *Magnificat* and *Benedictus* at the end as we now have it from a Christian copyist, it is probable that it already stood in the previous Jewish text as an additional hymnary for liturgical use.[1] We have already observed a quotation

---

[1] Of course the two Lucan canticles may themselves have already existed in the pre-Christian synagogue. *Codex Veronensis* adds five more canticles.

from Deut. 32.43 in Heb. 1.6, in a form which has an exact parallel only in the reading of the *Odae*.[1] There also the quotation occurs in a catena of psalm verses. Another line from the same verse of Deut. 32 occurs in Paul's second list of preaching testimonies, Rom. 15.10.

This agreement between Paul and Hebrews is the more notable when we observe another text from the same canticle. Both use for its moral value the phrase 'Vengeance is mine, I will repay' from Deut. 32.35 (Rom. 12.19; Heb. 10.30). What is more, both agree in reading ἐμοὶ ἐκδίκησις, ἐγὼ ἀνταποδώσω, against the Septuagint.[2] This stands closer to the Hebrew,[3] but probably comes from another Greek tradition, for the vocabulary is that of the Septuagint, and deliberate correction by both writers is scarcely conceivable. In Rom. 10.19 Paul draws from the same source once more, quoting Deut. 32.21.

## (g) Apocalyptic Scriptures

The second catena of Gentiles texts concludes with a quotation of Isa. 11.10 (Rom. 15.12). In the last chapter it was argued that this entered the Christian tradition not as a messianic text but by way of the conventions of the apocalyptic programme.[4] It was there noted that Paul's special interest in apocalyptic was the idea of the conversion of the nations. It is probable that Joel 3.5 (2.32) in Rom. 10.13 comes from the same field of thought. For it is the last verse of the long Joel quotation in St Peter's speech in Acts 2, which specifically asserts that the Day of the Lord has arrived.

Moreover in Rom. 11.26f. Paul expresses the missionary hope in apocalyptic form with the aid of Isa. 59.20f., conflated with Isa. 27.9. Even the Jews will be saved after the Gentiles have been gathered in, when 'the Deliverer' comes from Zion (presumably our Lord's Parousia is meant). The strange chapter Isa. 59, describing God's saving action as a mighty hero after a time when evil has been rife, could easily be read as an apocalypse. The pic-

---

[1] *Supra*, p. 211.

[2] LXX ἐν ἡμέρᾳ ἐκδικήσεως ἀνταποδώσω, reading ליום for MT לי. This is found in the Samaritan text and Qumran fragment, and is probably the true reading. Cf. 1QS 10.20. Of course Hebrews may be actually quoting from Romans.

[3] לי נקם ושלם. The Targum is interpretative, but is probably based on the same text, קדמי פורענותא ואנא אישלים.

[4] *Supra*, p. 202.

ture has given a phrase to Paul's description of the armour of faith in I Thess. 5.8, transferred, however, from the Lord himself to the steadfast readers.[1] It is possible that it is conventional language in such a context, in connection with the πειρασμός which precedes the End. If we are to see an allusion to Isa. 59.19 in Matt. 8.11 = Luke 13.29, we may take it as further evidence of the apocalyptic use of the chapter. Paul has also included quotation of Isa. 59.7f., which would be applied to the evils before the end, in his list of psalm verses concerned with moral depravity in Rom. 3.10-18. His composite quotation in Rom. 11.27 ends with words from Isa. 27.9. This is an eschatological chapter, and perhaps has supplied the trumpet in Matt. 24.31 and I Thess. 4.16.

There remain two more citations in Romans which do not fit into the above classification. Both come from Deutero-Isaiah, which assumed such importance in the vindication of the Gospel to the Gentiles. On the other hand both have a liturgical character, and so may have been taken over from synagogue usage. The first is Isa. 40.13, included in the doxology of Rom. 11.34-36. The latter part of it seems to be based on Job 41.3, but differs fundamentally from both the Hebrew and the Septuagint. The second quotation is Isa. 45.23 (with altered opening words) in Rom. 14.11. The same verse has an important place in the christological hymn of Phil. 2.10f.[2]

Finally, it should also be recalled that another theme of the earlier apologetic which Paul has adopted is the idea of the hidden mystery.[3] Characteristically he applies it to the admission of the Gentiles, which is an element of the divine plan of salvation which the idea of the People of the Law had obscured. This is expressed in Rom. 16.25f., and with very great effect in Eph. 3.3-6. It also appears in I Cor. 1.18-20, which contains the quotation of Isa. 29.14 referred to in (e) above, and in I Cor. 2.6-16. The latter passage contains a much altered version of Isa. 64.3, evidently shaped around the widely used Isa. 6.10, and also concerned with response.

---

[1] As in Wisd. 5.15-23. This passage has certainly influenced Eph. 6.14, where the eschatological motive has disappeared.

[2] It is interesting to note that Paul follows the text of LXX[A] in his quotation of Isa. 40.13, both here and in I Cor. 2.16, and also in both examples of Isa. 45.23. This supports the contention about the influence of LXX[A] in connection with Deut. 32 in (f).

[3] *Supra*, pp. 157f.

### 3. THE GOSPEL TO THE GENTILES

The analysis of quotations in Galatians and Romans has shown that Paul stands in the line of the Church's exegetical work, as well as in that of the synagogue and other Jewish traditions. His own work, however, takes it along special ways for his own purposes, and thereby contributes importantly to the development of Christian doctrine. It is striking that he does not reproduce the christological texts nor argue that Jesus is the Messiah. This is simply taken for granted as an assured fact. He is concerned to elucidate what is really implied when men commit themselves to this fact.

The Resurrection of Jesus proved that Jesus is the Messiah. But this victory could be put into different terms for other purposes. From one point of view it could be looked at as the reversal of the curse laid upon Jesus by those who condemned him. Paul has taken up this argument and shown that it logically entails the abrogation of the Law, so that the policy of the Judaizers is really a betrayal of the Gospel. Again, the Resurrection victory could be looked at as the fulfilment of the promise to Abraham and his seed. Paul similarly makes use of this to show that the scope of the promise had always been wider than the Jewish people as defined by the Mosaic Law.

Paul knows, and disapproves, the apocalyptic speculations in some Christian quarters. To him the important fact (eschatological rather than apocalyptic) is that in some sense 'the ends of the ages' have come upon his own generation (I Cor. 10.11). He accepts the general lines of the conventional apocalyptic programme, but uses it primarily for the needs of his readers in their present situation. Consequently he shows a tendency to treat the expected time of testing ($\pi\epsilon\iota\rho\alpha\sigma\mu\acute{o}s$) in a virtually timeless way, applied to temptation in the spiritual life (I Cor. 10.13; cf. Eph. 6.14). During the $\pi\epsilon\iota\rho\alpha\sigma\mu\acute{o}s$ the righteous must live by faith (Hab. 2.4). Paul sees this as the necessary condition *now*. And it is something that is available to the Gentile as much as to the Jew. The attitude of the Judaizers takes away this common factor and undermines the Gospel itself.

Another feature of the apocalyptic programme is the conversion of the Gentiles, as the only alternative to their destruction. The unknown prophet of Deutero-Isaiah had perceived that Israel's special position as God's own people was not only a privilege, but entailed a responsibility towards the whole inhabited earth. The largeness of the prophet's vision seems to have reached out beyond the racial barrier of the Law to a true universalism. But later Judaism, self-consciously fighting to maintain its identity, could not take so wide a view. So in the later period the prophecy was normally interpreted in the sense of a mission to the Gentiles to bring them within the covenant of circumcision before the End.[1] When Paul takes over the scriptural passages associated with these ideas he returns to the original universalism on the principle that Christ has abolished the distinction between Jew and Gentile. It is doubtful whether the first Christians perceived the importance of this. The Judaistic controversy itself shows that Paul's attitude was by no means self-evident to all. It took some time for men to understand the true nature of salvation. To make his point Paul draws on both the apocalyptic tradition and also on Deutero-Isaiah. We should also note that the Passion apologetic had been bringing this prophecy into prominence, through the increasing importance of the Servant passage, Isa. 53, in the thought of the early Church.

In these ways the later chapters of Isaiah became the prophecy of the Christian mission, and in Paul's hands that means the Gospel to the Gentiles. After his time it is regularly used to warrant the preaching to the Gentiles.[2] Moreover it had its effect on christology. References to Isa. 61.1f., with the closely associated 35.5f. and 58.6, are confined to Q and the Lucan literature.[3] It should be seriously considered whether this is not due to the influence of St Paul in placing the preaching to the Gentiles at the very centre of the proclamation of salvation. For this happens at the stage which was noted in ch. IV of this book, when the moment of messianic manifestation was pushed back to our Lord's Baptism. This gives messianic significance to his ministry, and so changes the idea of what the Messiah actually is. He ceases to be the inaugurator of the kingdom, in which the wonders of the times of the Messiah will come to pass, and becomes the actual agent of these wonders. Deliverance consists in the spiritual and physical

---

[1] I. L. Seeligmann, *The Septuagint Version of Isaiah*, pp. 110ff.

[2] The principal citations in allusions in Acts are at 2.39 (Isa. 57.19, with Joel 2.32), 10.36 (Isa. 52.7), 13.47 (Isa. 49.6), 15.15-18 (Amos 9.11f. LXX, combined with Isa. 45.21, cf. p. 35 n. 3), 26.18 (Isa. 35.5; 42.7, 16).

[3] Q passages: Matt. 5.3 = Luke 6.20; Matt. 11.5 = Luke 7.22. Lucan passages: Luke 4.18f.; Acts 4.27, 10.38, 26.18.

restoration of harmony which these wonders teach. The quasi-political idea of the kingdom had already disappeared by the time Paul wrote his Epistles, only surviving in Gospel material which has a continuous link with the older outlook, and in apocalyptic contexts which can be readily spiritualized. The signs of the kingdom have become the gracious acts of Christ, and the conversion of the Gentiles has become the acceptance of universal healing.

Paul's achievement also includes a new doctrine of the Church. Our study of the testimonies has shown that there was a tendency in the early days to slip into a sectarian outlook. This was aroused by the unexpected resistance to the message of salvation. We have seen that when Paul adopts the biblical material concerned, he can see that its fundamental application to the nature of belief and unbelief cuts across the distinction between Jew and Gentile. The Church is the new Israel, but this absolutely transcends the old Israel after the flesh.

From more than one point of view we have seen that the works of the Law have been superseded by faith in Christ. A corollary of this is the supersession of the Jerusalem temple and its cultus. It is interesting that none of the quotations in Galatians and Romans is concerned with this issue. The classic expressions of it are to be found in Acts 7 and Hebrews. Paul, in his later Epistles, uses sacrificial or temple phrases from time to time, but only in allegorical and moral applications. He never has to argue the point.[1] This may be due to his Hellenistic background, in which the idea of the supersession of temple and sacrifice already had its supporters even within Judaism. The development of theology, which saw that the need for atonement was achieved in Christ, had already taken place in the Hellenistic elements of the Church before Paul.[2] It is probable that similar ideas existed within stricter elements of Judaism as well. The Qumran Sect had a priestly organization apparently detached from actual participation in the temple and its rites. The comparative ease with which the Rabbis of Jamnia could rebuild Judaism after the devastating national defeat, by taking up all the meaning of the old structure of sacrifice into a religion of the Synagogue and the Book, also shows that the time was ripe for the development which had been achieved within Christianity.

[1] Col. 2.22, quoting Isa. 29.13, refers to universal ceremonial customs of the Jews, not to temple and cultus.
[2] M. Simon, *St Stephen and the Hellenists*, ch. V.

The importance of this is that here are things which appear to be as essential as the laws of circumcision and sabbath, but which could be cheerfully dispensed with by St Paul at the same time as he had to use all his resources to prove that circumcision itself was not necessary to salvation. Thus the development typified by Stephen could be widely acceptable, but yet it left the fundamental issue between Jew and Gentile untouched. St Paul was the creative thinker who first produced a theory that could overcome this barrier without loss of the essential place of Judaism in the hidden mystery of the divine plan of salvation.[1]

[1] This universalism is precisely the 'mystery' of which Paul is the chosen exponent. Cf. B. Rigaux, 'Révélation des Mystères et Perfection à Qumran et dans le NT', *NTS* 4, 1958, pp. 237-62.

# VII

## THE USE OF SCRIPTURE IN THE EARLY CHURCH

THE work of St Paul is the beginning of the datable New Testament literature, and so brings us to the end of the proper concern of this book. It now remains to draw the conclusions reached in the preceding chapters, and to show their significance for evaluating the books of the New Testament in which the quotations occur. It has been the aim of this study to use the Old Testament quotations as a clue to the thoughts and problems which occupied the Church in the period for which we have no written documents. It is hoped that this may supplement and confirm the results of other parallel lines of enquiry. It must be emphasized that no attempt has been made to give an exhaustive review of the quotations. Many have been omitted from consideration, as they were outside the scope of enquiry. The study has been confined to those which may have contributed to the early Church's apologetic.

### I. THE PRIMITIVE APOLOGETIC AND ITS DEVELOPMENTS

During the life of Jesus there were various estimates of him. Two popular descriptions of him were 'the prophet of Galilee' and 'the son of David'. It seems certain that by the end of his ministry his closest friends were convinced that he was the expected Messiah, and that he was just about to inaugurate the kingdom of God, which was the substance of his preaching. His teaching about his approaching death was calculated to prepare them for considerable difficulty in establishing the kingdom. But it would not lead them to suppose that the attempt would be an utter failure, and the claim of messiahship come to nothing. On the contrary there seems always to have been a note of optimism in the Passion

251

predictions. This was expressed in language derived from Hos. 6.2, but was no doubt also due to reflection on the prophecy of Isa. 53. When the Resurrection happened, it was these facts that provided the key to the meaning of it. The event was unexpected in itself. But as it was clearly the work of God's power, it had to be seen in the light of the promises of God, as these had been taught by Jesus himself. So the Resurrection was seen to be the speedy vindication of which he had spoken. It could also be regarded as the manifestation of his messianic glory, and therefore as marking the inauguration of the messianic kingdom. The End is determined, the Messiah has been revealed, the effusion of the Spirit in the Age to Come has already begun, and entry into the kingdom must be secured by an act of personal allegiance to the designated King.

The beginnings of apologetic are to be traced to the need to give a reasoned defence of this interpretation of the Resurrection-event. Several great messianic texts are used along with the Church's proclamation, and these are naturally quoted for apologetic purposes. Thus Ps. 110.1 defined the Resurrection as messianic manifestation and showed it to be the expected vindication. This text had special value for apologetic, because the Resurrection (however unexpected in itself) is the literal fulfilment of it. The same argument applies to our Lord's promise of Resurrection on the third day, derived from Hos. 6.2. Presumably the apocalyptic Dan. 7.13, which is a text of vindication, was also used from very early times.

Several other texts are used in connection with the Resurrection-proclamation in this earliest period. It has been noted that this is the first stage in the use of Ps. 2.7, Ps. 118, and Isa. 42.1, possibly also of Isa. 61.1. The argument from literal fulfilment also occurred with Ps. 16 in the speeches of Acts 2 and 13. Although we have here an excellent example of the most primitive form of apologetic, it is impossible to be certain that the use of this particular psalm goes back to the earliest phase, because it only survives in the comparatively late Lucan compilation. It is significant that no evidence was found of the use of specifically Davidic texts in this way.

The preaching of the apostles was addressed to those who had very recently crucified Jesus. The Crucifixion, though apparently a disaster for his followers, had turned out to be the prelude to the divine act of messianic revelation and vindication. The positive value of the Passion is thus an element of the kerygma from the first. Jesus is the righteous sufferer of Isa. 53, of the Passion Psalms, and of Zech. 11 and 12. This is the earliest component of the distinctively Christian messianic idea. It arises directly out of the historical facts. Although it is not without precedents in late Jewish speculations it is sufficiently novel and striking to be seriously questioned, and so it forms the subject of the earliest apologetic proper.

The very fact that an apologetic is needed has a further implication. In the first flush of triumph it might have been expected that the Gospel message could not fail to compel belief and acceptance. The apostles quickly discovered that this was not so. The question of unbelief thus enters in from the beginning. It seems that the apostles saw themselves in a situation somewhat parallel to that of Isaiah at the beginning of his prophetic ministry, and included the classic text on unbelief, Isa. 6.9f., in their intellectual armoury at an early date.

The second phase of apologetic development is like a move from prepared positions into a volley of fire in the thick of battle. The fundamental Resurrection claim has to be substantiated against the observation that Jesus, though said to be risen, is not visible as an earthly leader. Two dogmas answer this objection: that he is present in his rightful place at the Father's side in heaven, and that he is known on earth by the effusion of the Spirit, which is plain for all to see. These are two theological ways of expressing the fact of the Resurrection. The first is reached with the aid of Ps. 110.1, which now gains its definitive application to denote the heavenly session. The second makes use of various eschatological passages which mention the Spirit (Ezek. 36.27, 37.14, cf. I Thess. 4.8; Joel 3.1-5, cf. Acts 2.17-21). At some point which cannot be determined with certainty Ps. 68.19 is an important influence in framing an answer to the objection. Its value lies in the combination of the ideas of the Ascension and of the Gift of the Spirit in a single quasi-prophetic verse.

At the same time there is a host of objections raised against the manner of Christ's death. So the passages already employed in the Passion apologetic are worked over to provide the answer to each particular item. The composition of the Gospel Passion narratives, in which these scriptures are constantly referred to for details, has been influenced by this apologetic. As the first Christians defend the Passion in this way, their understanding of its redemptive efficacy is deepened. This work takes into account the mode of execution by crucifixion, and the various humiliations to which Jesus was subjected. The first use of the curse of Deut. 21.23 may have been at this time, though in the extant literature it only occurs in Galatians. A special element in this apologetic was the treachery of Judas. This constituted a much more embarrassing problem in the early days, when recollection of the emotions which the events aroused remained fresh, than later on, when it had little more than dramatic interest.

The second phase is also concerned to make the messianic claim more precise. This has to be done from two points of view. On the one hand there are theoretical considerations involved as wider use is made of established messianic texts. The three famous passages in Isaiah (7.14, 9.5, 11.1) were all naturally referred to the Messiah of the house of David. Micah 5.2, Ps. 89 and II Sam. 7 could also be adduced in this sense. Against this there are signs of resistance in the early Church, using Isa. 8.23-9.1 in favour of Galilean origin, and possibly Isa. 49.6 to support Nazareth. It seems that Ps. 110.1 was also used in this controversy. But the Davidic texts, which had not been employed in the earliest strata, eventually won the day.

The other issue is the need to prove definite messianic character in the known facts of the life and teaching of Jesus himself. Thus Ps. 118, which began by being a Resurrection text, and was quickly drawn into the region of the Passion apologetic, is used to give messianic significance to the Palm Sunday tradition. The eschatological prophecy of Zechariah, which has also been used in the Passion apologetic, becomes an essential part of the story, so that Zech. 9.9 is regulative of its interpretation. The tradition of the Baptism of our Lord has also been adapted to this purpose, the conflate version of Isa. 42.1 and Ps. 2.7 being transferred to it from previous usage in connection with the Resurrection. The development of the Transfiguration narrative, in which another version of the same words is used, is motivated by the same need, though it may be a slightly later development. We also find at this stage the use of Isa. 61.1f. to show the messianic character of our Lord's ministry.

Meanwhile the problem of the unbelief of many people, and the continuing hostility of the authorities, must still receive attention. This also has two lines of development. Both stem from Isa. 6.9f.

In the first place, because this testimony accounts for the fatal *porosis* that has affected men's hearts, it is the basis of a theory about faith and unbelief. The idea of the rejected stone (Ps. 118.22), which had been an element of the Passion apologetic, is applied to the rejection of the unbelievers. Other texts of response are associated with this, notably Isa. 28.16 (the precious corner stone) and Isa. 8.14 (the stone of stumbling), and also Isa. 29. From the angle of faith, the doctrine of rejection makes for an estimate of the believers as a privileged *élite*. This leads to a sectarian doctrine of the Church. It is presupposed in the Petrine material of Matt. 16. It is also the beginning of the Christian 'remnant' theology, to which Hos. 2.25 was originally applied.

The other line of development from Isa. 6.9f. is a necessary rider to the tendency to give direct messianic significance to the sayings and acts of Jesus. It is the idea that this character was always there, but could only be perceived by the spiritually discerning. Besides the use of Isa. 6.9f. in this sense, Isa. 53.1 was also employed, though it belongs to the Passion apologetic. The use of Ps. 78 preserved in Matt. 13 may be an aspect of the theme of revelation of a hidden mystery, which was also expressed with the aid of other scriptures.

Closely connected with the apologetic of response, and probably a very primitive feature of it, is the application of the curses of the Passion Psalms, notably Ps. 69, to those who refuse to believe. The passage about the Prophet like Moses (Deut. 18.15-18) was also originally used in contexts of solemn warning.

In the liturgical life of the Church at this creative stage, the scriptures of the Passion apologetic have considerable importance in the recitation of the new act of redemption. It is perhaps at this time that 'the blood of the covenant' was added to the eucharistic words from Zech. 9.11. The recollection of the acts of Jesus in commentary on the Old Testament lections seems to have helped to give messianic significance to them. This may be true of the Baptism and Palm Sunday stories.

At the same time the Hellenistic elements of the Church are asserting that, as a result of Christ's work of redemption and inauguration of the kingdom, the temple and its cultus are superseded. In any case they have long felt these to be obsolescent, and offensive to their intellectual approach to religion. It is presumably at about this time that our Lord's prediction of Resurrection on the third day is combined with his prophecy against the temple, so producing a saying which supports the Hellenistic point of view.

The third phase of development takes up all these themes, and adds both precision and complexity. If we may continue the strategic metaphor, it is as if the actual engagement in battle is over, and the two opposing sides are entrenching themselves in the positions which they have won or been forced back to. From now on the warfare is conducted with greater care and calculation. Much attention is given to the fortification of the basic positions. So internal developments in the life of the church assume much greater importance. The earlier Epistles of St Paul belong to this time.

The Passion apologetic is now virtually finished. It no longer has to be argued that Jesus is the Christ. It is accepted that he is a descendant of the family of David. These points will, of course, have to be stated afresh in each generation. They reappear in the speech of Acts 13, which may be an example of discussion with the Jews as it was still conducted after the time of Paul. They are highly developed in the anti-Judaic tradition represented by Justin's *Dialogue with Trypho*. But they are no longer the formative elements in the Church's evolution of its own doctrine, but solid pillars on which the structure can rest.

There is now a tendency for originally distinct concepts to be fused into larger composite wholes. An illustration of this is the Transfiguration narrative. It is evocative of a great wealth of Old Testament imagery. It also combines an allusion to the Prophet of Deut. 18 with the Resurrection texts of the divine words at the Baptism. The idea of the Prophet, whatever its place in primitive interpretations of the person of Jesus, here appears as an element in a new agglomerate christology. The tendency of apologetic is not to choose between various messianic expectations, but to take them up into the expanding concept of the person of Christ. This is illustrated at a slightly later stage by the way in which Hebrews treats Jesus as the Priestly Messiah. He is not indeed the Messiah of Aaron (1QS 9.11), but he is a priest 'after the order of Melchizedek' (Ps. 110.4). This is a new application of this psalm, dependent on its established usage in christology.

In the matter of messianic origins, the doctrine of pre-existence assumes theological importance. At the same time the tendency to push back the moment of messianic manifestation is taken further by transferring it from the Baptism to the moment of birth. Two Davidic texts are now used for these purposes. Ps. 89 supplies the word πρωτότοκος, now used in passages of speculative christology (Col. 1.15-20; Heb. 1.5). Isa. 7.14 dominates the traditions of the infancy of Jesus.

The application of Dan. 7.13 to the Resurrection, as the moment of vindication before God, now becomes transferred to the final Parousia at the consummation. This is soon to be the normal application of this and similar apocalyptic passages, replacing the 'inaugurated eschatology' which is preserved in the apparently primitive phrases of Acts 3.19-21.[1] So Zech. 12.10-12, which had been used in the Passion apologetic, is referred to the coming in judgment (Matt. 24.30; Rev. 1.7). Apocalyptic scriptures are used with their conventional future reference increasingly as time goes on. This may be illustrated by the conflation of Isa. 59.20f. and Isa. 27.9 found in Rom. 11.26f. It retains its future sense, even though Paul dislikes apocalyptic and is using this text for a different purpose.

The effect of the apocalypticizing tendency on theology is to stress the interim between the redemption and the End. Yet another application of Ps. 110.1 comes into prominence here, the subjugation of the spiritual enemies of the ascended Lord. With it is associated the similar phrasing of Ps. 8. The doctrine of the Church is also affected by it, because those who are bound together by sacramental pledge when they 'proclaim the Lord's death till he come', are one Body in him in a way that marks them out from the rest of humanity now and ensures salvation in the coming judgment.

At this point the further ramifications of previous exegetical work become extremely complicated. The Church is one Body with Christ because of the inclusive character of his redeeming work—an idea always implicit in the concept of the righteous sufferer found in Isa. 53, but now expressed with the aid of Ps. 8.3 (Matt. 21.16), and Ps. 22.23 (Heb. 2.12) from the Passion apologetic. The doctrine of the *élite*, which had arisen in the apologetic of response, now becomes a doctrine of the closely-knit character of the Church. So the rejected stone is the foundation of the true temple (new applications of Ps. 118.22 and Isa. 28.16), and the rebuilt temple of the body of Jesus is his Body, the Church (cf.

[1] J. A. T. Robinson, *Jesus and his Coming*, pp. 143-8.

John 2.13-22 and the Passion Psalm 69). Thus we have here contributions from the liturgical tradition, the Passion apologetic, the apologetic of response, and the messianic stone theme, to the kind of doctrine of the Church as the Body of Christ which is familiar to us in St Paul.

It is not surprising to find that by now the idea of the People of God is applied to the Church specifically in contrast to the rest of Judaism, whereas to begin with the People of God consisted of the disciples and the whole of Judaism potentially. The change is reflected in the Remnant theology based on Hos. 2.25 preserved in the later chapters of Romans. Other ways in which the link between Christ and the Church was perhaps expressed at this time may be found in the prior use of the *pesher* quotations of Hos. 11.1 and Jer. 31.15 which are incorporated in Matt. 2.

The apologetic of response is also the basis of solving the question of the admission of the Gentiles. All the scriptures previously used in connection with belief and unbelief come into play to prove the rejection of the Jews (now 'written off' as unbelievers) and the acceptance of the believing Gentiles. This also links up with the 'interim' theology, for the preaching to the Gentiles before the End is one element of the apocalyptic tradition, even though this originally meant conversion to Judaism. The apologetic of response now has an enlarging effect. By showing that personal belief is the real criterion in the sight of God, it makes for a genuinely universal perspective.

In this phase it is inevitable that the prophecy of salvation contained in Deutero-Isaiah should be specially applied to the burning issue of the Gentiles. It becomes a prophecy of the Gospel to the Gentiles, and is frequently employed for this purpose. In the earlier phase the interest had been mainly directed to Isa. 53 for the Passion apologetic. Similarly there is a wider study of the Psalms, which had at first been mostly used in the Passion apologetic. It seems that the use of the Song of Moses of Deut. 32 belongs to this literary labour in a Septuagint milieu.

This is a matter internal to the life of the Church, but the older apologetic has been applied to it. In the same way Paul is ready to use the synagogue arguments to settle the problem. Many of his paraenetic sayings, like those of Jesus himself, can of course be compared to rabbinic teachings. But these are ethical matters, which, like the moral quotations from the Old Testament, simply testify to the continuity of the Church with its Jewish origins.[1] But Paul's theology of the faith of Abraham, his argument on the Law, and his theory of justification, all owe something to the earlier apologetic, of which we see traces in Acts 3 and 7.

Finally a great many of the selected scriptures become so well known in the thought of the Church that they are adopted for homiletic use without regard either to the apologetic which produced them or to the theology for which they were such influential factors. This is specially true of I Peter. It shows many traces of the earlier apologetic, and also the tendency to accumulate messianic ideas around the person of Jesus, but always with the hortatory motive. The apologetic and the theology which accompanies it are things that can be taken for granted. We have now really passed beyond the third phase, and reached the point where the application of previous material coincides with the motive of the writing in which it is incorporated. Thus the use of formula-quotations in Matthew and John is governed by their own purposes as evangelists. This aspect of the matter merits consideration in a separate section.

## 2. FORMULA-QUOTATIONS IN MATTHEW AND JOHN

The treatment of quotations which forms the basis of the present work presupposes exegetical study at various church centres during the first century. Apologetic considerations are an important factor in it. There is a natural tendency for some texts to be specially favoured and widely used. The formula-quotations in Matthew have a special claim to be regarded as products of such work. This does not, however, mean that the Gospel itself can be explained as the scholarly production of a local 'school'. This is the theory of Stendahl's *The School of St Matthew*, a work to which I am deeply indebted. Stendahl's case necessitates an integral connection between the resultant form of a *pesher* text and its actual context in Matthew. The impression gained in the course of our search for dogmatic implications in the quotations has been that Matthew has not been interested even in the factors which gave them their

[1] Among numerous works on the subject may be mentioned W. D. Davies, *Paul and Rabbinic Judaism*[2], 1955, and D. Daube, *The New Testament and Rabbinic Judaism*, 1956. An interesting attempt to explain some of the arguments which I have included in this study of early Christian apologetic from the methods of the rabbis is to be found in J. W. Doeve, *Jewish Hermeneutics in the Synoptic Gospels and Acts*, 1953.

final shape. On the contrary he seems to have been guided largely by what I have called 'pictorial' considerations. This can be seen if these quotations are quickly reviewed from the point of view of their function in the Gospel.

The five *pesher* texts in Matt. 1 and 2 are generally held to stand apart from the rest because of their key position in the traditions of the infancy narratives. This is particularly notable in the case of the first, the citation of Isa. 7.14 in Matt. 1.23. In the discussion of this text in ch. V it was shown that it is primarily a messianic text from the early Christian point of view. As the key text of the infancy traditions, it was instrumental in drawing attention to the virgin birth, and raised the question of Messiah's name or titles. The story as we have it in Matthew has been evolved out of this discussion. But it is purely descriptive in motive (οὕτως ἦν). The story is thought of as a straight fulfilment of the prophecy (τοῦτο δὲ ὅλον γέγονεν ἵνα πληρωθῇ),[1] and there is no overt reference to the use of the text to prove messiahship.

The quotation of Micah 5.2 (Matt. 2.6) belongs to the *pesher* texts, although its place in the narrative causes omission of the formula. Again the final form has been reached before the narrative is written. In fact Matthew seems to be quoting from the rabbinic school in vv. 4b-5. First there is the question, 'Where is the Christ born?' Then the reply, 'In Bethlehem of Judaea'. And finally the evidence, 'Because it is written by (διά = בְּיַד) the prophet'. From this dialogue Matthew is able to insert 'in Bethlehem of Judaea' at the start of the narrative (2.1). Really he has not the least idea where Joseph came from, but simply assumes it from the theory demanded by the Davidic controversy. The reading Βηθλέεμ γῆ Ἰούδα in the quotation itself, rather than Βηθλέεμ οἶκος Ἐφραθά (LXX[B], cf. MT), is of no importance to him, but was already there in the form in which he received it. Nor does he take any notice of the other significant variations.

The quotations of Hos. 11.1 and Jer. 31.15 in Matt. 2.15, 18 have purely biographical interest. In both cases the textual evidence favoured the supposition that they were selected for some other purpose before being adopted by Matthew. That Matthew does not know what this purpose was is indicated by his misunderstanding of the second one (the weeping of Rachel).[2]

---

[1] This very full form of the introductory formula occurs only here.
[2] Cf. *supra*, pp. 217f.

The brief and enigmatic formula-quotation in Matt. 2.23 came to Matthew with such little explanation that he neither knows its source nor its proper wording. It merely performs the function of explaining the discrepancy between the nativity tradition (Bethlehem) and the usual topographical designation of Jesus (Nazareth).

It should be noted that these observations do not invalidate the claim that there is a theological purpose in these opening chapters of Matthew. It is still tenable that his collection of infancy traditions is intended to imply that the history of Israel ('God's son', Hos. 11.1) is gathered up into the history of Jesus. This aspect of the matter is independent of the fact that the actual text of the quotations points to a previous apologetic of which Matthew knows little or nothing.

The rest of these *pesher* quotations are insertions into the narrative taken over from Mark. The citation of Isa. 8.23-9.1 in Matt. 4.15f. disregards the subtlety of the text form as a proof of the origins, or first preaching, of the Messiah in Galilee. Matthew uses it to illustrate a prosaic comment that Jesus took up residence at Capernaum after leaving Nazareth. Mark 1.14 simply says that Jesus returned to Galilee and began his preaching ministry there. This is enough to prompt the use of the Isaiah quotation at this point. But as it mentions the seaside, it seems to Matthew to denote removal from Nazareth in the hill country to the port of Capernaum on the Sea of Galilee. The phrase 'beyond Jordan' also seems appropriate, seeing that Jordan was the scene of the preceding episode. These pictorial details appeal to Matthew's mind, but they have not in any way shaped the form of the text.

The next two formula quotations are at 8.17 and 12.17-21. In an earlier chapter it was shown that these two citations (of Isa. 53.4 and 42.1-4 respectively) have been inserted into the Marcan material to illustrate two points which are both contained in Mark 1.34, the healing of the sick and the command of secrecy. Here it may be added that, just as in the last case Galilee seems to have been the keyword which suggested the use of the quotation, so also both of these on the healings have been prompted by keywords. Matthew's text of Isa. 53.4 includes τὰς νόσους. This picks up the phrase ποικίλαις νόσοις of Mark 1.34 which he has omitted in his own rewriting of it. He has suppressed the command of secrecy at this point, because he wishes to use his other quotation when it is mentioned again in Mark 3.10-12. Here again his abbreviating version omits the cry of the demons σὺ εἶ ὁ υἱὸς τοῦ θεοῦ. But these words may well have reminded him of the words at the Baptism, and so suggested the use of his *pesher* text of Isa. 42.1-4, beginning ἰδοὺ ὁ παῖς μου.

Note further that immediately after this he continues with the healing of the (blind and) dumb man which introduces the Q version of the Beelzeboul controversy (Matt. 12.22f. = Luke 11.14). Matthew is here evidently influenced by Mark. Thus in his version ἐξίσταντο πάντες οἱ ὄχλοι replaces ἐθαύμασαν οἱ ὄχλοι, which has been retained by Luke. But in the Marcan parallel at this point there is the phrase ἔλεγον γὰρ ὅτι ἐξέστη. The people's jeer that Jesus is 'beside himself' has been softened to an expression of their amazement.[1] Then Matthew actually supplies their cry μήτι οὗτός ἐστιν ὁ υἱὸς Δαυίδ. This certainly represents yet another Matthean substitute for the words omitted when rewriting Mark 3.11; for here we have both the demoniac and the recognition of Jesus' sonship. No doubt this Davidic title expresses Matthew's own interpretation of Isa. 42.1-4, which he has just quoted. It is the conventionalizing tendency of a mind that is not alive to the delicacy of the form of the *pesher* text.[2]

Reasons for leaving Matt. 13.14f. out of consideration were given on p. 155, and so we now pass on to the quotation of Ps. 78.2 in 13.35. Here again there is a keyword connection (παραβολαῖς). The quotation has been inserted to give scriptural warrant to our Lord's parabolic method, a thing which Mark has heavily underlined.[3]

The next formula-quotation is Zech. 9.9 in Matt. 21.4f. Matthew has added it to the Marcan account of the entry into Jerusalem. As was shown in an earlier chapter, the form of the text has certainly been influenced by its application to this incident, perhaps in the liturgical tradition. But the work seems to have been completed before Matthew made use of it. On the contrary, he has

---

[1] Other Marcan influences in this section can be observed at Matt. 12.25b, 29, 31f.; cf. Mark 3.25, 27, 28f.

[2] Stendahl (*SSM*, p. 204) says, 'The adapted reading ἐν ταῖς πλατείαις in Matt. 12.19 formed a link with the context'. But the verbal links with the context are independent of the adaptation of the text, as has been shown.

[3] Here again Stendahl (*ibid.*) takes ἐρεύξομαι κεκρυμμένα as a reading selected to form a link with the context. But in fact Matthew shows no interest in this half of the verse, and the LXX φθέγξομαι προβλήματα would have been equally apposite.

used the text as his guide in rewriting Mark, as it seems to him to give the definitive picture.

The last of the series is the elaborate conflate citation concerning the fate of Judas in Matt. 27.9f. The analysis of this passage and its context in ch. III showed that three stages can be distinguished in the exegetical work on the text before Matthew made use of it. His own interest in it corresponds with the motive which was at work at the second stage, and he is unaware of the reasons which gave the quotation the final form which he uses. It was suggested that in this instance he is also making use of the *commentary* on the text, which already existed with it in the Church's *midrash pesher*. His motive is simply to describe the legend of Judas' bad end. The narrative in 27.3-8 uses such portions of the text and its commentary as were suitable for this purpose. It is even possible to distinguish between the source and Matthew's own writing. There is a clear difference between the special vocabulary of the passage, all of which is directly connected with the Zechariah text in its various transmutations, and the rest of the vocabulary, which is characteristically Matthean.[1]

Matthew's rewriting of this material contains three points which link it to the context of the Marcan Passion narrative into which he has inserted it. (*a*) The action of Judas in returning the money is the direct consequence of the condemnation of Jesus (Matt. 27.1, referring back to Matt. 26.66 = Mark 14.64). (*b*) The motive is evidently remorse, comparable to the reaction of Peter just described (Matt. 26.75 = Mark 14.72). (*c*) The condemnation of Jesus means that the money can already be regarded as 'the price of blood', which means that Matthew can introduce the reason why it could not go into the treasury, and so was used for the purchase of land. These are the significant factors in his own contribution

---

[1] In vv. 3 and 4 all the words are Matthean (for $αἷμα \ ἀθῷον$ cf. 27.24). In v. 5 $ῥίψας \ldots ναόν$ is quotation material; $ἀνεχώρησεν \ καὶ \ ἀπελθών$ belongs to Matthew; $ἀπήγξατο$ is *hap. leg.* In v. 6 $οἱ \ δὲ \ldots βαλεῖν$ belongs to Matthew, $εἰς \ τὸ \ κορβανᾶν$ and $τιμή$ to the quotation material; $αἵματος$ is common to both Matthew and the source. In v. 7 $συμβούλιον \ldots ἐξ \ αὐτῶν$ is Matthean, $τὸν \ ἀγρὸν \ τοῦ \ κεράμεως$ is quotation, and $εἰς \ ταφὴν \ τοῖς \ ξένοις$ is source. In v. 8 $διό$ and $ἕως \ τῆς \ σήμερον$ are not Matthean expressions, and $ἐκλήθη$ and $ἐκεῖνος$ are common to this verse and to Acts 1.19. This analysis differs from that of Kilpatrick (*The Origins of . . . Matthew*, pp. 44-46) only in (i) regarding quotation material as criterion of the source; (ii) seeing nothing Matthean in the use of $ξένος$ =*proselyte*; (iii) noting that Matthew's own expression for 'till this day' is $μεχρὶ \ τ. \ σ.$, cf. 11.23, 28.15.

to the story, which he has inserted because of his predilection for testimonies. But apart from the idea of fulfilment of prophecy which this necessarily implies, the motive does not seem to be theological, but biographical like all the rest. There is no hint of the choice of the text in the first instance for the messianic proofs of the Passion apologetic; and the use of text and commentary is so muddled that it no longer achieves the secondary purpose of showing that every detail in the history of the traitor was foreknown in Scripture.

A searching analysis of the last passage was necessary, because more than any other it supports Stendahl's thesis of the Gospel according to St Matthew as the work of a school. The results of the present study do not bear this out. Even in this test case the *pesher* text is complete before Matthew uses it, and the motivation is in line with the pictorial interest which has been apparent in every instance of formula-quotation. It should also be observed that the same motive was found in the quotation of Ps. 8.3 at Matt. 21.16.[1] This severs the connection between the formula-quotations as a distinct group and Matthew's use of quotations, which is pictorial for all alike. This raises the question: Why then does he draw attention to them so carefully by means of the formula, if he is not interested in the questions which were responsible for their textual formation? This question resolves itself into two issues, the pre-Matthean group of testimonies, and the reason for Matthew's use of the formula.

As a group, they only have to be listed to show that they are concerned with the basic factors in the claim that Jesus is the Messiah: Isa. 7.14; Micah 5.2; Isa. 49.6(?)[2]; Isa. 8.23-9.1; Isa. 42.1-4. Passion apologetic: Isa. 53.4; Zech. 9.9; Zech. 11.12f. Redemption of the People of God: Hos. 11.1; Jer. 31.15. Revelation of the mystery: Ps. 78.2. All except the last four are used elsewhere in the New Testament, or referred to by John, who also has formula-quotations. This suggests a certain fluidity of exegetical activity. Study goes on in various church centres. The main lines of the work, and the favourite texts, are common to them all. But also each centre has its own contribution to make. This explains why the four which are peculiar to Matthew are also the most remote from the central point of interest. The texts most favoured

[1] *Supra*, p. 168.
[2] Presumed reference of Matt. 2.23.

find their way into the various aspects of church life, liturgical, doctrinal and homiletic, as well as apologetic.

Matthew's use of the introductory formula is to be explained in the light of the whole purpose of the Gospel.[1] It is generally recognized that his approach has been influenced by the rise of rabbinic Judaism at Jamnia. The fact that he uses Mark as the basis is sufficient to prove that he aims primarily at presenting the life of Jesus as the Messiah, though he does not think theologically. His method of proving the messianic significance of the acts of Jesus to rabbinic readers is to draw on such testimonies from the messianic stock-in-trade as can be easily linked to particular episodes, so as to give scriptural warrants for them. The formula implies that when Jesus acted in a certain way he was fulfilling messianic expectations, because the scripture says so.

From this reasoning it follows that, if we think in terms of a Matthean school, we must nevertheless avoid the idea that the Gospel is a group product to which all the exegetical work has been directed. Matthew is a scribe in the Christian school, who has the task of revising the existing Gospel, i.e. Mark, in the light of further material collected at the school. He undertakes his work on behalf of the local church as a whole, possibly for liturgical use as a lectionary.[2] The school's stock of biblical quotations, used orally in its work of catechizing and apologetic, is naturally known to Matthew. He makes use of it along with other available traditions in his own way and for his own purposes, as has been indicated. But the fact remains that the Gospel is not the controlling factor in the formation of the *pesher* texts. Conversely, the writer of the Gospel is an individual with his own characteristic style and method, but is not one of the exegetes whose study has produced these texts.

### St John

No argument is required to claim that John (except ch. 21) is the work of a single writer, though we may justly speak of an Ephesian school as the source of the Johannine writings as a whole. A close follower of the author of the Fourth Gospel may have written the three Epistles and added John 21, or these may be the work of

[1] This question is coming to the fore in New Testament study today. See W. D. Davies, *The Setting of the Sermon on the Mount*, 1964.
[2] This is stressed by G. D. Kilpatrick, *op. cit.*, pp. 94f.

more than one person. Revelation also shows signs of stemming
from the same place, though it is hard to believe that the writer
had close personal contact with the author of the Gospel. This
school, like that of Matthew, has the common store of scriptural
material for its catechetical and apologetic work, and also its own
local developments. John's relation to the school seems to be less
formal than Matthew's. When he is using sources he exercises
much greater freedom and allows full scope to his personal skill
as a creative theologian. This appears in his use of the *pesher*
quotations.

The adducing of a text with a formula (γεγραμμένον ἐστίν) first
occurs at 2.17, where Ps. 69.10 is cited. The text follows the Septuagint and shows no sign of prior handling for other purposes.
But the significance of this citation is that it reflects the Passion
apologetic in its primary application.

The same kind of introductory formula is used when Ps. 78.24
is cited by the Jews in John 6.31. It belongs to the sphere of
thought in which the acts of Jesus are regarded as the revelation
of the mystery of redemption. It is thus equivalent to the pre-
Matthean usage of v. 2 of the same psalm, also a formula-quotation.

Jesus himself is reported as using this introduction when he
cites, or rather alludes to, Isa. 54.13 in 6.45. This is an example of
the universalistic usage of the prophecy of Deutero-Isaiah which
is a frequent feature of Romans.

A reference to the scripture, i.e. a particular text (οὐχ ἡ γραφὴ
εἶπεν), in John 7.42 introduces the allusion to Micah 5.2 and other
Davidic texts.

A christological citation of Ps. 82.6 occurs with biblical reference
in John 10.34. It is worth noting in this case that the context implies more of the text than is actually quoted, not only ἐγώ εἶπα
θεοί ἐστε but also καὶ υἱοὶ ὑψίστου πάντες. It is this which makes
the quotation really relevant, and prepares the way for εἶπον υἱὸς
τοῦ θεοῦ εἰμι in v. 36, which had not been stated so unambiguously
before.

None of these five passages has used the 'fulfilment' type of
formula, which is Matthew's practice without exception. All have
γεγραμμένον ἐστίν, except 7.42 as noted above. It is also remarkable that they are all very closely related to the context, so that
they give the impression of reproducing the rabbinic type of dis-
putation with which John was familiar at the school of Ephesus.

Something more will be said about them from the point of view of subject matter when we have examined the rest.

In John 12.14f. we have John's version of Zech. 9.9. This also has the short formula as in the preceding quotations, but the element of fulfilment is brought in and pressed home in v. 16, just as in 2.22. This places both this quotation, and Ps. 69.10 in 2.17, in the category of testimonies in the strict sense. In neither case is there the tendency to use the text to supply narrative details, which was found to be the practice of Matthew. Each text simply gives scriptural warrant to one essential element of the story. In the earlier instance the quotation accounts for our Lord's drastic action in cleansing the temple. In the present one it explains the meaning of his choice of an ass for his ride into Jerusalem. Both show Jesus to be the Messiah when he acts in these ways. They are thus true to the primary purpose for which they were selected.

John's first use of a fulfilment formula, very similar to Matthew's, is at 12.38. It covers two citations, Isa. 53.1 and Isa. 6.9f. Although the first is from the Passion prophecy, it is here used (like the second) to explain the unbelief of the Jews. It is in this respect closely akin to the secondary use of Isa. 53.4 which must be postulated *before* its incorporation in Matt. 8.17. These texts are used by John exactly as they would be employed in the apologetic work of the school. It was noted in ch. IV that John's text form of Isa. 6.9f. is likely to be ancient.

A briefer style of the fulfilment formula introduces Ps. 41.10 in John 13.18. The non-Septuagint text, and the correct application to the treachery of Judas, again prove John's fidelity to the primitive apologetic.

On the other hand there seems to be an intentional shift of application when Ps. 69.5 is quoted with a most elaborate fulfilment formula in John 15.25. But it still shows familiarity with the primary reference to the sufferings of Jesus in the Passion apologetic, even though it is included in this chapter to encourage the disciples in face of persecution. This has the effect of making the words apply to the inevitability of our Lord's sufferings, rather than just providing scriptural warrant for them.

The next formula-quotation is Ps. 22.19 in John 19.24. Here we have an elaboration based on the quotation quite similar to the practice of Matthew. It was argued in ch. III that John has distinguished between the clothes of Jesus and the seamless robe by

logical deduction from the poetic parallelism, because he has a particular point of symbolism in view. The exact Septuagint text
shows no sign of previous handling. As the parting of the garments
and the use of Ps. 22 are already fixed elements of the Passion
narrative,[1] it is unnecessary to suppose that the unit John 19.23f.
grew up in isolation from it. However it remains possible that John
is drawing on the *midrash pesher* of his 'school'. But there is good
reason to hold that it is in fact John's own work, because of the end
which the elaboration achieves. It draws attention to the fact that
the robe of Jesus was seamless. This means that it has the same
peculiarity as the high priest's robe. The point of this will appear
in the next paragraph.

The thirst of Jesus is similarly elaborated for symbolic reasons
in John 19.28-30. Here the formula occurs with the one word $\delta\iota\psi\hat{\omega}$,
probably a reference to $\epsilon\hat{\iota}\varsigma\ \tau\hat{\eta}\nu\ \delta\hat{\iota}\psi\alpha\nu\ \mu o\upsilon$ of Ps. 69.22. The purpose
clearly arises from the author's presentation of the person of Jesus.
He wishes to point the irony of our Lord's thirst by contrast with
the statement in 4.14. This suggests that a similar motive lies
behind the description of the seamless robe. It is the irony that
Jesus, the true high priest, was stripped of his priestly vestment
when he offered himself in sacrifice. The idea of sacrifice is entailed in the Passover references which dominate John's handling
of the Passion. It was observed in the discussion of the present
section on the thirst that this is present in the mention of hyssop
in v. 29.

The last two quotations both come under one introductory formula, and have sacrificial significance. They are Ps. 34.21 and
Zech. 12.10, quoted in John 19.36f. In the first case it was argued
that the quotation had originally a slightly different application in
the Passion apologetic from its present usage; and also that John
has himself adapted the form of text to allude to the regulations
for the Passover (Ex. 12.46, etc.). As it stands, it explains why the
practice of breaking the legs to hasten death was not used on Jesus.
John takes this to indicate that Jesus is the true Passover victim.
The second quotation shows signs of use at an early date, and
analysis showed that the original purpose for selecting it was identical with that of Ps. 34.21. They belong together in the apologetic
tradition. John, however, adopts it to account for two further facts
in his accompanying narrative, the piercing of our Lord's side and

[1] Mark 15.24.

the eyewitness (vv. 34f.).[1] This allows him to include in the sacrificial symbolism the libation of the blood of the victim, and also to
make allusion to the Church's sacraments. At the same time the
real death of Jesus is emphasized by the whole incident, which
counters the view of the Docetists.

The point of interest for our present investigation is the fact that
this pair of texts from the Passion apologetic provide the essential
items in the narrative to which they are applied, and so they advance the author's theological interpretation of the Passion which
he is describing. The factual elements in the story may be genuine
tradition. It is equally possible that they have been deduced from
the texts, already applied to the Crucifixion. This could be done
without falsification of the tradition, becuse it contains no mention of the breaking of the legs, which nevertheless might have
been presumed from Roman custom.[2] It is then not a gratuitous
fiction, but something that is congruous with the known facts and
may be assumed from the *argumentum ex silentio*. So also the blood
of Jesus undoubtedly flowed when he was pierced. There is thus
an interplay of tradition and interpretation, in which the quotations help to draw out the theological meaning of the facts that
Jesus' legs were not broken and that his blood was shed.

The above review of the Johannine *pesher* texts permit some
tentative remarks on the composition of the Fourth Gospel. In
some ways John is in touch with primitive Christian thought. He
most frequently draws on the stock of the Passion apologetic—
Pss. 69.10, 41.10, 22.19, 69.22, 34.21; Zech. 12.10. To these may
be added Zech. 9.9, taken from the Passion prophecy, and Isa. 6.9f.
All these belong to the generally accepted range of *pesher* texts.
It is normal to disregard the particular form of the text in Johannine citations, but in all these cases where the early apologetic is
used the text is chosen with care. He either has a primitive form
derived from previous usage (Zech. 9.9; Isa. 6.9f.; Ps. 41.10; Zech.
12.10), or else adheres strictly to the Septuagint, with the two exceptions of Ps. 69.22 and 34.21, which he himself adapts slightly
for readily explicable reasons. Micah 5.2, and other Davidic texts
alluded to at 7.42, should be added to this list of primitive apolo-

[1] Verse 35, which is missing in two Latin MSS (*e* vg^fuld), may perhaps
be an addition to the text. If so, the anti-docetic motive is post-Johannine.
[2] But the evidence for the *crurifragium* as the *coup de grâce* after crucifixion is slender. See T. Keim, *Jesus of Nazara* (ET 1873-83), vol. vi,
pp. 253-7.

getic material. The important thing about this whole group is that he knows what issues they are concerned with. He knows not only primitive material, but also primitive thought.[1]

A rather later impression is given by the citations which occur in rabbinic-type disputations. These are Ps. 78.24, Isa. 54.13, and Ps. 82.6. On the other hand the use of Ps. 78 is similar to the use postulated for a verse of the same psalm *before* its incorporation in Matt. 13.35. Moreover the use of Isa. 54.13 is closely parallel to Paul's use of Deutero-Isaiah. These two quotations, which use Septuagint words, are the only ones where there is loose quoting for no apparent reason. This becomes a frequent feature in the early patristic period. If it is recalled that John 8 contains the Abraham argument parallel to, but independently of, Paul in Galatians and Romans, it can be seen that the *matter* in these rabbinic-type disputes need not be later than Paul, while the *form* is certainly not as primitive as the other material which we have studied. Add to this the peculiar vividness of these chapters, and the strangely inhuman character of Jesus in them, and the impression is bound to be gained that here we have a reflection of the struggle of the Church in John's own time, rather than actual tradition of the life of Jesus.

We must now ask whether this quotation-material gives indication of a date *later* than the time of Paul. Two facts have to be taken into account here. First, John has been able to make use of four of the Passion scriptures as the foundation of theologically motivated incidents in his Crucifixion narrative. Secondly, he twice uses the fulfilment-formula, not with reference to the Scriptures, but of the prophetic words of Jesus himself.[2] This virtual canonization of the words of Jesus throws into relief the impersonal effect of the portrait in the dispute chapters. These are not proper criteria for plotting a date in comparison with St Paul, as there is nothing in Paul to set against them. But they do seem to militate against any attempt to ascribe an early date to the Fourth Gospel.[3]

---

[1] Compare with this the way in which John preserves the original idea behind certain NT expressions, e.g. the gift of the Spirit (*supra*, p. 58), the third day (p. 61), and a particular use of πορεύεσθαι (p. 62).

[2] 18.9, 32. Both refer back to words of Jesus which recur several times in the Gospel.

[3] For recent discussion of the problem see W. F. Albright, 'Recent Discoveries in Palestine and the Gospel of St John', in *The Background of the NT and its Eschatology*, pp. 153-71; J. A. T. Robinson, 'The New

On the other hand we have had another standard of comparison in Matthew's handling of testimonies. Much the same stock of quotations has been employed by both of them, but the apologetic interests with which they are concerned are living issues to John, but not to Matthew. Matthew presents his material as a Christian Pentateuch, and is careful to show that Jesus is the true fulfilment of the Jewish Scriptures by means of the *pesher* texts. He thus has one eye on the rabbinic opponents of the Church, although he never comes to grips with them. John, however, has an intimate knowledge of their arguments. Even though he is addressing a wide audience, Greek as well as Jewish, he presents the Gospel in relation to Jewish objections.

Before drawing a conclusion from these observations, one more point must be attended to. The quotations in John cannot be viewed in isolation from the numerous biblical allusions. John draws on a rich store of scriptural passages, which enable him to work out a number of great biblical themes, creation, the Spirit, water, the manna, the shepherd, etc., for his theological presentation of Jesus. These themes have no connection with the formula-quotations, except in so far as he has adapted some of the quotations to bring them into line with another theme of great importance to him, the Passover. Now all these Johannine themes, or nearly all of them, have their counterparts in the creative thinking of St Paul, though they are independent of him. Thus, besides the wide diffusion of a stock of favourite texts for apologetic purposes, there is also a common store of biblical themes, no doubt used for the catechetical exposition of the faith.[1]

The evidence from quotation material only permits a very limited conclusion. The relationship between John and Matthew cannot be expressed in terms of date, whether they are contemporaries or not. It can only be expressed in terms of intelligence. John's use of Scripture shows an awareness of the living tradition from which he derives his choice of texts, and this differentiates him from Matthew. Even if he is writing much later than Paul, he can think himself into the time of Paul with a degree of historical imagin-

Look on the Fourth Gospel', in *Studia Evangelica*, pp. 338-50 and *Twelve New Testament Studies*.

[1] For the biblical material see J. Guillet, *Thêmes Bibliques*; for its continuation in the church Fathers, J. Daniélou, *Sacramentum Futuri*, 1950, and for its importance in the liturgical life of the Church, the same writer's *Bible et Liturgie*, 1951.

ation which commands respect. None of the quotation material
necessitates a date later than the time of Paul. Some of the ideas
seem to be older. As a man of culture and intelligence, sifting the
traditions of the school of Ephesus, John has produced a book
which ranks as a first-rate source for early Christian apologetic.

The phenomenon of formula-quotations in Matthew and John
does more than demonstrate a close link between John and pre-
Matthean material. It also indicates the kind of texts which were
considered most valuable in the early Church. This is something
which has been studied in this book from the point of view of the
development of doctrine. But it also raises the question why *these*
passages should be chosen for use in this way. Dodd's *According to
the Scriptures* has shown that when we turn our attention to this
question we must not confine ourselves to the isolated texts. The
whole blocks of Old Testament scriptures from which they are
chiefly drawn must be taken into account. In the next section an
attempt will be made to estimate the significance of this larger
background of choice of scriptures for the primitive apologetic.

### 3. THE CHURCH'S SELECTION OF SCRIPTURES

The *pesher* texts in Matthew and John, which have such great
importance for this study, are drawn almost exclusively from the
Psalms, Isaiah and Zechariah. Matthew also has one each from
three other prophets, Jeremiah, Hosea, and Micah. There are none
from the Pentateuch, historical books or Wisdom literature. But
we have not confined our attention to these testimonies, and so
must take care to keep this striking fact in proportion. However,
a glance through the summary of the primitive apologetic, which
forms the first section of this chapter, will show that it is almost
entirely based on quotations from the Psalms and Prophets. The
exceptions are the Abraham references from Genesis, the Prophet
from Deut. 18, and the messianic texts from II Sam. 7, none of
which belong to the most primitive stage. This is not to say that
only these books were used in the primitive apologetic. But it is
clear that they are regulative in laying down the chief lines of the
apologetic. The reasons for this can be shown by first contrasting
the use that is made of the rest of the Old Testament.

### *The Pentateuch*

The Five Books of Moses were the Bible proper of the Jews.

The Sadducees held that no other books were of equal authority, the later rabbinic Judaism made them the chief object of study and elucidation, they were the principal interest of the Qumran Sectaries, and the Samaritans recognized no other Scriptures. The early Church simply accepted them as canonical Scripture, especially for moral guidance. It is from this point of view that quotations occur in the New Testament, both in the sayings of Jesus himself and in other places. It is true that Jesus was radically reinterpreting the requirements of the Law, and that this is a matter which lies at the heart of Christianity. But the *legal* citations form an entirely separate category from any of the interests revealed in the *pesher* texts. In Mark all the Pentateuchal quotations belong to the legal class.[1] In Matthew and Luke the Q material exemplifies this fact even more clearly.[2] This tradition is continued in the Epistles.[3]

The legal class does not exhaust the Pentateuchal quotations. The speech of St Stephen in Acts 7 includes a series of them in the course of an historical retrospect. This constitutes a particular genre of literature which may be termed *the rewritten Bible*. The characteristic of this type is the presentation of well-known facts with a deliberate tendency. The classic example of this is I and II Chronicles, which aim at bringing the sacred history into line with the ideas of the writer's own age.

But the motive may be much more topical, to persuade the readers to accept a radical innovation. Thus *The Testaments of the Twelve Patriarchs* are a *midrash* on Genesis, aimed at making out a case for Levi as the ruling tribe, in support of John Hyrcanus.[4] *The Book of Jubilees* rewrites Genesis and Exodus from the opposite point of view, showing that although Levi has pride of place, the secular government belongs to Judah. It is thus a protest against the Hasmonean claims.[5] An earlier example of this genre is Deuteronomy itself, rewriting the wilderness history to promote religious reform. A shorter poetical example is Ps. 78. This reviews the sacred history as a catalogue of the divine mercy in the face of Israel's continual backsliding.

[1] Mark 7.10, 10.4, 7f., 19, 12.19, 29-33. The citation of Ex. 3.6 in 12.26 occurs in a theoretical question of doctrine in rabbinic style.
[2] Matt. 4.4, 7, 10 = Luke 4.4, 8, 12; Matt. 5.21, 27, 33-35, 38, 43, 48, 18.16.    [3] E.g. Rom. 13.9; II Cor. 13.1; Gal. 5.14; Eph. 5.31, 6.2f.
[4] *Test. Reuben* 6.7-12; *Test. Levi* 8.11-15; 18.3.
[5] The motive of the rewriting is to combat the tendency to Hellenism, and the idea of the messianic kingdom has little place. However the Messiah is expected to spring from Judah, *Jub.* 31.18-20.

This last example brings us close to the theme of Stephen's speech. It virtually asserts that the Deuteronomic law of the single sanctuary is the climax of disobedience—a highly provocative point of view, to say the least.[1] The interesting thing about the argument for our purpose is that there is nothing specially Christian about this tendentious rewriting of history at all. A free-thinking (presumably Hellenistic) Jew could have said the same without drawing Stephen's conclusion that Jesus is the true *locus* of worship, or that the Crucifixion is the ultimate disobedience. This means that it is not the Pentateuchal history that is regulative of the Christian application of the speech.

Paul's speech in Acts 13 is even more instructive. It retells the history in order to lead up to the promise made to the house of David. But then the claim that Jesus is the Messiah is made, not from these historical considerations, but from the normal stock of citations from Psalms and Prophets.

The Christian interpretation in Stephen's speech likewise depends on prophecy. The one thing that points to Jesus is the introduction of the Prophet of Deut. 18. This is from the Pentateuch, it is true, but its Christian usefulness is derived from the development of the figure in Malachi. It may be added at this point that two other Pentateuchal items in fact fall into the category of prophecy, and so stand apart from the use of the Pentateuch in general. These are Num. 24 (the prophecy of Balaam) and Deut. 32 (the Song of Moses). The latter may have had liturgical use along with the Psalter.

There is still one more category of the use of the Pentateuch, and this is *typology*. It is not used in the most primitive apologetic, but is a factor in the developing christology once the main positions have been established. Quotations from the Pentateuch for this purpose are a special feature of Hebrews. Paul quite often quotes the Pentateuch in this way, notably in II Corinthians. John only has allusions.[2] The foundation of typology is the prophetic view of history. When Jesus is shown to be the fulfiller of events in the wilderness, it means that the Pentateuch as a whole is being treated

---

[1] The speech makes use of haggadic embellishments, which show affinity with the Samaritan Version, but are now known in Jewish circles from fragments found at Qumran. It is a normal device of this class of literature.

[2] In the Synoptic Gospels typology is rare. In the Q account of the Temptations the quotations are 'legal' in effect, though the motivation of the whole episode is typological.

as prophecy. The entire record of God's dealings with Israel is a *Heilsgeschichte*, culminating in Jesus. The evidence of quotations suggests that this idea was the fruit of reflection after the Psalms and Prophets had been employed to lay down the fundamentals of christology.

This leaves only the arguments concerning the seed of Abraham and the curse of the Law as possible candidates for a primitive apologetic based on the Pentateuch. The evidence is slender, but both these issues seem to go behind St Paul's handling of them in Galatians to previous usage not necessarily in connection with the Judaistic controversy. But whether these arguments were employed to support a 'non-messianic' christology, independently of the arguments from quotations in the Psalms and Prophets, is a question on which we can only speculate.[1]

## The Historical Books

Quotations from these books are extremely few, and can be quickly dealt with. There are naturally some references to them in the speeches of the 'rewritten Bible' category. But the only important ones are II Sam. 5.2 and 7.8-16, which are used in *Davidic* contexts. As we have seen, these have a particular place in the apologetic concerning the proper credentials for messiahship. They supplement similar quotations from the Psalms and Prophets. Besides these, a *typology* based on the figures of Elijah and Elisha in I and II Kings may be traced in certain incidents in Luke, but no explicit quotations are used. Where John the Baptist is concerned, such allusions are drawn from the prophecy of Malachi.

## The Wisdom Literature

The quotations and allusions are mostly taken from Proverbs, and can be classified as *moral apophthegms*. This is a thing which the early Christian literature shares with its Jewish antecedents. The Psalms are also used in this way from time to time, as some of them fall into the category of Wisdom literature. It thus becomes a nice problem whether the quotations from Ps. 34 in I Peter 2.3, 3.10-12 are simply drawn from this tradition of ethical usage, or have a real connection with the Passion apologetic, as was sug-

---

[1] Cf. J. A. T. Robinson, 'The Most Primitive Christology of all?'; H. J. Schoeps, *Theologie und Geschichte des Judenchristentums*, pp. 87ff.; L. E. Elliott-Binns, *Galilean Christianity*, p. 49.

gested in ch. III. As christology develops, there is a growing tendency to adopt the concept of Wisdom to show the metaphysical aspects of the person of Christ. This is found in the opening verses of Hebrews and in Colossians. It also has its counterpart in Q (Matt. 11.25-30), where again a high christology is presupposed, though the precise interpretation of the passage is obscure.

### The Prophets and Psalms

By contrast with the other parts of the Scriptures, these books, and certain parts of them in particular, are the basis of all the creative theology of the very early period. It will be clearer *why* this should be so if we again first pay attention to the Jewish precedents. This at once introduces a category not mentioned in the case of the other books, that of *apocalyptic eschatology*.

The Jews of the Greek and Roman periods were living in an age of greater international perspectives. They were bound to be conscious, even in the brief spell of the Hasmonean ascendancy, of the gulf which lay between their religio-political convictions and the actual state of affairs. Today we are schooled to think of the prophets as *forthtellers* rather than *foretellers*, but the men of that age knew no such distinction. To them it was enough that the prophets had had a message in times of national distress, and the parallel with their own situation inevitably invited application of it to themselves. The Psalms also, with their oscillation between individual and corporate expressions of personal need, were felt to be directly concerned with their own circumstances.[1] There is thus a strong tendency to reinterpret these books during this period. Eschatology, which had a respectable history in religious aspirations,[2] was now dressed up in apocalyptic guise, in order to give it an immediate reference to the writer's own time. For example, the later chapters of Daniel contain expressions of distress from Jeremiah and use visual images drawn from Ezekiel. The note of expectation, which characterizes this reinterpretation, imparts a smouldering fire of passion. This is specially noticeable in the *Hodayoth* of the Dead Sea Sect, which contain numerous verbal allusions to the Prophets and canonical Psalms.

---

[1] The composition of psalms continued right through into the first century, if we include besides the canonical Book of Psalms the Qumran *Hodayoth*, the *Psalms of Solomon*, and the Gospel Canticles.

[2] Cf. S. Mowinckel, *He that Cometh*, chs. V and VIII.

In this time of eschatological expectation the precise form of kingship assumed importance because of the claims of the Hasmonean rulers. The prophecies concerning the dynasty of David made it doubtful whether anyone of another tribe or family could qualify to be the Lord's anointed ruler in the restored kingdom. Today scholarship has become very guarded about the use of the title 'the Messiah'. After all, priests as well as kings were anointed all through Israel's history, and the use of the term cannot be confined to a specific person expected in the future. This warning is valuable when a particular context is studied in which the word is found. But the reaction must not be allowed to go too far, to assert, for instance, that the idea of *the* Messiah is a Christian invention. The truth is that the word may have a priestly or regal connotation in general, but when the context is concerned with the future restored kingdom, it naturally refers to an individual who is to come. Of course in this case it may mean the future king, or high priest, or both.

Consequently, although apocalyptic-eschatological passages may describe the coming kingdom without reference to a particular individual known as the Messiah, whenever such an individual historically presented himself he must necessarily be tested by the standards appropriate to messiahship. The 'messianic prophecies', which otherwise might have no special importance within the whole range of prophetic expectation, suddenly come into prominence. Thus *Test. Levi* 18, although it is describing the coming of the priestly Messiah, regards him as the king as well, and so applies to him phrases from Isa. 11.1-9. *Test. Judah* 24.1-3,[1] which probably also refers to Levi, has allusions to Ps. 45 and Zech. 9.9. The fragment which follows in *Test. Judah* 24.5f., implying a king from Judah, also makes use of Isa. 11.1 and Ps. 45.6. The Davidic Messiah appears in *Ps. Sol.* 17 and 18. In the Dead Sea Scrolls there is mention of the 'Messiahs of Aaron and Israel', but the interpretation of the phrase is difficult to assess.[2] However, the fact that rulers in the future polity are meant is clear enough, although no messianic texts are applied to them to show what should be their credentials.[3]

[1] Both this and *Test. Levi* 18.3 also contain clear allusions to Num. 24.17, which of course is treated as prophecy.

[2] In CD the singular form מֹשִׁיחַ is used before the two names, which raises the question whether a single individual is meant.

[3] CD 12.23, 13.21, 14.19, 19.11, 20.1; 1QS 9.11; 1QSa 2.11ff. However

Nevertheless the Qumran texts do make use of a number of passages from the Prophets which have great importance in the primitive Christian apologetic. Here at last there is the possibility of a real standard of comparison. For this purpose only those documents which belong together as the work of the Sect are relevant. These are primarily the *Damascus Document* and the *Manual of Discipline*, to which must be added the single page of 4Q*Testimonia* and the fragmentary 4Q*Florilegium*. Other documents (the *War* scroll; the *Two-Column Fragment*) do not contain relevant quotations. But notice should be taken of the *Pesharim*, or *Commentaries*, because they show the general position with regard to the Psalms and Prophets in the early Church, i.e. the application of Scripture to the writer's own day as the time of eschatological fulfilment.

The *Manual of Discipline* contains three allusions that are important for the New Testament. But first we must notice the occurrence of Isa. 65.17 ('the making new') in 1QS 4.25, for it sets the note for the whole aim and purpose of the Sect as an eschatological society. And this is equally true of the early Church, which also made use of this passage.[1] With this in mind, we can observe the way in which the three allusions *differ* from the use made or them in the New Testament. Thus Isa. 40.3, on 'preparing the way of the Lord', is twice used to show the eschatological purpose of the Sect's special task of study of the Law.[2] In the New Testament this passage is applied specifically to John the Baptist, to define his relationship to Christ, whom he precedes. Moreover the Sect, when seen from this angle, is described as the 'elect', in a phrase closely parallel to Isa. 42.1, and as the 'precious corner stone', undoubtedly alluding to Isa. 28.16.[3] Both of these texts are used christologically by the early Church, though the second is also applied to the Church itself in a way quite similar to what we have here.[4] In all these three cases a testimony employed by the Qumran Sect with reference to itself is used christologically by the Church; and the link between the two different kinds of interpretation is the common eschatological motive.

In the *Damascus Document* there is a passage which includes several quotations that are relevant to the New Testament, though

we find the messianic texts in 4Q*Testimonia* and 4Q*Florilegium* (see below), and no doubt more will appear in fragments yet to be published.
[1] II Peter 3.13; Rev. 21.1.     [2] 1QS 8.14, 9.19.
[3] 1QS 8.6, 7.     [4] Matt. 16.18; Eph. 2.20; Rev. 21.14.

they differ in the two recensions.[1] In the A text Isa. 7.17 is quoted to express the coming eschatological visitation.[2] This belongs to the same prophetic unit as the virgin birth text, Isa. 7.14, which is not used messianically in the Scrolls. However it is likely to be in the background of thought in the beautiful poem on the 'messianic travail' in the *Thanksgiving Psalms*.[3] This shows, therefore, a pre-Christian eschatological use of the prophecy, without pressing the implications of it for messianic theory, as we find it later in the Church's apologetic.

The B text does not have Isa. 7.17 here, but more aptly substitutes an eschatological warning against the disobedient, using Zech. 13.7. This includes the words 'Smite the shepherd, and the sheep shall be scattered' quoted in Mark 14.27 = Matt. 26.31. Here the shepherd is identified with the *wicked* rulers, contrary to the interpretation presupposed in the Gospels.

The two recensions follow up these diverging quotations in different ways. The A text asserts that the precise historical situation visualized in Isa. 7 will be repeated in the coming time of visitation. This is pressed home with a very strained exegesis of Amos 5.26, expounded with the aid of Amos 9.11 and Num. 24.17. The two Amos passages occur respectively in Acts 7.42f. and 15.15-18. These are the only proper citations from Amos to be found in the New Testament. It is astonishing that they should occur together in the *Damascus Document*. In the latter, a play on words is used so that the two commentary texts (Amos 9.11 and Num. 24.17) fix the meaning of Amos 5.26 as a cipher for the Sect itself: it will escape 'beyond Damascus' in the coming tribulation. This alters the meaning of the passage from a threat of punishment to a promise of deliverance. But its eschatological reference is presupposed. In Acts 7.42f. it is used to show the nemesis that will come upon Israel's idolatry. Here Damascus has been changed to Babylon, which is quite unnecessary for the purposes of the argument, and may indicate prior usage. The other Amos passage (9.11) comes in

---

[1] It has to be remembered that both the Cairo Genizah manuscripts of CD were written in the Middle Ages, so that we cannot be sure that both recensions are early material. The fragments of the work found at Qumran differ from both, but support substantially the A text. On the other hand a few fragments give the end of the first part of the work, which is missing from A, but found in B. See J. T. Milik, *Ten Years of Discovery in the Wilderness of Judaea*, ET (SBT 26), 1959, pp. 38f., 58-60.

[2] CD 7.11; also quoted in 14.1.

[3] 1QH 3.3-18.

Acts 15.15-18 to warrant the preaching to the Gentiles. It is thus to be classed with the Deutero-Isaiah texts, which speak of the coming redemption, and are adopted for use in the Gentiles controversy. Thus, although the quotations are used for very different purposes in the *Document* and in Acts, they share a common background of eschatological interpretation.

Meanwhile the B text arrives at much the same meaning in a less complicated way. Having denounced the wicked shepherds in the words of Zech. 13.7, it describes the Sect itself in terms of Zech. 11.11, 'They that give heed unto him are the poor of the flock'. Here again there is contact with the New Testament, for Zech. 11.13 is the basis of the elaborate account of the death of Judas, and the idea contained in 11.11 is used of the Church (e.g. Luke 12.32, 'Fear not, little flock'). Once more the real link is the established eschatological interpretation of the prophecy. After two more quotations (Ezek. 9.4; Lev. 26.25), which compare the conditions of the coming visitation with those of the time of the Captivity, the B text joins up with the A text.

At this point the two recensions have a quotation of Hos. 5.10 as a promise of destruction of the wicked. The words in their proper context belong to a prophecy of the impossibility of healing without return to God. The A text actually uses the metaphor of healing at this point, though the words may be an addition to the original text (recension B has its own different additional phrase here). This is the prophecy which concludes with the promise of revival on the third day (Hos. 6.1-3), which had an important bearing on the very earliest proclamation of the Church's faith. As before, scriptures which the Church used christologically have a general eschatological reference in the Qumran literature.

Specifically messianic texts are included in the single page known as 4Q*Testimonia*.[1] It begins with Deut. 5.28f., which is an exhortation to obedience. Then follow Deut. 18.18f., Num. 24.15-17, and Deut. 33.8-11, which are testimonies appropriate to the three persons mentioned in 1QS 9.11, the Prophet and the Messiahs of Israel and Aaron.[2] Finally there is an adapted version of Josh. 6.26,

[1] Published by J. M. Allegro, 'Further Messianic References in Qumran Literature', *JBL* 75, 1956, pp. 174-87, Document IV. The title *Testimonia* is a trifle too *nuancé*, as it is by no means clear that we have here the sort of document proposed by Rendel Harris.

[2] F. M. Cross, Jnr., *The Ancient Library of Qumran*, p. 112, holds that the quotation of Num. 24.17 here is intended to refer to both the priestly

followed by a very obscure *pesher* of it which seems to be an apocalyptic warning.[1] Allegro asserts that the leaf has been written by the same hand as the *Manual of Discipline*. This suggests that it served a practical purpose in the life of the Sect. The three central testimonies may have been the normal scriptural warrants for the Sect's messianic expectations. They have here been put together in the framework of a solemn warning.[2] At any rate this frame certainly provides a perspective of eschatological expectation. Of these three texts we have seen that Num. 24.17 has its place in the story of the Magi (Matt. 2.2).[3] Deut. 18.18 also enters into the Church's christology. Deut. 33.8-11, the blessing of Levi, which suggests the priestly Messiah, is significantly absent from early Christian writings.

4Q*Florilegium*, fragmentary as it is, contains portions of more than one work. The first is a *midrash* of II Sam. 7.10b-14, using other texts as commentary.[4] One of these is Amos 9.11, which we have just seen was used in the A text of the *Damascus Document*. It is thus closely akin to the *pesher* writings of the Sect. Definitely messianic interpretations have been found in some of the fragments of *Pesharim*, notably 4Q*Patriarchal Blessings* (on Gen. 49.10) and 4QpIsaᵃ (on Isa. 10.22-11.4).[5] It should be observed that these are in any case messianic passages.

The general picture that emerges from study of these texts is of

and the secular Messiahs, the *star* and *sceptre* being distinguished. Then Deut. 33.8-11 (the blessing of Levi) refers to the Teacher of Righteousness.

[1] This has been identified as a quotation from a pseudepigraphic work styled *Psalms of Joshua*, of which fragments survive in the Qumran finds, cf. J. Strugnell's contribution to the report 'Editing the Manuscript Fragments from Qumran', *Biblical Archaeologist* 19, 1956, p. 94.

[2] Could the document have served a practical function, e.g. to be read to prospective members of the Sect in the initiation ceremony?

[3] Cf. II Peter 1.19; Rev. 2.28, 22.16.

[4] 4Q*Florilegium* is Document II in Allegro, *art. cit.* The other work is a *midrash* on Pss. 1.1 and 2.1. In a short note on this document in *JBL* 78, 1959, pp. 343-6, W. R. Lane has drawn attention to the hermeneutical method employed. For instance, the first part largely consists of II Sam. 7.10b-11a; Ex. 15.17-18; II Sam. 7.11b; II Sam. 7.11c-14a; Amos 9.11 (cf. CD 7.16; Acts 15.16). But this is not really a *florilége* of texts. Ex. 15.17f. and Amos 9.11 are distinguished from the rest by the introductory formula 'as it is written'. It is, then, a running commentary on II Sam. 7.10b-14a, incorporating other passages as comments. The reader will observe the parallel with the analysis of Peter's speech in Acts 2 earlier in the present work (*supra*, pp. 36-45).

[5] Allegro, *art. cit.*, Documents I and III.

a community of men supported in a common aim by fervent apocalyptic expectation. The Prophets and Psalms, and other prophetic passages (Gen. 49; Num. 24; Deut. 32), which are also the Church's favourite scriptures, are combed in order to throw light on the present and the immediate future. The Sect's convictions include messianic expectations, and naturally enough messianic passages are interpreted in this way.

We are now in a position to estimate the significance of the Church's selection of scriptures. Those that were found useful for the immediate apologetic needs were those which formed the basis of the contemporary apocalyptic-eschatological interest. Jesus had himself preached the kingdom in a way which was bound to appeal to this interest. Predisposed to believe that the time of the End was near, the first Christians found it true when the Resurrection actually proved Jesus' messianic dignity. And this meant that all the prophecies concerning the future referred to *this* time. This makes the person of Jesus central to the eschatological affirmation. It is this which accounts for the essential difference between the Church's use of the Prophets and the pre-Christian literature with which we have been comparing it. In the pseudepigrapha the messianic references are incidental to the main theme. In the Qumran literature they fall into a larger pattern of eschatological expectation. Several passages which the Church used messianically are applied to the Sect itself.

This means that, apart from 'royal' texts which are necessarily messianic when placed in an eschatological perspective, the greater number of the testimonies used messianically by the Church were in fact primarily simply eschatological passages. Such a passage, applied to the person of Jesus, thereby becomes a messianic text. Everything hinges on the claim about Jesus. The earliest apologetic was in connection with the Passion, and for this the 'righteous sufferer' sections of Isaiah and the Psalms were used. In the Qumran literature these are frequently drawn on in the *Hodayoth* to express the suffering that attends the formation of the eschatological community, and the characteristic oscillation between individual and corporate meaning remains. In Christianity they are applied specifically to Jesus as the Messiah, and only have a corporate meaning in a derivative sense. Similarly the heedlessness and unbelief, which in all the other literature are a matter of disobedience to the writer's interpretation of the Law, are now fastened on the question of acceptance or rejection of the revelation of the Messiah in the Resurrection of Jesus.

From this centrality of the person of Jesus, two further points follow. In the first place, if there are necessary qualifications for messiahship, e.g. the Davidic texts, then they must be made to fit the facts of the Messiah as he has actually been made known. And secondly, the Church's present experience—of forgiveness and acceptance with God, of the power of the Spirit and the joy of table-fellowship with the living Lord, and of the unity of all and the reconciliation of one with another—such experience is the truth about the promised blessings of the messianic kingdom. It is true that the theory that the eschatological age has dawned, resulting from faith in the risen Lord, controls the interpretation of these facts. But the facts themselves master the theory and transform it. It is in this sense that the Christian idea of the Messiah is something new, which no previous messianic concepts are adequate to explain.

The selection of scriptures for apologetic needs in the early Church is governed by a single factor, the established use of the Prophets and Psalms in eschatological speculation.[1] The significance of this is that the disciples felt from the first that the work of Jesus and their own experience could only be expressed adequately in eschatological terms, and proceeded to defend their belief on that basis. This means that an eschatological interpretation of the person of Jesus is the foundation of Christian doctrine.[2]

## 4. CONCLUSIONS

The main task of this book has been to expose the doctrinal significance of the form of the text of the Old Testament quotations. This has led to the consideration of a number of subsidiary interests. It may therefore be useful to give a brief summary of the general conclusions that have emerged in the course of this study.

---

[1] Dodd's classification of them (*Acc. Scrip.*, ch. III) as (i) Apocalyptic-eschatological, (ii) Scriptures of the New Israel, and (iii) the Servant of the Lord and the Righteous Sufferer, is useful to the student, but should not be allowed to obscure the essential unity of these concepts in early Christian thought.

[2] This fact is fundamental to Jean Daniélou's study, *Théologie du Judéo-Christianisme*, 1958: 'Le propre de cette théologie est qu'elle s'exprime dans les cadres de la pensée juive de l'époque, c'est-à-dire de l'apocalyptique' (p. 2). It is the late Jewish form of *Heilsgeschichte*, which is the key to O. Cullmann's *The Christology of the New Testament* (ET 1959).

(1) Modification of the text for the sake of the interpretation has been most frequent in the formula-quotations of Matthew and John, but has been found in a few other places as well. This has been detected in the quotations of Pss. 34.21, 68.19, 78.2, 118.22; Isa. 6.9f., 7.14, 8.23-9.1, 8.14, 28.16, 42.1, 53.4; Micah 5.1; Zech. 9.9, 11.13, 12.10, 13.7. In some cases this may be no more than the choice of an uncommon rendering. This seems to be true of Ps. 41.10, Hos. 11.1, Jer. 31.15. A recurring feature is the abbreviation of the text to limit its application to its specific function. So also Deut. 18.15-18 is abbreviated in this way. Paul's quotation of Deut. 30.12-14 is a paraphrase of midrashic type. Some of the features of these texts reappear when they are used in Justin Martyr's *Dialogue with Trypho*, which may earn for it a greater respect as evidence for the Church's debate with the Jews.

(2) Many of these quotations afford evidence of the use of the Hebrew Scriptures by the early Church. Some appear to indicate a Palestinian recension of the Septuagint. Where evidence for such a recension is sought it must be remembered that all the quotations which provide it are doctrinally coloured *pesher* texts. Elsewhere in the New Testament there are quotations which show the particular tendency of the Septuagint, notably the universalism of Deutero-Isaiah.

(3) In some cases it has been possible to uncover layers of interpretation, when a shift of application can be detected. The result of such analysis has tended to show that the primary interest was the nature of the messiahship of Jesus. The starting-point for considering this issue was the Resurrection. In attempting to recover the origins of Christian doctrine the Resurrection remains a fact that cannot be bypassed. A very primitive argument from literal fulfilment was found in this connection, but in no other.

(4) The scriptures used to defend the primitive faith were those already commonly employed in apocalyptic-eschatological speculation, which is thus the proper Jewish background to Christianity. The vital role of the person of Jesus made strictly messianic considerations far more prominent in the Church's apologetic than in any of the comparable literature.

(5) The first objections to the faith were concerned with the suffering and death of Jesus. This had immensely important consequences for the Church's understanding of its own proclamation. There is a traceable pattern of the development of christology, in

which the moment of messianic revelation is moved back from the Resurrection, first to the Baptism, and then to the Nativity.

(6) Several characteristic ideas of St Paul appear to be older than his use of them in the Epistles. There was evidence of this in the arguments on the promise to Abraham and the supersession of the Law, and also in the idea of the Resurrection as the salvation-event which discloses the hidden mystery of the wisdom of God. Moreover Paul's argument on the inclusion of the Gentiles has its basis in a universalism which had not yet faced the issue of circumcision. In contrast with the early Church's affiliation to eschatological thought, Paul is the first to state the faith from a rabbinic background.

(7) The Church inherited from the eschatological tradition the great typological themes of redemption, which greatly assisted the development of christology. On the other hand this seems to be a separate exploitation of scriptures from the use of texts in apologetic. In spite of the importance of the Passover as the time of the final act of redemption, the primitive messianic testimonies make no reference to it, but it only enters into them at a later stage, when they are used by John. The figure of the Prophet of Deut. 18 is only certainly applied to Jesus in the course of typological development. The primitive church shows no interest in the Levitical priesthood, which is so important in the Qumran literature and in some of the Pseudepigrapha. This also only comes in as a typological development, notably in Hebrews.

(8) The *pesher* quotations in Matthew and John have a common background in the stock of scriptures most frequently used for apologetic and other purposes in the principal church centres. A varied work of biblical exegesis, rather similar to the Qumran *Pesharim*, seems more likely than a Testimony Book, though the parallel should not be pressed too far. John's handling of the *pesher* texts is closer to the original meaning than Matthew's, and in general he reproduces the primitive apologetic with greater accuracy than is commonly recognized.

(9) Perhaps the most striking result of this study is the extent to which it was possible for the contemporaries of the first Christians *not* to believe the Gospel. In spite of the Church's conviction that the eschatological process had begun with the Resurrection of Jesus, there was nothing catastrophic to compel belief. Unbelief is a factor which demands attention in the earliest stage of the apolo-

getic. It had its effect on the development of the doctrine of the Church, making for a sectarian outlook. Many of the objections raised by the unbelieving Jews are the captious criticisms of those who are hardened in unbelief. It is well known that the anti-Christian motive becomes an important factor in Jewish exegesis from the second century onwards. The objections uncovered by our study of the New Testament testimonies may perhaps be the original form of this polemic.

Nevertheless the Church was unwavering in its conviction that Jesus had been raised from the dead. It is surely significant that, in spite of the numerous objections to the messianic claim about Jesus, there is no sign that the *fact* of the Resurrection was questioned in the earliest period. This only comes in slightly later, in the missionary situation at Corinth (I Cor. 15) and in the legend of the soldiers in Matthew's Resurrection narrative (Matt. 27.62-66, 28.11-15), which is manifestly an afterthought. The Resurrection is the vital historical fact for research into the origins of Christianity. The history of Christian doctrine begins with the debate concerning the interpretation of it.

# INDEX OF REFERENCES

## 1. OLD TESTAMENT

## 2. JEWISH LITERATURE

### APOCRYPHA

### PSEUDEPIGRAPHA

## QUMRAN

### RABBINIC AND OTHER WRITINGS

## 3. NEW TESTAMENT

## 4. PATRISTIC LITERATURE

### APOSTOLIC FATHERS

### GREEK FATHERS

## LATIN FATHERS

## OTHER WRITINGS

# INDEX OF NAMES